EMERGENT ERITREA

CHALLENGES OF
ECONOMIC DEVELOPMENT

EMERGENT ERITREA

CHALLENGES OF ECONOMIC DEVELOPMENT

Edited by
Gebre Hiwet Tesfagiorgis

THE RED SEA PRESS
Publishers & Distributors of Third World Books
15 Industry Court
Trenton, NJ 08638

Red Sea Press, Inc.
15 Industry Court
Trenton, N.J. 08638

Book Design — Jonathan Gullery

Library of Congress Cataloging-in-Publication Data

Emergent Eritrea : challenges of economic development / [editor]
   Gebrehiwet Tesfagiorgis.
      p.   cm.
   "Papers presented at a conference on economic policy options for Eritrea
held on July 22–24, 1991, at the University of Asmara" -
-Pref.
   Includes bibliographical references and index.
   ISBN 0-932415-90-3. -- ISBN 0-932415-91-1 (pbk.)
   1. Eritrea (Ethiopia)--Economic conditions--Congresses.
2. Eritrea (Ethiopia)--Economic policy--Congresses. I. Gebre Hiwet
Tesfagiorgis.
HC845.Z7E753   1993
338.963'5--dc20   93-8912
                                        CIP

CONTENTS

Chapter 5
Trade and Industry

Chapter 6
Natural Resource Development and Construction

Chapter 7
Technology And Information Systems

PREFACE

This volume compiles papers presented at a conference on economic policy options for Eritrea held on July 22–24, 1991, at the University of Asmara, in Asmara, the capital of Eritrea. The conference was held immediately after Eritrea's freedom fighters, under the Eritrean People's Liberation Front (EPLF), marched into Asmara, bringing to an end Ethiopia's thirty-year rule over Eritrea.

The idea for the conference was initiated by EPLF's leadership with the aim of providing a forum where the challenges of economic development facing emergent Eritrea can be freely discussed among policymakers, practitioners and scholars. Eritrea's independence occurred perhaps earlier than was anticipated. As a result, the conference, which was initially planned to be held in EPLF's base area, could be held in Asmara. And as Secretary General Issaias Afwerki stated, "one could not have wished a more appropriate time and place."

The conference was the result of a cooperative planning by the Department of Economic Planning and Coordination of EPLF (now the Provisional Government of Eritrea) in Eritrea and the Eritreans for Peace and Democracy (EPD) in North America, an association of mainly Eritrean professionals organized in 1989 to assist in publicizing Eritrea's cause. About forty papers were presented at the conference out of which thirty were submitted for publication and are compiled in this volume. It was the intent of the organizers of the conference that economic development be viewed in its broader sense. Thus, a broad range of topics is covered in the volume: ranging from human resource to oil resource, and from theories of regional cooperation to the theory of optimization.

This compilation does not represent a blueprint of economic development for Eritrea. Its importance lies in the fact that the collected essays raise many important problems of economic development. Nevertheless, each paper does provide, either explicitly or implicitly, some suggestions which Eritrean policymakers ought to give some consideration. To the outsider — including academics, potential donors and investors — this collection represents a window from which to peek into the collective thought of Eritreans about the future direction of their battered country.

As would be expected, opinions on several development issues were diverse at the conference; and this collection does reflect that diversity. However, some consensus did also emerge on some ideas, such as the following:

- Eritrea's economy should start as a mixed economy where both the public and private sectors will play important roles, but emphasis should gradually shift toward the private sector.

- Agriculture has been and will continue to be the backbone of the country's economy, but should be augmented by strategically selected and carefully planned industries.

- Regional cooperation, with emphasis on areas of comparative advantage, will work to the mutual benefit of Eritrea and its neighboring countries.

- Given its location and its industrious people, Eritrea can become a regional "hub" in industrial and commercial activities.

- Self-reliant strategy of development, which, by policy and necessity, served Eritrea well during the armed struggle, can serve peacetime Eritrea as well.

- The key resource Eritrea has is its human resource, which should be developed through well-planned educational and training programs, augmented by the introduction of appropriate technology.

- Social gains achieved by women during the armed struggle should not only be maintained, but advanced during the struggle for economic development.

- Industrialization and economic development decisions should take into account environmental and ecological factors right from the beginning.

- Hard evidence on the extent of Eritrea's natural resources is lacking; nevertheless, aggressive policies of exploration and of actual exploitation of known resources are essential.

- Establishment of an honest, corrupt-free and democratic government is necessary to create the type of sociopolitical environment conducive for economic development.

The volume is organized into seven chapters representing approximate economic sectors. The opening remarks by Haile Woldetensae, Secretary of the Economic Planning and Coordination, and the keynote address delivered by Issaias Afwerki, Secretary General of the Provisional Government of Eritrea, together serve as the introductory section of the volume. In his keynote address, the Secretary General, in his characteristically candid and precise manner, outlines Eritrea's immediate economic development problems and priorities. The priorities reflect the collective thinking of the Provisional Government at the time.

There are seven essays in this collection that were prepared by departments within the EPLF and were presented at the conference by their representatives. The departments are: Agriculture, Finance, Trade and Commerce, Industry, Water Resources, Marine and Ports, and Construction. The EPLF papers have more or less a common theme: they provide some background of the sector covered, assess the current situation with emphasis on the problems facing the sector, and provide short-run and long-run objectives and/or plans of action. Collectively, the seven EPLF papers are key to understanding Eritrea's economic reality. Four of the seven chapters in this volume start with an EPLF paper so that the reader is first introduced to Eritrea's objective conditions in the relevant sector. There were no EPLF papers that could anchor the remaining three chapters. Authorship of each EPLF paper has been assigned to the corresponding department in accordance with the wishes of the presenters. However, the names of the presenters are indicated in a footnote.

In Chapter One are essays that discuss Eritrea's economic development options at the macro level. Yohannes Habtu and Tekie Fessehatzion, in separate papers, call for regional cooperation in the Horn of Africa and contend that emergent Eritrea is destined to play a key economic role in the region. Yohannes emphasizes the broader context of Africa and its Horn region and Tekie concentrates on Eritrea and Ethiopia, stressing that peace and long-term development of the two countries are inextricably linked. Within the context of regional cooperation, Berhe Habte-Giorgis argues that given its location, human resource and predictably good government, Eritrea can become the "hub" of the region in industrial and commercial activities. Gebre Hiwet Tesfagiorgis contends that the self-reliant strategy of development, which, by design and necessity, served Eritreans well during the armed struggle phase can serve likewise in economic development. He suggests sets of criteria deemed appropriate for assessing economic performance in Eritrea.

Chapter Two deals with Eritrea's human resource. Gebre Hiwet Tesfagiorgis opens up the chapter by emphasizing the importance of education for human resource development, and raises several policy questions pertinent to the three levels of education. Yegin Habtes expands on education, and argues that empowerment of teachers, parents and local officials enhances the effectiveness and quality of education. Berhe Habte-Giorgis sees the rights of workers and harmonious employer-employee relations as important aspects of human resource development. He outlines labor policies that foster industrial peace and economic growth. Veronica Rentmeesters recognizes the important role women played during the armed struggle. She suggests development strategies that prevent backsliding on gender issues and advance the goal of women's equality.

Chapter Three covers agriculture and environmental issues, and is anchored by an EPLF essay that extensively analyzes current agricultural conditions in Eritrea. Tesfa G. Gebremedhin discusses agriculture in Eritrea with special emphasis on its potentials and constraints. He suggests policies for dealing with the constraints. Kidane Mengisteab analyzes socioeconomic factors, including land tenure systems, that have contributed to land degradation in Eritrea. He suggests changes needed to reverse the process and correct the damage. Ghermay Habte Selassie serves as the "conscience" of economic development. He urges that environmental impact should be an important factor in decisions on industrialization and economic development right from the beginning.

Finance and banking are covered in Chapter Four, anchored by a paper prepared by EPLF's Finance Commission. Arefaine G. Yohannes discusses concepts related to currencies and commercial and central banking in a manner a lay person can understand. He makes a case for the establishment of a national currency for Eritrea and offers specific policy suggestions. Brhane Tesfay introduces the concept of security exchange as a means of generating and allocating scarce financial resources. Araya Debessay expands on the same concept by stressing the importance of accounting and auditing standards for promoting securities market and enhancing the general efficiency of the economy. Based on the experiences of other countries and their own expertise, Brhane and Araya recommend specific security exchange, and accounting/auditing models, respectively, for Eritrea.

Chapter Five is devoted to trade and industry, and begins with a paper prepared by EPLF's Commerce Commission. Woldai Futur argues that Eritrea probably has a better comparative advantage in industry and trade than in agriculture. Basing his argument on the experiences of currently developing countries, Woldai suggests that Eritrea follow policies that are akin to free market. Gebre Gebrekidan and Tsegai Moges, in a jointly written essay, review industrial development experiences of developing countries from which they draw lessons for Eritrea. They discuss three phases of industrialization through which Eritrea should pass and suggest policies appropriate for each phase. Yacob Fisseha argues that small-scale enterprises are more appropriate than large-scale enterprises for Eritrea. He bases his argument on the experiences of several countries and his own expertise gained from extensive studies in the area.

Chapter Six deals with Eritrea's natural resource development and construction. Following an essay by EPLF's Water Resource unit, Berhane Abraha expounds the importance of water for economic development and suggests organizational setups and legislative enactments as necessary steps to deal with water resource problems. Ytbarek Cuddus briefly reviews the history of petroleum exploration in Eritrea and concludes on an optimistic note on the prospect of the discovery of oil along the Red Sea coast. He sees a need for detailed legislation on oil exploration and operation as the first step. Two EPLF papers, in addition to the one on water resources, are included in this chapter. They are on marine and ports, and construction. As previously mentioned, they provide important assessments of the current problems facing the units directing each sector.

In the final chapter, Chapter Seven, Woldai Futur introduces the concept of national technological capability. He argues that in the final analysis, it is Eritrea's human resource and its ability to absorb advanced technology that will compensate for the country's modest natural resources. He outlines policies for building a sustainable technological capability. Tewelde Zerom expresses his conviction that information technology can play a strategic role in promoting economic development and increasing productivity. Amdetsion Kidane introduces the concept of optimization theory, and using a hypothetical situation, demonstrates that it can be practically applied in Eritrea where necessity dictates that limited resources should be allocated to competing social services. Finally, Yemane Girmatzion argues that the mass media can play an important role by becoming an agent for mobilizing people in the reconstruction and economic development efforts. Following a review of mass media theoretical models, he suggests a model he considers to be appropriate for Eritrea.

Several people should be acknowledged for making the preparation of this volume possible. Special thanks should go to the fine sons and daughters of Eritrea, who, with their blood and ultimate sacrifice, brought independence to the country and made possible the convening of the conference in an ideal place. Special thanks should go to Haile Woldetensae and

Stephanos Habte, both from EPLF's Department of Economic Planning and Coordination, who tirelessly worked to organize the conference under unusual circumstances and provided effective logistical support. Thanks should also go to the University of Asmara and its fine staff for providing appropriate facilities and excellent services throughout the conference (the university was not even functioning at the time).

Thanks to the members of EPD's Executive Committee: Tekie Fessehatzion, Woldai Futur, Asgede Hagos, Araya Debessay and Haile Seyoum for their guidance and active participation in the preparation of the proceedings. Finally, thanks to Ruth Semmerling for applying her multiple talents in the process of preparing the volume for the actual production.

Gebre Hiwet Tesfagiorgis
Chair of EPD Publication Committee and Editor
August 1992

FOREWORD

Changing Role of EPD

The Eritreans for Peace and Democracy (EPD) is proud to have been a cosponsor of the historic economic policy conference on Eritrea. In the immediately following section, Woldai Futur, Vice Chair (former Chair) of EPD describes the planning for the conference and EPD's role in the process. As current Chair of EPD and participant of the conference, I would like to limit myself to a brief statement on EPD's future role and a couple of observations about the conference itself.

The EPD, an association of predominantly Eritrean professionals residing in North America, was formally established in August 1989 to assist in EPLF's efforts to publicize the cause of Eritrea. Now that Eritrea has achieved independence, there is a general consensus among the membership of the association that EPD should redirect its objectives and activities toward participation in the tasks of reconstruction and socioeconomic development of Eritrea. Cosponsorship of and active participation in the economic conference signaled the beginning of such a shift in direction.

The economic policy conference brought together Eritrean academics and senior members of the Provisional Government of Eritrea to assess the extent of the damage three decades of war had inflicted on the Eritrean society and economy. The aim of the conference was to identify the key obstacles to be overcome as free and independent Eritrea embarks on the mammoth task of reconstruction, resettlement and socioeconomic development.

The papers in this volume, particularly those presented by experts from the Eritrean government, are historic documents. These papers provide a snap shot of the collective thinking of the Provisional Government, barely two months after the liberation of Eritrea. Those of us, visiting academics, who participated at the conference were struck by the professionalism, insight and sober assessment that characterized these papers. Readers of the proceedings need to be aware of the fact that many of the government papers were drafted in the field when EPLF was a liberation movement, but presented when EPLF became the provisional government. And if some of the papers in the volume read dated, it could be because some of their recommendations have been implemented and have now become part of government policy.

Tekie Fessehatzion
Chair of EPD

The Road to the Conference

It took a coordinated planning on the part of EPLF's Department of Economic Planning and Coordination in Eritrea and the Eritreans for Peace and Democracy (EPD) in North America to organize the economic conference on Eritrea within a short period of time. Given the distance involved and the war situation in Eritrea, it was not an easy task.

The EPD was primarily responsible for locating Eritrean professionals and scholars as well as friends and supporters of the Eritrean independence movement in North America, Europe and the Middle East, and asking them to write papers on relevant topics related to their respective areas of expertise. The EPD was also responsible for organizing the general theme and structure of the conference in consultation with EPLF leadership, especially that of the Economic Planning and Coordination. The latter was responsible for the preparation of papers by the various sectoral departments within EPLF, and the logistics of the conference.

The conference was initially scheduled to be held in EPLF-controlled areas of the then Ethiopian-occupied Eritrea. Events moved so rapidly in the war of liberation that it became possible to hold the conference on the scheduled date, but at the University of Asmara, the helm of Eritrea's future excellence in higher education, in the capital city, instead of the base areas.

When held on July 22–24, 1991, the conference brought together Eritrea's policymakers and development practitioners, and scholars to exchange ideas on Eritrea's future development strategy options. As expected, the papers prepared by the various departments of the EPLF dealt with Eritrea's concrete situations. Presentations by the participants who came from abroad introduced conceptual and theoretical foundations of economic growth as well as useful empirical information from the experiences of several countries. Thus, the conference was well-balanced and presented an atmosphere that encouraged open, uninhibited exchange of ideas.

The conference was successful in the sense that it achieved the purposes for which it was organized. Most of the credit for the success should go to the Provisional Government, in particular the Department of Economic Planning and Coordination, for making it possible to hold the conference under difficult and unusual circumstances.

The economic conference was envisaged to be the first in a series of conferences to be organized in the future. As the first conference, and because of its timing, the economic conference opened up a new chapter, in that it marked the beginning of a democratic process for economic policy-making in new Eritrea. In that sense, it could be viewed as a prelude to the kind of democratic process Eritrea is likely to follow as it embarks on the arduous road of reconstruction and economic development.

Woldai Futur
Vice-Chair (former Chair) of EPD

INTRODUCTION

CONFERENCE OPENING REMARKS
AND
KEYNOTE ADDRESS

CONFERENCE OPENING REMARKS AND KEYNOTE ADDRESS

Haile Woldetensae, Secretary

Economic Planning and Coordination

Honorable Secretary General, Issaias Afwerki,
Respected Eritrean Provisional Government Officials,
Dear Conferees and Invited Guests:

It is with great pleasure and pride that I declare the opening of this first economic policy conference being held in free Eritrea. This is a unique conference as it is being held at a time when the Eritrean people, after a century of colonial rule and thirty years of vicious war and devastation, have an opportunity, for the first time, to decide their own destiny and future.

The culmination of war and colonization ushers freedom and peace, which, during the time of national economic reconstruction, accords Eritreans everywhere to participate in the making of the country's future economic policy by sharing and discussing openly and freely their studies and research findings. This occasion was made possible by all the heroic martyrs of our national liberation struggle to whom we must pay everlasting honor and respect.

Obviously, the liberation of our country was not an easy task; it required dedication and tremendous sacrifice. In this longest and bitter struggle of our time, the EPLF, galvanizing the Eritrean people, has cleared the way for freedom and peace and has heralded an era of peace and prosperity for the Eritrean people. However, major victories — liberation and tranquility — though necessary preconditions for the well-being of our people, are not sufficient in themselves.

Our people, victimized by years of colonial rules and a devastating war, have lived in abject poverty and misery. The betterment of living conditions is expected by the Eritrean people themselves, as it is neither right nor possible to live by merely waving a flag as a symbol of freedom.

In order to ameliorate the living conditions of our people, it is essential that the war-torn country and its economy be resurrected and rehabilitated. It is imperative that everyone be aware of the fact that this task is even mightier than the war of national liberation that we just successfully concluded.

As the EPLF depended on the diligence and commitment of its people during the national liberation struggle, so will the Front, through the Provisional Government of Eritrea, make sure the reconstruction of the national economy becomes a reality.

Because our pledges and promises are not enough, and in order to seriously embark on the task of economic reconstruction, the EPLF has convened this first economic conference in liberated Eritrea, designed to serve as a forum for economists — Eritreans residing inside the country and abroad as well as foreign friends of Eritrea — to discuss relevant issues and to forward views and proposals to the policy-making body of the Provisional Government of Eritrea. Now that Eritrean ears have been relieved from the deafening sounds of gunfire, which were the order of the day, an opportunity exits for free and constructive discussions on how to improve the living standards of the population through economic reconstruction. May I be allowed to extend my deepest congratulations, on behalf of this conference, to the Eritrean people.

Dear Participants:

The aim of this conference and the general economic programs drafted by the Provisional Government of Eritrea, as well as other issues of importance, will be discussed by the Secretary General, Issaias Afwerki, in his keynote address. The contents and proceedings of the conference will likewise be explained by Dr. Woldai Futur, Chairman of Eritreans for Peace and Democracy (EPD), in his brief introduction. In order to save time and to avoid repetition, I will confine my remarks to elaborating a couple of points in relation to the preparation of this conference and the underlying circumstances.

As you may be aware, the EPLF has in the past periodically carried out various studies and made assessments of economic policies and their implementations. All those endeavors were dictated, as they indeed naturally should be, by exigencies of the liberation struggle. As a result, they were essentially and necessarily economies of war, mainly geared to enhance and serve the tasks of liberation. More recently, however, preliminary researches to formulate economic policies for a transitional period as well as for long-term projections have been carried out.

In this spirit, the papers to be presented at this conference by the various sectors of the Eritrean economy were intended to focus on the experiences and lessons gleaned in the war economy, as well as proposals and policies appropriate for a transitional and long-term period. However, with the onset of the military offensive to entirely liberate Eritrea, and subsequent submersion in the tasks of assuming control and ensuring smooth operation of government institutions previously under the enemy, it was impossible to make adequate preparations.

I hope that the preparations made by Eritreans for EPD, other Eritrean economists from abroad, and our foreign friends will be more complete, though I realize that even in those instances, there were time constraints. Perhaps in the latter cases, the key problem lies more in the inevitable shortcoming of obtaining an accurate picture of the realities prevailing in Eritrea.

The EPLF could not undertake a detailed analysis and evaluation of economic-related government institutions due to time constraints resulting from the rapid military and political developments of the past few months.

Another constraint was the absence of contributions from those Eritreans with direct experience with the Ethiopian and Eritrean economic sectors under the Ethiopian colonial administration, but who until recently resided in enemy-controlled parts of Eritrea or are still residing in Ethiopia.

Nonetheless, because this conference is only the beginning, and not the final such effort, I sincerely hope and expect that it will result in useful proposals for the current Eritrean conditions and will lay down a solid basis for the future. In this three-day conference, where it is hoped that serious and intensive discussions will be carried out, your patience and active participation will be very much appreciated.

Dear Participants and Guests:

In conclusion, I would like to express my admiration and thanks to members of Eritreans for Peace and Democracy, who played a key role from outside Eritrea, in organizing this pivotal conference. Particularly indispensable was EPD's remarkable efforts in encouraging Eritreans and non-Eritrean friends, economists and other professionals, to participate in this conference.

I do expect, and am confident, that EPD will continue to play a role with such exemplary vigor and resourcefulness in our national economic reconstruction.

I hope that this first economic conference, being held under the theme "Yesterday in Liberation Struggle and Today in National Reconstruction," will be successful.

I now invite the Secretary General to open the conference by delivering his keynote address.

Awet Nehafash!

KEYNOTE ADDRESS

Issaias Afwerki
Secretary General
Provisional Government of Eritrea (PGE)

Dear Participants:

Allow me first to express my utmost pleasure for our ability to convene this conference in Asmara, the capital city of liberated Eritrea.

The convening of such a conference was under consideration for a long time, but could not materialize sooner for a number of reasons. Even though it is a sheer coincidence, rather than design, one could not have wished a more appropriate time and place for the conference. This conference is the first of its kind to be held at this historic moment. This is indeed the most appropriate occasion to talk about new Eritrea and its economic future.

Allow me now to proceed to outline some of the salient objectives of the conference:

- To collate and forward ideas that are essential for the formulation of the most appropriate direction of the economy of new Eritrea;

- To review existing knowledge about matters of economic policy in various sectors;

- To study, assess and learn from the experience of other countries;

- To ensure the effective role and participation of Eritrean professionals in the formulation of economic policy, economic reconstruction and management;

- To encourage and procure expert advice from friends of Eritrea; and

- To conduct continuous and frequent efforts rather than regarding this conference as the first and last forum.

Much effort has already been exerted to achieve most, if not all, of these goals. Thus, I would like to take this occasion to thank those individuals who have contributed in this effort. I shall proceed next to elaborate a general outline of the direction and approaches the Provisional Government of Eritrea has drafted on the economic matters, believing that they will have relevance to the proceedings of the conference.

It is sad, but true, to say that Eritrea has no economy today, devastated as it is by the thirty years of war and deliberate scorched-earth policy. In addition to the war, the manpower and economic resources of the country have been depleted by recurrent drought and other natural calamities. As there is virtually nothing, the first priority of the task is to formulate and lay the foundations for an initial economic framework. I discuss these policies in the order of their priorities: (1) agricultural development, (2) industrial development, (3) transport and communications, (4) mineral resources, and (5) education and health.

I. AGRICULTURAL DEVELOPMENT

Food is of a paramount priority. Before venturing into other big economic schemes, we have to ensure an environment in which we will be able to feed ourselves well through our toil on our land. As the welfare of the population comes before everything else, it is equally important to create conducive climate so as our human resources, persecuted and forced into exile and subjected to internal displacement, are repatriated, resettled and become productive citizens in the new setting. Specific objectives in agricultural development are:

- To rehabilitate agricultural land, rendered barren and uncultivatable, through various means;

- To provide oxen, agricultural implements, seeds and other essential materials;

- To expand the building of dams and irrigation canals as well as to exploit subterranean waters in order to alleviate water shortages and to effectively use our limited water resources in a manner that does not entail ecological imbalance and damage;

- To stem erosion and embark on afforestation;

- To preserve and maintain sustainable livestock and wildlife;

- To exploit the supply of seafood, primarily for internal consumption, without losing sight of its potential for export;

- To expand on cash crops as a source of foreign currency, but not at the expense of food crops; and

- To expand agricultural ventures that employ modern machinery, techniques and technology to reinforce and supplement, but not at the expense of the agricultural activities carried out by a broad participation of the population.

II. INDUSTRIAL DEVELOPMENT

Eritrea had a relatively robust industrial base, especially in terms of light industries and factories. That base has been destroyed due to a deliberate policy pursued by the successive colonial regimes over the years to induce stagnation and redundancy in the entire sector. Our specific objectives in this area include:

- To revive and renew these light industries to meet primarily internal demand;

- To build other basic industries in the consumer sector; and

- To find new and expand existing sources of energy with vigour since our economic development in general, and especially our industrial development as well as all our development projects targeted for raising the living standards of the population, depend on the availability of this currently rare commodity.

III. TRANSPORTATION AND COMMUNICATION NETWORKS

Both the war and deliberate negligence have rendered the main highways almost impassable and full of potholes; the railroads have literally been removed and the port of Massawa destroyed. All movements and transports were barred at the expense of the Eritrean community and geared to serve military purposes only. Thus, in order to facilitate internal and external trade, and to enhance economic development, rapid movement of people and goods and services is essential. Immediate objectives in this area include:

- To repair and properly maintain ruined transportation networks and build new ones;

- To build air and maritime transportation networks; and

- To build and expand efficient means of internal and external communication.

IV. MINERAL RESOURCES

The resumption and expansion of mineral extraction and surveying comprise another set of tasks that cannot be overlooked in order to strengthen the national economy, to reduce energy shortages and to procure foreign exchange.

V. EDUCATION AND HEALTH

Generations have been deprived of education, and our professional and skilled manpower has been paralyzed and made to lag behind. This is a very serious situation that requires immediate attention. The depletion of the productive capabilities of our people due to famine and other natural disasters is another matter of concern that must be redressed with the same emphasis. Efficient educational and health services and institutions have a vital role to play and can contribute to our economic development. Much effort must be exerted in these fields in tandem with other development schemes.

Dear Participants:

It is apparent that all these development schemes are ambitious, because we are starting from a scratch and with limited resources to support them. But, they do constitute timely tasks that cannot be postponed if our liberation is indeed to be meaningful. If nothing else, they are immediate tasks we have to at least brace for and start. At the same time, to be aware of the importance of various fields of development and to formulate comprehensive and appropriate schemes is not sufficient. For properly worked out schemes and plans to achieve their goals, good government and institutions, and effective administration and management are absolutely vital.

There are various controversial and challenging issues that crop up in connection with the latter. Should all the sectors of the economy be "commanded" and owned by the government or are these to be regulated by the private sector and market forces? Should the government interfere in all matters or should it have a limited role? Should there be an equitable distribution of wealth and economic development or should this be the preserve of narrow interest groups? Should we opt for "rapid development" pegged to external trade or prefer "gradual development" hinged on the internal market?, etc.

Although there are no ready answers and solutions to such questions, the general direction and premises of the Provisional Government of Eritrea may be summed up in the following words:

- Government ownership and control rights should be limited to land, mineral resources, transport and communication networks, educational, health and other social services, and some major agricultural and industrial enterprises. In the latter, the government has to encourage investment from local and foreign capital.

- The government should formulate a rational and effective tax and excise policies and seriously monitor their enforcement.

- The government and its institutions should abolish bribery and corruption.

- The government and its institutions should not be monopolized by few elites but should be characterized by a broad participation of the population.

- The distribution of wealth must be equitable and broad, and not characterized by a widening gap between an extremely rich few and the impoverished majority, which can only be a recipe for instability.

- We must ensure that economic development is not pursued at the expense of or to the detriment of our people and our natural resources.

- We must ensure that the interrelationship between internal and external trade — between the various sectors of the economy (government ownership, national capital, and foreign capital) and the various pillars of the economy — is balanced and appropriate, for the primary purpose of our economic development is to raise the standard of living of the population as a whole.

As I stated earlier, there are no ready-made answers to all these questions and problems. The general topics and details outlined above are open for debate and further study. Hoping that your contributions in all these matters will be useful and continuous, I wish your conference the best success.

Awet Nehafash!

CHAPTER 1

MACROECONOMIC FRAMEWORK

REGIONAL ECONOMIC COOPERATION AND INTEGRATION PROSPECTS FOR DEVELOPMENT IN THE HORN OF AFRICA:

THE CASE OF ERITREA AND ITS IMMEDIATE NEIGHBORS

Yohannes Habtu

I. INTRODUCTION

During the past thirty years of conflict, the Eritrean industrial infrastructure, transport and communications, power and energy, water and sewage system as well as the agriculture sector, have been severely damaged and effectively disrupted. The Derg deliberately de-industrialized Eritrea by dismantling and transporting, to Ethiopia proper, the whole lot set of factories, plants and equipment, leaving Eritrea bare of all its industrial establishments, when the thousands of displaced skilled Eritrean workers joined the Eritrean front en masse.

During 1977–88, the Eritrean People's Liberation Front (EPLF) expanded light industries in its Sahel base area, with the procurement of plants equipment and machinery and raw materials from the captured towns. Thousands of skilled and semi-skilled Eritrean workers were employed in the Sahel underground workshops in operating the newly acquired plants and equipment. The critical factor was the availability of a talented, committed, ingenuous and hardworking Eritrean work force. By the end of 1977, manufactured output in Sahel increased so much as to cover more than 80 percent of industrial consumption demand of the front.

Since then, the technical and technological capacity of the Eritrean front has reached a high level of industrial production and management, which augurs well in securing a viable strong foundation for establishing a sound and dynamic economy for a secure, peaceful and stable Eritrea. Self-reliant and self-sustained economic growth and social development remain a cornerstone of the new Republic of Eritrea.

With its strategic location on the Red Sea, in northeast Africa, Eritrea is in a position to play a crucial and effective role in its economic links and trade intercourse with its immediate neighbors; namely, Djibouti, Ethiopia, Somalia, and Sudan, which have a combined population of more than 75 million, availing a better opportunity and potential wider market for an accelerated and enhanced rate and level of industrial infrastructure and industrial production. Eritrea, as well as the other countries of the Horn, has to compete in terms of developing appropriate macroeconomic policies and strategies, establishing institutions, and educating skilled, knowledgeable, and

experienced technical staff and management in order to utilize these potential national and regional markets efficiently and effectively.

Mutually beneficial regional arrangements could extend to cooperation
and integration in economic sectors related to agriculture, industry, trade,
monetary and fiscal matters, transport and communications, energy, environmental issues, etc., once a genuine commitment for the common good prevails on all sides concerned. The past conflicts and hostilities in the Horn of
Africa could gradually be defused and eventually replaced by a spirit of mutual respect and cooperation in working toward the realization of an enabling
environment of harmonious relationship.[1] It is also crucial that appropriate
indigenous capacity is in place and relevant national and regional institutions
are created to facilitate and secure attainment of self-reliant and self-sustaining economic and social objectives. The endemic disasters of drought and
famine that continue to plague the Horn of Africa deserve to be tackled effectively and collectively on a priority basis.

II. ERITREAN ECONOMIC OVERVIEW

A. Eritrean Resources

The Eritrean human resource is the most important and valued economic factor and prime mover for stimulating growth and development and
for creating wealth — consumer and capital goods and services — for the
country. The Eritrean manpower, be it management or the skilled and semi-
skilled work force, has amply demonstrated its talents and skills in entre-
preneurship in business as well as in industry locally in Eritrea, Ethiopia,
and elsewhere.[2] The EPLF leadership and its highly disciplined and trained
army have proved their resilience, patience, hard work, creativity, inven-
tiveness, and innovation with meticulous planning and implementation of
assigned programs and tasks in development areas and in war activities.[3]

Eritrea possesses adequate natural resource endowments, including
agricultural and mineral resources. Its industrial structure and organization
has been buttressed by highly developed networks of transport and communications and its two main seaports of Massawa and Assab, interconnected
locally and with its neighbors — Djibouti, Ethiopia, Somalia, and Sudan.
There are local and international airports for internal and international airline services.

Economic growth and social development within Eritrea, in terms of
adequately feeding the population and providing basic needs such as education, health, housing, and productive employment, can and will be realized
through the process of determined, disciplined, committed, single-minded
efforts, and the ingenuity and hard work of its population, in optimum internal mobilization and efficient utilization of its scarce economic resources.
However, this will be neither adequate nor fulfilling for achieving its full
economic growth and social development potential. In order to accelerate the
rate and enhance the level and depth of economic growth and social development, through industrialization process, it becomes essential to complement and reinforce national efforts by mutually agreed upon and parallel
measures operating at subregional and regional levels. Eritrea with its cur-

rent resource base can significantly benefit from close economic links and possibly integration with its immediate geographical neighbors. Such economic links could encompass a combination of a variety of markets, supply of raw materials, movements of labor, or for access to supplementary routes to the nearest seaports.[4] Already, significant trade and movements of goods, services, and people are carried out among the countries of the Horn of Africa. Of concern now is the rationalizing, streamlining, and reinforcing intercourse of existing economic activities among the countries concerned.

B. Economic Sectors

Agriculture is the mainstay of the Eritrean economy. At least 75 percent of the population is engaged in peasant farming, growing mainly *taff*, maize, wheat, barley, fruits, and vegetables as food crops, and producing cotton, coffee, oil seeds as industrial crops. Livestock development, dairy, meat and meat products, and sea fisheries play significant roles in the economy. The highly developed commercial agriculture sector exports cotton, coffee, sisal, fruits and vegetables, fish, and dairy products to the neighboring countries, including Djibouti, Ethiopia, and Sudan. The agricultural sector is therefore the prime mover in the economy.

Industry in Eritrea was relatively developed, and by 1960 there were more industries in Eritrea than the whole of Ethiopia, Somalia, Sudan, and Djibouti put together. Eritrean industries were providing various consumer and industrial items. The quality of products produced in Eritrea were considered high and in great demand and appreciated by consumers in Eritrea, Ethiopia, Djibouti, and Sudan as well as others.

Potential for energy exploitation of oil, gas, and mineral resources exists in several parts of Eritrea but requires further studies, surveys, and mapping to determine actual location, reserve quantity, quality, and commercial viability of these resources. Oil and gas have already been identified in Dahlac Khebir, off the port of Massawa. Areas of particular interest in mining also exist in the Asmara area.

Potential mineral resources should be surveyed in greater detail for proper exploitation by the Eritrean government in collaboration with foreign capital and technology, on joint venture or similar appropriate arrangements as befits the interest of Eritrea.

The transport network, as well as the telecommunications system, is well-developed and properly maintained and serviced. The road system extends to about 600 miles of primary roads linking all the important centers of Eritrea. There are also more than 2,000 miles of secondary roads and trunks linking practically all towns and villages in Eritrea. The railway system runs from Massawa to the Sudan border via Asmara, Keren, and Agordat. One of the longest ropeways existed between Asmara and Massawa. The sea ports of Massawa and Assab are the principal sea outlets for Eritrea and are fairly well equipped to handle commercial shipping transactions. The country has local airports and one international airport in the capital city Asmara, with connection to all parts of the world.

III. THE STATE OF THE ECONOMIES OF THE HORN OF AFRICA

Eritrea, Djibouti, Ethiopia, Somalia and Sudan share similar initial economic conditions in that the mainstay of individual economy is based on agricultural and pastoral sector development. In Eritrea and Ethiopia, the agriculture sector contributes about 42 percent to GDP (1988). Similarly, in Somalia and Sudan the same sector contributes 65 percent and 33 percent respectively to GDP. In all five countries, the industrial sector is not yet fully developed and its contribution to GDP ranges from 9 percent in Somalia to 17 and 15 percent in Ethiopia and Sudan respectively. In contrast, the service sector contribution to GDP is relatively high in Ethiopia and Sudan, reaching more than 40 percent, and lower in Somalia, registering about 25 percent.

The five countries have natural endowments and potential for transformation of the agricultural sector in terms of land, water and human resources, and yet these countries have been unable to feed their populations, let alone to develop the agriculture sector as the engine for growth and development of the other sectors of the economy. This is primarily due to lack of adequate investment in research, education, extension, irrigation, land conservation, rural roads and related development infrastructure. Above all, it is because of absence of enlightened leadership, lack of prudent management and due to misallocation of resources. Consequently, the countries of the Horn of Africa import cereals and receive food aid in order to fill the food deficit.

The five countries place higher priorities and allot a substantial amount of resources in favor of defense and security matters. In Ethiopia, for example, defense and security issues consume more than 70 percent of annual budgetary resources, equivalent to 15 percent of GDP. Ethiopia is reported to have spent more than $11 billion for the purchase and procurement of the latest war machine to fight internal rebellions, but the Ethiopian army faced a humiliating defeat at the hands of the EPLF in Eritrea and the EPRDF within Ethiopia. Had the Ethiopian authorities been wise enough to have used half of the amount wasted on armaments, instead, on basic needs of the population — on education, health, housing, and building of infrastructure facilities — the people and the country would have enjoyed a higher standard of living. They would have been spared the humiliation and tragedy of falling to the level of perennial international food solicitors.

Between 80 and 90 percent of the exports of the countries of the Horn are primary commodities, mainly coffee from Ethiopia, livestock from Somalia, and cotton from the Sudan. The main destination of these commodities are Europe and the United States. Their structures of imports include food, fuel, intermediary goods, manufactured goods, construction, and equipment. In their efforts and intention to industrialize and stimulate increased rate and level of growth and development, these countries have heavily indebted themselves and borrowed much from bilateral and multilateral sources. As a result, they are heavily burdened with debt and debt services, which have paralyzed their capacity to further develop and pay back their loans. The Sudan is one of the heavily indebted countries in the Horn of Africa, reaching more than $11 billion in 1988, which was equivalent to more than 70 percent of its GNP at that time.

The five countries are listed within the UN league of least developed economies with average per capita income less than $500 per annum. They receive special support and assistance because they are considered severely economically handicapped countries with an extremely high levels of illiteracy, low levels of economic performance, and general poverty. For some years now, the same countries have been suffering from persistent drought, famine, malnutrition, and death of vulnerable groups of their populations, especially children, women, and the aged.

IV. THE DEFINITION, RATIONALE, AND SCOPE OF ECONOMIC INTEGRATION

A. Definition of Integration

Economic integration as a concept is widely interpreted and signifies a variety of stages of economic arrangements entered into between independent states, "ranging from economic rapprochement via cooperation and solidarity to amalgamation, fusion and unification," for greater stimulation and enhanced rate and level of development of economies.[5] The high implementation of the theory of integration is a post–World War II phenomenon and has been considered a leading aspiration of international economic policy in recent decades.[6] The European Economic Community is one of the successful models of economic integration schemes undertaken so far. But African experiences in the economic integration process have been limited in both scope and success.

Economic integration as a concept is basically concerned with resource utilization efficiency, with special consideration to the spacial aspect. Conditions necessary for its optimum realization involve (1) the freedom of movement of goods and factors of production and (2) the absence of discrimination.

B. Levels of Economic Integration

Economic integration can operate at three levels: (1) national integration, which involves the integration of regions within the boundaries of a national state; (2) international economic integration, which deals with the integration of separate nations in a regional bloc; and (3) worldwide integration, which takes place on a global scale. At the three levels of integration distinction exists between the integration of sectors such as agriculture, industry, transport, and communications, and the general across-the-board integration involving the entire productive activity. Our concern here is with the level of international economic integration.

C. Forms of Integration

Economic integration assumes several forms and varying degrees of union, ranging from a free trade area, to a customs union, a common market, an economic union, and complete economic integration. In a free trade area, tariffs (and quantitative restrictions) among member states are abolished, but each member state retains its own tariffs against third parties. In a customs union, there is free movement of commodities and harmonization of trade tariffs against nonmember states. Within a common market, restrictions in trade as well as factor movements are abolished, supplemented with some degree of harmonization of national economic policies, in order to remove discrimination due to disparities of policies. Finally, total economic integration assumes unification of monetary, fiscal, social, and countercyclical policies, with the precondition of creating a supranational authority whose decisions are enforceable over the member states.[7]

D. Rationale of Economic Integration

The case for economic cooperation and integration rests essentially on economic considerations related to economies of scale, diversity of resources, and natural geographical linkages, including river basin, or routes to the sea, for mutually beneficial economic welfare of the partner states, through broader and deeper rate and level of economic growth and development process.[8]

Two well-known theories on economic integration are introduced at this stage as essential and general frameworks for discussion of this paper. First is the orthodox customs union theory associated with Viner and which considers the effects of customs union on resource allocation, in terms of the trade creation and trade diversion that occur in trade flows. Trade creation refers to a union-induced shift from the consumption of high-cost domestic products in favor of low-cost products of the partner state. Trade diversion refers to a union-induced shift in the source of imports from low-cost external sources to high-cost partner sources. A union that is trade creating is regarded as beneficial to welfare, whereas a trade diverting union is regarded as detrimental. The analysis of the orthodox theory is not only static in its approach and consideration, but also has a limited use and bearing on the evaluation of gains from integration scheme in developing countries. The theory is limited to a study of the effects of customs union on welfare, without the other components of economic growth and development, including aspects related to equity, distribution of benefits, and costs.[9]

The second integration theory, a neoclassical analysis, considers integration among developing countries within a broader framework, which takes into account (1) economies of scale and (2) divergences between private and social costs of production. In this instance, benefits from integration are exploited on a mutual basis by market forces, within a customs union or common market, or other preferential areas without sacrificing structural development objectives of each member state.[10] The neoclassical analysis on integration is a definite improvement over the orthodox theory in its approach, consideration, and comprehensiveness in tackling integration issues between developing countries.

E. The Scope of Economic Integration

International economic integration arrangements have three main characteristics: (1) the suppression, in certain matters, of discrimination among the members, (2) the maintenance of discrimination against the rest of the world in various respects, and (3) the conclusion of agreements intended to have a lasting impact but which limit the independent use of certain instruments of economic policy. Institutions and organizations are created to identify, formulate, appraise, propose, implement, monitor, and evaluate the policies, program measures, and activities entrusted to the regional integration scheme.

The effects and the gains and losses that accrue to members of an integration scheme derive from a variety of sources, including: (1) increased output coming from a higher exploitation of scale of economies; (2) increased production realized from specialization based on comparative advantage; (3) improvements in the terms of trade of the group with the rest of the world; (4) efficiency changes from higher competition within the group; and (5) integration-induced changes affecting the quantity and quality of factor inputs, including increased capital flows and changes in the rate of technological advance.[11]

The overriding aim of the economic integration is the coordination and harmonization of policies and strategies of member states. Integration of general economic policy is based on three main concepts: (1) a free trade area; (2) a customs union, and (3) harmonization of specific aspects of policy to establish a common market. Emphasis is placed on harmonization of policies in order to merge members of separate economies into one.

The aims and objectives of an integration scheme can be achieved through one or a combination of the following specific economic processes: common external tariff, free trade between member states, a common agricultural policy, harmonization of tax system, free movements of goods, persons and capital, complete monetary integration, a common regional policy, a common transport policy, common rules on competition, and a community budget.

V. AFRICAN EXPERIENCE IN INTEGRATION SCHEMES AND THE WAY FORWARD

A. Nature and Variety

Pre-independent African struggle emphasized the need for pan-African movement, for forging strong inter-African links for promoting and consolidating political as well as economic independence and advancement of the African region as a whole. Post-independent African unity and economic cooperation aspirations are reflected in the existence of more than 230 institutional and organizational arrangements created for regional cooperation and integration processes scattered throughout the continent. More than 80 percent of these bodies are involved in inter-governmental organizations (IGOs) and the rest are nongovernmental organizations (NGOs). A majority of these regional organizations receive government support and subsidy as well as external assistance.

These organizations range from the most comprehensive in functions and membership (e.g., the Organization of African Unity [OAU]) to bilateral organizations (e.g., the Senegambia Confederation) or single-purpose organizations (e.g., the West African Rice Development Association). Their activities encompass collective security, regional integration, human resources development, and infrastructure development, as well as concerns of limited and specific nature, such as cooperation among wattle manufacturers in East Africa or highly technical and specific fields such as solar energy or mapping, surveying, and remote sensing.

Some, like the OAU and the Economic Community of West African

States (ECOWAS) are highly institutionalized with relatively large secretariats trying to solve intractable regional conflicts or implementing complex and highly technical trade liberalization arrangements. Several among them are, however, no more than one-man organizations, with post office box numbers, depending for their existence on a few individuals' dedication and a single government's intermittent and limited financial support. Their proliferation and diversity demonstrate that there is a widely shared and a deeply felt need for them. However, their tangible contributions have generally remained limited.

Several of these institutions were created in the immediate post-independence years without a great deal of planning or preparation. A few grew out of interterritorial links forged by a common colonial administration. Over the years, the significance of those links has diminished.

Since the early 1970s a more focused and comprehensive approach to regional economic integration and cooperation has emerged. These include the Economic Community of West Africa (CEAO) and ECOWAS in West Africa. In East Africa, however the collapse in 1977 of the once promising East African Community (EAC) had dampened for a time enthusiasm for economic integration. This is now changing, following the adoption of the Lagos Plan of Action (LPA) in 1980. A Preferential Trade Area has been established for East and Southern Africa. It has been followed by the Economic Community of Central African States (CEEAC) in Central Africa. The Southern Africa Development Coordination Conference (SADCC) and the more recent Indian Ocean Commission (IOC) represent new approaches to regional economic cooperation in Africa.

The Lagos conference, which led to the adoption of the Plan of Action and a Final Act, represents a watershed. It considered North Africa as one separate group and it divides sub-Saharan Africa into three subdivisions: West Africa, Central Africa, and East and Southern Africa. Before the final goal of continental integration is reached, it envisages each subregion to pass through at least the following three states: free trade, customs union, and economic community.

B. Constraints

The primacy of political over economic objectives has been a deeply ingrained feature of pan-African traditions. The other feature is the highly "personalized" nature of the political leadership's direction of inter-African cooperation.

Africa's high rate of political instability — as evidenced by the growing incidence of violent overthrow of government, military takeovers, insurgency, civil war, and ethnic strife — remains a major constraint to inter-African cooperation.

The proliferation of inter-African cooperation institutions has given way to duplication of functions, membership, efforts, and wastage of scarce resources. Although African governments expect institutions of cooperation to be vigorous in promoting common action, the governments are unwilling to give institutions of cooperation sufficient powers that would enable them to advance that goal. No African institution has been given supranational powers.

C. The Way Forward for African Economic Cooperation and Integration

Successive global development strategies in the past thirty years have caused stagnation in the African economies and increased their dependence on external sources. These economies have become vulnerable to externally generated shocks, by way of inflation, high interest rates, fluctuating exchange rates, and declining primary commodity prices, which contributed substantially to high and continuing external indebtedness and debt service burden that is beyond the capacity of the continent to bear.

Further, former traditional African markets have evolved into regional blocs and economic fortresses, buttressed with visible and invisible barriers that have effectively curtailed free flow of African goods and services. Tariff and nontariff barriers have effectively squeezed out African primary commodities, manufactured and semi-manufactured goods, from previously created international markets.

Hence, future African development strategy must be based on deliberate restructuring of the economic base and must also adopt a radical regional approach based mainly on collective self-reliance. The ultimate aim is to promote national economic and social development and regional integration of the African economies in order to achieve an increased level of self-sufficiency in the production and consumption of goods and services on a self-sustaining basis.

The vast majority of the African population, more than 80 percent, have no access to the basic needs of life, in terms of education, health, housing, and drinking water, which accounts for the abject poverty that prevails in the African continent as a whole. The conditions of underdevelopment, exacerbated by the prevailing drought and famine, have hit hard and debilitated the populations of sub-Saharan Africa. All this is happening "in the midst of plenty" — against the background of a continent potentially rich in agricultural, mineral, and human resources.

There are two interrelated policy issues that need to be tackled effectively for the smooth operation of an economic integration scheme in Africa. One policy issue involves resource allocation efficiency, with the workings of mainly based on comparative advantage, regional specialization, and investment. Another crucial policy issue is to design measures to produce an equitable and balanced interstate distribution of the benefits of integration process.

If the interests of interstate equity are to be served as well as those of economic efficiency, corrective policies to market forces will have to be employed to promote equitable and balanced development in a regional grouping, and appropriate instruments should be devised for this purpose.

VI. FUTURE ECONOMIC LINK MEASURES IN THE HORN OF AFRICA

In spite or because of the economic, political, and social crises that continue to plague the countries of the Horn, sensible and practicable arrangements of economic cooperation and integration process, internally generated, should be devised to help them out of their current difficulties and further contribute toward individual and collective welfare for the general populations.

There are several integration schemes in Africa where Eritrea, Djibouti, Ethiopia, Somalia, and Sudan will be or are members, one of which is the PTA, Preferential Trade Area for East and Southern African States, involved, among others, in trade liberalization process.

Within the framework of the Lagos Plan of Action, for the economic development of Africa in 1980, and in view of the economic integration models discussed above, and in the light of the African experiences in economic cooperation and integration schemes so far, the new Republic of Eritrea should be able to forge useful and productive economic links with its immediate neighbors, especially Ethiopia, Djibouti, and Sudan.

The significance of closer regional economic links among neighbors is generally recognized, as argued in this paper. The first and foremost action is the demonstration of genuine desire, efforts, and political will on the partner states. The political will should be effectively translated into a common structure, organization, and relevant institutions directed by capable and competent management and technical staff who will carry out the decision of the integration authorities.

There are several measures that members of an integration scheme need to take. The first task is to increase harmonization of macroeconomic policies, especially in monetary and fiscal issues. Second, allow countries to move forward whenever opportunity arises. Third, needless obstacles to movements of capital, labor and goods should be removed; simple administrative procedures and uniform national standards could facilitate economic progress. Fourth, whenever possible and practicable, the private sector can assist in disseminating market information; the role and contribution of the private sector in economic cooperation and integration process cannot be overemphasized.

All of the above measures will promote economic cooperation and integration across a broad range of issues, such as education, research, and watershed management. Regional centers of excellence should also be established for capacity building and technology training.[12]

At this juncture and time, Eritrea and its immediate neighbors, especially Ethiopia, should start with realistic, practical, and working development activities as a foundation for future regional development options and for mutual economic benefits. At present, there are several economic activities operational as common services. Such economic infrastructure relate to transport and communications, energy, monetary and fiscal cooperation, trade, the movements of goods, capital, and people, and environmental issues.

Transport and communications encompass policies, strategies, procedures, and rules and regulations related to roads, railways, shipping, airlines, and port facilities. The telecommunications system involves policies concerning telephone, radio, television, fax, and cable. Energy involves policies and strategies in power, electricity, gas, oil, etc. Monetary and fiscal cooperation are related to policies in currencies, exchange rates, and interest rates. Free trade area involves policies and strategies concerning free movements of goods, capital, and people. Environmental issues involve policies that affect afforestation programs and river catchment areas of common boundary.

VII. GENERAL SUMMARY AND CONCLUSIONS

The newly born state of Eritrea is destined to play a key regional economic role in the Horn of Africa, over the medium and long run. Its strategic location on the Red Sea, with a coastline of more than 1,000 kilometers, and two developed ports at Massawa and Assab, and its valuable economic resource base, especially its human resources, place it in comparative advantageous position.

The new Eritrean government vows to leave past hostilities and conflicts behind and replace them with an enabling environment of reconciliation and harmonious and good-neighbor relationship. The new relationship should be reinforced with the establishment of vital economic cooperation and integration scheme which facilitate social and economic intercourse among the partner states of the Horn of Africa. The relationship should be based primarily on collective self-reliance, and measures of self-sufficiency and self-sustainment.

The new Eritrean government has inherited stagnant, deteriorated, and distorted economy, destroyed physical and social infrastructure, devastated agriculture sector, dismantled industries and exported elsewhere to Ethiopia proper. The skilled and semi-skilled work force has been displaced throughout the world, but many individuals joined the EPLF and operated the Sahel industrial infrastructure.

Because the entire Eritrean economy is *tabula rasa,* economic rehabilitation and restructuring becomes a priority that demands the immediate attention and action on the part of the Eritrean government.

Eritrea is facing a challenge and opportunity of rehabilitation, restructuring, and transformation of a war-devastated economy. Its potential for economic growth and development is immense. Its comparative advantage stems from its natural resources, location, and the availability of a talented, hardworking, and ingenuous population. Initially external financial resources will be required for rehabilitation and restructuring purposes and also for the training and upgrading of entrepreneurial talents and to improve management and administrative capacities.

In order to exploit efficiently its comparative economic resource advantage, Eritrea must evolve and develop macroeconomic policies, strategies, and relevant institutions in favor of its key sectors of the economy, particularly agriculture, industry, trade, monetary and fiscal matters, and human resources.

A realistic and resource-constrained perspective plan can serve as an instrument of mobilizing and allocating domestic resources efficiently, and as a means of making the donor community aware of the priorities for external assistance.

Because Eritrean resources are limited, careful planning and sound financial management are essential. Great care and consideration must be applied to orderly priorities, with coherent and consistent policy and program implementation. An initial estimated fund of $1 billion might be needed to finance economic and industrial rehabilitation and restructuring in Eritrea.[13]

Although the fund required to rehabilitate the Eritrean economy is vast, it is essential that the provisional government solicits assistance and support from bilateral and multilateral aid donors, especially from the United States, the United Kingdom, Scandinavian countries, United Nations, UNDP, WFP, the World Bank Group, the ADB and the UN specialized agencies. In this instance, the Eritrean government needs to create a favorable economic climate, through fiscal, monetary, and other measures, in order to mobilize domestic resources and also to attract foreign investment. Approaches that might stimulate investment in economic and industrial rehabilitation and restructuring include, inter alia: (1) a dynamic and articulate national economic and industrial policy and strategy; (2) a system of incentives and other promotional measures; (3) replenishment of development banking institutions; and (4) harmonization of policy and incentive measures to promote specialization and complementarity in a regional framework.

NOTES

1. Interview of Issaias Afwerki, Secretary General, EPLF, in *Adulis* 7, 8 (October 1990).
2. Paul B. Henze, ". . . but let them develop their talents and skills . . ." Proceedings of the International Conference on Eritrea, EPD (November 3–4, 1990), Baltimore, Maryland.
3. Dawit Wolde Giorgis, *Red Tears: War, Famine and Revolution in Ethiopia,* pp. 80 and 102, 111.
4. World Bank, "Inter-African Cooperation and Regional Integration: Reshaping it for Development," Regional Integration Workshop, September 12–16, 1988.
5. Fritz Machlup, *A History of Thought on Economic Integration,* p. 4.
6. Peter Robson, *Economic Integration in Africa,* p. 11.
7. Bela Balassa, *The Theory of Economic Integration,* p. 2.
8. Hans Singer et al., *Challenges of South-South Cooperation,* p. 658.
9. Peter Robson, *Integration, Development and Equity: Economic Integration in West Africa,* pp. 6 and 7.
10. Robson, op. cit., p. 7.
11. Peter Robson, *The Economics of International Integration,* p. 3.
12. World Bank, *Sub-Saharan Africa: From Crisis to Sustainable Growth: A Long-Term Perspective Study.*
13. Author's estimate.

REFERENCES

Adedeji, Adebayo. 1989. *Towards a Dynamic African Economy: Selected Speeches and Lectures, 1975–1986,* compiled by Jeggan C. Senghor. Franc Cass.

Adulis, 7, 8 (October 1990).

Balassa, Bela. 1969. *The Theory of Economic Integration.* Watford: George Allen & Unwin.

EPD. 1990. Proceedings of the International Conference on Eritrea (November 3–4), Baltimore, Maryland.

Hogan, Michael J. 1989. *The Marshall Plan: America, Britain and the Reconstruction of Western Europe, 1947–1952.* Cambridge: Cambridge University Press.

Kraus, Melvyn B. 1973. *The Economics of Integration: A Book of Readings.*

London: George Allen & Unwin.

Machlup, Fritz. 1977. *A History of Thought on Economic Integration*. London: Macmillan.

Nkrumah, Kwame. 1963. *Africa Must Unite*. London: Heinemann.

Robson, Peter. 1984. *The Economics of International Integration*. London: George Allen & Unwin.

_____. 1983. *Integration, Development and Equity: Economic Integration in West Africa*. London: George Allen & Unwin.

_____. 1968. *Economic Integration in Africa*. London: George Allen & Unwin.

Singer, Hans, et al. 1988. *Challenges of South-South Cooperation*. Part II. New Delhi: Ashish Publishing House.

Timberlake, Lloyd. 1985. *Africa in Crisis: The Causes, the Cures of Environmental Bankruptcy*. London: Earthscan.

UNIDO. 1989. "Industrial Rehabilitation and Restructuring in Africa: The Case of the Food Processing Sub-sector." IPCT. (SPEC.), July 20, 1989. Conference document prepared by Dr. Yohannes Habtu, Senior Industrial Economist.

Wolde Giorgis, Dawit. 1989. *Red Tears: War, Famine and Revolution in Ethiopia*. New Jersey: Red Sea Press.

World Bank. 1988. "Inter-African Cooperation and Regional Integration: Reshaping it for Development." A paper prepared as background document for the World Bank–sponsored Regional Integration Workshop, Washington, D.C., September 12–16, 1988.

_____. 1988. "The Conceptual Framework of Regional Integration Analysis and Appropriate Technology." A background paper prepared by Professor Peter Robson of St. Andrew University, Scotland, for the World Bank–sponsored Regional Integration Workshop, Washington, D.C., September 12–16, 1988.

_____. 1989. *Sub-Saharan Africa: From Crisis to Sustainable Growth: A Long-Term Perspective Study* Washington, D.C.

PROSPECTS FOR REGIONAL ECONOMIC COOPERATION BETWEEN ERITREA AND ITS NEIGHBORS

Tekie Fessehatzion

I. INTRODUCTION

The future of emergent Eritrea and post-Mengistu Ethiopia will depend on the degree the newly independent state and Ethiopia are able to establish peaceful relations with each other and with their neighbors. Although the wounds from the thirty-year struggle would take a long time to heal, a concern for the region's future demands that the states in the region look ahead, bury the painful memories of the past and begin the gargantuan task of rebuilding their war-ravaged economies. A precondition for tackling the task ahead is for the future governments of Ethiopia and Eritrea to begin laying the groundwork for peaceful coexistence. Without peace the region's long-term development would remain unattainable.

The most effective way of achieving peaceful coexistence is through the mechanism of a regional arrangement, an arrangement designed to strengthen and deepen the interdependence of the economies of member countries. Although the history of regional economic integration initiatives in most of post-independence Africa is far from reassuring, there are certain dynamics peculiar to the Horn region that could make regional cooperation a success. As much as the thirty-year struggle has brought immense human sufferings, it also has created opportunities that could provide the framework for building enduring regional economic structures. The three states of the Horn (Ethiopia, Eritrea, and Sudan) share interlocking interests and needs. The degree to which the countries are interdependent provides the best persuasive argument for cooperation.

The proposal is based on the lessons learned from the regional economic groupings that have existed since the European Common Market was initiated in 1957. It also draws heavily from the experiences of the various regional economic initiatives that floundered in Africa over the past twenty-five years. This paper stresses economic cooperation over economic integration because integration imposes a degree of infringement on national sovereignty that may not be acceptable to any of the member states. Thus by eschewing economic integration for economic coordination, this paper is intentionally minimalist because such an approach has a much better chance of succeeding than the maximalist objectives often espoused by proponents of economic integration.

The central argument of this paper is that given the history of the relationship between Ethiopia and Eritrea during the past forty years, a relationship characterized by war and conflict, a way must be found to ensure that war and its consequences are things of the past. This means the new integrative scheme would seek to achieve political and economic objectives. The paper has four sections. Section I discusses, briefly, the theory and practice of economic integration. Section II reviews and identifies some of the reasons why some regional groupings succeed while others fail. Section III provides a sketch or framework of regional economic cooperation between Eritrea and Ethiopia. Section IV outlines activities for collective action as well as implementation strategies to make the scheme work. The framework, which would ultimately include the Sudan, Somalia and Djibouti, could be implemented in stages. During the early phases, Eritrea and Ethiopia, given their existing close trade and economic interdependencies, would form the core grouping. The discussion in this paper concentrates on Ethiopia and Eritrea.

II. GENERAL BACKGROUND ON ECONOMIC COOPERATION

Regional economic integration is a process by which two or more countries proceed to eliminate, gradually or immediately, existing trade discriminatory practices for the purposes of creating a single economic space. The ultimate goal of the process is to ensure that in the end there will always be free mobility of all factors of production and products within the new economic space or region. Generally, member states go through a series of steps before they are able to realize the full benefits promised by newly created larger economic space. Member countries may create a free trade area when they abolish all internal trade restrictions and agree to maintain different external tariffs against nonmember countries. The second step may be to form a customs union by adopting a common external tariff in addition to abolishing all restrictions to internal trade. The third step may be to add complete and free mobility of factors of production to the tariff restrictions already lifted to form a common market area.

A. Customs Union

A customs union stimulates trade among member countries in several ways. It permits substitution of high-cost products in a member state by cheaper products from other member states; when tariffs are abolished, products become cheaper and consumption is expanded, and finally, products from member countries are substituted for products from nonmember countries (Eilher 1983). Therefore, the countries that benefit the most are those that have a history of an interstate trade relationship. Furthermore, customs unions do better if member countries produce complementary products and minimize duplication of products. Also for customs unions to flourish it is important to abolish all nontariff, administrative barriers to trade. Even when the economic environment that binds member states is appropriate, for a customs union to succeed, the member states have to show a sustained political commitment to make the arrangement work.

The economic rationale that undergirds regional integration efforts is based on the following arguments: Integration (1) creates larger markets to permit economies of scale of production; (2) is a means of taking advantage of location and specialization; and (3) promotes efficiency. For many industries, especially those that employ modern technology, production costs steadily decline with increases in output thus accentuating the importance of access to large markets.

When two or more national markets are integrated into a large regional market, it provides the advantage of economies of large-scale production. Other important determinants include improved management, better organization of production, quality control, quality of labor force, etc., which impact a firm's unit cost of production. The best illustration of the importance of market size in promoting industrialization is provided by India and South Korea. Both countries have achieved high degree of industrialization because of their access to huge markets; India exploited its huge internal market while South Korea has had access to one of largest markets in the world, the United States of America.

III. REVIEW OF EXISTING ECONOMIC ARRANGEMENT

A. European Economic Community (EEC)

The experiences of the European Economic Community (EEC) provide the best examples of the interaction among trade liberalization, market expansion and industrialization for the benefit of a multistate region (World Bank 1990). The EEC, established in 1958 first to compete successfully with industrial and technological self-sufficiency and rapid increases in productivity, otherwise Western Europe would always remain under the economic shadow of the United States. Second, Europeans also feared that unless they remained economically strong, Western Europe could be vulnerable to Soviet expansionism.

The genesis of the EEC was a proposal in 1950 by Robert Schuman, the French foreign minister who proposed to merge the basic industries of France and Germany to make it very difficult for France and Germany to go to war against each other. According to Schuman, if previously warring countries were to form a new relationship based on economic interdependence, peaceful coexistence, and not war, would be the most likely outcome. The EEC was, therefore, as much an instrument for promoting economic growth as it was conceived as a tool for promoting peaceful coexistence.

According to the Treaty of Rome of 1958, the agreement that created the European Economic Community, the six initial signatories — France, West Germany, Italy, Belgium, the Netherlands and Luxembourg — agreed to form a customs union, adopt a common external tariff, and harmonize their domestic economic policies. The six signatories made it clear that their ultimate objective was a common market encompassing all the democracies of Western Europe. With the addition of Great Britain, Ireland and Denmark in 1973, Greece in 1981, and Spain and Portugal 1986, the original six members expanded to twelve.

Over the past three decades the EEC has grown into the second largest power in the world, with a gross domestic product (GDP) reaching 97 percent that of the United States. And with a population in 1986 of 324 million, exceeding the populations of the Soviet Union (285 million) and the United States (245 million), the EEC is a huge internal market (World Bank 1990).

The EEC is on the verge of moving its cooperation one step further — it is in the process of creating a common market by 1992. It proposes to eliminate all internal and administrative barriers, to merge twelve national markets into one huge common market. When the potential of the common market is fully realized, GDP in the member states is expected to grow by 7 percent. It is not surprising, therefore, that the EEC's success has been looked at for replication, mostly in the developing countries, who believed, rightly or wrongly, that if they could only organize along the lines of EEC, they too would see a robust economic growth.

B. Economic Cooperation in Africa

Africa has had its share of regional groupings that were established to emulate EEC's success. As of last count (1990), throughout Africa there were 200 organizations for regional cooperation (World Bank 1990). Unfortunately, progress toward regional market integration has been slow. The share of intraregional trade among member states has stagnated at the rate it was twenty years ago. A review of some of the most well known African economic organizations shows why African regional organizations have not succeeded in replicating EEC's success although they had adopted its integration model.

C. East African Economic Community (EAEC)

Three East African countries, Kenya, Uganda and Tanzania, established the East African Community (EAEC) in 1967 patterned after the EEC, although economic relationships among them were initiated early (1917) during the colonial era (Penaherrena 1978). The 1967 Treaty never became fully operational because two member states, Uganda and Tanzania, were dissatisfied with the distribution of cost and benefit of the integration. The flow of trade, industrial development and distribution of revenue were skewed in favor of the "stronger" state, Kenya, to the detriment of the two "weaker" member states. Early during the life of the Treaty, the member states' industrial export grew, although Kenya's share of the total grew disproportionately faster.

However, the perception that Kenya was taking advantage of its strong economic position created discord among the member states. Tanzania and Uganda felt that they could not afford to give Kenyan manufactured products unimpeded access to their markets. The two weaker states responded by erecting administrative barriers against Kenyan products, in opposition to the letter and spirit of the 1967 Treaty. Thus by 1973, intraregional trade had fallen from 32 percent in 1967 to 24 percent in 1972 share of Kenya's total export. For Uganda the decline for the same period was from 16 percent to 4 percent of its total export. Only Tanzania reported a modest gain, from 5 percent to 7 percent. The perception that the arrangement benefited one member to the detriment of the other two doomed the Treaty (Penaherrena 1978). Tanzania and Uganda, and the different social/economic systems between Kenya (capitalist) and Tanzania (socialist) finally sealed the EAEC's fate.

D. Economic Community of West African States (ECOWAS)

The Economic Community of West African States (ECOWAS) was established in 1975, during the waning days of the EAEC. With sixteen member states, ECOWAS is the largest multicountry economic community in the world (Ezenwe 1990). ECOWAS has committed itself to an ambitious agenda: elimination of internal tariffs, introduction of common external tariffs, trade liberalization and fiscal harmonization. ECOWAS has been patterned after the EEC model, although the West African countries lacked the EEC's extensive institutional, administrative, and technical infrastructure. Trade among the Western African countries was negligible before the formation of ECOWAS and remained so even after ECOWAS was created. ECOWAS member states continue to quarrel over the distribution of the costs and benefits of integration. Furthermore, the proclivity of member states to act unilaterally to protect their national interest and their inability to make short-term benefits has made if difficult for ECOWAS to realize its potential.

E. Why African Initiatives Failed

There are several reasons why the EEC has been a success while all the African initiatives failed. Traditional integration schemes such as the EEC's are based on orthodox trade theory built around the efficacy of customs unions for allocating resources. It assumes perfectly competitive economies in which large numbers of small firms work toward market-determined paces. In the long run, well-functioning customs unions are expected to expand the flow of trade, as it has already happened in the EEC. However, the customs unions model is inapplicable to the African situation (Longhammer 1990).

In most African countries in which trade between member countries was negligible before integration usually remains so after integration. There is not enough volume of trade that could benefit from removal of tariffs and other restrictions. The lack of consensus on the distribution of the costs and benefits of integration has undermined the search for an effective integration scheme in Africa. The perception that the stronger members of the economic association continue to reap the benefits of integration had encouraged weaker members to refuse to comply with some of the terms of the various integration treaties. Unlike the governments in the EEC, very few of the governments representing the various grouping in Africa are willing to expend the necessary political capital to sacrifice short-term benefits for long-term gains.

IV. ECONOMIC COOPERATION IN THE HORN OF AFRICA

Eritrea, Ethiopia, and to a lesser extent the Sudan have become economically interdependent. Over the past few decades infrastructure and transportation networks have been built, markets have been integrated, and strong trade links have been established. The massive population displacement that occurred in Eritrea during the past thirty years and the subsequent creation of Eritrean communities in the Ethiopian and Sudanese diaspora have integrated the economies of the three states to a degree that was unthinkable before the long war for independence had begun. Northern Ethiopia, Eastern Sudan, and Eritrea have evolved into a self-defining economic space, an integrated market — a market that could contribute significantly to peace and long-term development in the region if the three member states were to harmonize their economic policies on the basis of regional considerations.

A. Objectives of Cooperation

The fundamental objective of the proposed economic association among the countries of the Horn, particularly between Eritrea and Ethiopia, is to create the preconditions for making peaceful coexistence possible. Without peace and stability the countries of the region would be unable to solve their economic, political or social problems. Not unlike the 1950 Schuman proposal in which the French foreign minister proposed to integrate the basic industries of Germany and France to make it harder for the two countries to ever go to war again, this proposal aims at mutually benefiting from economic interdependencies between Eritrea and precluding the possibility of another devastating conflict.

The proposed association has something important the African initiatives lacked but the EEC always had: political commitment to make the arrangement work. Eritreans and Ethiopians who went through one of the most devastating conflicts in Africa have every incentive possible to insure that the conflict never reoccurs. It is therefore in their interest to make the new initiative succeed.

B. Political Basis For Cooperation

For Eritrea and Ethiopia, the proposed association is based on an appreciation of each other's vital needs. Both countries need peace to devote their energies to development and reconstruction. Eritreans know that Ethiopians are anxious whether they will continue to have unimpeded access to the Eritrean ports. Eritreans should be able to give assurance to Ethiopia that Eritrea would not block Ethiopian goods normal access to the sea and, if possible, provide written guarantees without compromising Eritrea's national sovereignty over the ports.

There are at least two ways of providing workable guarantees. One way is to declare Assab a free port zone in which goods passing through the port would be exempt from duties. This, however, has far-reaching consequences. Unless Massawa is simultaneously declared a free port zone, it is likely that trade will be diverted from Massawa to Assab. Massawa could quickly decline as a commercial port. However, even if Massawa is given similar status as Assab, there are several questions that have to be answered.

What happens, for example, to the goods in transit to Ethiopia? Would the Ethiopian government impose duties at its border? If duties are collected, then nothing much has changed from before except the customs collection point has been moved from the port to the Ethiopian border. And how will the Eritrean government view these goods if an attempt is made to re-export them to Eritrea? Would they be allowed entry to Eritrea duty free in light of the fact that the Ethiopian government has already collected duties on them? And would there be a duties sharing scheme in which Eritrea receives a share of the revenues to reflect the amount of goods re-exported from Ethiopia?

If Massawa is also declared a free port, would the Ethiopians collect duties at Adi Grat or Rama (on the Asmara-Gonder road) on all goods meant for Ethiopia? However, if Assab is declared a free port and Massawa is not, then how would the Eritrean government attempt to control the contraband activities that will certainly radiate from Assab to all points across Eritrea? Surely there are several other issues that have to be considered before Assab or Massawa are given permanent status of free port zones. Indeed any consideration of providing Ethiopia free access to the sea cannot be separated from agreements on all other economic and trade issues affecting both countries.

A second way of facilitating Ethiopia's access to the sea is through the establishment of a customs union in which all tariffs on internal trade would be eliminated and a common external tariff would be in place. Imports to Ethiopia would come through the ports, the way they did when Massawa and Assab were under Ethiopian control. The only difference between now and then is that customs revenue would not go to the Ethiopian treasury. Ethiopia, then, would still have access to the ports to the degree it did before the liberation of Eritrea. What Ethiopia has lost is sovereignty over the ports as well as customs revenues. However, the loss of the revenues is insignificant compared to the price Ethiopia had paid to maintain its control over Eritrea. There may not even be a net loss of revenues to Ethiopia because the additional flow of trade the agreement would generate would more than offset for the loss in customs revenues.

C. Economic Basis for Cooperation

Economically, economic integration will induce changes in the industrial structure. And it not only promotes industrialization, but it also provides stimulus to technical progress, which generates important spillover effects for the economy of the region. However, economic integration is not limited to taking advantage of economies of scale to expand markets. For Ethiopia and Eritrea and the other countries of the Horn, cooperation means the development of common resources such as river, transport, power generation, scientific research, and training and financial institutions.

Given the daunting economic problems the countries of the Horn face, there are very few alternatives to economic cooperation. And if they are to navigate successfully through the turbulent transition from today's crisis to tomorrow's sustainable growth, they need a new development strategy based on collective action. The new strategy calls for the coordination of economic activities and the harmonization of policies to insure that they make maximum use of resources available in the region.

Economic activities such as transportation, capacity building, and industrialization are so crucial that they can be profitably carried out at the regional level rather than at the individual country's level. Most of these activities require huge amounts of external assistance, which may only be available if the activities are carried out regionally.

V. ACTIVITIES FOR COLLECTIVE ACTION

The integration approach suggested for Eritrea and Ethiopia goes beyond the orthodox customs union approach. It incorporates a mix of activities designed to enhance the production capacity of the region to create the conditions necessary to expand intraregional trade. If the approach is to be of any use to Ethiopia and Eritrea first, and then to the rest of the Horn, it has to answer some fundamental questions. For example, how can regional cooperation assist Ethiopia and Eritrea and the countries of the Horn to achieve sustainable growth? Which economic activities can best benefit from the collective action of regional cooperation? To what extent do national policies need to be harmonized to ensure the proper implementation of regional economic activities? And what is the appropriate time frame for implementing the agreements?

Although definitive answers to these questions cannot be given now, it is possible to provide tentative answers to some of them. From the review of the effectiveness of the integrative schemes in the developed and developing world discussed in section III, it is possible to sketch the cooperation modalities most appropriate for Eritrea and Ethiopia. Cooperation is not new to the region. Long distance trade and informal exchanges were facts of life even before the advent of colonialism. Recently, informal trade and across-border exchanges have kept prices down through competition, alleviated shortages of supplies, and continue to promote entrepreneurial activities. During the difficult years of Mengistu's rule it was the informal, unofficial, across-the-border trade channels that supplied drought and war-victims with the necessities of life. Thus the integrative scheme suggested for Eritrea, Ethiopia and the Sudan will supply, formalize and expand the extensive informal trade already in existence.

The activities that can best benefit from collective action of regional integration include transportation and communication, food production, and industrialization. The logic of collective action is based on the following arguments: (1) activities in the sectors identified will expand markets to create the conditions for economies of scale of production; (2) expanded markets in turn will attract foreign investment; (3) joint activities will allow member states to optimize the use of their natural resources; (4) will permit member states to undertake projects regionally they may be unable to do so on their own; and (5) international lending institutions are likely to have preferences for funding multiregion projects (El-Egaily 1990).

A. Transportation and Communication

The Horn's physical infrastructure, inadequate to begin with, was badly neglected during the past twenty years. Eritrea, Ethiopia and the Sudan need to commit themselves to building and rehabilitating roads that could feed into a transport network to connect parts of Northern Ethiopia, Eastern Sudan and Western Eritrea. This area which conjoints the three countries contains some of the most fertile and underutilized land in the Horn. An expanded network of roads would open the area for extensive cultivation and would provide products easier access to markets. Furthermore, the three countries may wish to consider the feasibility of building a rail line connecting Kassala and Massawa to complement the network of roads, to open for cultivation the rich agricultural area of Humera, Wolkait, Barka and Sudan's Kassala Province.

Reliable aviation and communications service can open a region to foreign investors (World Bank 1990). Ethiopian Airlines is known throughout the world for its exemplary safety record, profitability and efficiency. It is a legitimate issue to raise whether Eritrea needs its own airline. The question is germane because it requires huge capital investment and highly trained personnel to initiate and operate a national airline. Shouldn't the capital required to start an airline be profitably invested elsewhere, say, to build an efficient road system? Given the general shortage of investment capital and the scarcity of highly skilled technical manpower in countries such as Eritrea, the need for a national airline is a doubtful proposition. However, a good case can be made that not only does Eritrea need its own national airline, but that it could even operate it profitably. Given the presence of a large number of Eritreans in the diaspora, who for personal and business reasons may want to visit home, and given Asmara's potential as a financial and commercial center in the Horn of Africa, the need for reliable aviation and communication services connecting Eritrea with the rest of the world cannot be overstated.

Although the scarcity of investment capital is real, most knowledgeable people are aware that Eritrean technicians, pilots and managers have played a key role in the development of Ethiopian Airlines. It is therefore not far-fetched to assume that if independent Eritrea wanted to initiate a new airline it would have access to the type and level of expertise required to initiate such an undertaking. And although during the near-term it may be in Eritrea's interest to explore an arrangement with Ethiopian Airlines or with any other carrier to examine whether the number of international flights to Asmara could be significantly increased, it is in Eritrea's national interest to start planning for its own airline.

B. Food Production

The Horn has become a metaphor for hunger and famine. Drought and wars have forced millions of Ethiopians, Eritreans and other peoples of the Horn to live on charity from the international community. This is tragic because there is a lot of truth to the worn-out cliché that Ethiopia has the potential to become Africa's breadbasket. With peace finally becoming a reality, the countries of the Horn need to take steps to increase their agricultural production and to attain self-sufficiency in cereals and other foods. The opening of the Humera, Wolkait and Barka regions for further cultivation, and the creation of a new network of transportation systems would make cereals and other crops available to a large number of people. As important as cooperation is for bringing more fertile land for cultivation, just as important is for the countries in the region to cooperate on ways to reduce food losses through pest control, storage and conservation systems. Cooperation is also needed in the establishment of agricultural centers to search for disease resistant crops appropriate for the area and to develop better management techniques to enable farmers to become efficient producers.

C. Industrialization

Industrialization enables member countries to expand their market to take advantage of economies of scale of production, which in turn leads to increased industrialization. Eritrean textile factories would be able to increase their demand for Sudanese cotton if they know they can sell it in a regional market twenty times the size of Eritrea's internal market. Integration also permits cooperating countries to exploit their raw and natural resources to a degree they would not be able to do on their own. The gas reserves in Dallol, not far from Assab, could be a suitable joint Eritrea-Ethiopia project. The gas produced at Dallol could either be used for export or could provide energy for industries in northeast Ethiopia.

D. Implementation Strategies

The European Economic Community's experiences of the past few decades show that effective coordination and harmonization of polices have been key to the EEC's success. It is not enough to define objectives and identify appropriate strategies; it is equally important to put in place clearly thought-out implementation strategies to ensure that regional objectives are achieved. Just as the EEC has successfully created an enabling environment for integration and cooperation, Eritrea, Ethiopia and the Sudan could harmonize their macroeconomic policy, administrative procedures and trade policy to reap the fruits of economic cooperation. Coordination and harmonization imply that members states have to surrender a small measure of their national sovereignty for the region's welfare. Most of the African initiatives floundered in part because some member countries took policy initiatives on their own and failed to implement, or were slow to act on an agreed-upon regional policy. The importance of policy coordination and harmonization cannot be overstated. At a minimum Eritrea and its neighbors should consider implementing policies that expand production, increase the flow of trade and encourage foreign investment.

E. Macroeconomic Policy Coordination

Although member states do not have to synchronize each other's policies on taxes, government expenditures, money supply and investment, it is important that they consult with each other periodically to avoid the occurrence of macroeconomic imbalances. A sound macroeconomic management practice could spare the countries of the Horn the pain of structural adjustment programs. Although individual countries can set their own policy on currencies and fixed exchange rates, the convertibility of the currency has regional implications. Convertibility is essential for carrying out payments and the settling of transactions between member countries. The young government of Eritrea will soon face important questions on the creation and management of a sound financial system and on the degree to which its currency is convertible. Unless Eritrea has a convertible currency or decides to utilize another country's convertible currency during a transitional period, Eritrea's ability to engage in trade would be hampered.

F. Removal of Trade Barriers

The primary tool for implementing market integration is the removal of existing internal tariff barriers and the adoption of a common rate against the nonmember states. At present there are no internal rates for the trading of goods between Eritrea and Ethiopia. The question, therefore, is not removing nonexisting tariff differentials, but agreeing to maintain the status quo of no internal tariff and coming to a consensus on a common rate against the rest of the world. The same is true with nontariff barriers: maintain the current policy of nontariff, administrative barriers. The absence of barriers would greatly facilitate the flow of trade between Ethiopia and Eritrea.

G. Harmonization of Administrative Procedures and Practices

One of the legacies of the Haile Selassie's and Mengistu's period was the multiplicity of rules and procedures that governed trade transactions. These practices and other bureaucratic obstacles should be streamlined, or simply be eliminated, in order to engage in international trade. They should be simplified because they add to the cost of doing business, making the area unattractive for foreign investment. Eritrea and its neighbors also need to harmonize their investment codes and procedures to facilitate the movement of foreign capital anywhere in the region.

Past Ethiopian government policy concentrated economic development activities in and around Addis Ababa. The northern provinces of Tigray,

Begemidir and Wollo were badly shortchanged primarily because of their distance from Addis Ababa and in part due to their proximity to Eritrea. Even before Mengistu Hailemariam shot his way to power, it was part of the official Ethiopian government position to steer new investment away from Eritrea and to shift economic activities from Asmara to Addis Ababa. The policy succeeded brilliantly in impoverishing Eritrea economically, although it produced unintended results. The economies of Tigray, Wollo and Begemidir were also hurt along with Eritrea's economy.

H. Free Movement of Labor and Capital

Some of the most effective regional groupings tolerate a small infringement on their national sovereignty for the greater good of the member states. The EEC countries have ceded some amount of decision making to the EEC's secretariat. And now by allowing free movement of persons within the EEC, member states have lost their authority to control emigration from member states. The unrestricted movement of capital from the capital rich (Germany) to the capital poor (Portugal) has benefited not only Portugal's economy but has also provided higher returns to German investors.

There are several reasons why Eritrea and Ethiopia may wish to adopt an open door emigration policy for each other's nationals and a free movement of capital. There are hundreds of thousands of Eritreans in Ethiopia who still have strong family ties in Eritrea, and restricting their movement either at the point of entry or exit would impose hardship. It would be both impractical and unwise to expect the Afar to carry passports every time they follow their camels/cattle across the Ethiopian/Eritrean border. Although it is the prerogative of a state to refuse undesirable aliens' entry into the country, in the Horn, any attempt to restrict the movement of law-abiding citizens from a neighboring country is likely to cause unnecessary friction.

Historically, Ethiopians and Eritreans have moved across borders without documentation. Eritreans, particularly, are a well-traveled people. Everywhere they go they have established a reputation for their entrepreneurial flair and innovations. Eritreans are so entrenched in the economic and business life of Ethiopia that if they were to leave the country in a sudden exodus, their departure could cause serious damage to Ethiopia's economy. A similar departure of Ethiopians in Eritrea would probably not cause economic damage of equal magnitude, but an exodus of Ethiopians would likely create labor shortages in Eritrea. Neither country would therefore gain by restricting the movement of people across the borders.

The dispersal of the nationals of the various countries of the Horn across the region could well be the very catalyst that could bring people of the region closer. For example, Eritreans in the diaspora have the capacity to build enduring trade and commercial links throughout the Horn. If given enough time, Eritreans can convert the region into one large consumer and financial market. If Eritrean entrepreneurs are allowed to move freely around the Horn, to invest and engage in trade, they could transform the Horn into an economically integrated prosperous region. When commercial and trade linkages are built from the ground up, they are much more enduring than those built by edict from the top.

V. CONCLUSION

The purpose of this paper was to provide an outline of a framework on regional economic cooperation between Eritrea and Ethiopia. The paper's essential premise is that for the foreseeable future, peace and long-term development in the Horn region will remain inextricably linked. The thirty-year struggle has created new economic, political and demographic realities that the states have to consider as they embark on the long and arduous journey toward economic development. The new realities are: the prevailing economic interdependence among the three states; Ethiopia's return to its pre–1950 status as a landlocked state, and the presence of large Eritrean communities in the Ethiopian and Sudanese diaspora. The new regional scheme would attempt to reconcile two interlocking objectives: permanent peace and a smooth transition from economic crisis to sustainable growth for the entire region.

The proposal advanced in this paper has a much better chance of succeeding compared to similar efforts in Africa primarily because it is based on a realistic assessment of existing economic interdependencies. The strength of the scheme is that it is built around pragmatic programs of specific and achievable objectives. Above all, this scheme is likely to succeed because its central objectives are consistent with the current enlightened thinking of the new leadership in Eritrea and Ethiopia.

REFERENCES

Axline, W. Andrew. 1977. "Underdevelopment, Dependence and Integration: The Politics of Regionalism in the Third World." *International Organization* 31, 1 (Winter).

Balassa, Bela, and Ardt Stoutjesdijk. 1978. "Economic Integration Among Developing Countries." *Journal of Common Market Studies* 14 (April).

Commission of the European Communities. 1990. "The Experience of the European Community." In *The Long-Term Perspective Study of Sub-Saharan Africa*. Washington, D.C.: World Bank.

El-Egaily, M. 1990. "Imperatives of Regional Integration" in *The Long-Term Perspective Study of Sub-Saharan Africa*, Vol. 4. Washington D.C.: World Bank.

Either, Wilfred. 1983. *Modern International Economics*. New York: Norton.

Ezenwe, Uka. 1990. "Evaluating the Performance of West African Integration Movements." In *The Long-Term Perspective Study of Sub-Saharan Africa*, Vol. 4. Washington, D.C.: World Bank.

Langhammer, Rolf J. 1977. "Regional Integration and Cooperation in Africa: A History of Disappointments?" *InterEconomics,* No. 9.

Machulup, Fritz (ed.). 1976. *Economic Integration: Worldwide, Regional, Sectoral.* London: Macmillan.

Penherrera, Germanico Salgado. 1978. "Viable Integration and the Economic Cooperation Problem of the Developing Countries." *Journal of Development Planning,* No. 13.

World Bank. 1990. *The Long-Term Perspective Study of Sub-Saharan Africa,* Vol. 4. Washington, D.C.

_____. 1990. *Sub-Saharan Africa: From Crisis to Substainable Growth — A Long- Term Perspective Study.* Washington, D.C.

SELF-RELIANT STRATEGY OF DEVELOPMENT: GOAL SETTING AND OBJECTIVE EVALUATIVE CRITERIA

Gebre Hiwet Tesfagiorgis

I. INTRODUCTION

The self-reliant strategy of development undoubtedly worked well during the armed phase of Eritrea's struggle for independence. There is reason to believe that the same strategy can serve peacetime Eritrea as well. Given that assumption, the purpose of this paper is to address goal setting and objective evaluative criteria in the context of a self-reliant strategy of development. Stated differently, the paper attempts to answer this question: Assuming that the strategy of self-reliance will continue to play a pivotal role in Eritrea's economic development, what criteria can be developed to assess performance toward achieving identified societal goals?

To answer this important question, the meaning of self-reliance is first delineated from the literature, followed by a general discussion of the circumstances under which self-reliance emerged as a strategy of development on the African scene. Then, an attempt is made to explain why self-reliance should continue to play a central role in Eritrea's development. Finally, a series of objective criteria are suggested for evaluating the performance of the economy in light of recognized goals in the context of Eritrea. A summary section concludes the paper.

II. SELF-RELIANCE: A NEEDS-ORIENTED STRATEGY OF DEVELOPMENT

Simply stated, self-reliance means to depend *primarily* on one's own human and material resources, and to determine one's own course of development. John Galtung, who has written on the subject widely, identifies three important elements which are basic to understanding of self-reliance:
1. the idea that development should develop human beings, not things. This means, development theory and practice have to be rooted in fundamental human needs — both physical and mental needs;
2. the idea that development can only take place through autonomy, and thus the need to rely on one's own creativity, one's own land, raw materials and capital, however limited they may be;
3. the idea that underdevelopment is primarily, though not exclusively, the product of an international structure, and that self-reliance becomes not merely an instrument of growth but also an instrument of changing this structure. (Monograph, undated)

Critics point out that if self-reliance is taken to its ultimate conclusion, the result is a world of mutually isolated states, devoid of sharing and learn-

ing from each other, and not cooperating for mutual benefit. However, current advocates of self-reliant approach to development contend that this
should not be the case. For example, Galtung states that self-reliance is
entirely compatible with horizontal trade (ibid., at 14). To support his suggestion, he states, "There is a big difference between exchanging tractors for
oil and tractors for transistors," the latter transaction being compatible with
self-reliance (ibid.).

III. GENERAL BACKGROUND AND
CONTEXT OF SELF-RELIANCE

A. An Alternative to the Old Economic Order

The concept of self-reliance surfaced in the continent of Africa in the
early 1960s as a post-independence reaction to the legacy of colonialism and
its related economic order, the most important characteristic of which is the
existence of centers and peripheries reflecting the international division of
labor. Many writers, of various ideological persuasions, have written on the
center-periphery dichotomy. They have described the relationship between
the two groups in such terms as colonialism, imperialism, neocolonialism or
their equivalencies. Regardless of the terms used, they have described an
international economic system which favors the centers at the expense of the
peripheries.

It was this situation which prompted African countries in the 1960s to
search for new strategies of development as alternatives to the traditional
export-oriented approach that placed them at a perpetual disadvantage in
their economic relations with the industrialized Western world. Self-reliance
was articulated as one of the viable alternatives and remains so, at least in
theory, as long as the situation that prompted it persists.

B. Ideological Context

The theory and analysis surrounding the self-reliant approach to development has been more akin to socialist-oriented than to any other ideological frame of thought. Indeed, the governments that made self-reliance their
watch-word espoused socialism of one form or another in their post-independence development strategies. Two examples of such countries are China
and Tanzania.

Currently, globally speaking, neither the general socialist approach to
development nor its central strategy of self-reliance, seem to be as appealing
as they were during the immediate post-independence era. In fact, the "third
world" success stories we hear about nowadays are the four East Asian countries of Hong Kong, Singapore, Taiwan and South Korea, and to a lesser
extent, the three Latin American countries of Mexico, Brazil and Argentina.
These are countries with development strategies more akin to open market
and capitalism than to self-reliance and socialism.

Nevertheless, the debate over the desirability of self-reliance as a strategy of development continues on the African scene. The debate is perhaps best
illustrated by two documents that came out in the early 1980s: the World
Bank's *Berg Report* (1980) and Africa's *Lagos Plan of Action* (1982). The Berg
Report evaluated Africa's economic performance in the 1970s and concluded

the performance was poor. The report squarely put the blame on the African countries themselves for following "misguided" policies. It called for an "open trade," and recommended an "outward looking" or "export-led" development strategy. The Lagos Plan, which is considered as the development theme for Africa for the balance of the century, called for the restructuring of the economy of Africa on the twin principles of national and collective self-reliance. The main theme of the document is that "Africa must actively strive to reduce its dependence on external nations and replace this dependence with a self-sustaining development strategy based on the maximum internal use of the continent's resources" (Browne and Cummings 1985:24–25).

The debate on self-reliance as an alternative strategy of development is not limited to developing countries. For example, in a colloqium held in Switzerland, whose participants came from many Western European countries, the strategy of self-reliance was accepted as "a legitimate theoretical and political alternative to the long dominant export-oriented nature of regional studies and regional policies" (Bassand et al. 1986).

Thus, in the global and continental contexts, self-reliance presents an interesting paradox: It does not seem to be as appealing as it was two decades ago; yet, it remains the collective development theme for Africa. What this perhaps means is that self-reliance should be considered in relation to the specific conditions of a country and the development needs of its people. Thus, we need to consider the specific context of emergent Eritrean.

IV. SELF-RELIANCE FOR PEACETIME ERITREA

That a self-reliant strategy of development has served Eritrea well during the armed phase of the independence struggle needs no elaboration (especially to an audience composed of people who are the architects and practitioners of that strategy). Evaluating how and why the strategy of self-reliance worked during wartime Eritrea is a very important step in considering the strategy for postwar Eritrea. It would be presumptuous to even attempt to do that in this paper, but the writer strongly believes that the strategy will work in peacetime Eritrea as well as it did in wartime Eritrea. This belief is not based on mere blind faith; there are at least three important reasons why the writer thinks self-reliance should work:

1. Current Eritrean Condition Calls for Needs-Oriented Strategy. Thirty years of devastating war has left the people of Eritrea in a dire condition. Food, health care and other basic necessities have to be met with a sense of urgency. Self-reliance, as previously described, is the strategy most oriented towards meeting such basic needs.

2. The Critical Human Factors Are Ever Present. Perhaps the most important set of factors for the success of self-reliance in Eritrea has been the human element. The dedication and competence of the young men and women involved in the struggle for independence, the effectiveness of the organization that led the struggle (the EPLF), the skills and farsightedness by which the leadership guided the activities of the organization — all combined accounted for the success. These human qualities are there and can serve peacetime Eritrea as well as they served wartime Eritrea.

3. Necessity Has Been and Will Continue to Be an Important Factor.

The people of Eritrea fought a difficult war for thirty years without any appreciable outside help, and against all odds. To rely on themselves, on their own resources and on their ingenuity was a *necessity*. There was no other way! The element of necessity will persist until Eritrea acquires what is known in international relations as "sovereignty" and becomes a member of the international community of states. Even when sovereignty is acquired, self-reliance will still be imperative. The 1990s are predicted to be rough years even for the Western industrialized countries. That means very few resources, in terms of aid or soft loans, will be forthcoming from those countries. Developing countries like Eritrea will therefore be obliged to basically rely on their own resources.

Thus, the strategy of self-reliance should take a center stage in a development plan for Eritrea. Assuming this is true, what kind of societal goals should be established to guide the economic development activities?

V. SETTING GOALS OF ECONOMIC DEVELOPMENT

This section attempts to explore parameters for desirable societal goals which should guide self-reliant strategy of development. But, it is important to first define development, or at least delineate the kind of meaning it should have in an African context.

A. Development in the African, and Specifically Eritrean, Context

Development is undoubtedly one of the primary concerns of our time, especially in the continent of Africa where most of the least developed countries of the world, including Eritrea, are found. Yet, there is no consensus on the meaning of development; it may mean different things to different people. Development has been described from economic, sociological and political perspectives, which have resulted in several definitions of the term (Pye 1966:31–48). What seems to be a common element to all the definitions is that development is seen as a process of change.

Sometimes "development" is used interchangeably with "modernization." Some sociologists, who use the tradition-modernity categories of social evolution, establish characteristics of modernity as goals and define development as a process toward achieving those goals (e.g., Lerner 1968:386–87). This notion of movement toward universal ends has been attacked as unrealistic because it ignores the existence of factors peculiar to particular societies. Consequently, some social scientists and practitioners have opted to define development as a process towards goals which are peculiar to a given society (see, for example, Nettl 1969:17). This second notion of development can therefore be broadly described as a process toward the attainment of known societal goals or aspirations, and it is this notion of development that is emphasized in this paper.

For the purpose of this paper, "societal goals" are equated with "national goals," expressed in national official documents. In practical terms this means, in the case of Eritrea, the goals articulated by leaders of the national independence movement and published in official documents could be taken as the societal goals during the armed struggle phase. Societal goals for post–armed struggle Eritrea are yet to be articulated. At the same time, additional goals can be inferred from the specific societal conditions. If hunger is widespread in the society, it is only logical that one of the societal goals should be the production of food to alleviate hunger.

B. Goal Setting in the Context of Self-Reliance

As previously described, national goals in the context of a self-reliant approach to development, should be needs-based goals. In other words, goal-setting should be built around a nucleus of basic needs satisfaction. In this context, one cannot even assume a single development pattern for the third world, or even for Africa for that matter, but many development patterns reflecting the diversity of cultures and social structures. According to Galtung, it is for each country to decide how self-reliance should work, and for third world or African countries collectively to learn from each others' experiences (undated monograph). The notions of commonality and specificity can be demonstrated by looking at examples of two sets of societal goals.

1. Societal Goals in Tanzania. Tanzania was the first African country where the strategy of self-reliance found its fullest expression, as expounded by former President Julius Nyerere in the Arusha Declaration in 1967. The societal goals formulated for Tanzania at the time were the following: (1) consolidate and maintain the independence of the country and the freedom of its people; (2) safeguard the dignity of the individual; (3) ensure a democratic socialist government; (4) mobilize all resources of the country to eliminate poverty, ignorance and disease; (5) facilitate the formation and maintenance of cooperative organizations; (6) give equal opportunity to all men and women regardless of race, religion or status; (7) eradicate all types of exploitation, intimidation, discrimination, bribery and corruption; (8) cooperate with other States in Africa to bring about African Unity; and (9) exercise effective control by the government over principal means of production (Second Five Year Plan 1974). The national leadership in Tanzania has viewed development as a movement toward these national goals.

2. Societal Goals in Eritrea. Eritrea, under the EPLF, has followed the strategy of self-reliance in its armed struggle against Ethiopia. The societal goals of Eritrea, as expressed by the EPLF, include the following: (1) establish a people's democratic state; (2) build an independent, self-reliant and planned national economy; (3) develop culture, education, technology and public health; (4) safeguard social rights including those of women, families of martyrs, disabled fighters and others needing social assistance; (5) ensure the equality and consolidate the unity of nationalities; (6) build a strong people's army; (7) respect freedom of religion and faith; (8) provide humane treatment of prisoners of war; (9) protect the rights of Eritreans residing abroad and respect the rights of foreigners residing in Eritrea, and (10) pursue a foreign policy of peace and nonalignment (National Democratic Programme 1987).

It is interesting to note in the societal goals of both Tanzania and wartime Eritrea, the emphasis placed on independence and self-reliance, on poverty, ignorance and disease, on social equality, and on education and other social services. This is an indication of the commonality of basic needs which need to be addressed by the development strategies of the two countries. But, it is also noticeable that the goals of building a people's army, safeguarding the welfare of disabled fighters, martyr's families, and human treatment of prisoners of war reflect the unique circumstances in which

Eritreans found themselves at the time. Currently, as we start the phase of peaceful development, revising those societal goals is a critical step in drawing an economic development plan for the country.

It should be noted that the purpose of citing the societal goals of Tanzania and wartime Eritrea here is not for evaluative purposes, but to merely demonstrate the common and the specific natures of societal goals. National goals, once articulated, become the context for developing evaluative criteria to assess the performance of a self-reliant or any other type of strategy of development.

VI. CRITERIA FOR ASSESSING PERFORMANCE OF SELF-RELIANT DEVELOPMENT

A. Inadequacy of the Gross National Product

The gross national product (GNP), usually expressed on a per capita basis, has traditionally been the most common measure of economic development performance. But it has come under increasing attack in recent years mainly because it fails to indicate the general well-being of the population and ignores how income is distributed. For example, by GNP measures alone, oil-rich Kuwait (that is, prior to the Gulf War) could be placed among the most developed countries of Western Europe and the Americas.

The deficiency of GNP as a measure of development is more dubious when one considers the fact that in the third world, the countries showing growth by that measure are accompanied by a widening gap between the poor and the rich (Ranis and Park 1979; Tesfagiorgis 1988). Thus, recently measures of distribution have been introduced as supplements to GNP. For example, the World Bank, since the 1970s, has incorporated employment and equality criteria (income distribution) in its development measures.

B. Evaluative Criteria Found in the Literature

Several attempts have been made by economists, political scientists and other social scientists to measure development. For example, Harry Eckstein identified: durability, civil order, legitimacy and decisional efficacy, as four criteria to evaluate government performance (1971). The Social Science Research Council (SSRC) suggested that development be viewed as the resolution of a series of "crises" encountered during the process of consolidation of the nation-state: identity, legitimacy, participation, penetration, and distribution (Binder et al. 1971). Both examples have problems: first, the criteria mentioned are too broad to be operationalized into measurable indicators; second, like GNP, they lack any indication of public general welfare as well as distributional aspect; and third, the analysis is akin to the notion of development as a movement from tradition to modernity, the shortcomings of which has already been discussed in section V.

Perhaps the most appropriate evaluative criteria of development for the African environment have been suggested by Crawford Young (1982:15–20). Following are the six criteria with brief restatements of Young's reasoning for choosing them and his suggestions of their appropriate measures:

1. Growth. Included mainly because African regimes, regardless of their ideological persuasion, consider growth as a central objective. But instead of the usual GNP, growth in the peasant agriculture is more appropriate to the African environment.

2. Equality of Distribution. Although recognizing that the traditional technical measures such as the Lorenz curve and Gini coefficient may serve a useful purpose, fiscal and pricing policies of agricultural commodities, degree of dispersion of social amenities into the country, mortality rates, established urban minimum wage, etc., can be equally revealing and appropriate.

3. Autonomy and Self-Reliance. Self-reliance is seen here as a manifestation of nationalism and is espoused by both aspirants of capitalism, such as Nigeria, and of socialism, such as Algeria. Possible measures of this criterion include indicators of inflow of foreign resources to meet state commitments, the debt burden on the state, degree of reliance on expatriate skilled personnel, degree of control over natural resources exercised by foreign enterprises.

4. The Preservation of Human Dignity. This criterion refers to the nonmaterial aspects of human needs. The prevalence of systematic and widespread abuse of human rights in the continent justifies this criterion. Suggested measures of this criterion include: the absence of large-scale, state-directed repression of individuals or groups, the number of people who abandon home and turn into refugees, and the size of the security forces relative to area and population.

5. Participation. This variable is intended to be an indicator of citizen access and involvement in the formulation and implementation of development policies. But its appraisal is possible only at a rather broad level.

6. The Expansion of Societal Capacity. This variable is aimed at measuring a propensity to adjust to new challenges faced during the developmental process. Understandably, the author falls short of suggesting any measurement.

Young's criteria of development effort definitely represent a significant improvement over the traditional aggregate measures typified by GNP. Granted, they are not specific enough for evaluation purposes; nevertheless, their relevance to the African environment is so striking that they should be considered in the context of Eritrean development process.

C. Suggested Evaluative Criteria for Eritrea in the Context of Self-Reliance

The evaluative criteria so far discussed are based on theoretical contexts of one form or another. To analyze development in the context of Eritrea, one can easily come up with additional criteria which are not necessarily grounded in any theory but which make sense under the given circumstances.

Following are such criteria which can be appropriately applied in evaluating the performance of a self-reliant strategy of development in Eritrea.

1. Alleviate Hunger. Hunger is now the number one problem in sub-Saharan Africa, including Eritrea. Thus, it makes sense that elimination of hunger should be a goal of high priority, and that an indicator of efforts to free the mass of Eritrean population from hunger should become a criterion to assess development.

The obvious measures of this variable are; food production, and the degree of importance attached to agriculture in a country's development policies. The importance of agriculture in the current situation in Eritrea lies not only in the urgent need to increase food production but also in the fact that the overwhelming majority of the people of Eritrea (about 80 percent) earn their living from agriculture. The degree of importance attached to agriculture is often considered very critical in the development policies of developing countries. China is often cited in the literature as an example where a high priority given to agriculture has enabled the country to adequately feed a population comprising a quarter of the world's total population (Brandt 1980).

2. Education. The subject of education is discussed by this and other writers in chapter two in more detail. For the purpose here, it will suffice to mention that the importance of education lies not only in its role as producer of skilled manpower, but also in its having "a nexus with democracy" (Galbraith 1983:16). That is, it produces enlightened citizenry capable of participating in the affairs of the state. The degree of commitment to the spread of education; the types of technical training provided and the way technically trained personnel are utilized for development purposes; and the degree of attention given to the contents of both general and technical education, to make them relevant to the particular developmental needs of the country, are all important indicators of development.

3. Health Services. The importance of the general health care of a population for economic development can hardly be overemphasized. The inadequacy of health services in sub-Saharan Africa is evident from the fact that the average life expectancy is only about forty-five years (Brandt 1980:54). Because a weak economy does not provide the necessary resources to provide adequate basic health services, the "chicken-or-egg" riddle between health and economic development is apparent in the Eritrean situation. Nonetheless, the emphasis given to health relative to other competing social services can be very telling. In particular, the distribution of health services between urban and rural populations, the balance between curative and preventive health services provided can be good indicators performance.

4. Improvement in the Status of Women. Development requires extensive public participation, and removing social barriers to women's participation means releasing the development potential of fifty percent of the population. Women in Eritrea, as is true in most developing countries, are far from being equal participants in development. This is so because traditional social barriers prevent them from having access to education, training, employment, land ownership, credit, business opportunities and even to nutrition and other social amenities. During the armed struggle, the participation of women has been one of the many success stories written about EPLF. Those policies that contributed to the success should continue during peacetime Eritrea. Policies which specifically address women's issues, and measuring the results such policies produce in the course of the developmental process, could be revealing indicators of the effectiveness of a country's overall development strategy.

5. Factors Specifically Unique to Eritrea. A country under consideration may be facing a unique problem which is so overwhelming that coping with that problem becomes extremely critical for the success of the development strategy being evaluated. Such was the case of Eritrea during the just concluded armed struggle. The Eritreans were conducting a lonely war of independence against all odds. In that context, survival assumed a high priority in the country's hierarchy of goals. It is important to identify such unique factors and accord them the degree of priority they deserve.

VII. SUMMARY AND CONCLUSION

Self-reliance is a needs-oriented strategy of development and emerged as an alternative to the traditional export-oriented approach to development. Although its emphasis is reliance on one's own human and material resources, the ultimate objective is improvement in the lives of the general population.

The strategy of self-reliance should take a center stage in any development plan for emergent Eritrea. Postwar conditions in Eritrea demand basic needs-oriented strategy, and the human factors which were primarily responsible for the success of self-reliance in wartime Eritrea can serve peacetime Eritrea as well. Once a development strategy, such as self-reliance, is set in motion to achieve identified societal goals, it is important to develop certain evaluative criteria to assess its performance. Several criteria have been suggested in this paper, some based on theory and the literature, and others inferred from the specific conditions in Eritrea.

REFERENCES

Bassand, M., et al. (eds.). 1986. *Self-Reliant Development in Europe.*
W. Brandt Commission. 1980. "North-South: A Programme for Survival." Report of the Independent Commission on International Development Issues.
Browne, R. S., and R. J. Cummings. 1985. *The Lagos Plan of Action vs. The Berg Report.* Monograph in African Studies.
Chenery, H. 1974. *Redistribution with Growth.* London: Oxford University Press.
Eckstein, H. 1971. *The Evaluation of Political Performance: Problems and Dimensions.*
Eritrean People's Liberation Front (EPLF), National Democratic Programme, March 19, 1987.
Galbraith, J. K. 1983. *Essays From The Poor to The Rich.*
Galtung, J. (No date). *Self-Reliance and Global Interdependence: Some Reflections on the "New International Economic Order."* Monograph. University of Oslo.
Lerner, D. 1968. "Modernization." In *The International Encyclopedia of the Social Sciences* 10:386-87. Edited by D. L. Sills.
Nettl, J. P. 1969. "Strategies in the Study of Political Development." In *Politics and Change in Developing Countries* 17. Edited by C. Leys.
Organization of African Unity. 1982. *The Lagos Plan of Action for Economic Development of Africa, 1980-2000.*
Pye, Lucia. 1966. *Aspects of Political Development.*
Stohr, W. B., and D.R.F. Taylor (eds.). 1981. *Development from Above or Below? The Dialectics of Regional Planning in Developing Countries.*

Tesfagiorgis, G. 1988. "Comparative Income Distribution and the Impact of Taxation," 42 *Bulletin* 281. Publication of the International Bureau of Fiscal Documentation, Amsterdam.

United Republic of Tanzania. 1969. *Second Five Year Plan and Social Development, July 1, 1969–June 30, 1974.* Vol. 1. Dar es Salaam: Government Printer.

Young, Crawford. 1982. *Ideology and Development in Africa.*

THE DIRECTION OF THE ERITREAN ECONOMY: SOME THOUGHTS ABOUT STRATEGY

Berhe Habte-Giorgis

I. INTRODUCTION

Independent Eritrea faces the challenge of reconstructing the economy and rebuilding the nation. The task will require a second "Eritrean miracle" equivalent to the military victory over Ethiopia.

Four decades of Ethiopian occupation and war have left the infrastructure in ruins and reduced the economy to the precolonial level. What used to be first-class paved highways are unusable for commercial traffic; health services have been outside the reach of Eritreans for some years, and education has been disrupted. All forms of modern economic activity have come to a standstill, creating an economy of full unemployment. The country is believed to have abundant mineral resources, but so far little prospecting has been done.

To complete the dismal picture, most of the machinery is too old. The average age of the enterprises is forty years (Haile 1991). Under direct Ethiopian government control, industries in Eritrea were mismanaged and fell into disrepair. All top-level managerial decision-making authority was centralized in Addis Ababa. The little managerial talent that was in Eritrea was now scattered around the world. What the Ethiopians left behind upon defeat was the outcome of decaying socialist mismanagement.

If one is to follow the traditional schools of economic development, Eritrea would be written off as a hopeless case. However, one may get consolation from the fact that there are not many examples where the theories of development themselves have worked (Lal 1985). Theories of economic development remain useful subjects for academic discourse (Smith 1979). What seems to have worked in other countries is different from what the theoreticians of economic development prescribed (Drucker 1989). Therefore, the realistic approach for Eritrea is to develop a strategy to suit its unique situation and its people's vision.

Experiences of countries that have managed to attain economic development recently can be used, if they are found to be compatible with the Eritrean requirements. Countries that have managed to industrialize in recent years are poor in natural resources but rich in human resources. Likewise, the answer to Eritrea's problems lies in its people. The "can-do" spirit of self-reliance and the sense of pride of the Eritrean people that were critical for winning the war are likewise essential for succeeding in economic development and nation building. Following the example of the newly industrialized countries of Southeast Asia, the free enterprise system, with government, unions, and management working together is a proven method for creating a thriving economy.

However, the market system operates when the forces of supply and demand are fully in place and all the conditions for a freely competitive market are met. In Eritrea, there is shortage of all commodities due to the limited productive capacity and limited imports for lack of foreign exchange. The price of whatever little is available is sky high. The situation is exacerbated by the fact that the exchange rate of the Ethiopian *birr* has gone down against foreign currencies although personal income has remained the same or even gone down. The net effect is lowering of purchasing power. The influx of Eritreans visiting from abroad and the remittances they send can create demand in some products with the attendant inflationary tendency.

Thus, there is an economic emergency in the country: government involvement in the economy is needed to prevent complete breakdown of the social and economic order. Besides, the current Eritrean government has inherited a fully nationalized economy from the Ethiopian government. Privatization of state-owned enterprises should be done slowly and in an orderly manner, if chaos of the type now taking place in the former Soviet Union and East European countries is to be avoided.

The policy of "mixed economy," if it is not properly defined, can become socialism by another name. Also, the term implies a permanent policy and not an interim measure. Viewed in this light, the outcome of a mixed economic policy may not be different from the failed policies of socialism. Predictions for the future economy in the world are that only less ideological economic policies will succeed (Drucker 1989).

This paper presumes that government involvement in stimulating the Eritrean economy within the tenets of a market-driven economy is essential. Hence, it focuses on the degree and type of involvement that is needed until the market starts functioning smoothly. The economy itself is expected to go over different phases until a sustainable level of economic growth is achieved. Each phase will require a different level and type of government involvement.

The paper also envisages Eritrea becoming a regional hub in the economy of the Horn of Africa. The advantages of such a strategy are obvious and will undoubtedly be supported by all countries if mutual advantage is assured. Eritrea can take the initiative by becoming the center that brings together the economy of the region.

II. PHASES OF RECOVERY AND DEVELOPMENT

Economic activities involving recovery from the devastations of war cannot be accomplished all at once. At any particular time there will be priorities that have to be addressed. Logically, the Eritrean economy may be viewed as moving through three phases. The first phase will cover the first two years after liberation. The next three years constitute the second phase, followed by the third phase, which extends indefinitely into the future.

A. First Phase

This phase is characterized by a collapsed economy and absence of essential services. A state of economic emergency exists. Consequently, the government will be required to provide the people with food and other basic necessities. To pull the people out of a state of dependency, the government has to come up with a policy that will enable it to jump-start the economy.

Most of Eritrea's manufacturing enterprises and service industries were put under government ownership and management by the Ethiopian government, and it will take some time before the Eritrean government can come up with a lasting solution to the ownership and management of the state-owned enterprises. Under of the current situation, the only reasonable option is to continue operating the manufacturing and service businesses. Trade, distribution, and transportation activities should be privatized without delay, because most of the hardship and corruption in the past came from government controlled distribution and transportation system. If the private sector is not ready to take over the distribution business fully, then the public and private sectors can run parallel for the short run.

Financial resources, especially foreign exchange, will be limited. As a result the government will be forced to allocate resources to activities and products of high priority. Businesses that have access to foreign exchange resources of their own should be encouraged to import products without dipping into the country's coffer. Such a measure will undoubtedly benefit the businesses and the economy. Increase in the supply of products will depress prices and keep inflation at manageable levels. Otherwise, skyrocketing prices will combine with shortage of goods to scuttle efforts at improving the economy.

Immediate relief may be obtained from aid donors who have been supplying famine relief. However, to get more aid the donor base has to be widened; which means, more governmental and nongovernmental agencies have to be approached. Help for the repatriation and resettlement of refugees may be obtained from United Nations Higher Commission for Refugees (UNHCR), the European Community, other countries, and international organizations. Long-term rehabilitation should start along with aid for immediate relief to avoid the socially debilitating condition of dependency.

Lack of foreign exchange, as already mentioned, will be a serious problem. Obtaining some form of loan from other countries may provide a partial solution. But, considering the political status of Eritrea it may not be easy. The easiest source of foreign exchange is the Eritrean community abroad. The Eritrean government's realistic exchange rate of one U.S. dollar to six *birr* is highly commendable. It has definitely put a check to the underground currency market.

Additional effort is needed to encourage Eritreans to send money for investment, deposit money in Eritrean banks, send remittance to relatives, buy savings bond, and make outright donations. Facilitating travel to Eritrea itself will definitely generate millions of dollars of foreign exchange. There will also be a marked impact on the domestic economy with thousands of Eritrean visitors spending money in Eritrea. Generally, money coming from Eritreans abroad can provide badly needed foreign exchange to pay for imports, and the rest can become the foreign exchange reserve base for establishing Eritrean currency in the future.

B. Second Phase

Main activities during this intermediate period will typically involve consolidation of the economic base and bringing all existing resources and productive facilities into full operation. At the same time, the foundation of the economy for the future will be laid down.

Operation of the factories, farms, and service industries at full capacity will lessen the shortage of goods, which resulted from the breakdown of the economy under Ethiopian rule. Above all, the threat of famine may be averted.

At this stage, the country is expected to have its own currency and should be able to apply appropriate fiscal and monetary measures to stimulate the economy. As a sovereign nation, it will be able to enter into various forms of agreements with other nations and international agencies. The groundwork for a constitutional government may be worked out and a stable government, elected by the people, put in place.

The policies of the government will have lasting impact on the country and its economy. Investor confidence in the stability of the country has to be established before any foreign investment can be expected to flow in. Government agencies, essential for developing and implementing government policies, will have to be established and staffed with skilled personnel. During this period the state of economic emergency must ease, relieving the government from direct involvement in the economy. Privatization of the economy must start in earnest and implemented.

C. Third Phase

Achievements during this period will determine the economic position of the country at the turn of the century and beyond. If everything goes well, some time during this third phase the country should be expected to gather the momentum needed for economic takeoff.

Experience gained during the previous five years will be useful in identifying the strengths and weaknesses of the economy and society. Long-term objectives and strategy are to be formulated and readjusted using past experience and projections of the future. The ultimate purpose of the strategy is to use areas of strength fully, and minimize or eliminate detrimental effect of weaknesses in the attainment of stated objectives.

The regionalization of the economy, within the context of the Horn of Africa, will be carried out during the various phases discussed here. At no time should national interests be sacrificed for the regions interest or vice versa. Regionalization should be carried out only to the extent, and at a speed, that is beneficial to the countries that join the association.

III. THE REGIONAL HUB STRATEGY

Conditions in the world economy are changing fast. Behind the globalization of markets there is a growing regionalization of the developed markets into economic blocs. The blocs in the triad —North America, European Community, the Pacific Rim — control most of the world production, consumption, and trade. These blocs are fortresses designed to protect their respective markets from outsiders. Developing countries are left out in the cold and they will remain indefinitely providers of primary products. Even without the blocs, international trade is going to be increasingly difficult (Reynolds 1986).

The world is also moving away from labor intensive industries to knowledge-based technologies. According to Alvin Toffler (1990), the knowledge era is the last stage in the development of societies, which started with agriculture and then moved to labor intensive smoke-stack manufacturing.

Traditionally, labor intensive production has been the starting point for developing countries. With the shift in technology, there will be less demand for products produced by such economies. As a result, there is bound to be intense competition for the limited and diminishing market among developing countries that strive to attain industrialization. One of the admirable accomplishments of the newly industrialized countries in Southeast Asia is that they used labor-intensive industries to gain critical momentum. Then, they moved swiftly to high-tech production. Countries like India stayed too long in the labor intensive economy and are still lagging (Drucker 1989).

With the globalization and regionalization of markets no nation will be able to either isolate itself from the rest of the world or even achieve a viable economy. Thus, Eritrean economic strategy should be regional in its base and export-oriented.

Creating some form of a regional economic association with the other countries in the Horn of Africa is appealing. The association has to be allowed to develop through a slow process of economic interaction to allow time for overcoming political, economic, and related obstacles. With democratization of the political process and privatization of the economy in each country, at first a customs union, followed by a regional common market, can be created. Depending on the long-term success of the common market, some form of political association can be contemplated. Apparently, this is the process followed by the European Community.

At the initial stages Eritrea can play the lead role and provide the nucleus for close economic cooperation and integration of the economies of the area. In this regard much can be learned from the strategy adopted by Singapore. Eritrea has a strategic location in terms of land, sea, and air communication links with the Sudan, Ethiopia, Djibouti, and Somalia. Eritrea's location becomes even more significant when the other neighboring country across the sea, Yemen, is considered as part of the group. Thus, Eritrea, taking advantage of its geographic location, becomes the "regional hub." Singapore has used the hub strategy with much success.

The appropriate long-term economic objectives of Eritrea will be to create employment in industry, transportation, and services, and raise the standard of living of its people by using appropriately its natural and human resources. Attainment of these objectives will require uplifting the economies of countries in the region; it should not be a situation where Eritrea takes advantage of the rest.

The hub concept works for production, trade, transportation and logistics, and regional location for multinational corporations operating in the area.

A. Production Hub

Assuming the return of sizable skilled Eritrean manpower from Ethiopia and other countries, and the availability of investment, Eritrea will be capable of producing high-quality products at low cost. Eritrea has accumulated experience in the production of beverages, specialized types of textiles such as knitwear, shoe and leather, processed food, glass and bottle, agricultural implements and tools, and construction materials. It can use these areas of production as the nucleus and launching pad for its industrialization.

Assembly of machinery and electronics can follow immediately. With the expansion and improvement of the educational system and vigorous pursuit of technical training programs it will be possible to develop knowledge-based industries. Although, countries in the region may have shortages of foreign exchange, the barter system can be used in economic transactions. Over time, these countries may develop areas of specialization for which they may have comparative advantage within the region. As a result, trade within the regional market will enable all countries to find a market for the products for which they have comparative advantage.

B. Distribution Hub

The tendency in business strategy is to reduce cost of storage and transportation and improve services by using distribution centers. Establishment of a distribution center for imported goods that will have to be distributed in the region will create an attractive cost advantage for companies that import and distribute goods in the region. Availability of land, sea, and air transport, combined with the centrality of its location, make Eritrea the ideal distribution center.

Storage facilities can be built at the coastal areas for goods that will be re-exported. In the case of products which require storage in cool and dry places, the temperate highland region around Dongollo and Ghinda, within a one-hour drive from the seaport, is suitable. None of the countries in the region can match these conditions.

C. Corporate Headquarters and Technical Services Hub

Many multinational companies operate from regional headquarters and service centers. So far, Nairobi has dominated the East African area. The other locations further north are Cairo, Athens, and Beirut. With increases in economic activities in the region, it may be economical to locate offices and technical services personnel somewhere in the region. Climate, living conditions, and political stability are some of the factors companies consider in trying to open offices in foreign countries. Asmara, with its beauty and climate, will undoubtedly meet their requirements. To make it even more attractive, travel and visa requirements for business people have to be relaxed and modern communication facilities installed.

Banking, insurance, stock exchange, and related service activities within the region will have to be developed to support the level of economic activity in the region. Eritrea can easily become the hub for such operations.

Improved telecommunications and high-speed computers are making possible the export of service jobs from developed countries to developing countries. For example, many banks and airlines have their labor intensive clerical work transferred to countries with low labor cost. This trend is expected to continue in the future. With some planning and continued emphasis on improving the educational standard, Eritrea can become a good candidate for getting the service jobs.

IV. SUMMARY AND CONCLUSION

The government will be a very important force in developing the Eritrean economy. Initially, its involvement in the economy will be more direct. It will aim at helping the people get basic means of sustenance and jump-starting the economy. Given the inheritance of nationalized economy from the now defunct Ethiopian Derg, the new Eritrean government will be obliged to manage temporarily the nationalized industries, hotels, banks, and insurance until the private sector takes over.

The process of privatization and consolidation of the Eritrean economy may take place in three phases, based on the amount and type of government involvement required. The current period of economic emergency will require direct government involvement in the economy and management of state enterprises. The second phase starts with the conclusion of the referendum on the status of Eritrea as a country. It will be characterized by full privatization of the economy, and government involvement to merely stimulate economic development. The last phase will be a long-term process. Socioeconomic development is expected to be at full swing.

The countries of the Horn can benefit from a regional economic alliance. Eritrea can play an important role in this process by making itself the regional hub. The purpose of the alliance will be to help member countries attain a critical mass in terms of market size and pave the way for closer cooperation in the future.

REFERENCES

Drucker, Peter F. 1989. *The New Realities*. New York: Harper & Row.

Haile, Tesfay. 1991. "Financial Management Implications to Rehabilitate Public Manufacturing Enterprises in Eritrea." Unpublished paper, Asmara University (May).

Lal, Deepak. 1985. *The Poverty of 'Development Economics'*. Cambridge: Harvard University Press.

Morishima, Michio. 1988. *Why has Japan 'Succeeded'?* Cambridge: Cambridge University Press.

Reynolds, Lloyd G. 1986. *Economic Growth in the Third World: An Introduction*. New Haven: Yale University Press.

Rosenberg, Nathan, and L. E. Birdzell, Jr. 1986. *How the West Grew Rich*. New York: Basic Books.

Semboja, Joseph J., and Lucian A. Msambichaka. 1990. "The Political Economy of State-Owned Enterprises in the Third World: The Case of Tanzania." In *Breaking the Links,* edited by Robert E. Mazur. Trenton, N.J.: Africa World Press.

Smith, Tony. 1986. "The Underdevelopment of Development Literature." In *The State and Development in the Third World,* edited by Atul Kohli. Princeton: Princeton University Press.

Toffler, Alvin. 1990. *Power Shift: Knowledge, Wealth, and Violence at the Edge of the 21st Century*. New York: Bantam Books.

CHAPTER 2

HUMAN RESOURCE
DEVELOPMENT

EDUCATION AND HUMAN RESOURCE FOR ECONOMIC DEVELOPMENT IN EMERGENT ERITREA: TOWARD POLICY ARTICULATION

Gebre Hiwet Tesfagiorgis

I. INTRODUCTION

The purpose of this brief paper is to articulate some educational and human resource policies in the context of economic development needs of emergent Eritrea. It should be pointed out at the outset that the Eritrean reality represented in this paper is likely to be a blend of what the writer remembers from eighteen years ago and what he has come to know from a distance through reading and word of mouth. Nevertheless, an attempt is made to relate the writer's own educational and professional backgrounds to such a reality. Such an attempt will hopefully generate some discussions out of which may emerge realistic policies grounded in the current realities of Eritrea.

The paper starts with brief statements of general principles, which serve as contextual guides. This is followed by an equally brief discussion of the need to establish national educational goals. Then general educational policy questions are raised, followed by level-specific policy issues, with answers hinted in the course of the discussion.

II. GENERAL PRINCIPLES ABOUT HUMAN RESOURCE

A. Education is the Main Ingredient of Human Resource

In its broadest sense, human resource encompasses education, better health and nutrition. Education is the process by which human resource is developed; any discussion of human resource thus necessarily focuses on education.

B. Human Resource is Critical to Socioeconomic Development

Generally, to expand education and raise the knowledge and skill levels of the general population is a good social policy. In an economically underdeveloped country like Eritrea, education acquires an added significance as it is expected to play a significant role in economic development. Economic development, for the purpose of this paper, is to be understood in its broadest sense to mean improving the general welfare of the Eritrean people. Human resource is so critical that many experts argue education is a precondition for economic development. This theory is supported by the experiences of several countries, including Japan and the currently fast developing countries of Southeast Asia (Hong Kong, South Korea, Singapore and Taiwan).

C. Education is an Investment in the Future

The implication is that educational activities have to be consciously and meticulously planned so that education becomes a worthwhile investment. Merely expanding educational opportunities may be a good social policy but not necessarily a good investment. Education, as an investment in emergent Eritrea, will be at its best if policies, and strategies for their implementation, are tailored to the specific circumstances in Eritrea and the specific needs of the people of Eritrea.

D. Education Should Be an Integral Part of a National Development Plan

An educational system should be developed as an integral part of a national development plan in order to be contributive to the national economic development effort. In wartime Eritrea, the strategy of self-reliance shaped the educational system of the time. The national economic development plan and related strategies for peacetime Eritrea should become the context within which the national educational system should be planned and implemented.

With these principles in mind, the remaining sections of the paper deal with some of the major challenges newly independent Eritrea faces in the areas of education and human resource, and raise some broad and specific policy guidelines that can serve as discussion points.

III. ESTABLISHMENT OF NATIONAL EDUCATIONAL GOALS

Assuming that an overall national development strategy is in place, and given the socioeconomic condition of the country, Eritrea's educational system must be anchored in clearly identified and articulated national goals. These national educational goals must be the result of inputs from all sectors of the Eritrean society and should reflect a national consensus. The goals should be realistic and attainable, assessable and revisable if necessary. Following are five goals that are illustrative of the kinds of national educational goals emergent Eritrea needs to establish.

1. Eradicate illiteracy from Eritrea so that by the year 2005 every Eritrean adult will be able to read, write and do basic arithmetic, and become functionally literate.
2. Achieve a free, compulsory universal primary education by the year 2000.
3. Promote Eritrean national unity by fostering a sense of equality among the country's diverse nationalities; develop a sense of Eritrean culture.
4. Produce skilled manpower with a balanced mix of general and technical/vocational education which are appropriate for the socioeconomic development needs of the country.
5. Establish and run a system of higher education with a mission to train highly skilled manpower, to serve as the center of basic and applied research, and to provide services that will make an impact throughout the country.

Such broad national educational goals become the parameters within which local educational goals can be drawn, taking into account specific local conditions.

IV. MAJOR EDUCATIONAL POLICY QUESTIONS

When establishing a national educational system, in order to achieve national goals such as those listed above, there are numerous challenging policy questions that policymakers should address. The following are such policy issues, which have relevance to the current situation in Eritrea.

A. Education Should Be a State Responsibility

Education, as previously stated, is so vital to the socioeconomic development needs of a country that it should be a state responsibility, guided from the highest possible level in the government structure. The position accorded education in the government structure can be an important factor in determining the degree of success of a nation's educational effort. In the United States of America — where education is considered to be the responsibility of the states, and not the federal government — educational activities by the federal government were guided by a mere commission within a large Department of Health and Social Services. The educational reform movements of the 1980s resulted in the creation of a Department of Education, headed by a cabinet-level executive, to enhance the role of the federal government in the national educational efforts.

State responsibility for education, however, should not preclude the establishment and running of private schools as long as they meet the minimum standards established by the state.

B. Education Is an Expensive But Worthwhile Investment

The debate on who benefits from education is very familiar. There is general agreement that the individual who receives educational services as well as the society at large benefit from education. Thus, theory would suggest that the public and the individual should share the cost of education. But in countries like Eritrea, the number of individuals who can afford to pay for their education is very small. Thus, reality dictates that the state carry the burden of the educational costs. Reality also dictates that education must compete with other equally worthwhile social services, such as health and agriculture. As a result, national financial resources will always be limited.

African countries have already invested heavily in education; between 1960s and 1980s, enrollments increased five fold. According to a 1988 World Bank report, many sub-Saharan African countries spend over 20 percent of the government budget on education. There is no basis to judge whether such a level of expenditure is sufficient or not, but it can serve as a point of reference when considering government budget priorities. Efforts should always be made to diversify sources of funding for education, including plans by which individuals who directly benefit from education can repay some of the costs through mandatory services after graduation.

C. Equity Should Become a Factor in Designing Access to Education

Equity will likely figure out prominently in the overall national economic development plan of Eritrea; and the equalizing function of education is well-known. If the goal of social equity is to be well-served by the educational system in Eritrea, education policymakers ought to pay particular attention to two problem areas. First, the imbalance between urban and rural areas; historically, the few educational opportunities in Eritrea were limited to the urban areas to the total exclusion of the rural areas. Second, the sociocultural barriers to women's participation in the educational process, especially past the primary school level.

D. Assessing Performance Should Become an Integral Part of the Educational Plan

Assessing the performance of the educational system, in light of the established national goals, is important for two reasons: first, to know how much progress is being made, and second, to get an opportunity to revise policy strategies and, if necessary, the goals. The idea here is not a matter of measurement but that of informed progress. In this respect, the importance of statistical information is obvious. For example, to assess progress towards the goal of universal primary education and the goal of literacy, we should initially know what percentage of school-age children are enrolled in school, and what percentage of the general Eritrean population is literate, respectively.

E. Adult and Nonformal Education Should Supplement Formal Education

In order to achieve the goal of universal literacy, educational activities should not be limited to schooling. Literacy campaigns, adult education, on-the-job training and other nonformal educational activities should provide to the large segments of the population the opportunity to gain new knowledge and skills or to enhance what they already possess. To concretize the need for nonformal educational activities, the writer would like to cite three examples from the memory of his school days in Eritrea.

Case 1. Haile Mariam is a lawyer at heart, equipped with the traditional skills of litigation he acquired through mere observation. An accident left him with a foot injury so that he cannot engage in farming. So he decides to earn his living by being a lawyer. He always carries in his pocket a book entitled, *Adkeme-Melegae,* the civil code that regulates property relations in the province of Serae in Eritrea. He can recite that code book from cover to cover. Every time he encounters a student relative, he invites the student to the tea shop. As soon as they sit at a table, he reaches for his pocket and pulls out papers and asks the student to read the contents to him, including those of the code book to refresh his memory. Every time he wants to file a lawsuit or respond to one, he sits with a professional writer and dictates his thoughts by paying a fee. Haile Mariam, at the age of 37, can neither read nor write.

Case 2. Tewolde Maasho is a happy go-lucky elderly man with a great sense of humor, and possesses a unique talent of composing poetry instantly. He is undoubtedly an accomplished poet. He can observe a situation and compose the most fascinating piece of poetry on the spot. On every major social occasion — be it a wedding, a holiday or a funeral ceremony — Tewolde Maasho would compose a fitting poem in commemoration of that occasion. For days, following the occasion, his compositions become the favorite topic of the community; men, women and children try to recite his pieces. I am afraid none of the works of this brilliant man will be recorded, and thus will be lost to the future generation forever. Tewolde Maasho too can neither read nor write.

Case 3. Saada Hassen is a widow and mother of two young children. She decides to earn her living and raise her children by starting a retail business of her own. Her business is very simple: during the harvest season, she buys crops from farmers in the open market and sells them to the merchants for a minimal profit. During the sowing season, she does the reverse. Imagine Saada dispensing to a customer from a huge pile of sorghum, using the standard of *melelik,* counting her numbers loudly so that there is no misunderstanding. When she reaches the desired count, she gives a long stare, at nobody in particular, but she is trying to calculate inside her head the total amount of the bill. At the end of the day she goes home and will still be thinking of some of the transactions about which she still has doubts, and will engage in a mental exercise to recalculate the bills. Her life would be easier if she knew how to do some basic arithmetic.

Common to all three cases is the denial of access to any kind of education. That denial has prevented Haile Mariam from becoming an effective lawyer, Tewolde Maasho from becoming an effective poet and writer, and Saada Hassen from becoming an effective entrepreneur. Nonformal education should be an integral part of the educational system so that no Eritrean citizen is denied access to some minimal functional education.

F. The Medium of Instruction Should be Selected Prudently

In selecting the medium of instruction in the educational system, the following factors should be considered: (1) the choice of the community; (2) the need to foster national unity and achieve commonality of knowledge; (3) the developmental stage of a given language, including its amenability to technical knowledge; and (4) the need for universality of knowledge and of skills.

If we superimpose these factors to the reality in Eritrea, it seems prudent that the medium of instruction at the primary school level should be a local Eritrean language, as determined by the community, and the medium of instruction at the secondary and higher education levels should be English.

G. The Educational Functions of Churches and Mosques Should be Sorted Out

The notion of separation of state and religion is a political issue and belongs to the domain of the national constitution. But, schools are the primary social institutions that give the notion its true meaning. It is a known fact that two major religions, Christianity and Islam, have dominated the lives of the Eritrean population so much that separation of politics from religion is easier said than done, and thus presents a formidable challenge.

The educational functions of the churches and mosques in the country are undeniable. Sorting out the educational functions and enhancing them, while leaving the faith-related activities to the individual adherents, presents a delicate problem. At any rate, educational policymakers should consider curricular measures by which koranic and church schools can be drawn into the primary school system.

So far, we have been dealing with general policy questions in the context of which Eritrea's educational system should be planned and implemented. Next, we turn to policy issues that are internal to the educational system itself.

V. POLICIES INTERNAL TO THE EDUCATIONAL SYSTEM

The subject of the structure of the educational system is not within the scope of this paper. But, we assume an educational system with three levels — the primary, secondary and tertiary (or higher education) — as a basis for organizing the thoughts in this section.

A. Primary Education

Primary education is a reference to the education given to children during the first four to six years. The primary level is the key to the success or failure of the national educational effort as it is the foundation upon which the whole system rests. Three problem areas stand out at the primary level:

1. Expansion of Access to Cope with Population Growth. Given the goal of free, universal primary education, the size and rate of growth of primary education will be driven by demographic factors. We do not know the exact birth rate in Eritrea, but it is safe to assume that is in the range of 2.5 to 3.0 percent, which is the estimate for most African countries. Accommodating the increasing number of children in the primary school system will require tremendous resources. Coping with the pressure will be a major challenge; it may require a combination of increases in public funding, cost containment, and sharing of expenses with the individual beneficiaries and the private sector.

2. Importance of Nutrition and Health Care. From the standpoint of human resource, school feeding and basic health programs are critical at the primary school level. The overwhelming majority of Eritrean parents do not have the economic means to provide nutritional food to their children. Moreover, traditionally the attitude of parents toward nutritional needs of children leaves much to be desired. Thus, primary schools need to give some attention to the nutrition and health needs of the young children they teach, if Eritrea is to develop the type of human resources it needs for economic development.

3. Equipping Primary School Graduates with Basic Skills. Not all primary school completers will proceed to secondary schools. The primary school curriculum should be such that the individual for whom a primary school certificate is terminal, is equipped with basic skills, habits and attitudes that will make him/her a productive citizen. That is to say, at the minimum, the primary school graduate should be functionally literate.

B. Secondary Education

Secondary education is the level of education children receive after primary education but before the higher education stage. This level again presents a set of several challenges to Eritrean educational policymakers.

1. The Dilemma of Access versus Resource Constraint. Eritrea's current developmental stage does not permit universal secondary education. Necessarily, access to secondary education will have to be limited. In Africa, national policies on access to secondary education vary by country. For example, in Tanzania, entry to secondary education has been very restricted (only about 1–2 percent of primary school completers). In Nigeria, the national development plan stipulates that 70 percent of primary school completers have some access to secondary education. Factors relevant to determining the degree of access to secondary education include: the demand pressure; availability of financial and other resources; the performance of the economy and its manpower needs. Perhaps the most prudent policy is to require minimum standards of educational achievements, develop standardized tests that reflect those requirements, and make secondary education available to those who pass such tests.

2. Making Educational Content Relevant. The relevance of the educational content to the Eritrean society at large, and to the country's development needs in particular, is even more significant at the secondary than at the primary school level. The colonial legacy of education in Africa is well-known, and Eritrea has had its share of that legacy. What is different in Eritrea, however, is that in the process of the armed struggle for independence, a new educational system has sprouted from the ashes of the colonial rule. This system can serve as a foundation for developing a curriculum which will serve Eritrea's socioeconomic development needs.

Particularly relevant to the secondary level is the balance between general education and vocational/training schools. Much debate and many experimentations have been going on for the past three decades over the question of priority between general and vocational education. The dust seems to have settled now, and the conclusion reached is that general education is at least as important to development objectives as is specific skill training, and that the former is a necessary complement to the latter (Psacharapoulos and Woodhall 1986). This has an important implication to the structure of secondary education policymakers contemplate for Eritrea. This may mean that general education for the first two years followed by vocational training for the last two years of secondary education may be a better approach than establishing two separate tiers from the very beginning.

Regardless of the structure, assuming the national economic development plan for Eritrea calls for laying a groundwork for a more technically-oriented economy, secondary education curriculum should place heavy emphasis on general mathematics and scientific skills.

3. The Paradox of Being Consumer of One's Own Product. The educational system is a major consumer of its own product. Teachers for the anticipated expansion of primary schools have to come from the secondary education level. Specialized teacher training schools are essential and should be the major sources of qualified teachers. But, it is going to take a while for such schools to meet the demand for teachers. Meeting the demand in the short run will require nothing short of a full implementation of EPLF's henceforth educational slogan: "the educated should teach the uneducated." In practical terms, this means secondary school completers should be used to teach primary school students even though they are not formally trained to be teachers. In the long run, teacher training schools should be expanded, and the teaching profession should be made attractive and respected enough to attract and retain qualified teachers. It is by entrusting children to qualified teachers that quality human resources can be guaranteed for Eritrea's future.

C. Higher Education (College/University Level)

Having advised African countries to streamline their higher education spending and redirect them to other levels of education, the World Bank and other international agencies now are stressing the importance of higher education to Africa's future (*Chronicle of Higher Education*, May 1991). In assessing the state of higher education in sub-Saharan Africa, such agencies conclude that African university graduates are of questionable quality and relevance to the continent's developmental needs, and that the pattern of financing higher education is inequitable and inefficient (World Bank 1988). Implied in those conclusions are important lessons that can be helpful in our deliberations on the establishment of higher education for Eritrea. Following are four general policy suggestions based on such lessons.

1. A Single National Higher Education System for Efficiency. Guiding the country's higher education activities from a single central administration offers the following advantages: (a) effective planning and effective linkage of universities to the economic development needs of the country, (b) minimization of administrative costs, and (c) avoidance of needless duplication of educational programs through better coordination.

2. University of Multiple Functions. The theoretical notion that institutions of higher education should have the three-pronged function of instruction, research and public service is well-known. The real question, however, is to make those functions a reality. Preparing young men and women for high-level positions by equipping them with requisite knowledge and skills is perhaps the obvious function of a university. But a university should also engage in research, both basic and applied, and the results should somehow impact the lives of the country's citizens. The service component of the function is also important in that a university should exist to benefit not only those few who are fortunate enough to gain access to it, but also the public at large. Particularly important is the need to establish ongoing linkages between university programs and their corresponding government and private sector functional areas.

3. University Presence Should Be Felt Beyond its Walls. This is related to the service function of the university. In the United States, there is an idea known as "the Wisconsin Idea," which, as its name suggests, originated in the State of Wisconsin. That idea can be best explained by the slogan that has guided the activities of the University of Wisconsin over the years: "The boundaries of the campus are the boundaries of the state." I think it is self explanatory. That slogan should be as appropriate to Eritrea as it has been to Wisconsin and other states in the United States.

4. Relevance of Programs to Justify High Costs. The importance of relevance of the curricular content of secondary education to the development needs of the country has already been emphasized. The question of relevance is even more critical at the higher education level because of the high cost involved. We can claim that the tremendous resource, which is likely to be invested in higher education programs in Eritrea, is a worthwhile investment only if the programs are relevant to the country's developmental needs.

VI. SUMMARY AND CONCLUSION

The importance of education for the socioeconomic development of a country like Eritrea is beyond question. From the standpoint of economic development, education should be viewed as an investment in the future. Such a view implies that Eritrea's educational activities should be consciously and carefully planned. The plan should start with the establishment of bold, yet attainable, national educational goals.

To guide the implementation of such national goals, educational policymakers need to develop policies and strategies that are grounded in the specific circumstances of Eritrea and the specific needs of the people of Eritrea. The educational system that has sprouted from the ashes of colonialism in the course of the just-concluded armed struggle can definitely serve as a basis for formulating the needed policies. At the same time, we can draw many valuable lessons from the experiences of other peoples as we chart the course of the educational activities for the people of Eritrea for the last decade of the twentieth century and beyond.

REFERENCES

Eritrean People's Liberation Front (EPLF). 1987. National Democratic Programme, adopted by the Second Congress of the EPLF, March 19, 1987.

Federal Republic of Nigeria. 1981. *National Policy on Education.* Lagos.

King, Kenneth. 1984. "The End of Educational Self-Reliance in Tanzania?" Occasional Papers, Center of African Studies, Edinburgh University.

Psacharapoulos, George, and Maureen Woodhall. 1986. *Education for Development: An Analysis of Investment Choice.* World Bank.

Thompson, A. R. 1981. *Education and Development in Africa.* New York.

World Bank. 1988. *Education in Sub-Saharan Africa.*

RESTRUCTURING EDUCATION IN ERITREA: POLICIES AND PRACTICES

Yegin Habtes

I. RESTRUCTURING ERITREAN SCHOOLS FOR DEVELOPMENT

A. Introduction

The new and rapidly changing Eritrean society and its economy require a very different worker and citizen than the traditional schools have been producing. In the traditional systems many students leave school without even minimal skills. These students always find it difficult to participate successfully and happily in the economy and society. Therefore, the aim of restructuring the school system in new Eritrea must be to make needed changes in schools so that the country educates all of its children for productive lives.

B. Defining Restructuring

Restructuring is distinguished as much by its philosophical underpinnings as it is by its structural or operational components. Its most salient characteristics are influenced by a belief system and a vision that require radically different responses to the problem of education than are possible within current forms .of schooling. Therefore, restructuring can be viewed as a process of institutionalizing essential, new beliefs and values in school mission, structure, and process. In other words, restructuring is about reconfiguring the basic functions, operations and organizations of schools.

Restructuring introduces fundamental changes in two key dimensions of schooling: (1) roles and relationships, and (2) programs and services for students. This paper discusses briefly these two fundamental factors in light of future Eritrean schools.

II. ADMINISTRATIVE ROLES AND RELATIONSHIPS

Self-management is a concept embraced by many successful businesses as a means for decentralizing the decision-making process to achieve a high level of productivity. Self-managing units have the authority to decide on how to meet established goals and how to allocate personnel and resources in order to do so. The concept of self-managing units can be applied directly to Eritrean public schools.

Self-management, which has been referred to as "site management" or "school-based management," is characterized by site autonomy, shared decision-making among school staff, enhanced roles for teachers and parents and regulatory simplicity (U.S. Department of Education 1991). The development of self-managing schools involves a shift in focus from individual methods of performing work to group methods. In other words, it entails attention to an increased quality of involvement.

To implement this concept in Eritrea, first, a large group of stakeholders appointed by the provisional government, must participate in running the school.

This body of stakeholders will be responsible for policymaking and will work with the Chief Educational Officer (CEO) (Minister of Education or Secretary of Education), who is also appointed by the provisional government. The CEO works at the pleasure of the provisional government and serves as a member of the cabinet. Together the body of stakeholders, which henceforth will be referred to as the "National Board of Education," and the CEO have the formal authority over the total public education and cultural effort of the nation. The board meets monthly or bimonthly depending on the need.

Specific responsibilities of the "National Board of Education" may include the following:

1. To delegate to the CEO responsibility for all administrative functions;
2. To support the CEO fully in all decisions that conform to professional standards and board policies;
3. To give the CEO the benefit of the board's counsel in matter related to individual board member's expertise, familiarity with the local school system, and community interests;
4. To hold all board meetings with the CEO or a designee present;
5. To consult with the CEO on all matters, as they may arise, that concern the school system and on which the board may take action; and
6. To provide the CEO with sufficient administrative help.

The CEO will serve as the head of the nation's department of education and is also an ex-officio member of the National Board of Education. He or she must be a professional educator. The major responsibilities associated with the Office of the Department of Education are likely to include the following functions:

1. Serve as the chief administrator of the nation's department of education and the national board;
2. Select personnel for the department (central staff);
3. Recommend improvements in educational legislation and educational budgets;
4. Arrange for studies, committees, and task forces as deemed necessary to identify problems and recommend solutions; and
5. Report on the status of education in the nation to the government and/or the legislature, and National Board of Education.

Directly under the CEO come the senior divisional educational officers and their staff (central office staff). It would be the responsibility of each divisional officer to create what was referred to earlier as the "self-managing units." In such schools, teachers take on a variety of leadership responsibilities, not only with respect to curriculum and instruction, but also with respect to the ways that resources are employed. Under such conditions, the principal who often serves as the school's chief executive officer, becomes responsible for supporting school team in exercising their expanded decision making authority and responsibilities.

According to Hackman (1986), a self-managing unit will exhibit the

following behaviors:
- Members take personal responsibility for the outcomes of their work and show in their action that they feel personally accountable for the results of what they do.
- Members monitor their own performance continuously, actively seeking data and feedback to learn how well they are accomplishing their task.
- Members supervise their own performance taking corrective action at their own initiative to improve their performance.
- When members do not have what they need to perform well, they actively and constructively seek from the larger organization the guidance, help, or resources they need for excellent performance.
- Although members make sure that their own responsibilities are being met, they also have a vested interest in reaching out to help others. They are willing to make effort to help members in other areas improve their performance, thereby strengthening the performance of the organization as a whole.

Effective self-managing schools are not created by simply professing democratic ideals, by simply turning down organizational hierarchies, or by instituting a "one-person, one-vote" decision-making process. Instead, such schools employ integrated top-down and bottom-up approaches to change. Organizational structures are based on networks and flexible work groups rather than hierarchies. Such self-managing schools will be run with the cooperation of all the constituencies in the school. Each school will have a representative group of parents, students, and teachers who formulate the matter of daily governance.

The group will be led by a coordinator (principal) who is recognized as an outstanding teacher. This officer will continue to teach (at least minimally) or will continue in office at the request and approval of the governance committee for the school.

Under such leadership, the school will emphasize basic principles of connecting classroom learning with the outside world and social responsibility to the school community as well as to the larger communities beyond the school.

III. RESTRUCTURING PROGRAMS AND SERVICES

A. Elementary Education

The purpose of the elementary education is to provide students with the experiences needed to promote life long learning in an interdependent world. It should focus on basic literacy skills, physical skills, thinking processes and aesthetic expression.

The appropriate learning sequence for the elementary aged child should be a continuing process connecting concrete experiences to abstract concepts. Instruction should provide learners with an abundance of manipulative materials, real life experiences, play, curiosity and challenges that are vital to the learning sequence.

Opportunities for independent and cooperative learning should be provided for all students. Learning experiences which encourage children to rely on themselves and on one another are essential to helping them become confident, independent and responsible.

Upon completion of the elementary program, it is expected that students will have acquired the following skills and abilities:

1. Use basic communication and mathematical skills for purposes and situations they will encounter throughout their lives;
2. Apply core concepts from mathematics, the sciences, the arts, the humanities, and social studies to situations they will encounter throughout their lives;
3. Become self-sufficient individuals;
4. Become responsible members of a family workgroup, or community and demonstrate effectiveness in community service;
5. Think and solve problems in school situations and in a variety of situations they will encounter in life; and
6. Connect and integrate experiences and new knowledge from all subject matter fields with what they have previously learned, and build on past learning experiences to acquire new information through various media sources.

In order to develop the above listed competencies in their students, teachers must make substantial adjustments in their instructional practices by including the methods described below.

First, infuse real-world learning and work into their instruction and place more responsibility on students to work both independently and collaboratively. In order to create a unified nation, teachers should plan lessons cooperatively so that students can work together to accomplish these daily goals and objectives. This will create a positive interdependence among students and develop the feeling that they can reach their learning goals if, and only if, the other students in the learning group also reach their goals (Deutsch 1962). This is much more desirable, than structuring lessons competitively so that students work against each other to achieve a goal that only one or a few students can attain. In competitive situations, there is a negative interdependence. Students perceive that they can obtain their goals if and only if the other students in the class fail to obtain their goals.

Second, design instructional alternatives to accommodate the range of abilities and talents. Good schools firmly believe that all students can learn and feel responsible for seeing that they do. They adapt instruction to the needs of the students and the situation (Heward and Orlansky 1988). It is perfectly acceptable to group students according to ability — both across grades and across classrooms. However, the grouping should be very fluid, where students can frequently move between groups, and extra attention can be given to slower students. It is also imperative that the schools provide special programs for academically talented students by broadening and enriching the curriculum with special in-depth courses, field trips, and independent study options (Gallagher 1981). Field trips in particular could be more beneficial in places like Eritrea because they would extend the classroom into the community (Clark and Starr 1986).

Third, reorganize instruction so that students truly understand the materials presented to them; experience more in-depth learning as opposed to rote learning and engage in higher order thinking and learning tasks.

Porter and Brophy (1988) suggest that effective teachers use published instructional materials in ways that contribute to instructional quality. Some teachers might say we don't have the money to purchase the necessary materials. This might be true but it should not be forgotten that teachers in excellent schools tend to develop their own instructional materials rather than purchase commercial packages (Wayson 1988).

B. Secondary Education

Although the goals of elementary schools are to provide students the experiences needed to promote life-long learning, secondary education should prepare all students for a life of work and learning. Accordingly, it is suggested that secondary schools in Eritrea should comprise of the school division following the elementary school which includes grades 9–12. The curriculum of such community secondary schools must be designed in such a way to meet the specific needs of the community. Such curriculum must be a shared vision of what student teachers, administrators and parents can accomplish together (Boyer 1983).

Eritrean secondary schools to be effective must be structured in such a way that there are two types of secondary school programs: (1) comprehensive high schools, and (2) specialized vocational schools.

Comprehensive high schools will offer courses in language, history (Eritrean history, African history, world history); civics, sciences, mathematics, and technology. These being the core courses, all students in comprehensive high schools will be given an opportunity to pursue their own unique aptitudes and interests. Specifically, the last two years of high school should be considered a "transitional school," program in which half the time is devoted to completing the common core and the other half to a program of "elective" clusters. These clusters will include five to six courses, and might range from "distribution" and marketing to business and office equipment and computers. Such programs could be offered in cooperation with local businesses and local arts centers.

Specialized vocational schools will offer broad vocational curriculum choices, such as agriculture, health, and industrial arts. These schools, to be successful ought to have up-to-date equipment as well as trained teachers.

Although it is important that graduates from such schools master their trade, the old philosophy that they must spend 80 to 90 percent of their time on "hands-on" activities might not be for the best interest of the students and the nation.

Looking to the year 2000, high school education might not be sufficient. As a result, specialized vocational schools must not focus on narrow skill courses that have little intellectual substance; courses that give them "hands-on" experiences while denying them a decent education. Instead, specialized vocational schools should provide their graduates with the knowledge and skills that they need for work and the pursuit of higher education.

IV. SUMMARY

Eritrean schools should be restructured in such a way that the system provides greater discretion to individual schools. The people responsible for the school must be responsible for enacting changes. Teachers, administrators, students and parents must take active role in shaping the school's program through involvement in decision making. They should be responsible for not only executing the task, but also for defining how the task will be structured and the resource needed to accomplish it. These are the tenants of a self-managing schools.

Restructuring Eritrean schools should also take into consideration reorganizing instruction so that schools provide new services that contribute to the child's overall well-being and productive life. Upon completion of the elementary program, the child should have acquired basic literacy skills, fundamental thinking processes and should have experienced aesthetic expression. Secondary education on the other hand, should prepare all students for a life of work and further education. It might not be for the best new Eritrea to track students into programs of "work bound" and "college bound." In the years to come secondary education might not be sufficient for most of the Eritrean work force. As a result, secondary education must give "work bound" students a solid foundation to move with confidence from school to work and if necessary from work back to higher education.

In conclusion, Eritrean teachers should structure lessons cooperatively so that students work together to accomplish shared goals. This will encourage not only positive interdependence among students in the classroom, but also will help the young men and women to work together as adult Eritreans in the years to come.

REFERENCES

Bamberger, Richard (ed.). 1991. *Developing Leaders for Restructuring Schools: New Habits of Mind and Heart.* Washington, D.C.: U.S. Department of Education, Office of Educational Research and Improvement.

Boyer, Ernest L. 1983. *High School: A Report on Secondary Education in America, The Carnegic Foundation for the Advancement of Teaching.* New York: Harper & Row.

Clark, H. Leonard, and Irving S. Starr. 1986. *Secondary and Middle School Teaching Methods.* New York: Macmillan.

Deutsch, M. 1962. *Cooperation and Trust: Some Theoretical Notes In Nebraska Symposium on Motivation.* Edited by M. R. Jones. Lincoln: University of Nebraska Press.

Gallagher, J. J. 1981. "Differential Curriculum for the Gifted." In A. H. Kramer, D. Bitan, N. Butler-por, A. Eryatar, and E. Landau (eds.), *Gifted Children: Challenging Their Potential.* New York: World Council for Gifted and Talented Children.

Hackman, J. R. 1986. *Educational Administration and Policy: Effective Leadership for American Education.* Englewood Cliffs, N.J.: Prentice Hall.

Heward, L. William, and D. Michael Orlansky. 1988. *Exceptional Children: An Introductory Survey of Special Education.* Columbus, Ohio: Merrill Publishing.

Johnson, W. David, T. Roger Johnson, Edythe Johnson Holubec, and Patricia Roy. 1988. *Circles of Learning: Cooperation in the Classroom.* Edwards Brothers.

Porter, A. C., and J. Brophy. 1988. "Synthesis of Research on Good Teaching:

Insights from Work of the Institute for Research on Teaching."
Educational Leadership 45(8):74–85.

Wayson, W. W. 1988. *Up from Excellence: The Impact of the Excellence Movement on Schools*. Bloomington, Ind.: Phi Delta Kappa Educational Foundation.

Wood, Fred H., and Sarah D. Caldwell. 1975. "Defining School Based Improvement in the Denver Public Schools." Unpublished Report. Denver: Colorado Public Schools.

LABOR POLICY
FOR A MARKET-DRIVEN ECONOMY

Berhe Habte-Giorgis

I. INTRODUCTION

Independent Eritrea faces the twin challenges of creating a democratic system of government and a viable economy. Both objectives can be attained, to some degree, in the workplace. Unless there is democracy in the workplace there cannot be democracy in the society at large. Assuming a country follows an appropriate economic policy under the right conditions, the performance of the economy will depend on the productivity of labor. Productivity itself is determined, among other things, by the prevailing employer-employee relations, motivation and skill of the human resources, and type of technology.

Employer-employee relations can be viewed as a system, with the workers, employers, and the government as the main components. Each component has important roles to play. At the same time, all components interact with each other and have to maintain a certain balance for the system to operate properly. The government, in addition to being one component of the system, has the duty to provide the general environment within which employers and employees can jointly establish smooth working relations and resolve conflicts peacefully. This paper attempts to identify ideas useful for the formulation of a labor policy that can foster justice, industrial peace, and economic growth. The paper assumes a free enterprise economic system as the context within which employer-employee relations exist.

Although the term labor relations implies labor unions, this paper covers both unionized and non-unionized workers. The industrial relations system is first examined from a historical perspective. Then the experiences of other countries are briefly discussed to provide a comparative view. Finally, labor relations in Eritrea, the main focus of this paper, is discussed.

II. HISTORICAL PERSPECTIVE

A. General Background

The origin of labor unions goes back to the Middle Ages in Europe when guilds were formed to protect the jobs of skilled craftsmen and artisans, and to provide quality assurances for their workmanship. Thus, guilds in their original form were exclusionary in character. Modern day craft unions followed the policy of their forerunners in their strive to monopolize the job market by creating union shops, which prohibited the hiring of nonunion employees.

The Industrial Revolution introduced mass production in few locations where coal, iron, and water, the most important natural resources of the period, were abundant. Peasants and craftsmen alike moved to the factories and mines seeking employment for wages. Similarly, mechanization revolutionized farming, transportation, and the marketing of goods. Thus, hundreds, even thousands of workers were employed by single employers, sometimes on the same site. Working conditions were subhuman, management style was little better than slave-driving, and "master servant" relations prevailed everywhere.

Workers, social thinkers, and activists reacted to the new phenomenon in varying ways. For example, the Luddites in England thought they could solve the problem by destroying the machines. Utopian socialists wanted to go back to the pre–Industrial Revolution type of small-scale production and communal living (Clegg 1971). Marx and Engels viewed the situation as an inevitable continuation of a long historical process. According to Marx and Engels, the plight of the workers can improve only when they own the means of production and stop exploitation of the surplus of labor by the owners of business. Social democrats sought political solutions through industrial democracy. Others looked at the problem from a pragmatic angle and advocated collective bargaining to resolve economic issues and working conditions. However, to be able to bargain with management, workers should have the right to organize. Employers resisted all forms of collective action by workers as infringement on the owners' right to property. To them, right to property was superior to any employee right. Common law supported the position of the employers. In the United States, where the idea of collective bargaining made strong headway, court decisions and legislation were used to institute the right of workers to organize and bargain collectively.

In the end, there were two major tendencies of labor unionism in the world: "bread and butter" unionism in the West and the socialist form in the Soviet Union and other countries of similar ideological persuasion. After seventy years' experience, the Soviet Union and its former satellites are going back to the western style of unionism. Thus, barring few lingering socialist systems, western-style unionism remains the mainstream of world labor unionism.

However, even in the West, unions are not as popular and as powerful as they once were. In the United States, for example, membership in labor unions has been declining for the past three decades due to structural changes in the country's industries and the loss of confidence in unions. The interest of the union in the twenty-first century is predicted to be concerned with "improving the total work and income security of its membership by enhancing their mobility and skill development" (Miles 1989).

In Africa and most third world countries labor unions emerged during the colonial era. In the struggle for independence many of the independence movement leaders were either labor unionists or used the unions as their power base. However, after independence many of the new governments, and especially those that professed one form of socialism or another, put the unions under government control. Ironically, African labor unions were denied the independent existence and minimum rights they enjoyed under colonial rule (Clegg 1971).

Now the wheel of history has come full circle. Dictatorial regimes in Africa are being overthrown or seriously challenged by labor unions in alliance with students and other enlightened segments of the society. They are demanding the restoration of democratic rights and multipartyism. At least in one country the leader of the labor unions was expected to win the presidential election.

B. Eritrean Labor Movement

Labor unionism in Eritrea, unlike the typical pattern in European colonies of the time, did not develop during Italian rule. A racial policy, similar to apartheid in South Africa, was enforced upon Eritreans. Many parts of the city of Asmara were out of bounds for the "natives." Eritreans were treated as subhumans, collectively referred to as *"moschi"* or flies. Had the war ended in their favor, the Italians would have realized their wish "to make shoe soles out of the skin of Eritreans." In terms of employment, the only use the Italians had for Eritreans was as gunfodders in the colonial army, as providers of cheap labor in the plantations, and as housemaids and servants. Thus, any form of assertion of rights or collective action was out of the question.

During the British military administration, which followed Italy's defeat in 1941, a labor office was opened and grievances of employees were handled on an individual basis. The only notable collective action was a strike by workers of the Eritrean Railways, which was settled through the intervention of the Bishop of the Orthodox Church, and ultimately through arbitration.

The first national union was formed in Asmara on December 1, 1952. It was a federation representing free trade unions whose main interest was the protection of Eritrea's autonomy. The veteran leader of the Eritrean independence movement, Woldeab Woldemariam, was elected the first president of the federation. At that time, the main concern of the trade unions was the preservation of the country's political autonomy. Ten days later he was shot point blank and seriously wounded by assassins hired by Ethiopia. While he was still in the hospital, the workers put his name in the ballot for a bi-election to the Eritrean Assembly. He won by a landslide. The Eritrean Chief Executive officially nullified the election results. Shortly afterwards, Ato Woldeab went into exile and embarked on a long process of struggle for Eritrean independence. Thus, from the very beginning the Eritrean labor movement was the nucleus of struggle for the independence of Eritrea.

After the departure of Ato Woldeab into exile, the confrontation between the labor movement and the government culminated in the General Strike of 1958. The immediate cause of the strike was opposition to a decree by the Chief Executive of Eritrea that made union leaders personally responsible for their members' involvement in "communist" activities. The government used the "communist infiltration" of labor unions as a pretext to nip the emergent movement in the bud and to preempt its involvement in politics.

After annexing Eritrea in 1962, the Ethiopian government enacted the 1964 Labor Relations Proclamation. The new law gave workers the right to organize and bargain collectively and set minimum working conditions. Eritrean workers that migrated to Ethiopia are credited for playing an important role in organizing labor unions within Ethiopia. In Eritrea, unions became subsidiaries of the Confederation of Ethiopian Labor Unions (CELU).

Despite the legislation, there was little improvement in the conditions of the workers, both in Eritrea and Ethiopia. Emphasis was given to keeping the labor unions docile instead of protecting workers' interests and rights. Corrupt government officials took side with the employers in suppressing the workers. Some of the Italian industrialists in Asmara were so powerful that they even controlled top government ministers in Addis Ababa. In addition to regular payoffs they entertained the government officials in their special villas in Asmara and yachts on the Red Sea.

The Derg, the military junta which took power in 1974, brought the unions under its direct control. Union leaders and members who attempted to maintain the autonomy of the unions were swiftly killed or imprisoned.

During the struggle for independence, Eritrean workers participated in the armed fighting and underground activities. The political program of the EPLF gave primacy to the protection of the workers' rights and interests, along with that of the general masses.

III. SUGGESTED GOVERNMENT POLICY

Government labor policy should aim at creating an environment that enhances the dignity of labor and enable employees and employers to work out mutually acceptable terms of employment. The policy should also aim at settling disputes, whenever they arise, with the least disruption of work and inconvenience to society. To this end, governments legislate minimum labor conditions and standards and the mechanism for dispute settlement, based on the principle of subsidiarity. That means all matters have to be handled at the lowest possible level and with minimum government intervention (Fossum 1982).

In Eritrea, as in other nonindustrialized societies, the political, social, and economic conditions are different from those of the industrialized countries where unionism emerged. Therefore, the labor relations system that evolves should reflect the particular needs and conditions of the society. History of the Eritrean society in general, and labor unionism in particular, along with the legacy of the thirty-year struggle for independence, constitute the foundation on which the new labor relations system should be built. Other conditions such as low industrial activity, high level of unemployment, and generally poor socioeconomic condition of the people have to be viewed realistically. But, these conditions should in no way be used as excuses by employers, who remind workers not to be "beggars choosers," to have their way. There is always a balance where the interests of investors and workers can be met.

The low standard of living and high unemployment situation makes those employed look much better off than the rest, creating the image of "labor aristocracy." Workers may be asked to sacrifice their immediate interests for long-term societal goals such as economic development. If care is not taken both by the government and labor, the situation can put both parties at loggerheads. Workers will be viewed as pursuing narrow personal or group interests and the government will use economic development and broader societal interest as excuses for assuming a repressive and anti-worker stance. In the end, an anti-union attitude can develop in the society.

Specific topics of legislation and other issues important for the development and maintenance of a healthy climate of labor relations in a country are outlined below.

A. Legislation

The main labor law should address the rights of workers to get organized and bargain collectively, the obligations of employers to comply with minimum working condition requirements, provisions for dispute settlement, training, safety, health, and other essential provisions. Unions should be independent and free from government intervention except regulations necessary to make the labor relations process function smoothly (Fryer 1986).

Unions should have the option to form their own national organizations by industry, and one or more confederations. The option to form one confederation only should be left to the unions. Workers in a plant, whose number is too small to meet the legal requirement for forming a union, should be entitled to have the national or regional industrial union bargain on their behalf. Such a provision is very important in situations where most of the workers in a country may be employed by small businesses. Resistance of employers to such a policy is to be expected but should not deter the government from following the right policy. Employers themselves have the right to form their own associations to help them work together on labor relations matters.

In dispute settlement it is important that a spirit of conciliation predominates. The laws as well as the entire labor relations system should reflect this spirit. However, if efforts in mediation and arbitration fail, there should be a labor court to adjudicate disputes.

The rights of employees not to join unions should also be respected. Union shop, or membership in a union, should not be used as a condition for employment. The common practice is that nonunion employees in a unionized company are required to pay a fraction of the union dues to cover for the services the union renders and from which they may be benefiting.

B. Right to Strike

The rights of employees to strike should be protected by law (Kennedy 1980). Strike, or the threat of a strike, is the only weapon unions have to force employers to bargain in good faith, and at times to concede. However, depending on the nature of the industry and the effect of a strike on the welfare of society at large, the economy and national security, the government may selectively use a variety of measures to preempt strikes. Mandatory cooling-off period, compulsory mediation and arbitration, and outlawing wildcat strikes are some of the means used. Legal and illegal strikes should also be carefully defined. However, care should be taken by the government not to appear favoring employers at the expense of unions.

The right to strike carries some penalty. The moment employees go on a strike they are forfeiting their employment with the company, because employers have the right to hire replacements for striking workers. Similarly, employers lose money if the plant closes even for a few hours. Thus, it is in the interest of the two parties to reach agreement. Normally, both parties may agree on a "no strike, no lockout" clause in their collective agreement. According to this clause, employees agree not to strike and employers agree not to shut the workplace unless forced by business or financial exigencies.

C. Minimum Wage

Arguments pro and con to the minimum wage issue abound. Nevertheless, it is beneficial to have a minimum wage, or perhaps two: one for agricultural and one for industrial workers. The impact on prices and on the overall economy should be assessed carefully before minimum wage levels are established.

Employers in developing countries are generally interested in a "fast buck." They do not want to invest in training their manpower. They use obsolete technology, and they themselves are mostly not even aware of the modern techniques of management and motivation. They pay huge bribes to bypass the law, and sometimes even to operate within the law. In addition, investors, who are usually the owner-managers, expect and get abnormally high profits. The burden of all the inefficiency and greed falls on the workers, who are forced to work for wages below the subsistence level. A minimum wage, that is a livable wage, forces employers to embark on effective management to increase productivity. High productivity is mandatory for survival in a competitive global economy and for economic growth. Low wages, on the other hand, do not necessarily result in low cost of production.

D. Safety and Health

Separate legislation may be required to emphasize the importance of safety and health to the workers and to society. The International Labor Organization (ILO) standards can be useful in this regard. Safety and health are areas in labor relations where the government needs to be actively involved. Otherwise, the damage inflicted on the working population will be higher than the benefits reaped from industrialization. The disaster at the Union Carbide plant in Ophal, India, in the 1980s, where thousands of people were killed, blinded, or maimed for life, is an example of what can happen when safety is ignored.

The government should specify the safe working conditions for each industry and make this observance conditional for giving license to operate a business. Society and government have to realize that there is no trade-off between safety/health and employment. This is true especially in the present era of chemicals and radioactive materials that can cause genetic deformities and death to thousands of people, if not an entire population, and the effect can be passed to future generations.

Health and safety cannot be confined to the workplace. The effect on the environment should be viewed with the same degree of concern. Industries and the products they put in the market can cause serious environmental problems. Establishment of standards and continuous enforcement of the standards, reporting systems, and swift action whenever violations occur should be part of a vigorous application of safety and health policy.

E. Union Corruption

Unions may become very powerful and fail to respond to the demands of the rank and file. Embezzlement of union funds, selling out to the employers, intimidation, and manipulation are some of the illegal practices that characterize corrupt union leadership. Corrupt union leaders entrench themselves in power the same way dictatorial regimes do. They use money to buy support and use force against those who oppose them. The power of the leadership becomes too formidable for the general membership to do anything.

In the case of unions, the government should have reporting and disclosure laws to prevent corruption and to safeguard the right of the individual union member.

F. Training Provisions

Except for workers who are trained in trade schools, most operative employees learn the skill of their trades from their place of employment. On-the-job training or other formal training programs are usually offered by the employer. Unfortunately, too often, employers in developing countries ignore the training needs of their employees. The end result is shoddy workmanship, waste, and low-quality output. Initial industrialization for countries such as Eritrea will be primarily in labor intensive industries, and thus well-trained manpower is a prerequisite.

The government may have to use incentives, such as tax credits, to motivate employers to train their workers. When deemed necessary, technical assistance can be given to employers. Labor unions themselves can play an active role in pushing for adequate training and cooperating with management in this endeavor. Labor unions can offer training programs of their own outside the company premises. Assistance from various international aid agencies is available and should be utilized to the fullest extent.

G. Employer-Employee Cooperation

Both employers and employees should view each other not as adversaries, but as partners with common interests. The situation is not a zero-sum game, where if one wins then others lose. If the right attitude prevails when one party wins then everybody, including society, wins.

The sphere of cooperation should extend beyond the structured and legalized relations. Part of the explanation for the success of the Japanese is their participatory style of management in which workers are involved in making decisions regarding production and quality control that are normally considered within the prerogative of management in most industrialized societies. In Japan the employer takes full responsibility for the workers, both in times of prosperity and hardship (Furstenber 1974).

In the developing countries "workers' participation goes back to government initiative and not trade union pressure" (Schregle 1985). Often, such approaches lead to suspicion and misunderstanding by the workers, who see government-imposed cooperation as a means of undermining the union. The lesson to be learned from this experience is that it may be advisable to put worker representation and cooperation in the labor law only as a recommendation and not as an imposition. In Eritrea, the legacy of people working together as equals and partners in the struggle for independence, the "*gedli*" sense of comradeship and diligence or "esprit de corps," should be maintained and spread to the rest of the society. Such positive self-image provides the basis for effective working relations and high morale. The Japanese achieved phenomenal success in their economy, an economy that is known as "samurai capitalism," by converting the warriors into captains of industry.

H. Organization of Government

The government needs to have an agency in charge of labor affairs. In many countries the agency is at a ministerial level. The function of the agency will be to develop and enforce labor policy and legislation. Various departments and autonomous agencies that deal with matters related to labor and labor relations can be accommodated within this agency. A labor relations board in charge of arbitration and even a separate labor court have to be established to handle disputes.

I. Unions in Politics

In a democratic society any group should have the right to form a political party. The party will have power only up to the degree of support it gets from the electorate. To this end labor unions should have the right to form their own political party. In practice, labor unions support candidates in elections and political parties that support the labor cause.

Union interest in politics varies to the extent that the unions think their problems are political in nature or have political solutions. According to Drucker, "unionism as a political force collapses as soon as the conditions disappear which trade unions have been developed to correct" (Drucker 1965). Thus, union involvement in politics is a function of the prevailing political situation and to what extent unions think their problems are political in nature. The government should refrain from bringing the unions under its fold or preventing them from participating in politics independently.

J. International Affiliation

During the Cold War international affiliation was based on ideology. The East and the West each had its own international federation. The International Confederation of Free Trade Unions (ICFTU) belonged to the capitalist bloc while the World Federation of Trade Unions (WFTU) belonged to the communist bloc led by the Soviet Union. Part of the Cold War was fought on the labor front by both groups trying to win labor unions in nonaligned countries over to their side.

There are many other international and regional associations and agencies, some representing only labor and others representing employers. The ILO, a UN agency, is the premier international organization. Membership with the ILO requires the representation of unions, employers, and the government. There are minimum labor standards and many conventions that have to be adhered to by member countries. At the same time members receive technical assistance, which, in situations like in Eritrea, can be very useful.

K. Public Employees' Representation

In the developed countries, employees of the different levels of government, including bureaucrats, teachers, policemen, and firefighters, have the right to form unions and bargain collectively. In most cases they have the right to strike, although for some types of jobs strikes may be illegal. In other cases the government may have the power to invoke some restrictive measures to avert strikes. It will not be long before the question of public employees forming unions becomes an issue in developing countries, including Eritrea.

IV. CONCLUSION

A smoothly functioning labor relations system is important for industrial peace, economic development, and the well-being of society. The tripartite system, whereby employers and employees interact freely with minimum interference from the government, is preferred. Unions should be independent from domination or coercion by the government. Still, workers have the right to form political parties of their own or support a party and candidates of their choice. Likewise, employers should have the right to form their own organizations. Minimum standards of working conditions, safety, and other pertinent matters, along with the appropriate enforcement agencies, have to be established by the government.

It is important to foster, right at the outset, the spirit of union-management cooperation instead of the damaging adversarial relations. Policies developed and decisions made now, be it in labor relations or other areas, will become the tradition for the future. It is, therefore, very important that the long-term impact of any policy measure is properly analyzed before its implementation.

REFERENCES

Clegg, Ian. 1971. *Workers Self-Management in Algeria.* New York: Monthly
     Review.
Drucker, Peter F. 1965. *The Future of Industrial Man.* New York: New
     American Library.
_____. 1989. *The New Realities.* New York: Harper & Row.
Dunlop, John T. 1980. "The Development of Labor Organization." In *Readings
     in Labor Economics and Labor Relations,* 4th ed., edited by Richard L.
     Rowan. Homewood, Ill.: Richard D. Irwin.
Fossum, John A. 1982. *Labor Relations: Development, Structure, Process,* rev.
     ed. Dallas, Texas: Business Publications.
Fryer, Bob. 1986. "Trade Unionism, Public Policy and the Law." In *Freedom
     and Fairness: Empowering People at Work,* edited by Ken Coates.
     Nottingham, England: Spokesman.
Furstenber, Friedrich. 1974. *Why the Japanese Have Been So Successful in
     Business.* London: Leviathan House.
Kawada, Hisashi, and Ryuji Komatsu. 1973. "Post-War Labor Movements in
     Japan." In *The International Labor Movement in Transition,* edited by
     Adolf Sturmthal and James G. Scoville. Champaign-Urbana: University
     of Illinois Press.
Kennedy, Thomas. 1980. "Freedom to Strike is in the Public Interest." In
     Readings in Labor Economics and Labor Relations, 4th ed., edited by
     Richard L. Rowan. Homewood, Ill.: Richard D. Irwin.
Mills, Raymond E. 1989. "A New Industrial Relations System for the 21st
     Century." *California Management Review.* Berkeley: University of
     California (Winter).

WOMEN AND DEVELOPMENT PLANNING

Veronica Rentmeesters

I. INTRODUCTION

The definition of development is the fundamental question underlying the issue of women's role in development. Strategies that lead to an improvement in women's position as well as condition employ a particular concept of development. This concept focuses on the quality of life as well as economic growth, and incorporates a broader conception of what the economic dimension encompasses. The economy is not limited to formally constituted work units: informal and reproductive activities are an essential part of it. Equity and growth are seen as compatible goals, that is, this is a win-win rather than a win-lose situation. Such strategies stress the need for a transformation of not only social relations of production but also family relations and relations of political power. This definition of development calls for some changes in traditional planning concerns.

The dominant paradigm equates development with economic growth. In some cases, this perspective also addresses issues of human resources, meeting basic needs, and poverty reduction. However, it downplays the relative importance of human resources in development and ignores the relationship between democracy and development. The resultant policies have had a negative impact on women as women. (Boulding 1981; Daly 1989; Kruks and Wisner 1989; Overholt et al. 1985; Seidman and Anang 1992; Young 1988)

This paper will review the basic findings of research on women and development, the distinction between women's interests and gender interests, the various approaches to gender issues used in planning, general research findings on actions that contribute to maximizing women's role in development, the importance of maximizing women's role in the Eritrean context, and some specific recommendations for Eritrea's policymakers.

II. WOMEN AND DEVELOPMENT: GENERAL BACKGROUND

The three basic findings of research on women and development are:
1. All societies have a division of labor by sex though what is considered a male or female task varies cross-culturally. There is no natural or fixed gender division of labor.
2. The integration of women's reproductive, productive, and community management work within the private sphere of the home and in the public sphere must be considered to appreciate the dynamics of women's role in development.
3. Economic development has a differential impact on men and women. The impact on women has, with few exceptions, generally been negative.

The first of these findings, a sexual division of labor, which is culturally specific, points out the need to look at the issue as one of gender not sex.

It is based on social relationships between men and women and not on their biological differences. Other than pregnancy and childbirth, the specific roles of men and women vary widely from society to society and over time within a given society. In Eritrea, for example, traditionally among the Tigrinya, men weave and women do not, while among the Rashaida the reverse is true. Among the Tigrinya, housing construction is a male responsibility, while among the Tigre it is a female one. Veiling was nonexistent among Sahel Tigre women 150 years ago and almost all cash income came from sales of women's products. In modern times, Tigre women veil and most cash income comes from men's wage labor and sales of men's products.

The second finding is that women's multiple roles — productive, reproductive and community management — must be considered in development planning. The development of labor markets under capitalism leads to a differentiation of roles with what are defined as productive roles assigned to men and what are defined as reproductive roles assigned to women. Misconceptions that hold that the sexual division of labor is biologically not socially based and that women are "natural" biological nurturers place the burden of reproductive work on the shoulders of women alone. They come to be defined as solely responsible for family and household maintenance.

The view that, once the above change has occurred in social relations, women's liberation lies in their incorporation into productive labor is invalid. Most women are active in "productive" labor —unpaid agricultural work or wage labor — as well as reproductive and community management (nurturing) roles. Frameworks that see nurture and liberation as contradictory either endorse only reproductive and community management roles for women and thus reinforce women's subordination, or they seek to liberate women by integrating them into the modernization process. Women, however, are already integrated into productive work — at the lowest levels and in unpaid or poorly paid occupations.

Without explicit recognition of women's multiple roles, women's subordination is strengthened. Wage employment does not reduce women's responsibility for reproductive and community management work but forces them to work a double day. It also reinforces the ideas that women are supplementary earners and therefore should receive lower pay; that child care, parental leave, protective legislation, etc. are applicable to women alone; and that reproductive roles are a duty for women only and not society as a whole.

Finally, because of their different roles, development impacts men and women in different ways. The overall impact on women as women has been negative. Generally development has marginalized women and deprived them of control over resources and authority without lightening their workload.

Here one must distinguish between women's condition and women's position. Women's condition is their material state; women's position is their social and economic standing relative to men. Overall, women's social position has worsened with their country's integration into the world market and modernization, regardless of whether their condition improved or not.

If we look at formal education, for example, the overall situation is one where initially both sexes lack formal education and have similar positions and low conditions. With development far greater proportions of men are

educated than women. The condition of the small group of women who are
educated may improve but women's overall position relative to men is worse.
As a case in point, in Eritrea it is estimated that 40 percent of men are literate compared to 10 percent of women.

This finding of a deterioration in women's position, and often in their
condition, associated with development and "modernization" is not limited to
the developing countries. In fact, it was first noted in research on Western
nations (see, for example, Momsen 1991; Afshar 1991; Fortmann 1981;
Hewlett 1986; Young 1988).

III. WOMEN'S INTERESTS AND GENDER INTERESTS

Molyneux's distinction between women's interests/needs, practical gender interests/needs and strategic gender interests/needs provides a useful and
generally accepted framework for identifying the costs and benefits of various approaches to the issue of women and development. (1986)

The concept of *women's interests* assumes that women have compatible
needs based on their biology. However women's needs are determined not
only by their biology but also by their class, religion, ethnic group, country,
etc. Their needs, and thus their interests, may be determined by these factors as much as by their biological similarities. This is not to say that women
do not share some common interests. However, these common interests
should be called *gender interests* to avoid the illusion of a false unity that the
term, women's interests implies.

Gender interests can be divided into those arising from strategic gender needs and those arising from practical gender needs. Strategic gender
needs are needs identified through the analysis of women's subordination to
men. Strategic gender interests express women's gender needs for an alternative, more equal and satisfactory organization of society in terms of both
the structure and nature of relationships between men and women.

Practical gender needs are needs formulated from the concrete conditions women experience in their engendered position within the sexual division of labor. Practical needs are usually a response to an immediate
perceived necessity identified by women in a specific context. Practical gender interests express women's gender needs for human survival.

For example, a day care center located at the mother's workplace meets
a practical gender need but, because it does not raise, much less address, the
question of responsibility for reproductive work in the gender division of
labor, ignores strategic gender needs. The same center located at the father's
workplace, because it is likely to mean that the father will take responsibility for dropping off and picking up the child, addresses both practical and
strategic gender needs. How the responsibility for dropping off and picking
up of children is allocated within the family will affect whether a daycare center located in the community meets strategic as well as practical gender
needs. Does the mother remain responsible for dropping off and picking up
the children? Is responsibility shared with the father? Do other household
members (siblings, grandparents, etc.) take responsibility for this? If so, is it
usually female household members who take the responsibility?

Meeting both practical and strategic gender needs has inherent problems. Because poor women, the majority of women, often are preoccupied with efforts to satisfy practical needs they do not have time to reflect on, and thus ignore, strategic needs. On the other hand, the focus on practical needs by both women and planners frequently serves, even if unconsciously, to preserve and reinforce the existing unequal division of labor and its adverse effects on development of women.

For example, many training programs for women focus on "women's occupations." These programs can meet practical gender interests for increased income, financial security, etc. At the same time they reinforce the unequal division of labor. Such programs may also have contradictory effects when seen in different contexts or over time. In the context of traditional Tigrinya culture, training women in sewing addresses both practical and strategic gender needs. This is traditionally a "men's occupation" and so such training addresses the strategic gender need to break down the traditional division of labor. On the other hand, when seen in the context of Eritrean Tigrinya women's role in the world market, the same program reinforces the sexual division of labor that dominates in the world economy where sewing is a "women's occupation" (Molyneux 1986; Momsen 1991; Moser 1989 and 1991; Young 1988).

This distinction between women's needs and gender needs and between practical and strategic gender needs is useful in evaluating the various approaches policymakers and planners have taken toward women and development.

IV. APPROACHES TO GENDER IN DEVELOPMENT PLANNING

There are five basic approaches to dealing with the issue of women and development. These approaches, described below, are closely related to various general approaches to development that have been popular over the years: growth, growth with equity, basic needs, structural adjustment, empowerment (Moser 1989:1808).

A. The Welfare Approach

This approach, which is associated with growth models of development, has been and remains the most common and most popular approach. It focuses on the areas of: (1) family survival through provision of food aid, (2) eradication of malnutrition through education and mother and child health programs, and (3) population control through family planning programs.

The welfare approach rests on the assumptions that: (1) women are passive recipients, (2) motherhood is women's most important social role, and (3) child rearing is women's most effective role in development. Welfare programs do not question women's "natural" role as solely responsible for reproductive welfare. Their top-down, handout character creates and reinforces women's dependency. Yet this remains the most popular approach because it does not question the existing division of labor and is thus politically "safe" so long as women do not mobilize against it whether due to lack of consciousness or lack of resources.

B. The Equity Approach

This approach is associated with growth with equity development models and stresses bringing women into the development process through access to employment and the marketplace. It sees the origin of women's subordination as lying in inequality in both family and marketplace relations. It has had limited viability because it emphasizes top-down legislative measures that meet potential strategic gender needs but often ignore practical gender needs.

C. The Anti-Poverty Approach

It developed along with the basic needs approach to development that was popular in the 1970s and encompasses basic needs and employment programs. This approach assumes that inequality is linked not to subordination but to poverty. Therefore, a focus on reducing income inequality in women's productive role should solve the problem. In practice, this approach has exacerbated problems for women by: (1) ignoring women's engendered roles in reproduction and community management, (2) concentrating on female-headed households (FHH) and sex-specific occupations that replicate the existing division of labor, (3) developing economically inviable projects, and (4) increasing the work burden of women.

D. The Efficiency Approach

This approach is associated with the currently popular structural adjustment programs emphasizing efficiency and productivity. It stresses that, as half the population, women must be used efficiently in the labor force to achieve economic growth. It operates on the assumptions that: (1) increased economic participation automatically results in increased equity; (2) women's lack of education and underproductive technologies are the predominant constraints on their full equality; and (3) women's unpaid labor is elastic.

Practically this approach may contribute to more rapid economic growth at least in the short-term, but it entails high social costs generally and there are serious questions regarding its long-term viability. It hits women particularly hard because it shifts costs from the paid to the unpaid economy through increased use of women's unpaid labor in reproduction and community management.

E. The Empowerment Approach

This is the approach least used by existing formal planning models. It enjoys a great deal of popularity with grassroots organizations but little with governments. It rests on the following assumptions: (1) Women face not only gender oppression but also different experiences of oppression by race, class, and current and historical position in the international economic and political order, and these structures and situations must be challenged simultaneously at different levels; (2) Power is not domination over others but is the capacity to increase one's own self-reliance and internal strength and the right to determine choices in life and to influence the direction of change through the ability to gain control over material and nonmaterial resources; (3) Integration into existing forms of development is undesirable for women, and it also does not necessarily help all men; and (4) Women's multiple roles in production, reproduction and community management must be recognized.

Implementation of this approach has relied on: (1) use of bottom up strategies involving women's organizations, political mobilization, consciousness raising, and popular education; (2) avoidance of direct confrontation and utilization of practical gender needs to build a secure support base and means through which strategic needs may be reached; and (3) rejection of rigid bureaucratic structures for nonhierarchical open structures even when these are not the most efficient organizational form.

It is the empowerment approach's use of particular strategically-planned improvements in women's condition to improve women's position that has contributed to its successes — to women benefiting from development and to a more sustainable and beneficial form of development for society as a whole (Brydon and Chant 1989:213–39; Buvinic 1983; DAWN 1985; Goetz 1991; Moser 1989:1809–14 and 1991; Schoepf 1992).

IV. GENERAL FINDINGS ON THE ROLE OF THE STATE

The state has an important role to play in maximizing women's participation in development. General findings on the role of the state and particular policies are described below.

Evidence indicates that without state intervention women and other socially subordinate groups lose out. Market (the efficiency/structural adjustment approach) and purely voluntary approaches perpetuate subordination by relying on unpaid labor and increasing the burdens of women's "double day." To improve women's condition as well as position, state intervention must specifically note gender interests and incorporate them into planning. If gender differences and the implications of various policy interventions on women are not explicitly noted at each stage of policy development and for all sectors, development not only bypasses women, it worsens their position and often their condition. (For specific examples, see Overholt et al. 1985; Rao et al. 1991; Feldstein, Sims and Poats 1989: Fortmann 1981; Dauber 1981; Warren and Bourque 1991; and Moser 1987.)

To be successful, the form of this intervention must include consideration of: (1) the relative costs/benefits of various options, not necessarily only programs specifically geared to women; (2) the efficiency and/or effectiveness of state provision, organizational and/or managerial capacity; (3) the relationship between meeting practical gender needs and strategic gender needs; and (4) the positive role of democratic political processes in advancing women's position.

Traditional planning rests on several problematic assumptions: (1) The household is defined as the basic unit composed of husband, wife and children; (2) Within the household, there is a clear division of labor with the husband in productive labor and the wife in reproductive work; (3) Within the household, men and women have equal control over resources and decision-making; (4) Men and women use their income in similar ways; (5) Access to resources automatically implies control over them as well as over the benefits that flow from them.

In fact however, men and women play different roles in society and have differential control over resources and their benefits; therefore they often have different needs and interests. Gender disaggregation is necessary in assessing benefits and costs of various policies and programs. Specific recommendations in terms of data collection for policy-making purposes include: reexamination of data collection categories; disaggregation of data by sex; data collection on the informal and domestic sectors; expansion of indicators to obtain a more realistic assessment of development; and valorization of the informal and domestic sectors.

Broader analytic research is also needed on the questions of: (1) women's position within the system of production and division of labor; (2) women's social identity, and how far that is organized around their differences from men as opposed to other forms of social difference (class, ethnicity); (3) sexuality and its development and regulation within various nationalities and communities as well as by the state; (4) role of externally introduced elements as well as the history of internal changes prior to the emergence of the modern world system; and (5) women's role in creating, sustaining, subverting, adapting or resisting changes in these areas.

Objectives and methods, ends and means, are closely bound together. Whether planning takes a blueprint or a learning process approach makes a significant difference for society as a whole and particularly for women. Blueprint approaches produce poor results because they: (1) require a degree of knowledge and consensus that is unattainable; (2) cannot take into account the wide variety of circumstances that exist so they impose a universal solution which may be good for one situation but is not necessarily good for others; and (3) cannot take into account the improvisation and innovations required in implementation so there can be no dichotomy between thinkers and doers, planners and implementers.

The more inductive and experimental learning process approach does not allow for the feeling of control over outcomes associated with the blueprint approach. It involves a degree of democratization that is not customary and faces the problems of the time limitations, lack of self-confidence, and lack of education of the majority of the population, including women. In practice, however, the sense of control associated with detailed blueprints too frequently proves illusory. The flexibility of the learning process approach is more effective in practice in the long-term. "To the extent that national institutions desire for . . . people what they want for themselves . . . building up local capacity helps both the center and the periphery to advance their respective objectives." (Uphoff 1986:218)

Finally it must be noted that integrated approaches, rather than compartmentalization and fragmentation, work to women's benefit. Compartmentalization (the assignment of the issue to a women's bureau or ministry) in practice excludes consideration of gender issues in development. Fragmentation ignores women's multiple roles, a major source of the problems with most of the present development models. (See, for example, Afshar 1991; Brydon and Chant 1989; Buvinic and Lycette 1988; Schoepf 1992; Seidman 1981; Stamp 1990:26; Uphoff 1986:192-218; Young 1988.)

V. THE ERITREAN CONTEXT

Today Eritreans are at a major turning point in their history, the end of one era and the beginning of another. It is a good time to look back and remember that the struggle was not for its own sake but "to uproot and change prevailing conditions of exploitation, oppression, degradation and the deprivation of our human rights. . . . So long as freedom is not equally and universally extended to all members of society, so long as there is oppression, there is struggle" (EPLF 1973). The concept of development that this goal entails is by definition one which seeks to empower women as equal members of society. This commitment to the full range of human rights for all members of society is in itself justification for an active effort to work for women's strategic gender interests as well as their practical ones.

However, other nations' experiences provide gloomy prospects for the future of Eritrean women in national development. A number of other revolutionary movements (for example, Mozambique, Nicaragua, VietNam) also had this commitment including an explicit commitment to improve women's position. Yet their post-independence periods saw a great deal of backsliding on gender issues. In Eritrea today, there are already objections to women's ownership of land and to their political participation, verified reports of women fighters being "returned to their families" because they were not virgins at marriage, etc.

One would hope that backsliding in Eritrea would not occur to the extent it occurred in the said countries. Compared to these other nationalist revolutions that stressed women's participation, Eritrea enjoys advantages in terms of the number of years women were active in the front, the proportion of the front that was female, the use of integrated units, the participation of women in all areas of the front, the number of years the mass organization existed and the proportion of the population involved in the mass organization. The success of the EPLF during the independence struggle, which was based on an empowerment approach stressing bottom up popular participation, is the other factor that makes backsliding less likely.

Again while some backsliding is to be expected, Eritrea has some relative advantages. The population in the urban centers may not have the same experiences as other parts of the county but it is not antagonistic to the EPLF. The "honeymoon" won't last forever but it offers more time to lay the groundwork for a positive direction. Secondly, the Eritrean struggle to a much greater extent than any other contemporary movement, was genuinely self-reliant. Foreign assistance was minuscule. EPLF depended on an empowerment approach for its very survival. This approach is deeply embedded in the consciousness of many, including the policymakers. It is reflected in the general orientation to move toward maximizing decentralization and ensuring a more equitable distribution of resources throughout the country.

Though it has many supporters, there is no consensus in Eritrea today to support a concept of development that necessarily incorporates women's strategic gender interests. However, there is an immediate practical issue in Eritrea that can work in favor of meeting women's strategic needs. All economic sectors in Eritrea have a stake in maximizing the use of the potential labor force in terms of both quality and quantity. In Eritrea this labor force is largely female.

Human resources, labor power, are key in any country's development efforts. This is especially true for Eritrea. Thirty years of war have done serious damage to agriculture, industry and infrastructure. Even if oil is discovered tomorrow, it will take many years before Eritrea is in a position to reap the gains. What is to be done today? Eritrea must depend on its strength — a hard working population — to improve its weaknesses.

Relative to other countries, Eritrea's population is small. Small countries face increased pressure to facilitate women's economic participation. Economies of scale are not only applicable to the issue of efficient use of technology as machines but also to the efficient use of human resources. Many but not all sectors can produce efficiently on a small scale. However, in countries with a small population, ignoring women's roles means that it becomes very difficult to develop those sectors where economies of scale are important along with others. Competing labor power demands rule out the development of these sectors unless the country is extremely wealthy and can effectively draw immigrant labor. Even then questions of long-term security remain. (Kuwait is an example.) Ignoring women's role or increasing the oppression of women in this low population situation limits economic development no matter what concept of development — even the simple growth models popular in the 1950s — is employed.

In Eritrea's case, this issue becomes even more important because of the demographic impact of thirty years of war. Eritrea has a disproportion in male-female ratios. Women are more than half of the adult population. While there are no national surveys, the percentage of female headed households is high by traditional Eritrean norms. What estimates or limited area studies exist for the former liberated areas run 10–20 percent FHHs and for the refugee camps in Sudan (most of whose residents are expected to return) run 15–22 percent FHHs. For the former enemy occupied areas, especially the cities, there are no estimates but the general impression is that the number of FHHs is high. The survey with the largest sample size was of over 17,000 recent returnees: 39.8 percent of these were FHHs. These figures have serious implications for the viability of the traditional gender division of labor for productive, reproductive and community management work.

Like most third world countries, Eritrea has a population age structure with a high dependency ratio. Eritrea has not completed the demographic transition that results in a fairly even distribution of age groups. Instead children under age 15 are almost half the population in Eritrea. The labor force must produce to meet not only their own needs but also those of their dependents. The dependency ratio has major implications for per capita income, purchasing power, markets, use of child labor, education, health and the quality of the next generation of the labor force.

The Eritrean labor force must not only meet its needs today but also make the demographic transition thus reducing its dependency ratio and increasing both the proportion and the quality of the labor force. The key to demographic modernization is not the overall level of economic development but widespread participation of the population in the development process through equitable distribution of food, health care and education; improvement in women's status; provision of career opportunities to women independent of child-bearing; and access for all to family planning services.

This is an efficiency argument and it is important to recall the problems of that approach mentioned above. Women play multiple roles in society and their labor is not elastic. Women are having difficulty surviving "double days."

They will not survive "triple days." A broader reconsideration of the gender division of labor is essential for sustainable development. (Afshar 1991:4; Berar-Awad 1984; Bondestam 1988; EPHP 1985; Findlay 1987; Gaim 1990; IBRD/World Bank 1984; Rentmeesters 1989)

VI. RECOMMENDATIONS

In the Eritrean context, implementation of the general findings noted above involves society as a whole — every department, sector, region, etc. It means incorporating gender consciousness into the Eritrean world view and definition of development.

Along with consideration of short- and long-term financial costs and benefits, environmental impacts, etc., the preparatory process for every policy, program, and major law should be required to incorporate a gender impact assessment. This assessment must consider not only the impact today but also the implications for the future for both practical and strategic gender issues. The information on the costs and benefits in terms of gender should be available to the affected community whether it is a single village or the country as a whole. In order to make these assessments, both appointed and elected officials must be aware of gender issues and be able to use that information in making decisions.

Data collection in all areas must be disaggregated by sex and include consideration of all relevant indicators. For example, this means that departments like industry must consider the differential impact of their policies/programs and must consider this impact not only on productive roles but also on reproductive and community management roles in society. If a new manufacturing plant is to be established in some area: Are both males and females being recruited as employees? Do work hours or location affect employment by gender? Are there gender differentials in pay scales? Are there gender differentials in occupations within the plant? What provisions are being made for child care? How will the establishment of this plant affect the informal sector (which is where women often gain their income)? How will it affect the division of labor among productive, reproductive and community management roles? How will it affect family income, the usage of that income and power relationships within the family?, etc.

On the other hand, departments like social affairs must consider the differential impact of their policies/programs on productive as well as reproductive and community management roles. For example, if responsibility for civilian disabled rests with the community, how is this responsibility allocated? Does this mean that care for the disabled will be provided by relatives? Which sex is responsible for financial aspects of care? Which for the time aspects of care? What are the implications for productive, reproductive and community management roles for both men and women in the community?, etc.

PGE should facilitate, commission or carry out the broader analytic studies noted in General Findings above to improve knowledge of what are the important social indicators and relationships in the gender division of labor.

PGE departments must provide selected staff with appropriate training in gender planning. This training can take various forms: training abroad at various institutes and schools that offer such programs, hiring expatriates or qualified Eritreans to provide short- and/or long-term training programs in Eritrea, developing relevant gender planning courses as part of the curriculum of the University of Asmara.

This information and training will not be put to use unless key policymakers, both elected and appointed, are conscious of the role of gender issues in development or face sufficient public pressure to force them to consider these issues.

PGE should sponsor informational programs for policymakers and the general public on women's role in development. These programs should use a variety of media to convey their message: seminars, radio and television broadcasts, newspapers articles, posters, exhibitions, information packets. They should include concrete and specific information about women's roles in Eritrea derived from the studies and data collection noted above. Local level women should be involved in both the formulation and presentation of the key issues. Where applicable, there should be a gender balance in both presenters and participants (see Thompson 1991).

The Department of Education and the University of Asmara should incorporate gender issues in the curriculum so that gender consciousness becomes part of the world view of the next generation. Throughout the curriculum, both males and females should be portrayed as role models in a multiplicity of roles and in all three role areas (productive, reproductive and community management). High school and introductory university-level sociology courses should include consideration of gender issues. These courses should be required core curriculum for all students whatever field they expect to enter.

PGE should reinforce the general tendency to emphasize decentralization with democratization and participatory approaches. Policy-making is overwhelmingly concentrated among males at the present time. Both historical factors and continuing sexual discrimination contribute to this situation. Because decentralization accompanied by democratization and participatory approaches shift power and policy-making to lower levels, where women are concentrated, they generally work to women's advantage. The resulting policies are more likely to reflect women's actual gender interests and needs and not male leaders ideas of what those interests and needs are.

If women are to gain rather than lose from development, they must be actively involved in designing policies and programs from the local through the national level. Precise prescriptions cannot come from above. They must be developed from below and take into consideration diverse circumstances.

The National Union of Eritrean Women and other concerned organizations must train and organize both their members and other individuals, male and female, to lobby for policies and programs that meet both strategic and practical gender interests. Some policymakers will consciously support the empowerment of women but many will not. If women's condition and position are to improve, women must struggle for their agenda. This will not be easy. However, the Eritrean independence struggle disproved the axiom that no small power can defeat a larger power without external support. There must be a sustained conscious effort by both men and women, leaders, planners and masses, to disprove the axiom that women's liberation cannot survive a liberation struggle. Ultimately, it is women themselves, through mobilizing pressure on the government to recognize them as equal citizens, who will be the key to a form of development that benefits all.

REFERENCES

Afshar, Haleh. 1991. "Women and Development: Myths and Realities." In Afshar (ed.), pp. 1–10.

_____, (ed.). 1991. *Women: Development and Survival in the Third World.* London: Longman.

Berar-Awad, Azita (ed.) 1984. *Towards Self-Reliance: A Programme of Action for Refugees in Eastern and Central Sudan.* Geneva: ILO.

Bondestam, Lars, Lionel Cliffe, and Philip White. 1988. *Eritrea: Food and Agricultural Production Assessment Study.* Leeds: Leeds University Centre of Development Studies, Agriculture and Rural Development Unit.

Boulding, Elise. 1981. "Integration into What? Reflections on Development Planning for Women." In Dauber and Cain (eds.), pp. 9–32.

Brydon, Lynne, and Sylvia Chant. 1989. *Women in the Third World: Gender Issues in Rural and Urban Areas.* New Brunswick, N.J.: Rutgers University Press.

Buvinic, Myra. 1983. "Women's Issues in Third World Poverty: A Policy Analysis." In Mayra Buvinic et al., *Women and Poverty in the Third World,* pp. 14–31. Baltimore, M.D.: Johns Hopkins University Press.

Buvinic, Myra, and Margaret A. Lycette. 1988. "Women, Poverty, and Development in the Third World." In J. P. Lewis et al., *Strengthening the Poor: What Have We Learned?,* pp. 149–62. New Brunswick, N.J.: Transaction Books/Overseas Development Council.

Daly, Herman E., and John B. Cobb, Jr. 1989. *For the Common Good: Redirecting the Economy Toward Community, the Environment and a Sustainable Future.* Boston: Beacon Press.

Dauber, Roslyn. 1981. "Applying Policy Analysis to Women and Technology: A Framework for Consideration." In Dauber and Cain (eds.), pp. 237–51.

Dauber, Roslyn, and Melinda L. Cain (eds.). 1981. *Women and Technological Change in Developing Countries.* Boulder: Westview Press and the American Association for the Advancement of Science.

DAWN. 1985. *Development, Crises, and Alternative Visions: Third World Women's Perspectives.* New Delhi: DAWN.

de Groot, Joanna. 1991. *Conceptions and Misconceptions: The Historical and Cultural Context of Discussion on Women and Development.* In Afshar (ed.), pp. 107–35.

EPHP (Eritrean Public Health Programme). 1985. *A Primary Health Care Programme for Eritrea: Guidelines for Infrastructure Development.* Orota: Department of Health.

EPLF. 1973. *Why Are We Waging a Struggle?* Vanguard I(1).

Feldstein, Hilary Sims, and Susan V. Poats (eds.). 1989. *Working Together: Gender Analysis in Africulture,* Vol. 1: Case Studies, and Vol. 2: Teaching Notes. Hartford, Conn.: Kumarian Press.

Findlay, Allan, and Anne Findlay. 1987. *Population and Development in the Third World.* London: Methuen.

Fortmann, Louise. 1981. "The Plight of the Invisible Farmer: The Effect of National Agricultural Policy on Women in Africa." In Dauber and Cain (eds.), pp. 205–14.

Gaim Kibreab. 1990. *The Sudan From Subsistence to Wage Labor: Refugee Settlements in the Central and Eastern Regions*. Trenton, N.J.: Red Sea Press.

Goetz, Anne Marie. 1991. "Feminism and the Claim to Know: Contradictions in Feminist Approaches to Women in Development." In Grant and Newland (eds.), pp. 133–57.

Grant, Rebecca, and Kathleen Newland (eds.). 1991. *Gender and International Relations*. Bloomington: Indiana University Press.

Hewlett, Sylvia A. 1986. *A Lesser Life: The Myth of Women's Liberation in America*. New York: William Morrow.

Hochschild, Arlie. 1989. *The Second Shift*. New York: Viking Penguin.

IBRD/World Bank. 1984. *Population Change and Economic Development*. New York: Oxford University Press for the World Bank.

Kruks, Sonia, and Ben Wisner. 1989. "Ambiguous Transformations: Women, Politics, and Production in Mozambique." In S. Kruks et al. (eds.), *Promissory Notes: Women in the Transition to Socialism*, pp. 148–72. New York: Monthly Review.

McKee, Katharine. 1991. "Linking Research with Policy Action." In Rao (ed.), pp. 85–89.

Molyneux, Maxine. 1986. "Mobilization Without Emancipation? Women's Interests, State and Revolution." In R. Fagan et al. (eds.), *Transition and Development*, pp. 280–302. New York: Monthly Review.

Momsen, Janet Henshall. 1991. *Women and Development in the Third World*. London: Routledge.

Moser, Caroline O. N. 1987. "Women, Human Settlements, and Housing: A Conceptual Framework for Analysis and Policy-Making." In Caroline O. N. Moser and Linda Peake (eds.), *Women, Human Settlements and Housing*, pp. 12–32. London: Tavistock Publications.

_____. 1989. "Gender Planning in the Third World: Meeting Practical and Strategic Gender Needs." *World Development* 17(11):1799–1825.

_____. 1991. "Gender Planning in the Third World: Meeting Practical and Strategic Needs." In Grant and Newland (eds.), pp. 83–121.

Nelson, Nici. 1981. "Mobilising Village Women: Some Organisational and Management Considerations." In N. Nelson (ed.), *African Women in the Development Process*, pp. 47–58. London: Frank Cass.

Oppong, Christine, and E. Haavio-Mannila. 1979. "Women, Population, and Development." In P. Hauser (ed.), *World Population and Development: Challenges and Prospects*. New York: Syracuse University Press.

Overholt, Catherine, Mary B. Anderson, Kathleen Cloud, and James Austin. 1985. "Women in Development: A Framework for Project Analysis." In C. Overholt et al. (eds.), *Gender Roles in Development Projects*, pp. 3–15. West Hartford, Conn.: Kumarian Press.

Papanek, Hanna. 1981. "The Differential Impact of Programs and Policies on Women in Development." In Dauber and Cain (eds.), pp. 215–27.

Poats, Susan V., Marianne Schmink, and Anita Spring. 1988. *Gender Issues in Farming Systems Research and Extension*. Boulder: Westview Press.

Rao, Aruna. 1991. "Incorporating Gender Issues in Development Training." In Rao (ed.), pp. 122–31.

_____ (ed.). 1991. *Women's Studies International: Nairobi and Beyond.* New York: Feminist Press at CUNY.

Rao, Aruna, Mary B. Anderson, and Catherine A. Overholt. 1991. *Gender Analysis in Development Planning.* West Hartford, Conn.: Kumarian Press.

Rentmeesters, Veronica. 1989. "Eritrea: Will Women's Liberation Survive the Liberation Struggle?" Presented at the Annual Meeting of the African Studies Association, Atlanta, November 2–5, 1989.

_____. 1990. "Women, Islam and Education in Halibet, Eritrea." Unpublished paper.

Rogers, Susan G. 1983. "Efforts Toward Women's Development in Tanzania: Gender Rhetoric vs. Gender Realities." *Women and Politics* 2(4):23–41.

Saito, Katrine A., and Daphne Spurling. 1992. *Designing and Implementing Agricultural Extension for Women Farmers.* Washington, D.C.: World Bank.

Schoepf, Brooke Grundfest. 1992. "Gender Relations and Development: Political Economy and Culture." In Seidman and Anang (eds.), pp. 203–41.

Scott, Hilda. 1984. *Working Your Way to the Bottom: The Feminization of Poverty.* London: Pandora.

Seidman, Ann. 1981. "Women and the Development of 'Underdevelopment': The African Experience." In Dauber and Cain (eds.), pp. 109–26.

Seidman, Ann, and Frederick Anang (eds.). 1992. *Twenty-First Century Africa: Towards a New Vision of Self-Sustainable Development.* Trenton, N.J.: Africa World Press.

Stamp, Patricia. 1990. *Technology, Gender, and Power in Africa,* 2nd ed. Ottawa: International Development Research Centre.

Thomson, Suteera. 1991. "Integrating Gender in Research and Policy for Development in Thailand." In Rao (ed.), pp. 89–100.

Uphoff, Norman. 1986. *Local Institution Development.* West Hartford, Conn.: Kumarian Press.

Warren, Kay B., and Susan C. Bourque. 1991. "Women, Technology, and International Development Ideologies." In Micaela di Leonardo (ed.), *Gender at the Crossroads of Knowledge: Feminist Anthropology in the Postmodern Era,* pp. 278–311. Berkeley: University of California Press.

Young, Kate. 1988. "Reflections on Meeting Women's Needs." In K. Young (ed.), *Women and Economic Development: Local, Regional and National Planning Strategies,* pp. 1–30. Oxford: Berg/UNESCO.

CHAPTER 3

AGRICULTURE AND DEVELOPMENT

PROBLEMS, PROSPECTIVE POLICIES AND PROGRAMS FOR AGRICULTURAL DEVELOPMENT IN ERITREA

The Agricultural Commission, EPLF[1]

I. INTRODUCTION

The biggest challenge facing the government of Eritrea is the enormous task of reconstruction and development of the war-torn and drought-ravaged economy. Over the years, the livelihood of the people of Eritrea in general and the peasantry in particular has been totally disrupted due to the intense military conflict and severe drought.

Agricultural production deteriorated drastically and hundreds of thousands of people died of hunger and malnutrition. Severe drought has substantially reduced the size of the livestock population of Eritrea. Consequently, the life of the Eritrean people has been one of misery and untold sufferings.

The EPLF, with meager resources at its disposal, has tried to mitigate some of the problems facing the rural population. But the basic problems are yet to be solved. In addition to the intensive war, and the severe and recurrent drought, EPLF's efforts have been hampered by shortages of capital and skilled manpower.

In this short paper, an attempt is made to identify the problems and characteristics of the agricultural sector, EPLF'S experience in agricultural activities, as well as policy choices and potential programs to deal with the situation. It is designed to stimulate discussion on the manifold issues of agricultural development with all its complexities and constraints. The problems are enormous and serious. They require practical and effective solutions. The points raised in this paper are, therefore, hoped to be thought-provoking and contributive to formulating practical policies and programs.

II. PROBLEMS AND CHARACTERISTICS OF ERITREAN AGRICULTURE

The economy of Eritrea, like those of other third world countries, is based on subsistence agriculture. More than 80 percent of the population is engaged in agriculture and related activities. The population derives its livelihood from crop farming and animal production. Over the past hundred years, Eritrean agriculture has been characterized by backwardness and uneven development. With the advent of Italian colonial rule, commercial farming was introduced to meet the consumption demands of the urban population, to supply local industries with raw materials and to generate foreign

1. Presented by Stafanos Seyoum

exchange earnings.

Although development of commercial agriculture may have contributed to the growth of the economy, as measured in terms of GDP, the chronic problems of poverty, hunger and unemployment among the rural population remained unaffected. Since the Italian colonial period, Eritrean agriculture has acquired a dual character in which an enclave of rich commercial farms coexisted side by side with the languishing traditional farms of the rural peasant economy. Generally, Eritrean agriculture is characterized by very low productivity, producing only at subsistence level. War and drought have disrupted the agricultural sector's established mechanisms of production and distribution. Almost all of the infrastructures have been destroyed. Furthermore, no services were rendered to the farmers and pastoralists apart from the very little provided by the EPLF.

The main problems now facing the Eritrean agriculture can be summarized as follows:

1. War and Drought. Because of the prolonged and intensity of the war, hundreds of thousands of Eritreans either died or fled their country and became refugees. Farming activities stagnated and production declined. Thus, over the years the war has totally disturbed the established social fabrics of the Eritrean society. The drought over the past ten years has resulted in severe losses of both the human and animal populations of the country. In the 1980s, it is estimated that production of crops had declined by 40 percent and the number of livestock reduced by 50 percent. The situation was further exasperated by the exceptionally low (subnormal) rainfall in 1990; consequently, the rural population was left practically without oxen and seeds for the next planting season, thus, presenting a serious threat of mass destruction to people and animal life.

2. Archaic and Traditional Farming Methods. This is the main cause of low productivity of agriculture in Eritrea. Eritrean agriculture has remained basically at a subsistence level with its rudimentary farming technology. Human and animal power are the only sources of energy. Throughout the colonial period, peasant agriculture was totally neglected and there was no opportunity for any structural transformation by intervening through new technological inputs and training.

3. Traditional Land Tenure System. Several land tenure systems existed in Eritrea. Throughout the colonial period, no attempt was made to change the structure of the systems, so as to encourage land holders to produce more by taking the initiative to improve their methods of farming. Starting in the mid–1970s, the EPLF, the ELF and the Ethiopian Derg had carried out land reform programs on areas they controlled. Although there were marked differences in approach among them, basically land was made available to those who work on it on an equal basis. However, the redistribution of land among members of the community created problems of fragmentation of holdings and lack of incentives for making improvements on land, thereby rendering the holdings less viable.

4. Agricultural Degradation. One of the main causes of low productivity of the Eritrean agriculture is the depletion of soil fertility through erosion, and the cutting of trees for fuel and energy. Throughout the years, no effective measures were taken to control soil erosion, improve soil fertility or safeguard the environment through afforestation and reforestation programs. As a result of this policy of neglect, the whole ecological resource base of the country has now reached a critical stage.

5. Low Productivity of Livestock. Like crop farming, livestock production in Eritrea has suffered due to lack of inputs to improve its quality and lack of measures to protect it from various diseases. The war and the drought have substantially destroyed its size. As a result, livestock as a source of income to the people has drastically deteriorated and has become insignificant.

6. Lack of Research and Training Programs. Eritrean agriculture never had the support of research institutions. The few research centers that had been established by the Italians were either closed down or totally neglected and became nonfunctional. Similarly, there were no agricultural training institutions that could provide technical education to agricultural workers and farmers. Thus, the lack of agricultural research and training has left the people of the country without an appreciable knowledge of modern ways of farming and animal husbandry.

III. EPLF'S EXPERIENCE IN AGRICULTURAL ACTIVITIES

The organizational setup of agriculture was off to a good start in 1975 when the EPLF established the Agricultural Commission to implement a policy of self-reliance. In the initial period, the EPLF sought to be self-sufficient in food production for its own consumption. With respect to the civilian peasantry population, the front's efforts were directed at alleviating the problems of food shortages in the country. From the middle of the 1980s onwards, however, EPLF's direct engagement in food production was deemed unrealistic. The greatest effort of the front was then diverted to helping the peasantry solve its production problems.

The severe drought of 1984–85 in the Horn of Africa awakened the whole international community to the plight of the people of the region. Several nongovernmental organizations (NGOs) not only provided relief aid but also became very much involved in financing rehabilitation and development projects.

The EPLF, aware of the gravity of the drought situation, had tried to direct all of its available resources to combating the problem and its after-effects. Regional rehabilitation and development projects were submitted to several NGOs and promptly accepted for funding. Up to the present time, the objective and effort of the EPLF, in cooperation with the different NGOs, has been to revive agricultural production with the goal of attaining food security and tackling the root cause of drought.

Currently, EPLF's agricultural activities can be categorized into the following programs: (1) food production, (2) soil and water conservation, and afforestation, (3) extension services, (4) plant protection, (5) animal health and husbandry, and (6) research and training.

These programs were adopted as a policy in response to the food crisis and environmental degradation created by the continuing drought still affecting most of Eritrea. However, efforts of the EPLF at implementing these programs were constantly hampered by the war and drought. When there was sufficient rain, as was the case in 1988, spectacular results were attained and the program set out by the EPLF proved effective. Nonetheless, working under the twin burdens of drought and war, the EPLF and the people of Eritrea gained vital experience in dealing with the problems of agriculture in the country.

IV. IMPORTANCE AND FUNCTIONS OF THE AGRICULTURAL SECTOR

Over the past twenty years the agricultural infrastructure of Eritrea has been obliterated by war and drought. Consequently, the majority of the Eritrean people are hungry and undernourished and have became dependent on emergency food aid supplies. The government of Eritrea, in its development policy, will necessarily assign a central role to the promotion of agriculture and rural development. The aims and functions of the agricultural sector in the process of economic development in general, and that of rural development in particular, may be summarized as follows:

1. The Agricultural Sector Must Produce Sufficient Food. As already stated, the number of the hungry and undernourished in Eritrea has already reached an alarming proportion. With a high growth rate in population, the problem of feeding the people has been compounded, placing additional pressure on the agricultural sector.

2. Agriculture Can Create Employment. Agriculture has a major function in solving unemployment problems. Appropriate economic and monetary policies and the provision of suitable technology will improve agricultural production, resulting in the creation of employment opportunities. There are also secondary and tertiary benefits in terms of employment through the expansion of trade, rural industry, transportation systems, administration and other services.

3. Agriculture as a Basis for Development of Trade and Industry. Increased agricultural production enables countries of the third world to develop their trade and industry. Agricultural products can be marketed locally and, in some cases, processed to generate additional value. Plants and industries developed on this basis are usually less capital intensive and easier to plan and manage. Increased purchasing power leads to increased demand for production inputs, consumer goods and services in agriculture, which in turn leads to further build up of small business and industries.

4. Intensification of Agriculture Leads to Diversified Economy. Through intensification and expansion of production, agriculture contributes to the necessary diversification of the national economy. In this way it can initiate a development process, which can lead to the structural change necessary in the country.

5. Agriculture Can Become a Basis of Foreign Trade. In developing countries, agriculture remains the most important sector of foreign exchange earnings. These earnings, if they are not spent on the importation of food stuffs or nonessential consumer items, can be valuable sources of capital investment for developmental purposes.

For the above-stated functions of the agricultural sector to materialize, long-term prospective plans and short-term sub-plans have to be drawn carefully to serve as a guiding strategy and plan of action.

V. POLICIES AND PROGRAMS FOR AGRICULTURAL DEVELOPMENT IN ERITREA

Over the past years, EPLF's agricultural policy was dictated by the then prevailing war and drought situations in the country. In addition, the EPLF was working in an economy of its own almost detached from the rest of the world. Domestic markets, due to the war, ceased to function normally. There were neither exports nor a national currency in the liberated areas. Whatever was produced by the EPLF was consumed by the front itself.

The EPLF had an "isolated" economy with no prospective plans. Pressed by a volatile and shifting military situation, it only tried to implement isolated annual programs to mitigate economic problems of the people and the front.

At present, with the winding down of the war, the people of Eritrea achieved peace and independence. The need arises, therefore, to have a country-wide long-term prospective economic plan put in place in which the agricultural sector could play the role assigned to it. The critical question now is, in view of the prevailing sociopolitical conditions in Eritrea: What alternative policies and programs could be formulated to rehabilitate Eritrean agriculture and set it on the road to recovery and development? It has been pointed out that the EPLF's experience in matters of policy-making and implementation was too limited to be of great help for the emerging situation.

However, in order to solve the problems of hunger, unemployment, environmental degradation and other related matters, and to guide the country toward recovery and development, there is an urgent need to initiate a comprehensive long-term plan and the attendant policies and programs.

Several studies have to be undertaken to identify constraints and to prepare appropriate policy measures in the agricultural sector. In the meantime, certain key policies and programs have to be determined from existing knowledge to serve as a guiding strategy for our short- and long-term activities.

A. Key Policies and Programs for Rural Agricultural Development

Agriculture and rural development are crucial for economic and social progress in Eritrea. Under the current socioeconomic conditions in the country, rural development can be regarded as a means of fighting poverty through a better utilization of local resources. Policies and programs toward this end may include the following:

1. Mobilize farmers to use their knowledge and physical potential for self-supporting and development process.
2. Provide farmers with basic services and new technological inputs such as oxen, seeds, fertilizers, farm implements, credit and marketing information.
3. Help farmers establish rural and agriculture-related industrial enterprises to create additional employment.
4. Encourage small farmers to engage in subsidiary agricultural activities to generate additional income, activities such as vegetable gardening,

fisheries, poultry and dairy production.

5. Initiate technical transformation of agriculture by introducing new technologies and training farmers in modern methods of farming.

6. Integrate research findings with extension services and help farmers improve agricultural productivity.

7. Organize and train farmers in plant protection measures, such as pest and disease controls, and provide the necessary equipment and chemicals for the task.

8. Develop project plans for financing by multilateral agencies for the purpose of producing surplus food and modernizing agricultural activities in rural areas.

B. Key Policies and Programs for Environmental Conservation

Environmental degradation by soil erosion and deforestation, as already mentioned, is one of the most crucial problems of Eritrean agriculture. The following policies and programs may be considered as protection and rehabilitation measures.

1. Undertake soil erosion control measures extensively to prevent soil depletion.

2. Introduce rational land-use methods of agriculture so that land holdings and tenure systems may not discourage efforts for increasing production and investment.

3. Expand irrigation activities in crop production through the construction of diversion canals, dams and embankments, and other water control and management methods.

4. Protect environmental degradation by undertaking afforestation and reforestation measures and economic utilization of forest resources.

5. Extend to farmers training and technical facilities in soil and water conservation and afforestation activities.

C. Key Policies and Programs of Animal Husbandry and Fisheries

The livestock population of Eritrea showed a dramatic increase following the introduction of medical and veterinary services by the Italians. However, over the past twenty years and with the intensification of the war and recurrent drought, its size declined drastically. In addition, due to the poor quality of livestock, its productivity is very low. Therefore, in order to protect the animal population of the country from the main killer diseases and to improve its quality, the following measures could be considered for this subsector.

1. Extend an expanded medication and vaccination service to protect the nation's livestock resource from the dangers of various diseases.

2. Introduce a rational utilization of pastures and watering points for sustaining livestock without creating conflicts with crop farming.

3. Establish pilot hybrid projects to help change the poor quality of cattle and their products.

4. Encourage the establishment of livestock-related industries such as preparation of feeds, dairy processing plants, meat canning enterprises, tanning, etc.

5. Establish credit marketing, storage and transportation agencies to help increase the quantity and quality of livestock and livestock products.

6. Provide training and technical services to livestock owners on improved

methods of animal husbandry.

D. Key Policies and Program on Commercial and State Farms

Commercial agriculture, including agro-industrial enterprises, existed in different parts of Eritrea. Initially, these enterprises were exclusively Italian-owned, but later foreigners as well as members of the Ethiopian and Eritrean ruling class joined the venture in larger numbers. The commercial farms produced vegetables, fruits, milk and other dairy products, cotton, sisal, coffee, oil seeds and sorghum. Though primarily export-oriented, commercial agriculture has also been meeting the demand of the urban population. In addition, it has employed thousands of local workers.

Presently, commercial agriculture can play an important role as a source of increased food production and of raw material for local industries, as well as a source of employment and income opportunities. In addition to these contributions, commercial agriculture is an earner of foreign exchange. For Eritrean commercial agriculture to recover and develop, implementation of the following policies and programs will be necessary.

1. Encourage people to rehabilitate abandoned farms and start normal production.
2. Allow small and medium size commercial farmers to obtain concessions from the government on favorable terms so that they engage in production.
3. Invite foreign investors to participate in agricultural and agro-industrial enterprises either on the basis of joint ventures with the government or on their own.
4. Establish state-owned commercial farms in critical areas of food production or production of industrial inputs.
5. Promote national and foreign investment ventures in agriculture, with favorable taxation and profit remittance provisions.

E. Key Policies and Programs of Research and Training

Agricultural research is essential for sound agricultural development. It is a catalyst that can generate needed improvements in the rural sector. During the periods of successive colonial rule in Eritrea, research work on food crops had been completely neglected. Thus, there is a total lack of information and an urgent need for research work.

No educational and training institutions existed to produce agriculturalists with needed expertise, extension workers and enlightened farmers. It is, therefore, not surprising for the agricultural sector to remain stagnant in the absence of research and training support.

For research and training tasks to function and serve the agricultural sector properly, the following policies and programs are worth considering:

1. Establish an agricultural institute to deal with research on the different problems and aspects of Eritrean agriculture in general and those of food crops in particular.
2. Undertake research activities on different crops based on the different ecological zones of the country with the aim of increasing productivity.
3. Examine traditional farming methods and implements and improve by introducing new technologies.
4. Identify crop pests and diseases, and develop measures of controlling them.

5. Establish higher and middle level educational and training institutions to provide needed agriculturalists and extension workers and other agricultural professionals.
6. Establish close linkages between the educational and training institutions and the research and extension activities for effectiveness.
7. Provide frequent extension training programs to farmers to effect cultural and technical transformation in the rural areas.
8. Strengthen the national research and educational institutions by establishing linkages with related international organizations.

VI. SUMMARY AND CONCLUSION

The problems of poverty and unemployment in today's Eritrea are massive. The solution lies primarily in the adoption of a strategy for comprehensive development of the agricultural sector, covering not only crop production but also associated subsidiary activities and rural industries. Conditions that favor the expansion and growth of crop production seem to exist, provided much effort is made to introduce new inputs such as fertilizers, improved seeds, farm implements and price incentives. Further, crop production, apart from rain-fed farming, can be raised steadily by expanding irrigation farming using appropriate water control and management practices.

The opportunities of exploiting the livestock resources in Eritrea also are vast. The demand for meat and dairy products is high. Scientific practices in animal husbandry, combined with appropriate price and marketing policies and technical support, will help to modernize and to increase the contribution of the animal resources subsector to the national economy.

The role research and training play in the agricultural sector cannot be overemphasized. However, there is an enormous shortage of skilled manpower capable of handling the task of research, training and related activities. It thus becomes imperative to initiate manpower development programs as soon as possible.

Development of sustainable agriculture depends on rational utilization of natural resources. Unless the degradation of the environment through erosion and deforestation is checked by measures of afforestation and reforestation, soil and water conservation programs, the productive capacity of the entire agricultural sector could be seriously affected. Therefore, due attention must be paid to the problem of maintenance and improvement of the environment.

The Eritrean economy in general, and that of the agricultural sector in particular, is in a state of shambles. The overwhelming majority of the population is faced with acute and serious shortages of food that could be met only through emergency aid supplies or imports from abroad. Achieving self-sufficiency in food production becomes the immediate and primary concern of an agricultural policy, which requires a strategy for increasing agricultural production.

Attempting to increase food production by introducing inputs and improved technological innovation is not a sufficient course of action to solve the problem. The long-term goal of establishing sustainable agriculture should necessarily consider various issues and their proper combination of applications so that the root causes of poverty and unemployment can be solved and the whole agricultural sector structurally transformed. Key policy issues to be taken into account in relation to attaining sustainability of agriculture include:

1. Changing the Land Tenure System. The peasant agriculture sector in Eritrea includes a communal land holding system. The frequent redistribution of land among members of the community has caused fragmented and variable plots of land. Furthermore, the short period of redistribution of five to seven years has created insecurity of tenure and thus become an impediment to investing in new inputs and technology for improvement of farming practices. Unless a land reform program to consolidate fragmented farms and provide security of tenure is undertaken, progress and development in agricultural production will not be realized.

2. Environmental Constraints. In considering the broad framework for strategies of agricultural development in Eritrea, it is essential to consider the country's particular environmental constraints. The relationship between environmental deterioration and agricultural stagnation in almost all countries of Africa is a well-established fact. Environmentally conscious agricultural planning is, thus, a key element for a sustainable agriculture in Eritrea.

3. Development of River Basins. Potentially productive agricultural areas along the main river basins of Eritrea still remain undeveloped. To generate surplus food production, supply industries with raw materials and produce export commodities, the development and exploitation of the potential river basin areas is an important task to undertake.

It should be reiterated that the economic infrastructure of the entire Eritrea is almost destroyed. The country is starting from scratch, with little development experience and inadequate background information and studies upon which to base policies and programs. It is therefore necessary to undertake a survey and studies of the whole agricultural sector prior to the preparation of a prospective long-term plan.

Solutions to the problems of rural poverty and unemployment and the task of improving the standard of living of the Eritrean people must be given the greatest possible attention. But, because the problems are vast, realization of appreciable improvements in the reduction of poverty and unemployment will take time.

Accompanying the process of agricultural development, certain policy issues, which do not appear to be important at this moment, may emerge as critical problems with social and political implications. Such issues include:

1. How to reconcile the policies of growth of production with those of equity and social justice.
2. Interpersonal and interregional disparities due to unequal land holdings among farmers and resource endowment of land and water differences among regions. A need for a policy instrument to narrow the emerging disparities is thus necessarily a social and political issue.
3. With the need to expand crop production, continual encroachment of farming into traditional grazing areas creates serious conflict between agriculturalists and pastoralists. A policy problem then arises on how to resolve this potential conflict without creating political problems.
4. Eritrea's shattered and subsistence-level economy has a narrow possi-

bility to generate capital for investment, especially in the initial period. It is important, therefore, to invite foreign investment to play a role
in certain critical areas of the agricultural sector. What policy options
of foreign investment are available and how should they be formulated?

5. State-owned and managed agricultural enterprises are usually centers
of controversy. In Eritrea, there are certain commercial farms and agro-
industrial enterprises inherited from the Ethiopian regime. A policy
issue arises related to the merits and demerits of whether they should
be run by the government or the private sector.

6. Organization of agricultural planning and implementation procedures
are important elements in determining the success or failure of plans.
The issue involved here is the degree of centralization versus decentralization. Taking the Eritrean case into consideration, how far can
planning and implementation procedures be centralized and decentralized? What organizational infrastructure can be set up for the
administration and implementation of agricultural plans and programs? Policy issues relating to these problems need to be addressed
and developed.

Given the present Eritrean agricultural conditions, the problems and
policy issues stated above need to be critically considered by undertaking in-
depth studies of various aspects of the agricultural sector. There are no ready-
made policy prescriptions to deal with the complex problem of agricultural
development. However, there is a need to recognize the interrelationship
between various policy instruments. As such, a mechanism for integrating
them must be provided.

AGRICULTURAL DEVELOPMENT IN ERITREA: ECONOMIC AND POLICY ANALYSIS

Tesfa G. Gebremedhin

I. INTRODUCTION

In Eritrea agriculture provides most of the employment and livelihood of the population. Four fifths of the total Eritrean population of 3.5 million earn their living from the land, either from settled agriculture or livestock production. Agriculture is represented by subsistence farming, livestock rearing and fisheries. Over a third of the Eritrean people directly depend on raising cattle, sheep, goats, poultry, and camels for sustenance. A great potential exists mainly in increasing the volume and variety of livestock production and developing related domestic processing industries, particularly for meat, dairy, and other livestock products. Eritrea also has natural conditions suitable for the production of a wide range of agricultural, horticultural, and industrial crops such as barley, sorghum, wheat, maize, millet, coffee, oil seeds, pulses, cotton, and a wide variety of fruits and vegetables. The major rivers namely Setit, Gash, Barka, Anseba, and Mareb have great potential for crop production through small-scale irrigation schemes. According to a recent estimate, of a potential cultivable area of at least six and a half million acres, not more than three million acres have been under cultivation since 1970. In addition, the Red Sea has been a great resource for coastal fishing as an important food potential and future major industry in Eritrea (EPAC 1988; Firebrace and Holland 1985). Thus, for the foreseeable future, agriculture is likely to remain the main source of employment and the major contributor to the national economy in Eritrea.

A country's potential for economic and social development is greatly influenced by its physical and human resource endowments, technical innovations, and institutional evolutions (Todaro 1981; Ghatak and Ingersent 1984; Tweeten 1972; Sen 1985; Singh 1987). Israel, with a "sand pile," and Japan, with a "rock pile," have also demonstrated that economic development is possible without a rich endowment of natural resources (Tweeten 1972). But these countries are endowed with people constituting a dedicated, conscientious, and hardworking labor force willing to seize investment opportunities and eager to take reasonable risks for economic gains. The attitudes of their people also influenced their government institutions to provide the requisite atmosphere of stability, freedom, justice, and security. Compared to Israel and Japan, Eritrea is endowed with relatively rich natural resources in which agricultural development can succeed to evolve through technical change and institutional innovation. The general aspiration and work ethics of the Eritrean population show a great potential for agricultural and general economic development.

II. DEVELOPMENT CONSTRAINTS

A. Traditional Farming Methods

Inappropriate farming techniques can threaten the agricultural productivity and food security of a country. Farming in Eritrea is still traditional; not amenable to the requirements of the economic life of modern society. The whole farming system — the preparation of the land through clearing the field, planting of seeds, harvesting and transportation — is primitive with total absence of mechanized operation. It is a system operated by human power supported by traditional hand tools, animal-drawn implements, and rudimentary techniques. Over 90 percent of subsistence farmers rely heavily on draught animal power. Currently, the shortage of animal power is becoming the biggest problem for the majority of Eritrean farmers. The absence of improved farming techniques and implements have always been a hindrance in food production for Eritrea (Green 1974; Gebremedhin 1976).

B. Climate and Topography

Because Eritrea lies in the Sahelian rainfall zone of Africa, its agriculture has been vulnerable to frequent years of drought. Rainfall in Eritrea has been poor for most of the past twenty years. In some villages farmers have harvested practically nothing in some years. Most farmers have lost their meager means of production. Their draught animals have died, their farm tools and implements have been destroyed, and their capacity to retain seeds from harvest has been diminished. The lack of various farm inputs and the inability of farmers to engage in farming are the main reasons why the food supply in Eritrea is inadequate. Further, desertification due to deforestation, bush burning, overgrazing, and overcultivation is currently a major problem in Eritrea.

Almost all Eritreans rely on fuel-wood for cooking. A considerable amount of forest has been consumed to meet the demand for fuel, building materials, and farming land. The overutilization of forests and the overgrazing of the vegetation cover have left the land exposed and barren. Only about 10 to 13 percent of the country is covered by natural vegetation (ERA 1989; IBRD/IDA 1973).

Eritrea has a climate and topography of great variety and extremes. The country's rugged terrain and the lack of transportation facilities isolate various regions of the country from one another. Consequently, contacts among many of the highland regions are minimal. Although progress has been made by the Eritrean People's Liberation Front, poor communication is a serious problem retarding agricultural productivity. The supply of feeder roads and bridges is certainly inadequate, and those currently in operation are in poor condition. The majority of the farm population in the country are isolated and most of the farms are located far from major or feeder roads. The pack animals — donkeys, mules, horses, and camels — are still the most important means of transportation in the rural areas. Consequently, most farmers produce what they consume and consume what they produce (Gebremedhin 1976; Gilkes 1973).

C. Traditional Social Institutions

A variety of social factors have also acted to retard the rate of development in agriculture. Tradition is a common phenomenon in Eritrea's rural areas, and the behavior of the agricultural population is governed both by the tradition and its related institutional laws. Rural labor is linked with the multiplicity of religious holidays, and observers of such holidays are forbidden to perform any kind of labor work on those holidays. Moreover, excessive fasting and religious pilgrimages severely hamper the effectiveness of the rural labor force. In sum, traditional practices in rural Eritrea are development constraints. As a result, agricultural development has been very slow and productivity remains very low (Pankhurst 1970).

This strong adherence to tradition can generally be attributed to lack of education in the rural areas. A large proportion of the Eritrean population is illiterate. A significant size of the rural population continues to depend on some traditional medical practices. Malnutrition, particularly among children, is widespread. Generally, the rural social services are inadequate and need the necessary facilities to initiate economic development in Eritrea (IBRD/IDA 1973).

D. Land Tenure System

Among the leading factors identified as major constraints of agricultural development in Eritrea is obviously the complex and counter-productive land tenure system. Family land holdings are very small in size, severely fragmented and dispersed at significant distance among them. Communal or village land ownership (*deissa*) is the most dominant land tenure system in Eritrea. The great majority of the Eritrean farm population falls under this ownership system. Private land, which has the rights of ownership and cultivation, can be an incentive to increase production and generally to develop the farming system.

In addition, information related to the agricultural sector is inadequate. There are no proper systems of measurement and registration, either of deeds or titles of lands. No land records exist apart from the tax registers, which contain no reliable detail on lands as to their locations. Generally, the records are fragmented, incomplete, and inconsistent. The position and boundaries of any particular parcel of village land can be satisfactorily located only after an inquiry to determine what land is under individual title and what land is in the undisputed ownership of the whole village. Procedures for dealing with land issues are cumbersome; disputes are numerous, and the cost in terms of time and money is considerable.

E. Marketing and Pricing

Agricultural development can not be carried forward without constant attention to pricing and marketing practices. Marketing services in Eritrea have not been developed. Costs of producing farm products are unduly high because farmers do not produce more than their subsistence and minimal cash needs. A large proportion of most farm commodities is produced on small subsistence farms resulting in low yields. Any surplus produced in excess of family requirements tends to be very small and probably credit-linked. Storage is a necessity whether the farm yields are produced for domestic consumption or export market, but facilities are still rudimentary. It has been estimated that about 25 percent of the farmers' produce, mainly grains, is lost in the process of preparing and storing for the market (Nekby 1971; Gebremedhin 1976). Adequate markets and marketing facilities could be a major incentive for increasing output.

III. DEVELOPMENT PROCESS AND CONDITIONS

A. General Development Goals

Economic development, in any society, is concerned primarily with enhancing the well-being of the people by meeting basic human needs. The first major objective of economic development is to increase the production of goods and services to meet those basic needs and improve the standard of living. The second major objective of economic development is to distribute income more equitably among the people. A concentration of income and wealth among a small segment of the population usually is not sustainable politically. Consequently, more egalitarian sharing of the fruits of economic progress is another important goal of development of countries regardless of their ideological persuasions.

B. Economic Development Process

The development of a modern agricultural sector capable of contributing to overall economic development is a dynamic process. Public investment is essential to increase the productive capacity of agriculture, to improve efficiency in product and input markets, and to provide basic social services, especially education and health. The provision of these services induces increased private investments in the production and marketing of agricultural goods and services. Consequently, the integrated investments increase the productivity of the agricultural sector and facilitate the intersectoral flows of products and inputs. Sustained increases in agricultural productivity result in a "surplus," which in turn helps the development of the nonagricultural sectors. The falling prices of increasing supply of agricultural products put pressure on owners of productive resources to shift them out of the agricultural sector and cause the real incomes of consumers to increase (Ranis and Fei 1961; Jorgenson 1966; Nicholls 1963).

The development process spearheaded by agriculture supports industrial development in several important ways. First, rising productivity permits agriculture to release part of its labor force for industrial employment while meeting the increasing food needs of the nonagricultural sector. Surplus labor released from agriculture tends to be relatively more productive in other sectors than in agriculture. Second, productivity in agriculture raises real incomes in both rural and urban areas, thereby creating the purchasing power needed to buy a wide range of new industrial goods, and create savings which can be mobilized, by direct or indirect means, to finance further industrial development. In urban areas, increases in real income result only from decreases in the price of agricultural products. The savings occasioned by reduced agricultural prices may also be viewed as an increase in the real income of urban consumers. This increased income will be available for purchase of food and investment goods produced in the nonfarm sectors and for more desirable agricultural products. The result of this process is an increase in demand and investment in those sectors, with increased markets and more incentives for rapid general economic development.

Likewise, decreases in the price of food and increases in agricultural productivity both affect real incomes in the rural areas. Just as in urban areas, decreases in the prices of food tend to reduce the expenditures for food and increase the real income of the rural consumers. Because rural consumers are also always producers, their farm incomes are simultaneously being reduced by decreasing prices induced by a higher level of agricultural productivity. Thus, increases in income from decreased food costs tend to be offset by decreases in farm revenues. Technical changes in agricultural production, however, could cause costs of production to fall faster than farm revenues. The combined effect can result in increased real income for producers who adopt cost-saving technologies. In addition, increased incomes in the rural sector can be invested or used to purchase a wide range of other consumption goods. The impact of such increases in real incomes can be significant given the fact that the large proportion of Eritrean population is concentrated in agriculture. Rising real incomes in both rural and urban areas lead to broader and deeper national markets and contribute to the development of the services and industrial sectors (Whitaker and Colyer 1990).

The production of an agricultural surplus through sustained increases in agricultural productivity can have four important impacts for economic development. First, price decreases tend to shift the distribution of income in favor of the low-income people, who constitute the majority of the Eritrean population. This happens because low-income people tend to spend a larger proportion of their income on food than high-income people do. Second, the nutrition of the population tends to improve as consumers gain access to nutritious food products due to lower prices. This leads to an improved health of the population, which in turn leads to further increases in productivity and efficiency. Third, products of the agricultural sector become more competitive in the world market with subsequent increases in exportable farm products, and thus foreign exchange earnings, and an increase in domestic production of previously imported goods. Fourth, agriculture supports industrialization with resource transfers in the form of food to a growing industrial sector, surplus labor and raw materials, and provides a market for domestically produced industrial goods. When agriculture fails to meet the full resource transfers required by the industrial sector for economic development, it becomes a drag on industrialization (Ruttan and Hayami 1984). Thus, both the agricultural surplus labor and real incomes are fundamental to the initial development process because they provide a source for shifting productive resources to the nonagricultural sectors, without reducing agricultural output for the market. In addition, subsequent resource transfers, enhanced by public investments, lead to increased levels of production in the economy of the country as a whole.

C. Induced Technical Innovations

The principal challenge of successful agricultural development is to attain an efficient path of technological change that saves the relatively scarce factor of production (Hayami-Rutton 1985). There is clear evidence that technology can be developed to facilitate the substitution of relatively abundant (hence cheap) resources for relatively scarce (hence expensive) resources in agriculture. For example, if labor is the limiting resource in the development process, as is the situation in Canada, United States, and Australia, then an efficient path of technical innovation must be labor-saving. If land is relatively the limiting resource, as evidenced by the situation in Japan and Taiwan, then biological and chemical technology must be land-saving (Ruttan and Hayami 1984). Chemical and biological innovations permit various technical inputs (such as improved seeds and fertilizers) to substitute for the scarce land, thus increasing the land's productivity and the use of relatively abundant labor. Farmers usually seek technologies that save the scarce and expensive inputs and reduce their production and marketing costs. They turn to both public research agencies for improved technical knowledge and to the private commercial and industrial sectors for improved inputs which can substitute for the limiting factor of production. This development process permits the continuous and sustained substitution of new technical knowledge and inputs for the scarce factor of production.

Based on the importance of agriculture in fostering overall economic development, increases in agricultural productivity and market incentives are identified as critical elements in the development process. However, concurrent development of the various sectors of the economy, rather than total dependence on agriculture, also is recognized as necessary for rapid and sustained social and economic development in Eritrea. Rapid increases in agricultural productivity can be achieved primarily through improved technology. To sustain such a development strategy, the following steps are needed: (1) development of a publicly supported science-based research on agriculture; (2) production of modern or improved inputs (seeds, fertilizer, farm implements); and (3) education of farmers in the adoption and utilization of new technology. Economic and social returns to investments in agricultural research, extension and education programs have been shown to be uniformly high in both developed and developing countries (Whitaker and Colyer 1990). Thus, in Eritrea, the application of induced technical and institutional innovations in agricultural production can contribute substantially to the entire social and economic development of the country.

IV. POLICY IMPLICATIONS

As already emphasized, agriculture is the base for economic development in Eritrea because the majority of the country's population depends on agriculture. It is clear that agricultural progress is one of the preconditions for a viable and sustainable economic development. To attain and sustain agricultural economic development in Eritrea, the following comprehensive policy measures are suggested.

A. Appropriate Agricultural Technologies

If improved technologies are to have the most desirable and productive results in agriculture, they must be adoptable and affordable by a majority of traditional subsistence farmers. Thus, their selection should meet certain criteria: First, technologies should be based on existing farm conditions and knowledge of agro-ecological and socioeconomic characteristics of the agricultural sector. Agricultural technologies should be well-suited to the needs of subsistence farm operations and farm families, for whom capital is scarce and expensive and labor is relatively plentiful and cheap. Second, technologies should initially be low-cost and low-risk until the market input supplies and delivery systems to farmers are improved and their productive capacity for economic and social survival are enhanced by the central government.

Agricultural technologies should be economically feasible and socially desirable to advance over a broader base of land and wider range of farmers than to impose high cost inputs and expensive imported technologies on poor farmers who cannot bear the costs of these technologies.

B. Research and Extension Services

The future level of agricultural and rural development in Eritrea depends in large measure on the level and capacity of agricultural research and the distribution of effective extension services. The critical link between farmers and research institutions is essential to foster development and application of scientific and technical knowledge on traditional agriculture (Ghatak and Ingersent 1984). Shifting from a subsistence farming to a modern system of agricultural production involves technical innovation and institutional evolution in production agriculture consistent with the available natural resources and cultural endowment (Schultz 1984). The central government is required to initiate technical and institutional innovations and promote agricultural development by providing the necessary public facilities and services. The public sector will have to undertake most of the investments in research and establish agricultural research institutions to stimulate resource productivity in the agricultural sector. The main responsibility for organizing and financing research and extension services falls on the central government because the prospective commercial payoff from agricultural research and extension programs is too small or uncertain to attract the private or commercial sector. Consequently, the agricultural research institutions will be required to develop a viable system capable of producing, extending, and adopting continuous flows of new technical knowledge to make positive changes in agriculture. The success of such a development process, represented by agriculture as the initial and principal sector, and its development by introducing appropriate agricultural technology must be locally tested and generally acceptable by the majority of farm population in Eritrea (Whitaker and Colyer 1990).

C. Human Resource Development

It is also evident that human resources of any country, rather than its capital or its material resources, ultimately determine the character and acceleration of its economic and social development. Human resources constitute the ultimate basis for the economic vitality and social viability of a country. Capital and natural resources are positive factors of production; human beings are the active agents who accumulate capital, exploit natural resources, build social, economic and political organizations, and carry forward national development. Clearly, a country which is unable to develop the skills and knowledge of its people and to utilize them effectively in the national economy will be unable to develop agriculture or any other sectors (Harbison 1973; Todaro 1981). Thus, it should be realized in Eritrea that the most fundamental policy measures with regard to manpower planning and the development of an effective strategy for the efficient utilization of human resources is to relate the entire educational and health systems at all levels to human resources development. The principal institutional mechanism for developing human skills and knowledge is, therefore, the efficient and sufficient delivery of these services in order to initiate a social and economic development in the country.

D. Land Reform and Development Programs

Land reform has been viewed as essential to the mobilization of human resources and the generation of increased productivity in any kind of development perspectives. The main public policy for agricultural development rests on the acquisition and distribution of land to farmers (FAO 1979). A predominant owner-cultivator system allocates resources more efficiently and makes a great contribution to the national economic development than any other system. Land in Eritrea is the single most important property to the farmers from the economic and social perspectives. Social norms and economic survival are deeply entrenched in the land tenure system. Consequently, land reform is a major concern in Eritrea, which is counting on agriculture to drive its economic development. If agriculture is to play a positive role in facilitating economic development, there is a need to establish institutional innovation to modernize the land tenure relationships and improve the modes of production (De Janvry 1984). In addition, if land reform policy is to play an important role in development programs, it should also be concerned with improvement in agricultural economic institutions, which are not confined to the registration and redistribution of land for the benefit of subsistence farmers and farm workers, but also undertake many other integrated farm and rural development programs. Such development programs include the regulation of land rents or leases and farm wages, the provision of effective rural credit institutions, the establishment of progressive land taxation system, the formation of farm cooperatives, the promotion of soil and water conservation services, the establishment of land-use zoning practices, the preservation of pasture lands, forests and wildlife, and the protection of the environment.

E. Marketing and Pricing Policies

The marketing and pricing system must also reflect the actual scarcity of products and factors of production in allocation decisions of public and private sectors if an efficient path of technical and institutional change is to be attained. Price distortions in farm product and factor markets resulting from principal macroeconomic and sectoral government policies and interventions usually limit the prospects for more rapid and sustained agricultural and general economic development. Consequently, there is a large and growing body of evidence that the macroeconomic and agricultural sector policies utilized by many developing countries during the past decades significantly constrained public and private investments in agriculture. These countries almost uniformly adopted policies to promote industrialization and agricultural development through import substitution. The results indicate clearly that sectoral and macroeconomic policies have substantially discriminated against agriculture in almost all the countries (Krueger, Schiff, and Valdes 1988). Distortions inherent in misguided public policies must be removed by adopting more rational macroeconomic and sectoral policies. Policy measures must be consistent with the realities of the international economy and the economic and social characteristics of the country if agricultural development is to contribute to national economic and social development.

V. CONCLUSION

Economic development is more than economic growth; it entails meeting basic human needs. Increasing farm output has become the accepted basis for assuring food security and agricultural development. Agriculture, first and most important, serves society as a chief source of food supply (Ghatak and Ingersent 1984). Eritrea has to fulfill the most fundamental condition of its development —the achievement and maintenance of an adequate and reliable agricultural food needs for local consumption. Until Eritrea succeeds in achieving a dependable food supply for its people, it has not fulfilled the fundamental preconditions for economic development. With food-first as a policy to meet basic human needs, agricultural economic development will be measured in the welfare of its people.

From a social, economic, and political perspective, there is increasing recognition of the importance of agriculture to the whole economy and the possibilities for exploiting the great potential of this sector. Eritrea has adequate natural and human resource endowments to promote agricultural economic development. It has a great potential to revitalize its economy by introducing appropriate agricultural technology and establishing the productive capacity of the natural and human resources. Thus, better and continuous flows of farm technology due to increasing human knowledge at scientific, technical, and general levels will obviously be a major challenge and foundation for the development of a productive and sustainable agricultural industry in Eritrea.

REFERENCES

De Janvry, Alain. 1984. "The Role of Land Reform in Economic Development: Policies and Politics." In Carl K. Eicher and John M. Staatz (eds.), *Agricultural Development in the Third World.* Baltimore: Johns Hopkins University Press.

Eritrean People's Liberation Front (EPLF). 1977. *The National Democratic Program of the EPLF.* (February).

Eritrean Professionals Action Committee (EPAC). 1988. *Facts on Eritrea.* Public Relation and Communications Task Force. (October).

Eritrean Relief Association (ERA). 1989. *Annual Report 1988.* Khartoum, Sudan. (May).

Firebrace, James, and Stuart Holland. 1985. *Never Kneel Down.* (Drought, Development and Liberation in Eritrea.) Trenton, N.J.: Red Sea Press.

Food and Agriculture Organization (FAO) of the United Nations (UN). World Conference on Agrarian Reform and Rural Development. 1979. Rome.

Gebremedhin, Tesfa G. 1976. *A Critical Analysis on the Land Reform Policy — Ethiopia.* (Unpublished M.Sc. Thesis) Fort Collins: Colorado State University.

Ghatak, Subrata, and Ken Ingersent. 1984. *Agriculture and Economic Development.* Baltimore: Johns Hopkins University Press.

Gilker, Patrick. 1973. "Ethiopian Farmers: Not Getting Their Share." In *African Development.* London (October).

Green, David A. B. 1974. *Ethiopia — An Economic Analysis on Technological*

Change in Four Agricultural Production Systems, No. 2. East Lansing: Michigan State University (April).

Harbison, Frederick H. 1973. *Human Resources as The Wealth of Nations.* New York: Oxford University Press.

Hayami, Yujiro, and Vernon W. Ruttan. 1985. *Agricultural Development: An International Perspective.* 2nd ed. Baltimore: Johns Hopkins University Press.

IBRD/IDA. 1973. *Agriculture Sector Survey — Ethiopia.* Vol. 3 (unpublished) IBRD, Washington, D.C. (January).

Jorgenson, Dale W. 1966. "Testing Alternative Theories of Development of Dual Economy." In Irma Adelman and Eric Thorbecke (eds.), *The Theory and Design of Economic Development.* Baltimore: Johns Hopkins University Press.

Krueger, Anne O., Maurice Schiff, and Alberto Valdes. 1988. "Agricultural Incentives in Developing Countries: Measuring the Effect of Sectoral and Economywide Policies." *The World Bank Economic Review* 2(3):255–71.

Nekby, Bengt, CADU. 1971. *An Ethiopian Experiment In Developing Peasant Farming.* Stockholm: Prisma Publishers.

Nicholls, William H. 1963. "An `Agricultural Surplus' as a Factor in Economic Development." *Journal of Political Economy.* Vol. 71 (February).

_____. 1964. "The Place of Agriculture in Economic Development." In Carl Eicher and Lawrence Witt (eds.), *Agriculture in Economic Development.* New York: McGraw-Hill.

Pankhurst, Richard. 1970. "Some Factors Influencing the Health of Traditional Ethiopia." *A Journal of Ethiopian Studies* (pamphlet), Addis Ababa, Ethiopia.

Ranis, Gustav, and John C. H. Fei. 1961. "A Theory of Economic Development." *American Economic Review* 51:533–65.

Ruttan, Vernon W., and Yujiro Hayami. 1984. "Induced Innovation Model of Agricultural Development." In Carl K. Eicher and John M. Staatz (eds.), *Agricultural Development in the Third World.* Baltimore: Johns Hopkins University Press.

Schultz, Theodore W. 1984. "The Economics of Agricultural Research," pp. 335–47. In Carl K. Eicher and John M. Staatz (eds.), *Agricultural Development in the Third World.* Baltimore: Johns Hopkins University Press.

Sen, B. R. 1985. "Development Through Aid: A Strategy for Surplus Utilization." In *Food Aid for Development.* FAO, Economic and Social Development Paper, No. 34, Rome.

Singh, Harjinder. 1987. *Agricultural Problems in Ethiopia.* Delhi, India: Gian Publishing House.

Todaro, Michael P. 1981. *Economic Development in the Third World.* 2nd. ed. New York: Longman.

Tweeten, Luther G. 1972. "Elements of Economic Growth in Rural Areas." In *Research Application in Rural Economic Development and Planning,* by James S. Plaxico (ed.). Research Report P-665. Stillwater: Oklahoma State University (July).

Whitaker, Morris D., and Dale Colyer (eds.). 1990. *Agriculture and Economic Survival: The Role of Agriculture in Ecuador's Development.* Boulder: Westview Press.

REHABILITATION OF DEGRADED LAND IN ERITREA'S AGRICULTURAL POLICY: AN EXPLORATORY STUDY

Kidane Mengisteab

I. INTRODUCTION

Desertification and land degradation have reached dangerous proportions in Eritrea. Although global scale atmospheric changes have contributed, social, political and economic factors have played a major role in the desertification process. The objectives of this study are to analyze briefly the socioeconomic factors that have contributed to land degradation in Eritrea and to explore what kinds of socioeconomic changes need to be introduced to reverse the process. More specifically, the study aims to investigate (1) why the peasantry's traditional conservation measures have failed,[1] (2) why land tenure reforms such as privatization are not feasible at the present time, and (3) what role the state needs to play in order to help the peasantry reverse the land degradation process. Although the exploratory nature of this study allows only tentative conclusions, it is hoped that it will contribute in raising and defining some important issues for further research.

II. LAND TENURE SYSTEMS

Conservation measures generally lose their effectiveness when they are not modified to cope with the changing socioeconomic conditions. In Eritrea the traditional conservation measures have essentially remained stagnant while the socioeconomic conditions have changed drastically. To demonstrate this discrepancy, the traditional conservation measures and the changes in socioeconomic conditions, including demographics, are examined. Because the conservation measures cannot be fully understood without relating them to the land tenure patterns, the most common land tenure systems in Eritrea are briefly described first.

Land tenure systems in Eritrea are rather complex and vary from one locality to another (Nadel 1946; Zekarias 1966; Gebre-Medhin 1989). Nevertheless, three types of land tenure systems are predominant. These are village ownership (*diessa*), kinship ownership (*risti*), and state ownership (*demaniale*) tenure patterns. In the *diessa* system each village is virtually autonomously administered by its *shimagle* (village elders), who are elected every year, and the *chiqa* (village judge), who is appointed by the district administrator. Arable land is periodically (usually every seven years) redistributed relatively equally among all households in the village. Every male member of a village is entitled to a *gibri* (a share of arable land) when married. Single widows/widowers, spinsters and orphans are also entitled to one-half of a *gibri* from the village land, and married females share their husband's *gibri*.

In order to ensure some degree of fairness, the village land is categorized into fertile, semi-fertile and poor lands, and each household gets a plot of each kind. Pastureland is left for communal use. Land is never sold or inherited, but *gibri* holders can lease their share of land for any number of years until the next rotation of land.[2]

In the *risti* tenure system ultimate ownership of arable land resides in the extended family of remote ancestors, who are believed to have pioneered the settlement in the area.[3] An individual holder of land does not have the power of making a will to determine respective shares going to different off-springs nor can s/he disinherit any of them. A *risti* holder can (in most types of *risti*) cultivate or lease the land but cannot sell or give away as a gift any portion of the land outside of the extended family without the consent of all its members. This rule is at times disregarded particularly during periods of economic hardship. However, since land transferred by sale can be claimed by relatives of the seller, buyers are often reluctant to purchase *risti* land due to fear of long litigation.[4] Individual *risti* holders thus do not have absolute control over their lands. Moreover, as in the village land tenure system, pastures are communally used in most of the *risti* systems.[5] For these reasons, this tenure pattern also can be regarded as communal.

Several advantages are attributable to these two communal land tenure systems. The *diessa* tenure produced a society with relative equality of holdings and a spirit of community within the village at least until population pressure began to undermine it. There are, however, inequalities of holdings between villages as the lands of some villages are bigger than those of others in proportion to their population density. Furthermore, equality of holdings does not necessarily translate to an egalitarian society as land is only one among many other factors of production, including labor, plow-oxen, seeds, and livestock. Thus, village ownership is not entirely egalitarian but it moderates inequality and provides members some degree of social security.

In the *risti* tenure system, every male member of the extended family is entitled to plots of land from the kinship land upon starting a family. The size of holdings of arable land, however, varies significantly depending on the number of households within a kinship. Both tenure systems generate fragmentation of holdings depending on population growth rates. Nevertheless, they both prevent landlessness and are economically and socially valuable since in subsistence agricultural economies a person's rights, status, and standard of living are determined by his/her relations to land.

Demaniale is land appropriated by the Italian colonial state (1890–1941) and retained as state land by the subsequent governments. *Demaniale* is predominant in the lowlands but is found throughout Eritrea. Despite its legal control, the state does not strictly restrict access to such lands. Peasants thus have essentially open access to state lands both for farming and for grazing their animals.

III. TRADITIONAL CONSERVATION MEASURES

Access to both the *diessa* and *risti* communal lands is restricted. Nonmembers are prohibited from farming, grazing livestock or cutting trees in these lands. Both systems also regulate use by members for conservation purposes. Among the most common traditional conservation measures are the following:

1. Members of a village and a kinship group are expected to exercise restraint in cutting trees. They are allowed to cut trees for their own construction needs but, in most cases, they are prohibited from cutting trees in order to sell wood and charcoal in the urban areas. They are also expected to use only dry wood for their fuel needs.

2. Many villages, particularly those in high density areas, also attempt to reduce overgrazing by preventing cattle, except milk-cows and plow-oxen, from grazing in village lands during certain months of the year. Owners thus take their cattle to the state lands in the eastern lowlands (*Bahri*) in the winter and to the southern lowlands near the banks of the Mereb river in the summer.

3. *Diessa* villagers as well as *risti* owners fallow some land in order to restore its vegetation and fertility. They also practice terracing, especially in the highlands, to prevent soil erosion.

Enforcement of these traditional conservation measures often varies. In most cases, however, it is very loosely organized. For example, rarely are guards appointed to patrol nonmembers from cutting trees in *diessa* or *risti* lands. Rather all members are responsible for stopping violators if they happen to see them. There are also no viable mechanisms for preventing members from lopping leafy tree branches for livestock feed, which, during drought periods, occurs at alarming rates with severe deforestation impacts. Despite these implementational problems, the traditional measures were adequate until the turn of the twentieth century when political, social, and environmental conditions changed drastically, rendering them ineffective. We now briefly examine the most important of such changes.

IV. CHANGING SOCIOECONOMIC CONDITIONS

With the colonization of Eritrea by Italy in 1890 a number of changes with important consequences to the environment began to take place. One such change was land expropriation by the successive colonial governments. One of Italy's designs for Eritrea was to turn it into an Italian settlement. Implementation of this policy was rather slow and by the end of the Italian occupation in 1941 there were only 70,000 Italians in Eritrea (Trevaskis 1975:22).

Despite strong opposition from Eritreans, land expropriation continued under the British Administration in order to settle Italians displaced by the war (Pankhurst and Pankhurst 1953:71). Accurate figures of the amount of expropriated land do not exist. Nevertheless, a considerable amount of land, mostly in the lowlands but also in the highlands, was expropriated from the population by the colonial state (R. Pankhurst 1964; 1966; Tsegai 1978; Gebre-Medhin 1989:58).[6]

Rapid population increase is another important change that has taken place since the turn of the century. The Eritrean population, which was estimated at about 330,000 in 1900, rose to about 510,000 in 1928 and to 760,000 in 1941 (Longrigg 1974:134). By 1952 the population was estimated at 1,031,000 (Trevaskis 1975:133) and in 1991 the estimate was about 4,000,000.

In company with the alienation of land by the colonial state, this rapid population growth led to a severe shortage of arable land. Many households have been left with plots of arable land that are too small to support a family. With such mounting shortages of land, fallowing land for purposes of restoring its fertility has been largely discontinued. Thus, in much of Eritrea, land is farmed and grazed continuously with serious consequences on its fertility and vegetative cover.

Improved veterinary services provided by the colonial state, which viewed livestock exports as part of the colony's economic potential, also led to rapid increases in the number of livestock. Between 1905 and 1946 the number of cattle in Eritrea increased by over 300 percent and the number of goats and sheep rose by over 200 percent (Gebre-Medhin 1989:59). With the rapid increase in population and livestock, overgrazing and overmining of forests became serious problems, especially in the highlands where mixed farming — crop production and livestock rearing — are common practices. In these areas, because livestock are grazed on communal pastures with no user fees, each household attempts to increase the size of its livestock, thus reducing the land's carrying capacity. Even in the lowlands where population density is low and pastoralism is the mainstay of the population, increases in stock and declining rainfall have led to severe overgrazing.

The various wars fought in Eritrea since the late nineteenth century, including the Italian wars of occupation, the Italo-Ethiopian war of 1935–36, the Italo-British war in the Second World War, and the Ethio-Eritrean war, which lasted from 1960 to 1991, also harmed the environment in several ways. These wars led to the destruction of forests for security purposes. They also removed a significant portion of the Eritrean labor force from agriculture, resulting in neglect and poor maintenance of land. During Italy's invasion of Ethiopia in 1935, for example, over 65,000 *askari* were conscripted by the colonial state (De Bonno 1937:313).

Perhaps one of the most important changes and one that is the most difficult to overcome is the perpetuation of economic structures that are exploitative and negligent of the peasantry by the successive colonial states in Eritrea. Since the Italian colonization the poorly organized and poorly informed peasantry has been subjected to an exchange with a modern capitalist system. Such an exchange deprived the peasantry of economic resources through unfavorable pricing as well as through neglect in the resource allocation process. This deprivation limited the ability of the peasantry to withstand the challenges of its changing environment by moving from its extensive farming and herding practices to more intensive methods. The same traditional practices were thus maintained with the obvious effect of declining standards of living.

In addition to deprivation of resources, the Eritrean peasantry frequently faced the burnings of its villages and crops as well as the looting of its property by military forces, especially during Ethiopian rule. Impoverished by the confluence of all these factors, the peasantry has been forced to over-exploit and undermaintain its environment. The worsening economic hardships in the countryside and the growing demand for charcoal and wood for fuel in the urban areas have led many people to cut trees for fuel wood and charcoal to sell in the urban areas without planting replacements and without paying any compensation to the village or the kinship. Villages have found it difficult to stop members, whose families are threatened by famine, from cutting trees to sell as wood or charcoal. Such cutting of trees in company with the growing shortage and irregularity of rainfall have destroyed the vegetative cover of much of the land.

The declining standards of living have also led to a process of semi-proletarianization of the peasantry. Many peasants, particularly those near urban areas, have sought seasonal employment to supplement their subsistence existence, often neglecting the proper care and maintenance of their farms. There is thus a vicious circle where the impoverished peasantry is forced to overexploit its land, and the overexploitation of land, in turn, leads to further decline in the peasantry's standard of living.

Overexploited and undermaintained, much of the land in Eritrea is presently at a serious risk of becoming a wasteland. Poor and/or insufficient farming and grazing lands have already become major problems in many areas. Even drinking water and firewood have already become extremely scarce in some areas. In addition to lowering the level of subsistence of the peasantry, the shortages and deteriorating quality of land have generated considerable conflicts among communities. Left unchecked this ecological crisis has also the potential to lead to a broader political crisis. There is thus little doubt that the ecological crisis should be given top priority in this emerging new nation.

V. CONSERVATION WITHOUT TRANSFORMATION OF THE PEASANTRY

Traditional ("nonrational") farming and grazing practices and excessive population growth have often been viewed as the primary causes of land degradation. Population controls, sedentarization of nomads and reduction of the size of livestock have thus often been regarded as the most important solutions. Although the present rates of population growth and the existing practices of farming, grazing and overcutting of forests are clearly unsustainable, there is a serious omission with this type of prescription. As already noted, the causes of land degradation are not limited to factors internal to rural communities. State-level resource allocation patterns, which have impoverished the peasantry, have also played a crucial role. Policy measures that are only aimed at correcting the "irrationalities" of the traditional sector are thus doomed to fail.

Despite their negative impacts on the environment, under the present socioeconomic conditions, large family sizes, nomadism, and large stocks are rational efforts to obtain economic security and avert risk for the peasantry. In the highlands of Eritrea, where mixed farming is practiced, households need children to help in cattle rearing, herding sheep and goats, feeding plow-oxen and draught animals, as well as in farming. Peasants also need several children to ensure economic security in their old age. They are thus unlikely to reduce the number of children and deprive themselves of helping hands in their farms or risk old age misery. As Mahmood Mamdani argues (1972), people are not poor because they have too many children, rather they have too many children because they are poor.

Nomads are also not likely to reduce their stocks as long as they view their subsistence threatened by it and they are unlikely to become sedentary as long as they only have access to marginal lands. The peasantry is thus unlikely to adopt policies of population and stock controls and sedentarization unless broader socioeconomic changes that improve its standard of living and transform its mode of production are initiated. This is evident from the lack of success of population control measures in many developing countries.

Privatization of *diessa* has also been suggested as a necessary change to mitigate land degradation in Eritrea (Abraham 1990:113). If implemented carefully to avoid the displacement of poor peasants, privatization of state-owned arable land may, by restricting its access, reduce its abuse and degradation. It may also encourage private small- and large-scale commercial farming. By contrast, the relevance of privatization of *diessa* land is very doubtful. Girmai Abraham's suggestion is based on Hardin's "tragedy of the commons," which predicts that communal ownership leads to abuse and degradation of the property (Hardin 1968). However, more recent research has shown that the tragedy is related to open access and not to common property in which access is restricted and use is regulated (Bromley 1989).

Girmai argues that privatization of *diessa* land would overcome the problems of absentee ownership, fragmentation, and overexploitation of land that the *diessa* system generates. There are several problems with this argument.

First, the identified problems of absentee ownership, fragmentation, and abuse of land are not limited to the *diessa* tenure system. *Risti* land also generates all three problems. In fact, the problem of absenteeism is much easier to correct in the *diessa* than in the *risti* tenure system. Elimination of absenteeism in *diessa* lands can be achieved by requiring full residency and compliance with residency obligations in order to acquire a *gibri*. Some villages have already undertaken such measures and government legislation can reinforce their initiative. In the *risti* tenure system, however, because absentee owners have the option of selling their holdings, they may demand compensation.

Second, there are two aspects of land fragmentation: dispersion of holdings to various locations and shrinkage of the size of holdings due to growing number of households. As already noted, one rational for the dispersion of holdings in the *diessa* is to minimize inequality in the quality of holdings. Another purpose is to reduce risk. For example, if it rains in certain parts of the village land and not in other parts, it ensures that a household will have at least a small plot in the area where it rained. In any case, if further research shows that consolidation of holdings is economically desirable, it can be achieved without privatization. Villagers only need to be convinced of the benefits of consolidation. The problem of shortage of arable land also cannot be solved by privatization since after privatization there would be the same number of households with the same area of land as before. Only developing alternative sources of employment and rapid improvement of land productivity through the provision of extension services to the peasantry can overcome the problem of shortage of arable land.

Third, privatization of arable land does not protect pastureland. Moreover, it is impractical to privatize pastureland as long as the present types and numbers of livestock are maintained. Privatization would not only fragment pastures, it would also generate conflict within villages because every household would have to spend considerable labor time guarding its plot from unauthorized use by its neighbors.

Finally, it is not clear if privatization would be supported by the peasantry. The only survey available, which was conducted in 1969, shows that the peasants overwhelmingly opposed privatization (Ministry of Land Reform 1969).[7] It thus seems that privatization of *diessa* lands, at this point in time, is counterproductive although it may be expected to promote long-term investment in land.

VI. POLICY RECOMMENDATIONS

Selective privatization of some state lands is feasible, as already noted, but privatization of the communal lands is impractical in the short run. The preceding discussion suggests that reversing land degradation in these areas requires, among other things, three simultaneous measures. One such measure is adopting policies that improve the standard of living of the peasantry. As Michael Horowitz and Muneera Salem-Murdock point out, poverty of the peasantry is clearly a primary cause of environmental degradation (1987:96). It is thus imperative that the new state in Eritrea transforms the subsistence sector into a surplus-producing exchange economy by facilitating the peasantry's access to credits, fertilizers, improved seeds, improved farm implements and improved breed of livestock. The state also needs to encourage the development of irrigation systems where appropriate. Such policies are capable of improving the standard of living of the peasantry while keeping rural people in agriculture until alternative employment is developed.Development experience clearly suggests that in peasant-dominated economies, such as Eritrea's, successful and sustained development is not likely without the transformation of the subsistence sector. Moreover, a genuine democratization of the country requires the peasantry's access to resources, including the power to influence decision-making. The Eritrean People's Liberation Front has, despite severe resource limitations, demonstrated remarkable initiatives in providing some extension services to the peasantry. In independent Eritrea, such measures need to be undertaken on a much larger scale as soon as possible.

Another crucial and urgent measure is to promote exploration for alternative sources of energy such as natural gas to replace wood, particularly in urban areas. The reliance of urban people on wood for fuel energy is simply unsustainable.

A third measure is mobilizing the peasantry to improve its conservation measures and to develop more effective ways of implementing them. With a strong commitment on the part of the state, the peasantry, which is already mobilized as a result of the long liberation struggle, can clearly formalize the implementation of the traditional conservation measures and augment them with new ones. As the peasantry's standard of living improves, policies such as afforestation, sedentarization of nomads, population controls and reduction and changing the types of stock would be easier to implement. The peasantry would also be in a better position to adopt changes such as new designs of houses to replace the traditional *Hidimo,* which is highly taxing on the country's scarce forest resources. In the longer run, as alternative sources of employment absorb more rural people, privatization of *diessa* land may also become more feasible.

NOTES

1. The term peasantry is used in this paper to refer to subsistence producers in rural areas, including small farmers and nomads.
2. Origins of *diessa* are not very clear. Some scholars (Cohen and Weintraub 1975:29) believe that *risti* holders developed it in order to correct the fragmentation of plots and inequalities of holdings and to end the numerous land feuds created by the *risti* land tenure system.
3. There are several variations in the *risti* system. For details, see Nadel (1946), Ambaye Zekarias (1966) and Jordan Gebre-Medhin (1989).
4. Land litigations are frequent and long in the *risti* land tenure system. The number of court cases regarding land feuds in the Serae province, where the land tenure system is predominantly *risti,* was greater than in all the other seven provinces in Eritrea put together (Lundstrom 1976:57).
5. The *Tselmi* type of *risti,* which is individual ownership of land (*risti* subdivided among kinship members), is the exception.
6. The state lands are not inaccessible to the peasants and thus have severely suffered from overgrazing and overexploitation of forests. With urbanization and the growing need for fuel wood the state has also been issuing concessions to loggers at prices that do not necessarily reflect social costs.
7. A 1969 survey by the Ethiopian Ministry of Land Reform and Administration shows that a great majority of the farmers wanted to maintain the communal ownership system against the option of privatization of land. Although unlikely, it is possible that the peasants may have changed their views on privatization since 1969. A new survey is thus very important.

REFERENCES

Abraham, Girmai. 1990. "The Privatization of the Diesa in Independent Eritrea: Towards an Agricultural Research and Policy Agenda," pp. 99–116, in *Proceedings of the International Conference on Eritrea,* EPD, Baltimore: November 3–4, 1990.

Bromley, Daniel W. 1989. "Property Relations and Economic Development: The Other Land Reform," *World Development* 17(6):867–77.

Cohen, John, and Dov Weintraub. 1975. *Land and Peasants in Imperial Ethiopia: The Social Background to a Revolution.* Assen, Netherlands: Van Gorcum.

De Bonno, Emilio. 1937. *Anno XIIII; The Conquest of An Empire.* London: Cresset Press.

Gebre-Medhin, Jordan. 1989. *Peasants and Nationalism in Eritrea.* Trenton, N.J.: Red Sea Press.

Hardin, Garrett. 1968. "The Tragedy of the Commons," *Science* 162:1243–48.

Horowitz, Michael M., and Muneera Salem-Murdock. 1987. "The Political

Economy of Desertification in White Nile Province, Sudan," pp. 95–114, in *Lands at Risk in the Third World,* by Peter D. Little and M. M. Horowitz (eds.). Boulder: Westview Press.

Little, Peter D. 1987. "Social Science Perspectives on Land, Ecology, and Development," pp. 1–16, in *Lands at Risk in the Third World: Local-Level Perspectives,* by Peter D. Little and M. M. Horowitz (eds.). Boulder: Westview Press.

Longrigg, Stephan H. 1974. *A Short History of Eritrea.* Westport, Conn.: Greenwood Press.

Lundstrom, Karl J. 1976. *North Eastern Ethiopia: Society in Famine.* Uppsala: Scandinavian Institute of African Studies, Research Report No. 34.

Mamdani, Mahmood. 1972. *The Myth of Population Control.* New York: Monthly Review.

Ministry of Land Reform, Imperial Government of Ethiopia. 1969. *Report on Land Tenure Survey: Eritrea.* Addis Ababa.

Nadel, S. F. 1946. "Land Tenure on the Eritrean Plateau," *Africa* 16, 1 (January):1–22.

Pankhurst, Richard. 1964. "Italian Settlement Policy in Eritrea and Its Repercussions 1889–1896," in Jeffrey Butler (ed.), *Boston University Papers in Africa History,* Vol. 1. Boston: Boston University Press.

_____. 1966. *State and Land in Ethiopian History.* Addis Ababa: Haile Selassie I University and Oxford University Press.

Pankhurst, Sylvia, and Richard Pankhurst. 1953. *Ethiopia and Eritrea: The Last Phase of the Reunion Struggle, 1941–1952.* Woodford Green: Lalibela House.

Tsegai, Araia. 1978. "Exposition and Analysis of the Colonial Economic History of Eritrea." Mimeograph.

Trevaskis, G.K.N. 1975. *Eritrea: A Colony in Transition: 1941–52.* Westport, Conn.: Greenwood Press.

Zekarias, Ambaye. 1966. *Land Tenure in Eritrea.* Addis Ababa: Addis Ababa University Press.

SOME ENVIRONMENTAL ASPECTS OF DEVELOPMENT WITH SPECIAL REFERENCE TO ERITREA

Ghermay Habte Selassie

I. INTRODUCTION

The question of environment has become urgent and is currently placed high on the agenda of international conferences dealing with economic development matters. Generally, the impacts of economic and technological advancements on environment have been felt the most in the developed (technologically advanced) countries, although of late, the developing countries also have started to have their share of environmental problems of one form or another.

During the past ten years, much attention has been given to environmental pollution and destruction because of the magnitude of damage that has resulted from humankind's careless and often selfish exploitation of natural resources and the disposal of dangerous waste products.

In Eritrea, environmental damage has been occurring for years, but has been much more pronounced during the war of liberation over the past three decades. The war forced thousands of Eritreans to be displaced and misplaced from their permanent areas of residence. Farms have been abandoned, resulting in poor or ńo harvest at all. Coupled with drought, the outcome has been mass starvation and the death of hundreds of people and livestock.

For generations, Eritreans have used wood for fuel and building materials, with little concern for conservation. Italy, as a colonizer, contributed to the destruction of Eritrea's once rich vegetation by cutting trees to produce charcoal, which was necessary for running factories. More recently, during the past thirty years, the occupying Ethiopian army caused irreparable damage to the flora and fauna of Eritrea. The careless cutting of trees, along with overgrazing and overuse of farm land, has set in a process of desertification in Eritrea, turning several areas of the country into barren land.

To the problems of deforestation and desertification are now added those of environment pollution and destruction, which come as by-products of economic and technological development, such as air pollution, noise and water contamination.

Eritrea is emerging as an independent nation and needs to strive for rapid economic development. However, while attempting to achieve economic and technological advancement, attention has to be given to the consequences on the environment. Preventive measures should be considered from the outset. If goals of economic development are guided only by growth and quantitative measures, then the right path has been missed. In this regard, what Schumacher said bears some relevance: "[W]e should think twice before we embrace the materialism of modern economics and question whether the path of economic development laid down by modern economics will take us where we want to be" (Schumacher 1978:65).

In the remaining sections of this brief paper, an attempt is made to assess some environmental aspects of development with regard to production, consumption, population and agriculture.

II. PRODUCTION

What is produced and how the production is carried out are very important considerations when it comes to the question of environment, because it is during the process of production that nature can be violated.

So far, one does not associate Eritrea with enormous pollution problems. This is largely because (1) there have not been many industries, and (2) no follow-up has been made on the quantity of waste from the existing factories. Furthermore, there has been no strict environmental rules regulating the operation of some firms.

It is evident that production is necessary. One of the questions faced is: Should it be capital intensive or labor intensive? With capital intensive, it would mean using up scarce foreign exchange to import foreign capital goods, less employment opportunities and perhaps environmentally unfriendlier means of production. With labor-intensive production, on the other hand, it would mean more employment opportunities and less use of imported capital. Here a distinction has to be made between heavy and light industry, and between the modern and non-modern sectors of the economy. In order to avoid polluting the environment, it is necessary to enact laws that require firms to have cleaning and filtrating facilities installed as a means of reducing any dangerous waste to acceptable levels. Such waste limits should be strictly adhered to and must be regulated at regular intervals by a designated government authority. Failure to abide by such environmental regulations should be subject to penalty, either in the form of financial compensation or reparations for any damages. This would be consistent with what has come to be known as the "polluter pays principle" (PPP).

Now that Eritrea is peaceful and on the verge of becoming formally independent, it may become attractive to foreign investment. There is the possibility that some investors may want to establish factories or other enterprises if they are accorded attractive investment incentives such as tax exemptions for a certain number of years, remittance of profits earned, and cheap labor. In this situation, government authorities must adopt economic policies that take into account the environment and above all the welfare of the Eritrean people. In other words, firms wishing to establish themselves in Eritrea should be scrutinized not only economically, but also environmentally, bearing in mind the general welfare of human beings. They have to be judged from the perspective of a long-term plan. Will such firms create healthy working conditions for their employees? Will the workers be entitled to medical care and holidays? Will the employers have pension schemes for their employees? The answers to these and other related questions should be in the affirmative before such firms are licensed to operate in the country.

Attention should be paid especially to firms in the mining, manufacturing and transportation industries, and assembly plants. In all cases, the environment can be affected in one form or another. With regard to the mining industry, for example, the manner in which mineral exploitation is carried out in many third world countries is very hazardous, both to the miners and to the ecology of the area. Care should be taken of miners' health, ensuring that they receive regular medical check-ups. Moreover, the mining areas should be designed in such a way that they can be restored to their normal conditions when the mining operations are terminated. Otherwise, depending on the chemical nature of the minerals exploited, the result can be much damage to the environment, including contamination of water and killing of vegetation. In addition, the holes left behind could become attractive breeding grounds for insects that cause malaria and other diseases.

In the manufacturing and/or processing industry, a good example is the oil refinery in Assab, which was built by the Russians as a technical aid to Ethiopia on Eritrean territory. Waste from the refinery is dumped directly into the Red Sea, and one wonders how much damage has been inflicted on the portion of the Red Sea around Assab, especially considering that the Russians are not reputed for their environmental care. There is thus reason to fear that some damage is already done to the marine flora and fauna in the vicinity of the oil refinery at Assab.

In Eritrea, the location of factories has been concentrated in and around towns and cities like Asmara, Massawa, Keren, Dekemhare and Assab. It is known that these urban areas do not have proper sewage treating facilities. In the ports of Massawa and Assab, waste from households and factories is dumped into the sea. In the inland cities and towns, waste is deposited in the wilderness. In Asmara, for example, the sewage is dumped into Maibella (a stream which runs through the city), which after running for several kilometers is used as irrigation water in some parts of the Province of Hamasien. This situation cannot continue especially if more factories are built and thus increase the amount of industrial waste. A central waste treatment unit should be established, to which all waste from households and industries should flow, and be physically, biologically and chemically cleaned at the site before release. The cost of building and maintaining such a central waste treatment unit could be financed through fees paid by households and firms in accordance with the user principle.

Among the hazards that can result from untreated sewage waste are contaminated drinking water and food. Heavy metals, like mercury, which are widely used in several industries, can easily pollute some of the sources of food such as fish and vegetables. For example, some 650 people reportedly died in Minamata Bay, Japan, from eating fish contaminated with high levels of mercury (Worldwide Church of God 1990:14).

Planning industrial production by establishing factories in and around urban areas, giving preference to capital-intensive investment, presents the risk of neglecting the countryside where many people will remain unemployed. This can lead to social as well as political unrest. Desperate people will migrate to the cities in search of employment. There are already thousands of Eritreans who have been refugees in the Sudan and many more displaced in many parts of the country. Now that the war is over, there will be a big influx of people into the cities. This would mean the creation of slums such as Edaga Arbi and Geza Tanica neighborhoods in Asmara, plus an increase in crime and other undesirable social problems. Further, there is the risk of epidemics, like tuberculosis, due to poor nutrition and housing conditions. Asmara and the other urban areas in Eritrea are not equipped to receive any influx of people from the countryside or returning refugees. Under such a situation, letting the number of inhabitants in Eritrean cities grow beyond 300,000 would mean degradation of human life.[1]

The need for striking a balance between cities and the rural areas in economic development is obvious. As Schumacher stated: "It is necessary . . . that at least an important part of development effort should by-pass the big cities and be directly concerned with the creation of an agro-industrial structure within the rural and small town areas" (1978). This means the use of intermediate technology also should be considered in industrial development strategies for future Eritrea.

III. CONSUMPTION

Consumption, both in amount and pattern, is as important as production when it comes to the question of conserving resources. Man's destruction of nature depends on how numerous and complicated his demands are. If there is a desire to satisfy oneself by simple means, then the tendency is to use less resources. However, if one's demands are complicated, then more resources will be used and nature will be disturbed. A comparison between the lifestyle of a rural dweller in Eritrea and a middle class city dweller in Sweden, for example, can easily show a big difference. The former tries to maximize his satisfaction by an optimal pattern of consumption, while the latter tries to maximize consumption by an optimal pattern of productive effort (Schumacher 1978:56).

For most Eritreans who are returning from industrial countries, the consumption pattern they adopt is like that of the city dweller describe above. They have been influenced by the availability of an excessive diversity of consumer items in the market. They have seen people buying goods aimlessly and throwing away useful items because they get tired of them, and they want to buy new things again in order to be "happy." Piles of discarded refrigerators, radio and television sets, pieces of furniture, plastic bags, empty cans, abandoned cars, etc., are common daily sights in the Western world — they are all threats to the environment. This type of consumption should not be allowed to develop in Eritrea. Simplicity is needed in our consumption pattern. Few and necessary items are adequate for the market. There is no need to have fifteen brands of soap, ten brands of tea bags, twenty brands of disposable plastic cups and plates or that many trademarks of beer. An important aspect of consumption is the need to recycle; that is, produce and use recyclable items.

IV. POPULATION

The size of population and its rate of growth have tremendous impact on resources. Eritrean policymakers will have to consider various measures to deal with the question of population growth. Family planning, with heavy emphasis on education and understanding, should be initiated. People should be discouraged from having too many children, which they do as a means of social and economic security for old age.

Economic development brings about resources that can be used to improve education and public health. These improvements, together with other social changes, result in reducing the mortality rate. Such socioeconomic developments in turn create a conducive environment for family planning and thus a balanced development.

Generally, poverty encourages high population growth because poor parents with little or no income, or any kind of social security, need children to work for them and to take care of them when they get old. This situation is also true in Eritrea, where there is no social security system. In this respect, it is necessary to establish a social security system by which people in their senior ages could be supported, and laws that prohibit child labor. Moreover, general health care and child care programs should be improved so that it will be unnecessary for parents to have "extra" children as a security measure against possible mortality (*Var gemensamma framtid* 1988:122).

For economic development to succeed, it requires people to change their values and attitudes toward the environment and development. This can be achieved through a general education for the whole population, regardless of age, gender and ethnic differences. In this regard, one of the main objectives of the educational system in Eritrea should be to eradicate illiteracy completely. If that objective is achieved, it would mean an increase in each individual's productivity and income, and a better understanding of health, nutrition and family planning issues. This in turn could lead to a greater understanding of environmental problems (Nisbet 1991:272–81).

V. AGRICULTURE

To judge a country's progress, one has to know how its land is used. The aim of agriculture should be not only to produce the food stuff and other necessities for survival, but also to keep humankind in touch with nature, of which it is a part.

In Eritrea, where a variety of land tenure systems have existed, people's attachment to the land has been for mere survival. Land was more or less used excessively until it became unproductive. Trees were cut for firewood and pastures were overgrazed. Conservation measures were near absent in agricultural activities. Such agricultural practices were carried on for generations, and the end result has become apparent: deforestation, desertification and barren land in many parts of the country. This has been aggravated by the war situation during which time no development activities have been carried out.

Eritrea's agricultural lands can be roughly divided into two main groups: the main agricultural lands owned by individual families, and big farms formerly owned by successive colonial governments. Many of the private holdings have been subjected to land reform under the Eritrean People's Liberation Front (EPLF) during the war of liberation and they can be further reformed into viable farm units to enable groups of farmers to use better farming equipment and methods jointly. The big farms could be operated with more advanced farm machinery as their sizes justify economic use of such machines.[2]

The question of irrigation and artificial fertilizers and pesticides is also something that must be considered both from environmental and economic perspectives. There are areas in lowland Eritrea where agricultural production is possible through irrigation. However, a careful study has to be made beforehand in order to avoid the kind of mistakes observed in the experience of other countries. For example, the Food and Agriculture Organization (FAO) and UNESCO estimate that as much as half of the irrigated fields in the world suffer from salinity, alkalinity and swamp, as a result of improperly established and utilized irrigation systems (*Var gemensamma framtid* 1988:144).

It is known that artificial fertilizers and pesticides play a big role in increasing agricultural production. However, if used on a large scale, they can also cause greater hazards. For example, nitrogen and phosphate leakage from use of fertilizers have caused great damage to drinking water sources and groundwater (Lantbruk utan lackor 1987:27). The use of chemicals as pesticides, weed killers and the like does increase production. However, such use of chemicals also threatens the health of people and wildlife. Furthermore, continuous and long exposure to chemical agents and residues in food stuffs, water and air can be very dangerous, especially to children.

In developing countries, about 10,000 people die yearly due to poisoning from chemical agents and about 400,000 people suffer from serious illness (Var gemensamma framtid 1988:143). The effects of chemical agents are not limited to the place of usage alone; they can also spread to the food production process. In addition, certain fish species and some useful insects, which live on other harmful insects, can be totally eradicated. Further, bird life can be threatened. Continuous use of chemicals in the form of pesticides may even fail in the intended use, in that some of the targeted insects build up resistance to the pesticides.

There is, of course, an alternative to using chemicals; agricultural production can be increased by using organic substances effectively. The use of organic plant-food substances should be encouraged as substitutes to chemicals. Pests can also be fought by natural methods.

Nevertheless, to implement such a change in countries where commercial fertilizers and pesticides are well-established, a change in the general policy and attitude is necessary.[3] In Eritrea, some chemical fertilizers have been used in some concession farms, and one does not know the effect on the environment. During the so-called Malaria Eradication Programme in the 1960s, large quantities of insecticide, known as DDT, was sprayed over vast areas in the country. The impact on people and livestock living in those areas is not yet known.

At the minimum, the use and importation of chemical products should be governed and regulated through special laws. The Eritrean government should adopt an agricultural policy that encourages use of organic fertilizers and, at the same time, inform and educate farmers on the use of organic fertilizers. Agriculture should, as much as possible, be made free from commercial fertilizers. There would also mean a substantial saving of the scarce hard currency.

VI. SUMMARY AND CONCLUSION

Environment and economic development are interrelated. Any economic development activity has some effect on nature. It is therefore important that an economic development policy take into account the environment right from the beginning.

Eritrea, as a newly emerging nation, should learn from the mistakes of other nations. Wholesale imitation of Western patterns of production and consumption, both of which are not compatible with Eritrea's size, capacity and cultural heritage, should be avoided. Many developing countries are currently entangled in economic problems because they simply imitate the Western patterns of consumption with catastrophic consequences on the environment.[4]

Thus, there is a need to develop in Eritrea special import regulations specifying standards on consumption goods and services that should be allowed to enter the country. All imported items should satisfy certain quality and safety requirements. It would be unwise to accept all imports and make the country a dumping place for products of inferior quality or questionable safety.[5] The establishment of an institution with responsibility for testing and verifying quality and safety of products is essential.

Environmental pollution is a problem with no specific boundary, especially with regard to air and water pollution. Of course, Eritrea and the other countries of the Horn of Africa, so far, have no serious environmental problems related to industrial development. However, with regard to the Red Sea, it is high time that regional cooperation is undertaken to prevent pollution.

The task of caring for environment is not simple; it is a complicated and time-consuming job. Moreover, it requires expertise in different fields of study. The establishment of a government office to deal with environmental issues would be a step in the right direction as emergent Eritrea tackles the arduous tasks of reconstruction and socioeconomic development.

NOTES

1. Schumacher suggests half a million inhabitants as the desirable upper limit (1978:65).
2. The provision of credit for the purchase of farm equipment is envisaged for both types of farms.
3. We have to keep in mind that corruption and bribes do come into the picture when one wants to change an established system.
4. The Eritreans living abroad have certainly adopted Western patterns of consumption, and once returned could potentially become contributors to the threat on environment.
5. This writer regrettably has noticed with concern the littering of some places in Asmara and other towns with empty beer cans, which in fact were marked with "recycle" signs. Such cans are made, among other metals, of alumninum and thus can be hazardous to people's health if left to decompose in the open. Because the country does not have the capacity to recy-

cle such cans, the best thing would be to import bottled beer instead. Bottles can be reused or recycled at the glass factory in Asmara, and can be supplied to the local brewery when operations return to normal.

REFERENCES

Dor skogen. "Is the Forest Dying?" In *Kalia,* No. 21, 1985.
Fisk eller olja ur havet. "Fish or Oil from the Sea." In *Kalia,* No. 20, 1985.
Habte Selassie, Ghermay. 1988. *Environmental Pollution and Destruction.* Sweden: Molndal.
Lantbruk utan lackor. "Agriculture Without Leakage." In *Kalia,* No. 29, 1987 (Publication from Forskningsradsnamnden, Swedish Governmental Research Advisory Committee.)
Nisbet, E. G. 1991. *Leaving Eden: To Protect and Manage the Earth.* Cambridge, Massachusetts.
Schumacher, E. F. 1978. *Small is Beautiful: A Study of Economics as if People Mattered.* London.
Var gemensamma framtid. "Our Common Future." 1988. Report of the World Commission for Environment and Development, Hagerhall, Bertil.
The Worldwide Church of God. 1990. *Planet Earth Beyond Repair?* United States of America.

CHAPTER 4

FINANCE
AND BANKING

CHALLENGES OF THE FINANCIAL SECTOR IN ERITREA

Prepared by

The Finance Commission, EPLF[1]

This short paper attempts to focus on the urgent tasks confronting us as we try to fill the administrative vacuum created by the demise of the former colonial regime. It neither pretends to suggest a development strategy nor does it endeavor to raise all the various problems awaiting solutions. It is a modest attempt to highlight the salient problems currently confronting us and to suggest solutions based on our limited knowledge and experience.

I. THE ROLE OF THE CENTRAL BANK

Assuming that we will continue to use the Ethiopian currency, *birr,* until a referendum is conducted to determine the future of the country, the role to be played by our national or central bank will necessarily be different from what it would be if we had our own currency. Specifically, several issues will have to be jointly settled with the National Bank of Ethiopia before our Central Bank can discharge its responsibilities successfully.

A. Supply of Money

In most countries, central banks are responsible for the issuance of notes and coins. Obviously, the Central Bank of Eritrea will not be playing this role in the near future. Given that the medium of circulation will entirely consist of Ethiopian currency for the next two years, some sort of mechanism must be introduced to afford us the possibility of regulating the supply of notes and coins in response to the demands of the Eritrean economy. Inward remittances by Eritreans living in foreign countries are bound to increase the demands for Ethiopian currency. Similarly, gold production, although negligible at present, can increase significantly in the near future, thereby increasing the demand for Ethiopian currency.

Then there is the question of foreign aid. In the early stages of the postcolonial era, we will need massive foreign aid, without which it will be practically impossible to rehabilitate many sectors of the economy. Although we know from past experience that such foreign aid is usually given in kind, a substantial amount can be expected to be furnished in cash, for no other reason than to cover local costs associated with the aid in kind. At any rate, the aid received in cash will add to the demand for *birr*. Finally, notes and coins judged to be unfit for circulation because of wear and tear can also increase the demand for *birr* as they are replaced with new notes and coins. These examples suffice to show the need for the Central Bank of Eritrea to be provided with an ample stock of Ethiopian currency in order to be able to meet demands by the public.

---

1. Presented by Ghebriel Fassil

The Central Bank will also have to bear the responsibility of making sure that the money supply facilitates the circulation of an ever expanding output of commodities. The Central Bank will have to carefully gauge the rate of economic growth and adjust the supply of money accordingly. As a peripheral institution, the Central Bank of Eritrea has never had to assume this function before. At any rate, the Central Bank will have to be furnished with an abundant supply of Ethiopian currency to which it can have recourse as the need arises.

B. Risk in Using the Ethiopian *Birr*

In order to avoid inflationary pressures, it is obvious that the quantity of money in circulation should be increased in line with the increase in output. In the past, the Ethiopian government resorted to the printing press whenever taxes failed to finance the war it was waging against us. Because taxes were not sufficient for this purpose, it meant that the government had to frequently increase the quantity of money arbitrarily, with the result that the Eritrean population using the *birr* as a medium of transaction saw its standard of living decline without interruption. It must be emphasized, therefore, that if the present regime in Addis Ababa does not pursue a prudent monetary policy, our efforts to put the economy in order will not bear fruit, given the fact that we will continue to have a common currency with the Ethiopians.

A similar irresponsible behavior was responsible for the continued depreciation of the Sudanese Pound, again victimizing those Eritreans using it in the marketplace exclusively. Since the historical reasons that made the supplanting of *birr* by the Sudanese Pound possible do not exist any longer, however, it is our view that the *birr* will soon regain its former position as the sole medium of transaction both in the western lowland and Sahel regions of Eritrea.

The Central Bank of Eritrea must be permitted to determine not only the quantity of money in circulation but also its composition. With sinister political ends in view, the former Ethiopian regime used to deliberately restrict the circulation of higher denominations, thereby making trade cumbersome. Therefore, the Central Bank of Eritrea must be permitted to order freely the types of denominations which in its view are required for efficient circulation.

C. Need to Control Credits and Interest Rates

Because demand deposits, which are created by commercial banks, are also part of the supply of money, the Central Bank must be empowered to control credit in a manner that will promote economic growth, stable prices and high employment. Obviously, this will mean fixing the level of the various rates of interest in such a way that these goals are achieved. Again, the Central Bank of Eritrea must be able to arrive at an understanding with its Ethiopian counterpart with regard to interest rate levels. If interest rate levels in the two countries are set wide apart then there will always be danger of capital flight out of or into Eritrea in search of higher returns, with the result that intended goals will not be achieved. Ideally, interest rate levels in our countries must be the same and should be permitted to fluctuate equally and in the same direction. On the equation of credit, we also feel additional measures are required.

Ethiopia's former regime, like all corrupt regimes, had its pampered pets, the top beneficiaries being members of the workers party, of the army and of the security services. The credit policy of the commercial, mortgages and development banks served to pamper these groups; therefore, it is our considered view that outstanding loans be recalled and renegotiated according to business criteria, with the aim of canceling those that fail to meet the test. As for the future, we feel it will be necessary for the Central Bank to specify in general terms the nature and terms of loans that the commercial, mortgage and development banks can each safely extend. The Central Bank must of course be authorized to check whether these banks are complying with guidelines. Appropriate measures can then be taken against delinquent bankers.

D. Reserve Requirements

Reserve requirements to be imposed on commercial banks must also be fixed by the Central Bank of Eritrea in a way that will benefit the economy of the country. Again, it will be necessary to impose the same reserve requirements on both sides of the border as these will have a direct bearing on the quantity of money in circulation. In our view, an average of 20 percent reserve requirements on the various classes of deposit liabilities is reasonable for the moment.

E. Foreign Reserves

After taking into consideration the various competing views on the question of the management and control of the foreign reserves, we believe that the Central Bank of Eritrea must be given the monopoly of dealing in foreign currency. All foreign currency earned from exports and inward remittances must be under the control of the Central Bank. All imports must also be solely financed by the same bank according to priorities set by the policymakers. The Central Bank can, of course, authorize the commercial banks to deal in foreign exchanges on its behalf. The Central Bank of Eritrea has been functioning as a branch of the National Bank of Ethiopia and obviously had no mission other than serving the interests of the Ethiopian government. If it is to serve the Eritrean people effectively, it must be empowered to enter into direct correspondent relationships with foreign banks, where foreign earnings can be deposited in accounts maintained in its name and out of which it can pay for imports. In addition, the bank can investigate the possibility of investing its idle foreign funds in short-term securities and can take measures to effect whenever it believes it is profitable to do so. Servicing of foreign loans can also be undertaken in association with these banks.

With the approval of the Central Bank, commercial banks may also enter into correspondent relationships with foreign commercial banks in their own right.

F. Rate of Exchange

One of the most pressing problems confronting us today is one of deciding on the exchange rate of the *birr* against the dollar, which, taking all things into consideration, would be most advantageous to us. With regard to the appropriate level of the rate of exchange of *birr* against the dollar, we believe that this is a very delicate matter which should be decided very carefully. On the one hand, taking the wide disparity between the official and the black market rates of *birr* against the dollar into consideration, it would seem logical to devalue the *birr*. On the other hand, when we consider the fact that imports will be dearer if the *birr* is devalued, it would seem illogical to revise the present rate. At any rate, whatever official rate is adopted, it should be equally binding on Eritreans and Ethiopians.

G. Type of Reserve

The question of what type of reserve we should have has probably been answered: already, established trade practices have made the dollar the major foreign reserve asset, and at present we see no need to change its dominant position. We, of course, realize that the purchasing power of reserve predominantly consisting of dollars will vary with the fortunes of the dollar in the international market. But, then this can also be said of all reserves.

As to the size of the reserve, we believe that we must strive to build it up to a level that would enable us to import six months' need.

With regard to our trade dealings with the Ethiopian government, we believe we must have the option of being able to convert any *birr* we might earn through exports or invisibles into a hard currency of our choice, otherwise we will be forced to use our *birr* to import goods from Ethiopia even when we can import the same commodities at a cheaper price from other countries.

Bilateral trade on a barter basis can help us economize on our scarce foreign reserves, and we believe the possibility of this type of trade must be explored and every opportunity seized.

H. Managing the Public Debt

Although a market for securities hardly exists, today we believe that there will be modest need for the introduction of certain types of securities, if for no other reason than that the government might benefit from them should taxes fail to cover expenditures. In other words, the bank can be entrusted to manage the public debt on behalf of the government.

With regard to monetary policy, we believe it is safe to predict that open market operations, which are the major tool of monetary policy, will not in the foreseeable future be conducted satisfactorily for lack of a developed securities market; the Central Bank will have to resort to other measures to steer the economy toward desired goals.

I. Bankers' Bank

The Central Bank can also assume the role of lender of last resort to commercial banks. This is a function it never had to assume because reserve requirements were not even perfunctorily enforced in the past. If it ever had the legal right to enforce reserve requirements, this was only as agent of the National Bank in Addis Ababa. In order to protect the interests of the clients of commercial banks, we believe that the Central Bank of Eritrea must be empowered and required to enforce reserve requirements stringently.

J. Fiscal Agent of the Government

Central banks have traditionally acted as fiscal agents of the government and the Central Bank of Eritrea can also be called upon to play this role. To be sure, it has been playing this role — although in the service of the Ethiopian government. All that is needed in this respect is to reinforce this role through legal provisions.

II. THE ROLE OF COMMERCIAL BANKS

A. The Immediate Order of Business

The first order of business with regard to the commercial banks, both in Eritrea and Ethiopia, we believe, is to have the accounts closed as of May 24, 1991, the date Eritrean liberation forces entered Asmara, and then have the books audited by external auditors acceptable to both parties. On the basis of their reports, claims and counterclaims of both parties can be established, following which the party owing can be asked to make good on the balance. Although the books have yet to be audited, preliminary figures nevertheless indicate that the Ethiopian commercial banks owe the Eritrean commercial banks tens of millions of *birr*. Until a major portion of this amount is actually transferred from Addis Ababa to Asmara, the Eritrean banks will not be able to conduct normal banking operations and the present partial paralysis of the banking system will persist with the result that the effects will eventually and inevitably spread to the rest of the economy, leaving untold damages in its wake. Obviously, this is a situation requiring the most urgent attention!

B. Credit Policy

The lending practices of the Commercial Bank left much to be desired by way of providing adequate protection to depositors. As the experience of the recent past confirms, political expediency was given precedence over banking principles. The Commercial Bank kept on providing overdraft facilities to mismanaged nationalized factories even though loans previously given had no hope of being collected. The amount extended in this manner runs into tens of millions of *birr*. Some of these factories had borrowed so much that their working capital was showing a negative balance. By providing such loans irresponsibly, the Commercial Bank was endangering the public's deposits and its own future. Obviously, the prudence that bankers are supposed to exercise cannot be taken for granted.

One result of the above-mentioned loans will be that, if it is ever decided to sell some of these factories now, cash will hardly reach the treasury because these loans will have to be settled first. Therefore, it would be helpful if these factories, which have yet to start production, begin operating now and reach their optimum output as soon as possible because only then can the outstanding loans be reduced and eventually be settled. Some of these factories will, of course, require additional capital to start production. At any rate, it would only be profitable to sell them after the loans are repaid.

C. Secondary Reserves

Once treasury bills are introduced, we believe that commercial banks must be encouraged to participate actively in this market. Proceeds from the sale of treasury bills will help the government to finance its deficits while providing profitable investment to commercial banks. These investments also serve as secondary reserves, thereby protecting the public's deposits profitably.

Furthermore, time deposits can also be profitably loaned to the savings and mortgage bank, which has not been able to expand its activities for lack of funds.

III. ROLE OF OTHER FINANCIAL INSTITUTIONS

A. Housing and Savings Bank (Mortgage Bank)

The type of service the savings and mortgage bank offers to the public is the passbook savings account. Because the funds collected in this manner have not been substantial, this bank has hardly been able to expand its activities.

In the case of the mortgage bank, as was the case with the commercial banks, political considerations were given precedence over business criteria by the former Ethiopian government. The rate of interest charged to home builders is 4.5 percent, but the interest paid on savings accounts is 6 percent. Because time deposits of commercial banks are a major source of funds for the mortgage bank, the latter must charge home builders more than 6 percent if it is to repay its debt. This is an anomalous situation that defies all business principles and thus needs to be remedied speedily. The outstanding loans of this institution must be recalled and renegotiated so as to guarantee its long-term solvency.

Another problem the mortgage bank has been facing is the fact that when many borrowers had their homes nationalized, the *Kebeles,* which were collecting income by renting these very homes built by loans obtained from this bank, refused to repay the outstanding loans. Therefore, this situation also has to be remedied in order to render the bank solvent.

As for the future of this bank, we believe that through the growth of insurance companies and the establishment of pension funds, sources will become available to the bank guaranteeing its long-term growth — provided it utilizes them judiciously.

B. The Agro-Industrial Bank

The Agro-Industrial Bank has hardly played any role with regard to agriculture for obvious reasons, but it has made a modest contribution to the development of industry in Eritrea. The sources of funds of this bank have been soft loans obtained from abroad and extended to the head office in Addis Ababa. Therefore, if this bank is to contribute to the financing of agricultural and industrial development in Eritrea, direct access to these external sources must somehow be found. Because development loans take a long time to repay, it is practically impossible to obtain domestic funding for them. With regard to additional financing, some of the nationalized factories can be seriously considered as potential sources. If it is decided to sell some of these factories, we suggest that the sale be effected in dollars and the proceeds given to the development bank so that it can be used to start new factories in partnership with local private capital.

C. The Eritrean Insurance Corporation

Preliminary figures of the branch operated by the Ethiopian Insurance Corporation in Asmara show that it has been operating at a loss for quite a while. This is hardly surprising given the fact that the area the Eritrean branch was supposed to cover has been a theater of war for a long period of time. At present, the Eritrean Insurance Corporation has a substantial amount of outstanding claims which can never be settled from its own resources. Because all of the outstanding claims resulted from accidents that occurred before or on May 26, 1991, our view is that the Ethiopian Insurance

Corporation must be asked to settle these claims. According to our information, the majority of these claims originated in connection with damages sustained by large trucks. As these trucks are required to transport urgent food aid supplies within Eritrea, the Ethiopian Insurance Corporation must be asked to settle these claims as soon as possible.

As for the future of the Eritrean Insurance Corporation, we believe that if it is provided with a modest capital, it can soon become self-financing, although for certain classes of insurance a direct reinsurance arrangement with foreign insurers must be immediately started. In order to evaluate the long-term prospects of the Insurance Corporation and to organize it along efficient lines, we suggest that the help of experts be solicited.

IV. FISCAL ADMINISTRATION

A. Budget for Each Level of Government

With regard to the public finances, the different levels of government must be required and empowered to organize the fiscal administration of their respective areas. The central, regional and municipal governments must each prepare and execute their own budget. The budget prepared must then be presented to the highest legislative authority or any other competent authority of each level of government for approval, following which it can legally be implemented for one budget year.

The last budget of the colonial government has just lapsed, but this in no way prevents us from reactivating it for the current year. We can simply decide to maintain the current expenditures that we consider are justified. We believe that the practice of spending without a budget must be avoided.

Not only should the budget take the various levels of government into consideration but it should also encompass both ordinary and capital expenditure of each level of government. We should also strive for a consolidated budget avoiding fragmentation.

B. Taxes

A country like Eritrea, which has just disengaged from a long war, needs massive financial resources to rehabilitate its economy. In addition, there are always pressing needs calling for new investments, which, due to the extremely low per capita income of our people, can hardly be undertaken privately. Moreover, there is always the need to finance a bureaucracy with an in-built tendency to grow in size. If the government were to single-mindedly aim at the achievement of these goals, then it would have no choice but to impose heavy taxes on the population. However, there are serious reasons militating against heavy taxes. First, the tax base had narrowed drastically over the years as many once economically viable businesses and agricultural outfits ceased to operate either partially or completely. Second, agriculture, the economic sector employing the majority of our people, and thus constituting an important source of tax income for the government, has been suffering from a long and malignant drought. Finally, there is the need to attract foreign investment by offering a tax holiday.

Taking into consideration the above-stated financial needs and tax constraints, one can see how difficult it is to decide on an optimum tax regime.

The difficulty of choosing the right tax mix, notwithstanding, the task of revising the entire tax regime, which was singularly introduced to serve colonial aims, is an urgent one. Meanwhile, it is our view that as far as customs and excise duty are concerned, the one proclaimed last year should be imposed throughout the country and the colonial one legislated out of existence.

C. Compositions of Tax Revenues

In the West, direct taxes, which are considered to be progressive, rank first in terms of contribution toward the budget. In the third world countries like Eritrea, however, in spite of the fact that they are generally judged to be regressive in nature, indirect taxes contribute the most toward the budget simply because they are easy to collect. From the point of view of equity, it is desirable to reverse this situation. But as it will not be practical to do so in the short run, indirect taxes, especially customs' duties, will have to contribute the major share to the budget. Meanwhile, measures must be taken to eventually make direct taxes, especially income taxes, contribute the lion's share. At the same time, expert advice must be sought to reorganize the tax collecting departments along efficient lines.

D. Composition of Expenditures: Salaries and Pensions

In third world countries, it is common to have a huge army of civil servants on the payroll, the result being that salaries and emoluments generally absorb practically the entire revenue, leaving hardly anything for development. It is our view that we are lucky we have been provided with the opportunity of paring the civil service to the bare minimum, should we wish to do so. If we are not careful today, we will be repeating mistakes of other third world countries. Due to the low per capita income in our country, our government has no choice but to initiate capital formation through taxation. But if this capital is to be available for investment, we must keep the size of the civil service to the bare minimum.

In Eritrea, there is a large army of pensioners today. These pensioners have been inherited from the former government. With regard to expenditures on pensioners, we propose the following: As far as booklet-owning pensioners are concerned, we believe that the Ethiopian government must itself pay them regularly. Advisably, it can create a fund for this purpose in Asmara, or delegate the Eritrean Pension Department, making sure that it transfers enough funds regularly. Those who will be pensioned off in the future, but who happened to have contributed to the pension fund in Addis Ababa and later in Asmara, can have their case individually studied in order to determine Ethiopian or Eritrean liability. In the meantime, we must create a pension fund by regularly contributing our share so that future pensioners can be paid promptly. The present arrangement where the employee contributes 4 percent of his salary and the government contributes another 6 percent is reasonable.

E. Public Debt

We believe that the government must be empowered to borrow in order to finance temporary deficit if and when the need arises. In other words, we should single-mindedly aim to balance the budget. Although such temporary borrowing can be used to finance deficits on ordinary expenditure, borrowing on a relatively large scale may be beneficial for capital expenditure. The latter can, of course, be obtained from domestic as well as foreign sources.

F. Processing Foreign Assistance

As mentioned earlier, we believe that foreign assistance can and must play an important role in the rehabilitation of various sectors of our economy. Every department may already have rehabilitation proposals in the pipeline, with foreign financing in mind. Although it is proper for proposals to be initiated by the various concerned departments, we believe that requests for foreign aid must be processed in a centralized manner in order to avoid duplication and to keep centralized records. Moreover, if the assistance is in the form of long-term loans, terms can be negotiated in a centralized manner. Therefore, we propose that a section be created in the Finance Department to deal specifically with foreign assistance and foreign and domestic loans.

V. MISCELLANEOUS CHALLENGES OF THE FINANCIAL SECTOR

A. Managerial-Level Vacancies

With the departure of Ethiopians who were holding managerial-level posts, a critical shortage of qualified manpower has begun to be felt. We can state with authority that the financial sector is in need of able people to lead it in the direction the Provisional Government may chart for it. We believe that in other sectors also managerial posts are crying to be filled. We have two proposals to make with regard to filling these posts once an exhaustive list of these is carefully prepared.

First, the possibility of rehiring pensioned personnel on a contractual basis should be seriously considered. The colonial government had a policy of retiring personnel at the age of fifty-five. Surely, for an underdeveloped country like ours, it is unjustified to retire people at such an early age, particularly when they possess specialized skills.

Second, we understand that there are many qualified Eritreans working abroad who can be prevailed upon to take employment here. Therefore, we propose that a committee be formed to approach them in order to convince them to take employment in Eritrea. Of course, employment conditions must be made reasonably attractive enough for them.

B. Corrupt Officials

It is often reported that we have inherited corrupt officials from the colonial government. Our view with regard to this question is that all former employees of the former government be required to submit an exhaustive list of the assets they own. Those who are proven to have amassed wealth illegally can be compelled to hand over these assets to the state. Again, a committee, in which members of the judiciary are heavily represented, can handle the matter swiftly and efficiently.

CURRENCY AND BANKING
FOR AN EMERGING ECONOMY

Arefaine G. Yohannes

I. INTRODUCTION

An efficient financial system is essential for economic growth and development. The financial system includes money and various short-term and long-term financial instruments, banks and other financial institutions, a central bank and financial markets. The focus of this paper is on money (currency) and commercial and central banking.

The functions of money in a monetized economy are well-known. Money serves as a medium of exchange or means of payments, a unit of account and a store of value. As a means of payments, it facilitates exchange and promotes specialization. Specialization increases productivity, which in turn speeds up economic growth. As a unit of account or standard of value, money simplifies business and national economic accounting.

Commercial banks provide a number of important services in both developing and developed countries. However, their main functions are to mobilize savings and provide loans to various sectors of the economy.

Central banks issue currencies, supervise banks, manage foreign exchange resources of an economy and regulate the economy's supply of money and credit. They also perform other functions.

The purpose of this paper is to discuss some key issues related to currencies, commercial banking and central banking in an emerging economy like Eritrea. The ideas presented in this paper are designed to stimulate discussion of some of the relevant issues and simplify the task of formulating appropriate policies with respect to currency and banking.

II. A NATIONAL CURRENCY

The currencies that are used in different countries of the world today, including Eritrea, are fiat currencies. The currencies are not backed by gold or other precious metals. People accept those currencies because they believe they can use them to buy other goods and services.

The responsibility for minting coins and printing and issuing paper currency is, typically, given to the central bank. Assuming that a popular referendum in Eritrea leads to the independence of Eritrea, the establishment of a new central bank and a new national currency will have to be considered.

A. Benefits of a National Currency

Aside from the psychological pride of having a national currency, there are economic benefits to establishing a national currency. First, the central bank would have greater control over the amount of currency issued and the supply of money. This type of control would be essential for promoting stated macroeconomic objectives such as economic growth, stability of prices and foreign exchange rates.

Second, the issuing of currency can be a profitable activity for the central bank. The cost of minting coins and printing paper currency is relatively small. The costs are smaller than the face values and the difference between the face values and the costs represent profit to the issuer — the treasury or the central bank. Furthermore, the currency is a liability of the issuer and as long as people have confidence in the currency, they will be willing to hold it without any explicit interest. In other words, the issuer does not have to pay interest on its liability. People will be willing to forego the interest income so they can use it for transactions purposes. On the other hand, the central bank acquires interest-earning assets with the currency issued and the spread generates income to the central bank.

B. Currency Unit, Denominations and Other Features

The currency should have several denominations to facilitate exchange. Divisibility of the monetary unit is one of the advantages of monetary exchange over the much less efficient barter system. Assuming that the basic unit of a new Eritrean currency is an Eritrean *kirshi* (dollar), it could be defined in decimal format to equal 100 *santeem* (cents or pennies). Coins with face values of 1, 5, 10, 25 and 50 santeem (cents) could be minted and paper notes with face values of 1, 2, 5, 10, 20, 50 and 100 can be printed and issued.

In some countries, there are dollar coins (e.g., Canada) instead of dollar bills. The coins reduce the cost of issuing the currency because they have longer expected lives than dollar bills. The dollar bills tend be the most frequently used bills compared to the higher denomination bills and thus have the shortest expected lives. In one study, the average life of a U.S. dollar bill was estimated to be 1.81 years.[1] In some countries, plastic currencies are being used to increase the durability of the currency and to discourage counterfeiting; this is something that may have to be explored.

The paper bills in some countries also have different colors (e.g., Ethiopia). In countries with high illiteracy rates, people can recognize bills with different face values by just looking at the colors. Furthermore, the variety of colors makes it difficult for counterfeiters to produce counterfeit currency in different denominations.

C. Introducing the New Currency

If the new national currency is to be the sole legal tender in Eritrea, other currencies that are used in Eritrea, notably, the Ethiopian *birr* and the Sudanese *pound*, would have to be converted into the new currency and withdrawn from circulation. The currencies can be converted at some stated ratios. For example, the Ethiopian *birr* can be converted into an Eritrean *kirshi* at par, if inflation rates in Eritrea and Ethiopia are comparable. The Ethiopian *birr* and the Sudanese *pound* may then be shipped to Ethiopia and the Sudan respectively. In exchange for the Ethiopian *birr* and the Sudanese *pound*, Eritrea would receive convertible currencies like the U.S. dollar.

There should be extensive advance publicity of the conversion from other currencies into the new Eritrean currency. People should be advised to convert the currencies that they hold within a specified period of time. A period of up to six months may be adequate for this purpose.

D. Foreign Exchange Arrangements

The new Eritrean currency would have to be priced in terms of other national currencies in the foreign exchange markets. The new Eritrean currency could be pegged to another major currency or basket of currencies. Alternatively, its price in terms of other currencies could be determined by market forces. The first approach is called the fixed exchange rate system and the second is called a flexible or a floating exchange rate system. In a fixed exchange rate system, the government defines the currency in terms of another major currency or a basket of currencies and the exchange rate remains fixed until the government revalues or devalues it to deal with serious external imbalances (primarily trade deficits or surpluses.

1. Fixed Exchange Rate Systems. The major advantage of a fixed exchange rate is that it promotes international trade. On the negative side, serious imbalances in the external sector may force policymakers to use fiscal and monetary policy instruments to reduce external imbalances and such policies may conflict with domestic economic goals of full employment and price stability. They may also result in trade and capital controls. Furthermore, the local currency may be fixed relative to the currency to which it is pegged but its price will vary relative to other currencies that float. Moreover, currencies of many countries tend to be overvalued and there is resistance to devaluations. As a result, parallel (black) markets have developed in economies where currency overvaluation exists. Finally, if devaluations occur after a major external imbalance occurs, the magnitude of the devaluation required to eliminate the imbalance may be disruptive.

2. Flexible or Floating Exchange Rates. There are three major arguments in favor of flexible exchange rates.[2] First, exchange rate changes will tend to automatically correct disequilibrium in the balance of payments and this allows the policymakers to pursue independent fiscal and monetary policies to deal with domestic economic problems such as unemployment and inflation. There would also be less need for instituting trade restrictions and controls on capital flows to deal with external imbalances.

Second, flexible exchange rates tend to insulate the economy from external shocks such as high inflation rates and high interest rates.

Third, prior to the introduction of the floating rate system in 1973, exchange rates in a flexible exchange rate system were expected to change gradually. As a result, exchange rate changes were not expected to be disruptive.

However, the experience with floating exchange rates since 1973, has shown that the above advantages were overstated.[3] Exchange rate changes failed to correct external imbalances. For example, the depreciation of the U.S. dollar could not eliminate the large current account deficits after 1985 and there was political pressure within for import controls in the United States and export restraints in the trading partners. Moreover, domestic economies continued to be adversely affected by external shocks. In the mid-1980s, high interest rates in the United States led to the appreciation of the dollar, which in turn led to inflationary pressures in some European countries. Those countries were forced to tighten monetary policy to control the inflationary pressures despite high unemployment rates.

Finally, there was a marked increase in the volatility of exchange rates and there is evidence that the volatility of exchange rates has limited international trade in both developing countries and industrial countries.[4] In the industrial countries, the presence of forward markets may have reduced the adverse effects of volatile exchange rates on international trade. In the developing countries, however, forward markets are limited and the volatility of exchange rates and the uncertainty associated with it may have produced a more negative impact on international trade.

3. Current Exchange Rate Systems of Developing Countries. Many countries peg their currencies to other currencies like the U.S. dollar or the French franc or to a basket of currencies of countries which are major trading partners. As of December 28, 1990, 26 currencies were pegged to the U.S. dollar, 14 were pegged to the French franc, 35 were pegged to a basket of currencies, and 6 were pegged to SDR's (Special Drawing Rights issued by the International Monetary Fund).[5]

Developing countries that have floating exchange rate systems describe their regimes as managed floating arrangements, independently floating arrangements and exchange rates adjusted according to a set of indicators.[6] In the managed floating arrangement, the central bank adjusts the exchange rate frequently. The adjustments are frequent and they are made judgmentally. The adjustments are based on factors such as the level of international reserves, balance of payments condition and developments in the parallel markets.

In the independently floating arrangement, the exchange rate is determined either by negotiations in the interbank market or on the basis of an auction. Finally, in the third type of floating arrangement, there is a well-defined procedure for adjusting the exchange rate and the changes may be predetermined. The changes are based on a set of indicators such as the difference between the domestic inflation rate and the world inflation rate, the level of international reserves, and balance of payments performance.

4. Recommended Foreign Exchange Rate Arrangement for Eritrea. The managed floating arrangement is appealing, initially, but the pegged system may be better for Eritrea. The stability of the exchange rate would tend to favor international trade. The *kirshi* would have stable purchasing power in terms of the goods and services in Eritrea's major trading partner(s). The Eritrean *kirshi* could be pegged to the U.S. dollar or to a basket of currencies of countries which are expected to be major trading partners. The latter might offer greater stability of purchasing power but it depends on the degree of concentration of trade and on how the currencies in the basket correlate with each other.

E. Common Currency with Ethiopia

The use of a common currency by countries that have close economic relations offers some benefits to the countries that use the common currency. One such benefit is that it reduces transaction costs and facilities trade because individuals and businesses do not have to deal with currency conversions.

Furthermore, the growing globalization of national economies and the stiff competition among the different countries of the world necessitates greater economic cooperation between Eritrea and Ethiopia and the other countries of the region. The increased economic cooperation could then form the basis for gradual economic and monetary integration.

However, although the use of a common currency may have to be explored, the implementation of such an idea may be very difficult in practice.

III. CENTRAL BANKING

Central banks play very important roles in the economies of developed and developing countries. Their specific functions may vary from country to country. In general, however, the functions of a central bank are to issue a national currency, to serve as the banks' bank and the government's bank, to supervise commercial banks, to manage foreign exchange resources and to stabilize the foreign exchange rate, to regulate the supply of credit and money, and to provide check-clearing facilities. In developing countries, additional functions may be to develop financial markets (money and capital) and financial institutions such as credit unions.

Central banks perform a number of important functions, but the most important function of a central bank in a developed country is the regulation of the supply of money and credit. The money supply is manipulated to achieve specific macroeconomic objectives such as full employment and stable prices. To manipulate the supply of money, they use three general monetary controls: open market operations, legal reserve requirements and the central bank discount rate.

In addition to the general monetary controls, the central bank utilizes selective credit controls to control the flow of credit to specific sectors of the economy. These credit controls are interest rate controls and margin requirements.

The use of open market operations requires the existence of a well-developed financial system, i.e., financial markets and financial institutions. In developing countries, however, the financial markets are not well-developed and open market operations would not work well.

A. Alternatives to a Central Bank

Because of the absence of well-developed financial markets and other reasons, alternatives to a full-fledged central bank have been suggested.[7] The alternatives are a transitional central banking institution, a supranational central bank, a central banking institution for a currency enclave and a central banking institution for an extremely open economy. The transitional central banking institution is a type of central bank somewhere between a currency board established by a colonial power for its colony and a full-fledged central bank. It has more powers than a currency board and may include loans to the government and bank supervision.

A supranational central bank acts as central bank for a group of countries that belong to a monetary union, characterized by, among other things, a common currency and limited restrictions on capital mobility.

In the third type, the currency enclave uses the central bank of a major trading partner as the central bank. In addition, a domestic central bank is established to perform some limited functions. In a situation like this, the currency of the trading partner also circulates in the currency enclave.

For an economy with open commodity and capital flows, a central bank with limited powers with respect to lending to the government and regulation of financial institutions may be needed.

B. Proposed Monetary Authority for Eritrea

As in many developing economies, there are, obviously, no financial markets or institutions that would allow open market operations. As a result, a full-fledged central bank in Eritrea would not be able to employ all the general monetary controls that are employed by central banks in developed countries. Nevertheless, it would be advisable to establish a central bank in Eritrea with the responsibilities that are enumerated above. Specifically, its functions would be to issue the national currency, to hold bank deposits and make loans to banks, to serve as the government's bank, to supervise banks, to manage foreign exchange reserves and stabilize the foreign exchange rate, to regulate the supply of credit and money, to authorize the opening of new or branch banks, to close banks and to promote the development of financial markets and other financial institutions (such as credit unions, *ekubs* and development banks) that are essential for economic development.

Because the use of open market operations would not be available, the central bank would have to rely on credit guidelines and legal reserve requirements to achieve its macroeconomic objectives.

The central bank should refrain from financing budget deficits. If loans are advanced to the government they would have to be limited with respect to amount and repayment period. The loans should cover temporary budget deficits and they should not be used as sources of long-term finance. In some countries central banks have financed deficits of state enterprises and caused major inflationary problems. As a result some people have recommended the replacement of such central banks by currency boards because currency boards would not be able to print money to finance deficits.[8]

The implementation of many of the functions of the proposed central bank would require skilled personnel and other resources. Given the limited resources and the absence of financial markets, it will take some time for the central bank to perform all its functions fully. However, the framework that is created should permit the central bank to grow overtime and exercise its powers and responsibilities more fully as it grows.

The central bank should probably be an independent entity led by a board of governors, rather than within the finance ministry. For continuity of monetary policy, the governors could be appointed, in a staggered manner, for long periods of time. However, to ensure proper policy coordination, the minister of finance should be a member of the board of governors of the central bank or at least an ex-officio member.

IV. COMMERCIAL BANKING

Commercial banks play a vital role in economic growth by mobilizing savings from the surplus units in the economy and channeling the savings to the deficit units. They offer demand deposits, saving deposits and time deposits or certificates of deposits with various denominations and maturities. The funds deposited with them are used to finance consumer loans, business loans and real estate loans.

Other functions performed by banks include the purchase or sale of foreign exchange, issuing of credit cards, provision of trust services, and the renting of safe deposit boxes.

Much of the urban population in Eritrea has been exposed to banking. Individuals as well as the economy as a whole can benefit from expanded commercial banking services in different parts of the country. The banks can encourage people to open various types of accounts and provide loans to different members of their communities. They can offer loans for the purchase of cars, loans for the purchase of homes or for home improvements, secured or unsecured short-term and long-term loans to businesses.

Many people may not be familiar with the services that banks offer or they may not have confidence in banks. To deal with these types of problems, the banks should hold seminars for the public and explain to them how they can benefit from the services of banks.

To supplement the activities of commercial banks, the central bank should encourage the establishment of a development bank, credit unions and *ekubs*. The purpose of the development bank would be to raise funds by borrowing long-term and making industrial and agricultural loans. The purpose of the credit unions and the *ekubs* would be to encourage people to save.

A. Safety Factors

The safety of the banking system can be enhanced by requiring banks to maintain acceptable minimum capital ratios and by periodic examinations and audits. Another safety feature of a banking system is deposit insurance. Deposit insurance is the most important safety feature in the United States. Although deposit insurance may be too costly for the banking system in Eritrea, it is something that could be considered.

B. Foreign Banks

Foreign banks can also play a very important role in the economic development of Eritrea.[9] First, the foreign banks would bring expertise such as management and other skills. They would also help in training local personnel. Second, they would promote international trade and direct foreign investment. They are in a better position to meet the needs of importers, exporters and direct foreign investors. Because of their networks, they may be able to attract foreign exchange into the economy.

Some countries impose restrictions on the activities of foreign banks. For example, they may require that at least 51 percent of the capital of a bank be owned by local nationals or they may require foreign banks to include local nationals on their boards of directors. Their activities may also be limited to certain geographical areas.

Although it is important to ensure that the activities of foreign banks are consistent with the overall economic development objectives of the policymakers, excessive controls or restrictions could be counterproductive. They would discourage international banks from investing in Eritrea.

V. FORMING A SPECIAL COMMISSION

Establishing a new monetary authority, introducing a new currency and formulating a banking policy are complex matters. Establishment of a special commission may be advisable. The commission would consist of experts in central and commercial banking.

The commission could then make specific recommendations on the organizational structure, powers and responsibilities of the central bank, the monetary unit and appropriate foreign exchange arrangements as well as commercial bank policies. The recommendations would also include specific procedures for operationalizing their recommendations and time frames for implementation.

VI. SUMMARY

In this paper, the importance of printing and issuing one's own national currency is explained. Moreover, it is proposed that an Eritrean *kirshi*, consisting of 100 cents, be the basic currency unit and that various denominations of it be issued.

It is also proposed that a central bank be established to issue a national currency and to perform other functions that are performed by a central bank.

Finally, the expansion of domestic commercial banks and the encouragement of foreign banks would help in mobilizing savings. The savings can then be used to finance consumer loans, such as car loans, business loans and real estate loans.

NOTES

1. Explaining the Cash Explosion," in Federal Reserve Bank of Atlanta, *Economic Review* (March 1982):16.
2. J. A. Whitt, Jr., "Flexible Exchange Rates: An Idea Whose Time has Passed?" in Federal Reserve Bank of Atlanta, *Economic Review* (September/October 1990):6–8.
3. Ibid.
4. P. De Grauwe, "Exchange Rate Variability and the Slow-Down in Growth of International Trade," *IMF Staff Papers* (March 1988). P. D. Grauwe and De Bellefroid, "Long-run Exchange Rate Variability and International Trade," in S. Arndt and D. Richardson (eds.), *Real Financial Linkages Among Open Economies* (Cambridge: MIT Press, 1987). P. Kennen and D. Rodrik, "Measuring and Analyzing the Effects of Short-run Volatility in Real Exchange Rate," *Review of Economics and Statistics* (May 1986). J. Williamson, "The Case for Managed Exchange Rates," in J. Adams, *The Contemporary International Economy,* 2nd. ed. (New York: St. Martin's Press, 1985):308. J. A. Whitt, Jr., op cit.
5. IMF, *IMF Survey* (April 1, 1991):96
6. P. J. Quirk, "The Case for Open Foreign Exchange Systems," *Finance and Development* (June 1989):30–31.
7. C. Collyns, *Alternatives to the Central Bank in the Developing World* (Washington, D.C.: International Monetary Fund, 1983).
8. S. H. Hanke, "Argentina Should Abolish its Central Bank," *Wall Street Journal,* October 25, 1991, p. A 15.
9. D. Germidis and C. A. Michalet, *International Banks and Financial Markets in Developing Countries* (Paris: Organization for Economic Cooperation and Development, 1984).

SECURITIES EXCHANGE AND MONETARY SYSTEM FOR AN EMERGING NATION: ERITREA

Brhane Tesfay

The status of the Securities Exchange and Monetary System (SEAMS) of the United States, immediately after its independence from Britain, is described. The problem of the U.S. SEAMS that led to the enactment of the 1935 Securities Exchange Act is examined. Based on the historical analysis and the examinations of several studies, related to the early SEAMS of the United States, an Eritrean SEAMS is recommended.

I. INTRODUCTION

Securities Exchange and Monetary System (SEAMS) is a system where currencies, notes, bills, bonds, stocks and other similar commercial instruments are traded. Although, notes and bills have much shorter maturity period than bonds, they are commonly classified as "bonds." The primary purpose of the system is to raise capital and allocate it to the different means of production. The system is expected to help a nation pool resources to some central places and then distribute the resources to those who build plants, roads, hospitals, schools, etc.

The primary purpose is analogous to that of *"Ekub"* in Ethiopia and in Eritrea or "Chit fund" in India. *Ekub* is a method of raising funds from members who voluntarily join for the purpose of pooling funds and distributing them to the members. Typically, twelve or more people get together and elect a secretary, treasurer and a judge. They agree to each contribute a certain amount of money monthly to the *Ekub*. For our purpose, let us assume that the contribution is $100 per month per person. The pooled $1200 per month is then given to whoever wins the lottery for that month. This process continues until every one receives $1200 per month. The Chit fund in India is similar in principle. However, the Indian government requires all Chit funds to be officially registered, which implies that the government has some interest in regulating them (Tesfay 1970).

The fundamental difference between an *Ekub* and a security exchange system is that in joining an *Ekub* an individual who pays his/her share of $100 per month does not receive a certificate or document that assures that sometime during the twelve months the payee will receive back the $1200. In other words, the member of the *Ekub* is giving someone unsecured funds based on faith, and hopefully all members will pay the $1200 that they promised to pay.

A study of *Ekub* by the author showed that about 25 percent of *Ekub* members lose their funds because they could not take their case to court to enforce the terms of the *Ekub* (Tesfay 1970).

All securities, be they stocks, notes, bills, bonds or other commercial papers, specifically state the value for which they have been purchased and the terms, period and other requirements to ensure that the payee knows in advance what to expect out of his/her purchases, including the possibility of losing all the investment in some cases. The key difference is that with securities, terms of sale and purchases are well-known to all parties and therefore become contracts enforceable by courts, but with *Ekub* there is no such contract.

II. THE SECURITIES EXCHANGE AND MONETARY SYSTEM DURING THE EARLY YEARS

The strength of any SEAMS is a function of the "synergy."[1] A well thought out synergy will result in a constructive and useful SEAMS. However, unless the synergy includes some ethical standards and cherished societal values, SEAMS cannot, on its own accord, include values that were deliberately left out by its designers. Like all systems, SEAMS will achieve only the synergy that it was designed to achieve. In some ways it is analogous to capitalism. Capitalism is a system of economy that depends on the free market concept of supply and demand. In capitalism all resources and wealth are allocated by the "invisible hand." As such, it is theoretically devoid of "value." Democracy and the "Rule of Law and Fairness" are the processes that instill value and discipline in capitalism. Thus, the political process and governmental apparatus become critical mediators in a capitalist economy. A review of the SEAMS' early years in England and the United States illustrates how critical the correct relationship of SEAMS to the political decisions and governmental policies are.

The earliest markets in England and the United States started with the primary markets (West and Seha 1971). The primary market is the market where newly issued stocks, notes, bills and bonds are traded. There are two types of stocks: common stocks and preferred stocks. The common stocks are shares with clearly stated par values intended to raise immediately needed funds by a corporation. Shareholders are holders of certificate of ownership of a company and are entitled to voting rights and dividends. Preferred stocks have the properties of stocks and debts. Owners of the preferred stocks may receive dividends. The dividends, however, are fixed at the time the stocks are issued. This is similar to the fixed interest that a bond holder may expect at the time of the maturity of the bond.

Although common stockholders may get more dividends, when the company does well, preferred stockholders get the fixed rate of dividends. This makes preferred stocks less attractive than common stocks. Companies may deduct interest paid in bonds for tax purposes but cannot do so with the dividends paid on preferred stocks. This makes preferred stocks less attractive than bonds. These are some of the reasons that the issuing of preferred stocks is dwindling year by year.

The earliest recorded issues of stock were made sometime in the middle of the thirteenth century in England (De Bedts 1964). The abuse of stockbrokers in the selling of stocks prompted the English parliament to enact the 1697 "Pernicious Art of Stock-Jobbing." The act required that all brokers take a "fiduciary oath," limit their commission to 10 percent, and a metal token properly stamped by the authorities for identification. The law also restricted the number of stockbrokers to one hundred for England. The stock market was instrumental in raising funds through the dispersion of owner-ship to finance new industries and also colonization. For example, in 1711 the South Sea Company raised all the funds it needed to carry out its activities — including slave trading. This was done through the London Stock Exchange, which was established in 1696.

By 1852 the stock swindlers disease had reached the United States. Massachusetts had to prohibit by law some fraudulent activities of stock-brokers. In 1911 a Kansas legislature warned that if left unregulated, the stockbrokers of his day would sell shares in the "blue sky" above. By this time the federal government's concern was expressed by the House of Representatives Committee, chaired by A. D. Pujo of Louisiana. His investi-gation revealed two key problems in the stock market. The first problem was the "speculation" aspect of the market. The committee reported that a vast waste of capital resulted when substantial quantity of investment funds went into the pockets of a few speculators instead of into the productive industry. This phenomenon in conjunction with the so-called "poll syndication" exas-perated the impatience of the federal government. Poll syndication is the process by which stock values are increased artificially because a few big buyers and sellers decide to create an atmosphere that favors either buying or selling. This process of manipulating the stock prices is often achieved through well-placed rumors and threats to buy or sell (U.S. Government Press 1913).

The final blow, which resulted in part in the October 1929 Great Crash, was excessive "insider trading" practices. Even though by this time there were laws of incorporation and full disclosure, the practice of sharing vital stock information within selected groups of associates and friends by "insiders" was common. An "insider" is a person who often controls a corporation by owning at least 10 percent or more of the company stocks and gets privileged inside information. The insider is often a director or an elected official of a corpora-tion. In 1935, the Security Exchange Act was legislated. This act created the Security Exchange Commission (SEC) to implement all the details of the act. There were numerous studies and hearings that uncovered several problems associated with the creation of SEC, the principal regulatory agency of the U.S. SEAMS. There is a 400-page book that lists the titles of the papers, state-ments, and countless debates in the U.S. Congress. Given the distrust of any governmental regulating agency by the U.S. public, it is not surprising that the subject commanded so many studies and so many debates. The idea of reg-ulating a market of any kind, in a land whose markets are supposed to be run by the "invisible hand," is contrary to the foundation of the capitalist econo-my. Yet the U.S. Congress passed the 1935 SEC Act to precisely do so. This implies that the problems associated with the unregulated securities exchange market were so severe that they might have been perceived as threatening the very existence of capitalism and democracy as they did during the Great Crash of 1929 and the subsequent great depression.

III. SUMMARIES OF THE STUDIES OF THE SEAMS PRIOR TO THE 1935 U.S. SECURITIES EXCHANGE ACT

Several of the serious studies and papers (e.g., Harvey 1932) identified the "systemic" problems associated with SEAMS. These were related to the fundamental problems of any system. First, the synergy or the expected prime purpose of creating a SEAMS was either unclear or open for exploitation by the participants in the system. It was not clear if the public wanted the system to help in investment or speculation.

Second, the functional interrelationship of all the variables or parts in the system was not clearly defined. (See Figure 1.) Thus, instead of the SEAMS working in a synchronized way to achieve the intended synergy, some parts were countervailing the efficiency of others. For example, some banks that should have directed funds to the proper investment channels were found laundering[2] funds.

Third, the hierarchy of the different governmental agencies and market institutions was so vague that the lack of chain of command was apparent. As in the case of the 1929 crash, no one took the ultimate responsibility of what happened. Individuals and firms did not know whom to hold responsible when things got out of hand.

Fourth, there was no well thought out method of dealing with the tendency of "entropy" of the system. Entropy is the natural tendency of a system to decay or degenerate. Such degeneration of a system is delayed by designing a proper feedback system. The feedback system, like the three elements of any system mentioned above is determined by the degree of "openness" dictated by the imperative of the intended synergy. The problem of "pool syndication," which amounted to the monopoly of some of the securities market by some, and the insider trading issues were directly the result of the lack of a properly designed feedback system. Nowadays, thanks in part to the third generation of computers, such activities as the pool syndication and insider trading are monitored by SEC every minute of the day.

Even though there will always be individuals, and firms, who will attempt to exploit the "openness" of the U.S. SEAMS, they often get caught. For example, Levine and Boisky of Drexel Lambert Brokerage were caught and fined hundreds of millions of dollars. They also had to spend some time in federal prison for illegal insider trading practices. Most of the credit for their arrest and conviction is given to the third generation computers, which quietly tracked their illegal activities and transactions during the course of several months.

The Grand Synergy (GSY) can be assumed to be ranging from the maintenance of the free enterprise system to the allocation of resources and distribution of wealth in the United States as well as enhancing continued public confidence in the U.S. SEAMS. It is also used by many as an economic gauge and by some as a ground for speculative practices. Each element of the model has its own small "synergy" (SY), which is functionally interrelated to the Grand Synergy (GSY). In other words, the value of the small synergy must contribute positively to the Grand Synergy or else it has to be corrected to do so. What dictates this is the hierarchical nature of synergies or the weights assigned to each synergy in the system. The key variables in the U.S. SEAMS are:

1. The markets, such as primary, secondary and tertiary markets (SY = free);
2. The instruments such as stock, bonds, notes and bills (SY = authentic)
3. The intermediaries, such as brokers; financial institution (SY = dependable);
4. Users of funds and sources of funds such as individuals, firms, governments or a combination of any of these (SY = adequate);
5. The media, such as print, broadcast (SY = independence);
6. Regulating agencies such as SEC, Federal Reserve Bank (U.S. Central Banks), Treasury, U.S. Economic Advisor's office, that monitor and adjust the system (SY = monitor and adjust); and
7. Credit rating agencies such as Standard and Poor (SY = integrity) (Standard and Poor 1983).

Figure 1

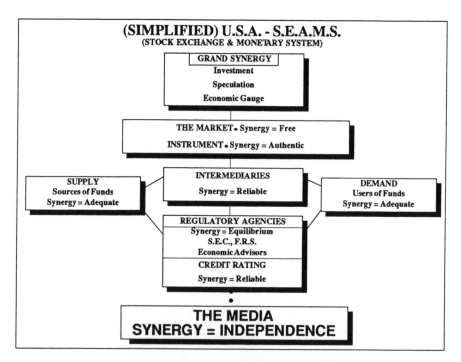

Some of the studies, conducted years after SEC and other regulatory agencies were in place, kept observing some recurring problems associated with specific issues of some instruments, particularly the bond-type of instruments, and the secondary and tertiary markets. In the United States, bonds are issued by firms after they are rated by credit-rating firms such as Standard and Poor Inc. The yield or return expected from each dollar invested in bonds is relative to this rating, which presumably assigns the risk an investor is taking in purchasing the bond. Lately, especially in the 1970s and 1980s, some "junk bonds" with a low credit rating of BB (AAA being highest rating) but with higher yield possibilities have been issued and sold to the public. Unfortunately, many of these bonds have proven to be useless, leading to the loses of savings of many, especially the elderly who invested in them (Cooner 1987).

The secondary markets are markets where the connection between the investment or purchase of a stock or bond is more remotely related to the issuer than in the primary market. None of the funds from this market go to the issuing company. The tertiary market, where options and futures are traded, is even more remotely related to the issuer of the instruments than both the primary and the secondary markets. To illustrate the basic difference, let us assume a firm issued a $50 share and sold it at the primary market. The primary concern of the buyer is how strong the firm is now and how much stronger it may be in the future. Thus, the buyer has to examine the "prospectus" of the firm and read the 10-K reports. (The 10-K reports are the official annual reports that each firm must submit to SEC). In addition, the buyer must obtain some data on the firm's market share (both current and future) and find out the industry growth rate and the credit worthiness of the firm (Schwartz 1988).

In the secondary market this $50 share has a life of its own. The buyer has to study the supply and demand data of this share in the market. Whether the firm that issued it is doing well is secondary to how well the share is being traded.

However, it should be noted that as part of the U.S. SEAMS, these three markets are functionally interrelated. In order for the primary market to achieve its synergy, both the secondary and tertiary markets have to work well. This of course assumes that the system has been designed to have the three markets. There are markets in some countries such as India, China, and the USSR that do not include the tertiary markets. Even in the United States there are states that have made the trading of option future and other highly speculative trading illegal (Pitts and Fabozzi 1990).

IV. SEAMS FOR AN EMERGING NATION: ERITREA

An emerging nation has some imperatives that it has to consider. These imperatives range from the lack of capital to the scarcity of general resources. But the demand for goods and services is so great that the various markets are ready to absorb almost any thing that is supplied. The combination of the two imperatives should force policymakers and strategists to be extremely prudent and cautious without unnecessary interference in the SEAMS.

In the case of Eritrea, the above scenario of emerging nation is complicated by the thirty-year war of independence. The harsh realities of war and the continuous adjustment processes that the leadership has to make in order to utilize extremely scarce resources to the maximum might have engendered the need for highly centralized planning and the excessive prudence and cautiousness that goes with it. These have to be recognized and the negative aspects of these to the Eritrean SEAMS have to be minimized.

Given an economic system that would encourage private ownership and management but also allow public ownership and management of enterprises, Eritrea's economic priorities should be obvious. Its number one economic goal should be to mobilize its most important resources, its people, provide them with the necessary capital, and harness the natural resources to improve the quality of life of all Eritreans. The purpose of an Eritrean SEAMS, that will be considered in this paper, is capital accumulation and proper allocation of that capital to the sectors that will contribute to the improvement of the quality of life of all Eritreans. Therefore, the Grand Synergy of the Eritrean SEAMS for at least the first ten years should be capital accumulation and proper allocation of that capital to the basic industries and services. An example of the basic industry is manufacturing of the basic goods and examples of the primary services are health and education. Because the GSY is unambiguous, the Eritrean SEAMS can be designed to be simple and easy to understand and monitor. All those confusing elements experienced by the U.S. SEAMS since its inception can be avoided.

The suggested model of an Eritrean SEAMS is shown in Figure 2. Figure 2 is intended to achieve two purposes. First, to simplify the understanding of an Eritrean SEAMS so that constructive criticisms can be provided to improve the model. Second, and perhaps more important, is to provide policymakers and legislators a basis for legislative action and formulation of strategies and policies to deal with the Eritrean SEAMS. For example, the GSY (Grand Synergy or Mission) for the Eritrean SEAMS, as stated in the chart, is to combine investment and economic gauging. Given this GSY, legislators may enact laws that may restrict the GSY of the Eritrean SEAMS to the above two, thus making speculation in the stock market illegal.

Figure 2

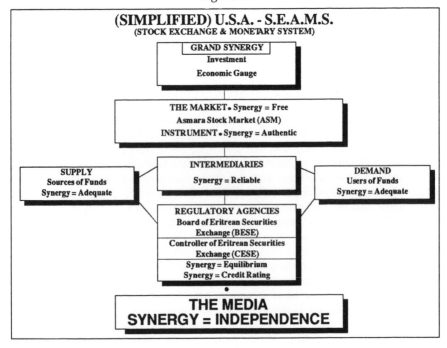

The two markets that should exist in the first ten years are the primary market and the secondary markets. The secondary market should be allowed to grow only if the primary market is directly benefiting from such growth. However, care should be taken not to interfere with the basic goal of the markets, which is to remain free and competitive. It is probably wise to have only one central market such as the Asmara Stock Market (ASM).

The instruments should be common stocks, bonds and foreign currencies. Stocks such as preferred stocks, unrated stocks should not be traded. In fact, it might even be wiser to allow only publicly traded certified stocks to be traded in public until the public trust and confidence in the market is well established. Bonds should be either government bonds, such as municipal bonds, or corporate bonds. Corporate bonds should be restricted to those bonds secured by mortgage of real property, such as building or debentures secured by a company's earning power. Convertible bonds are to be considered only if the primary market has gained the trust of the public. Convertible bonds are bonds that can be exchanged for shares of the issuer's stocks.

Foreign currencies, which should be traded during the first ten years, should be the currencies that comprise the or special drawing right (SDR) of the International Monetary Fund (IMF). Currently the SDR is composed of 42 percent U.S. dollar, 19 percent West German mark, and 13 percent each of the British pound, French franc and Japanese yen. Thus, the foreign currencies that should be in the market are: the U.S. dollar, German mark, British pound, French franc, the Japanese yen, or any other currency that can be easily converted to one of them (Schwartz and Smith 1990).

The participants, as the sources of funds and users of funds, are the same. They are: individuals, corporations, communities, trade and professional associations, chartered agencies, and governmental units. Again, the freedom of everyone to join or get out of the market must be protected. Associated with participants are the agencies that rate the credit standing of the participants either when they issue stock and bonds or they buy them. In many western countries these agencies are private agencies. In the Eritrean case, appointed but independent credit rating members of a three-person commission might serve the purpose adequately for a limited period of time. This could work well in conjunction with a free and independent media. It is of paramount significance to ensure that all market activities, including the monthly activities of the commission of credit raters, are published regularly and widely circulated.

The intermediaries, such as individual brokers and brokerage houses or companies, should be licensed and supervised by the Board of Controllers of the Eritrean SEAMS. There should be a three-person board, appointed by but independent of the executive branch. The term of office should be limited to no less than four years. The board's primary function is to develop the appropriate regulations to maintain the desired equilibrium in the market. This has to be done in order to minimize the possibility of the traumatic experience of the U.S. stock market crash of 1929 ever occurring in Eritrea. This function may include the board's active participation in the market in buying and selling some of the instruments to affect the supply and demand. Even though the major abusers of the market are likely to be the intermediaries, as was the case in the United States, this board and the country's media should be vigilant and monitor their activities.

Enough cannot be said as to how critical the role of an independent media is to the assurance of freedom in general and freedom in the stock market in particular. It has to be recognized, however, that the media, if run by the private sector, will also have its stocks and bonds traded in the same Asmara Stock Market (ASM). Consequently, it is going to face the associated conflict of interest problems. For this reason, the ASM should have its own official publication.

The final question is: Who should *own* and *manage* the ASM? As a general rule, it should be the membership of the ASM, such as traders, brokers, representatives of brokerage houses, and some banking officials. In the case of Eritrea, it is recommended that ownership be 51 percent government and 49 percent the private sector for the first ten years. It is further recommended that ASM be a chartered agency with rights and responsibilities for Eritrea spelled out and legislated.

V. CONCLUSION

The above recommendations are to be used as the basis for future policy discussions. The future policymakers and policy implementors must have sound training in the mechanics of the SEAMS (Henderson 1988). Luckily, there are several institutions in the West and also in Japan that are willing to provide scholarships to train such people if asked through the governmental channel. It has to be noted that many of the western countries, specially the United States, both on private as well as on governmental levels, strongly feel that the establishment of a stock market and the commitment of a given country to the free enterprise system are highly correlated. The stock market is probably the only market where the "invisible hands" of supply and demand are regularly operating as the great accumulators and distributors of capital.

The stock market is the closest to the perfectly competitive market. It acts as the financial barometer signifying the health of the economies and the soundness of the spirit of the free market in the Western world, including the United States. Therefore, if any country wishes to demonstrate to the rest of the world its commitment to the free market system, the stock market and its successful operation are the proper route. Given the many failures of experimentations with Marxism-Leninism by developing countries, the West has had reasons to require proof that such practices are passe. The stock market provides an excellent opportunity for an emerging nation, such as Eritrea, to address this issue concretely. Such a concrete method of demonstration of commitment to the free market, even within the framework of a mixed economy, could result in the generous donation of financial and technical aid from the European Economic Community, North America, Japan, and the World Bank.

NOTES

1. Synergy is a mission or a goal which is achieved by systematically combining several variables whose individual impact even when added together have less impact than that which was systematically combined.
2. Laundering funds is the process of transferring funds through several financial institutions to conceal its illegal source.

REFERENCES

Cooner, J. J. 1987. *Investing in Municipal Bonds.* New York: John Wiley & Sons, pp. 29–43.

De Bedts, R. 1964. *The New Deal's SEC. The Formative Years.* New York: Columbia University Press.

Harvey, E. J. 1932. *The Victims of Fraud — A Plea for a New Law: Notes of the American Law.* Oxford University Press.

Henderson, J. W. 1988. *Obtaining Venture Financing: Principles and Practices.* Lexington, Mass.: Lexington Books, D. C. Heath and Co., pp. 233–313.

Pitts, M., and F. J. Fabozzi. 1990. *Interest Rate and Future and Option.* Chicago: Probus Publishing, pp. 3–45.

Schwartz, R. A. 1988. *Equity Markets: Structure, Trading and Performance.* New York: Harper & Row, pp. 3–15.

Schwartz, R. J., and C. W. Smith, Jr. (eds.). 1990. *The Hand Book of Currency and Interest Rate Risk Management.* New York: New York Institute of Finance, pp. 7.1–7.21.

Standard and Poor. 1983. *Credit Overview Industrial Ratings.* New York: Standard and Poor Corp., pp. 3–11.

Tesfay, B. 1970. "Ekub Today and Tomorrow, National Lottery Administration."

The Wall Street Journal. 1990/91. Educational Edition.

West, R. R., and M. T. Seha. 1971. *The Economics of the Stock Market.* New York: Praeger, pp. 1–4.

U.S. Government Printing Press. 1913. "House of Representatives — Report on the Committee Appointed Pursuant to House Resolution 429 and 504," pp. 44–45.

THE ROLE OF ACCOUNTING, AUDITING, AND REPORTING REQUIREMENTS IN PROMOTING AN ACTIVE AND EFFICIENT SECURITIES MARKET IN ERITREA

Araya Debessay

This paper briefly discusses (1) the role of securities markets in economic development, (2) the necessity to establish accounting and auditing standards and other reporting requirements, (3) accounting and auditing requirements in other countries, and (4) policy recommendations toward promoting an efficient securities market, and the establishment of uniform accounting and auditing standards in Eritrea.

I. THE ROLE OF SECURITIES MARKET IN ECONOMIC DEVELOPMENT

In the context of the current situation in Eritrea, a securities market can be viewed in its simplest form as the stock market, where securities (shares, stock and bonds) of varying types are traded openly and where one can purchase or sell any of such securities with relative ease.

Large corporations can play an important role in economic development and national reconstruction by providing much needed goods and services and employment opportunity to a large number of people, which in turn results in further economic stimulation and recovery. Because of the nature of the operations of large corporations, the amount of capital needed to finance their operations is very substantial and can only be met by pulling together the savings of a large number of individual investors. As is being demonstrated in the case of Nacfa Corporation in Eritrea, one can raise enormous capital by issuing shares to a large group of shareholders.

In the Eritrean context, publicly owned share companies can serve as effective vehicles for injecting much needed development and national reconstruction capital, particularly if appropriate measures are taken to encourage participation of Eritreans residing abroad.

Establishing a securities market that is perceived as being well-regulated, with all the necessary rules and regulations that govern both the primary and secondary markets, is absolutely essential for the smooth operation of the capital markets. To actively participate in the securities market, investors must feel safe and protected. Without confidence in the country's securities market, many potential investors would be reluctant to part with their hard-earned savings and participate in the economic development of their country. In this sense, a properly regulated securities market is a prerequisite for economic progress and development.

The opportunity that the stock market offers for the subsequent trading in newly issued securities is a major factor facilitating capital mobilization. The ready marketability feature that the stock exchange bestows upon listed securities minimizes any inhibitions a would-be investor may have in considering participation in the securities market. It is therefore equally important that the secondary market for the exchange of securities also be developed. Investors should feel that their share holdings can be converted into cash by selling their shares in the secondary market.

Investors need to have information that will enable them to assess the potential return and risk involved. This information is provided through properly audited financial statements and the disclosure of other pertinent information.

II. THE ROLE OF ACCOUNTING INFORMATION

Accounting is often called "the language of business." It is the process of recording, classifying, and summarizing the financial activities of businesses in a logical manner. A company's financial information is presented in a series of reports called financial statements, which include the balance sheet, income statement, cash flow statement, and other supporting statements and notes.

In the context of securities markets, the overall objective of accounting is to provide financial information that is useful to present shareholders, potential investors, creditors, and other users in making rational investment, credit and similar decisions.

Financial reporting is expected to provide information about an enterprise's financial performance during a period and about how management of an enterprise has discharged its stewardship responsibility to owners. In this way, accounting information assists in identifying those organizations that employ their resources efficiently and effectively, and thereby helps to ensure that resources are channeled to those organizations that are efficiently and effectively managed — consistent with the best interest of the society at large.

If limited societal resources are allocated to those organizations that employ these resources more efficiently producing goods and services, then society's standard of living will be raised, and society will in general be better off. The scarcer the resources are, the more important it is that these resources are not misdirected or misappropriated.

Thus, "though accounting itself, as a service activity, cannot feed the hungry or cure the sick or bring enlightenment to the illiterate, yet, it can serve society an important role by contributing to the proper utilization of societal resources" (AAA 1978:viii).

III. THE NEED TO ESTABLISH ACCOUNTING AND REPORTING STANDARDS

For accounting information to be useful to economic and investment decision making, it must have two main qualities: comparability and relevancy. For comparability to exist, the principles used by firms in the same industry should be similar, thus facilitating comparison between two or more economic entities. Without comparable accounting information, it is difficult to distinguish those firms that are successful from those which may not be effectively using their resources. Because of this, it is important that the financial statements be prepared adhering to some generally accepted uniform accounting standards and procedures.

Thus, one of the important steps that a country interested in developing its capital markets needs to do is to establish accounting, auditing, and reporting standards, and to take measures to ensure that the rules are enforced.

IV. THE AUDIT FUNCTION IN SOCIETY

The primary purpose of *auditing* is to ensure that the financial statements issued by a given company are prepared in accordance with generally accepted accounting principles and procedures; that the financial statements are not misleading, and that they reflect fairly the economic events that occurred during the accounting period, and that they properly show the financial position of the company and the results of its operation.

In effect, the auditor enhances the credibility of the financial statements by independently verifying the fairness with which the financial statements are prepared so that users may comfortably rely on the financial statements. In this sense, the audit function is important in establishing the users' confidence in the financial statements.

For users of financial statements to rely on the auditor's report, however, it is necessary that there is a widely known, well-defined set of auditing standards that auditors are required to adhere to in the performance of the audit function. In the absence of such clearly stated auditing standards, it is not clear how much credibility can be attached to the report. The audit standards should spell out educational qualifications and training requirements for auditors, and should provide general guidelines that should be followed in the conduct of the audit.

A well-defined set of generally accepted auditing standards will go a long way toward allying the user's apprehension about the quality of the audit work being done. It is believed that with such credible, properly audited financial reporting, there will be a more positive attitude toward securities market activities.

V. LESSONS TO LEARN FROM OTHER COUNTRIES

A. The United States

In the United States the operation of the securities markets is controlled by the Securities and Exchange Commission (SEC), which is an independent agency of the U.S. government. The SEC was established in 1934 to help regulate the U.S. securities market. Its establishment was primarily in response to the public outcry arising from the great decline in stock prices between 1929 and 1933 (Skousen 1987:5). The overall purpose of the SEC is to assist in providing investors with reliable information upon which to make investment decisions.

Prior to the stock market crash of 1929, the stock market in the United States was characterized by rampant abuses and fraudulent and deceptive practices by greedy corporate officers who took advantage of lax conditions that existed at that time. Many innocent investors lost a great deal of their hard-earned savings because of price manipulations and fake trade activities that allowed those involved to reap huge profits at their expense. There were also cases of outright deceit, where false and misleading statements were issued to defraud unsuspecting investors. Moreover, there were reported cases of misuse of corporate information by corporate officials and other "insiders" that led to instability in the securities market. All these manipulative practices had as their objective the making of unfair profits at the expense of unwary investors. These conditions were factors that lead to the 1929 stock market crash in the United States and the serious financial crisis that ensued (Skousen 1987:4). Thus, with the view of restoring investors' confidence in the securities market and with the intent of protecting investors, the U.S. Congress passed the 1933 Securities Act.

The SEC was given the duty to ensure "full and fair" disclosure of all material facts concerning securities offered for public investment. The Commission's intent was not necessarily to prevent speculative securities from entering the market, but to insist that investors be provided with adequate information. The SEC disclosure regulations are intended to give investors the confidence that they are getting the whole story and thereby contributing to a more efficient securities market.

The SEC has considerable influence in setting generally accepted accounting principles and disclosure requirements as a result of its authority for specifying reporting requirements considered necessary for fair disclosure to investors. In addition, the SEC has power to establish rules for auditors who audit statements of publicly owned corporation. In practice, however, the Financial Accounting Standards Board (FASB), a private independent body, sets accounting standards, and the American Institute of Certified Public Accountants (AICPA) sets auditing standards in the United States.

B. Accounting in Developing Countries

The status of accounting practice in developing countries varies widely. India and Pakistan, for example, are considered developing countries by most standards based on economic statistics. Yet both countries have highly regarded accountancy professions and well-developed systems of accounting (AAA 1978:13). In most third world countries, however, we find that an underdeveloped economy goes hand in hand with an underdeveloped accounting establishment (AAA 1978:5–11).

The condition of the accounting establishment in a particular country will depend on many environmental factors. One of the most important is the influence of accounting exercised by former colonial powers. Thus, we find that most countries that were formerly British colonies have been greatly influenced by British models of accountancy education and financial reporting systems. A similar influence can be found in countries that were formerly part of the French colonial empire.

Another factor is the level of the accounting education in most developing countries, which has yet to develop sufficiently to influence the degree of sophistication of financial reporting present in most of these countries. This is directly related to the critical shortage of trained manpower in the accounting field — bookkeepers, accountants, internal and external auditors.

Another serious problem area for most of the indigenous enterprises in developing countries is the poorly designed accounting systems and the lack of uniformly accepted accounting procedures. Consequently, most financial statements are seriously deficient. Many annual statements are often late by one to three years, and in some of cases may not even be produced at all. The information needs of shareholders, creditors, and the government are therefore seldom satisfied.

Although the above is general to most developing countries, the financial reporting environment differs from one country to another. The following is a discussion of some of the developing countries that have taken measures to improve their financial reporting practices.

1. Nigeria. Every company incorporated under Nigeria's Companies Act of 1968 is required to keep proper books of account to show a "true and fair" view of the company's affairs and to explain its transactions.

The Companies Act of 1968 requires that the following documents be presented to the annual shareholders at least once every year: income statement, balance sheet, audit report to the shareholders, and a director's report. Financial statements must be approved by the board of directors, give a true and fair view of the company's affairs, and comply with the minimum requirements of Schedule 8 of the 1968 Companies Act.

Under the Companies Act, all limited liability companies must be audited by a duly recognized auditor. To be appointed as an auditor it is necessary to be a member of the Institute of Chartered Accountants of Nigeria and to be in public practice. In order to be admitted to public practice, an auditor must obtain the necessary professional experience and be granted a practicing certificate from the Nigerian Institute.

The Nigerian Institute of Chartered Accountants controls entry into the profession through its examinations. Anyone who has passed the institute's examinations may apply for membership in the institute. The institute has not issued any auditing standards and in practice follows those adopted by the United Kingdom.

The Nigerian Institute is a member of the International Accounting Standards Committee (IASC) and from time to time adopts IASC standards. These standards are then mandatory for members of the Nigerian Institute, and any significant departure from them must be disclosed in the financial statements.

2. Egypt. In the early 1970s, the Egyptian government adopted an economic policy towards a more market oriented approach, including easing restrictions and encouraging the participation of the private sector in the economy.

The Egyptian government adopted an open door policy or "*infitah,*" hoping that it would bring technological development and rapid industrialization, promote exports, and elevate the living standard. But to accomplish this, the government had to change its philosophy so as to attract private capital.

The government's desire to increase the rate of national economic growth required a major change in the political and economic structure.

These changes were also accompanied by majors changes in the Egyptian accounting and reporting system.

Consequently, the government decided to set accounting standards and the financial reporting requirements. In 1964, Egypt established the Central Accounting Agency (CAA) as an independent institution reporting directly to the president. In 1966, through the efforts of the Central Accounting Agency, laws for uniform accounting were introduced in Egypt.

The Central Accounting Agency establishes and periodically studies and evaluates Egypt's accounting standards. To do this, the CAA must present a draft of the proposed new standard (in the form of a draft of a new law) to the People's Assembly, which sends it to an appropriate committee for comprehensive analysis and appraisal. The draft law is sent to the Egyptian Council of State for legal advice. After this, the draft law is sent back to the People's Assembly for final approval. Once approved, it becomes effective as law from the date of its publication in the official government journal.

VI. HARMONIZATION OF INTERNATIONAL ACCOUNTING STANDARDS

There is diversity of accounting principles from one nation to another. International diversity in national accounting principles has the potential to diminish the international flow of investment capital that might be essential in accelerating economic development. Given the need for international investment, comparability of accounting principles in a global sense should be given a high priority.

Recognizing the need to harmonize international accounting standards, there is an organization called the International Accounting Standards Committee (IASC) that has actively taken steps to achieve this objective. The objective of the IASC is to issue international accounting standards to be followed in the presentation of audited financial statements. Each member country has pledged to use its "best endeavors" to see to it that IASC standards are adopted and followed in its accounting practices. Basically, the IASC has two objectives: (1) to formulate and publish international financial accounting standards, and (2) to promote their worldwide acceptance and observation (Choi and Mueller 1984:180).

In countries whose accounting standards have not yet been set, the IASC's standards may be adopted as the country's own standards. The following developing countries have adopted the IASC's standards: Bahamas, Fiji, Malaysia, Nigeria, Pakistan, Singapore, Trinidad, and Zimbabwe. These countries do not have the financial or technical resources required for formulating their own accounting standards and thus may have derived the most benefit from IASC activities.

Similarly, the need to harmonize auditing standards at international level has led to the formation of the International Federation of Accountants (IFAC). This organization was set up in 1977 to develop uniform auditing standards worldwide. Many countries that do not have the resources and expertise to develop their own auditing standards have adopted the standards issues through this body.

VII. POLICY RECOMMENDATIONS

To accelerate the national reconstruction and economic development in Eritrea, the formation of publicly owned corporations should be encouraged. As is already evidenced by the formation of publicly owned corporations, such as the Nacfa Corporation and others that are in the process of being formed, the Eritrean policy makers are fully aware of the need for the development of the securities market. Such corporations can play a vital role in funneling individual savings from Eritreans residing abroad. Thus, in order to encourage Eritreans living abroad to actively participate in the securities market in Eritrea, the Eritrean government should take steps to create confidence in the securities market and ensure that the securities market is orderly and efficient. To this end, the following suggestions are offered.

1. Establish an Eritrean Stock Exchange Commission (ESEC). The Commission will have broad and direct authority over the accounting principles used by publicly owned corporations, and that will have significant authority over the auditing standards that should be followed in the audit of the financial statements of such publicly owned share companies.

All publicly owned corporations should be registered by the ESEC before their shares are sold to the public. The law should be designed in such a way that the prospective investor is provided with adequate information for making investment decisions. The ESEC should issue regulations regarding disclosure requirements that will ensure that investors have "full and fair" disclosure of pertinent information in connection with security offerings. The disclosure requirements should be designed in such a way to be able to prevent misrepresentation or fraud in the sale of securities. These objectives are generally accomplished by requiring disclosure of specified financial and other information regarding the issuer of securities. The Commission should prescribe the detail and form of the financial statements included in registration statements, as well as the method of accounting to be used in preparing the statements.

In addition to laws regulating the primary issuance of securities, there should also be laws that regulate the secondary markets — the trading of securities that have been previously distributed. Such laws should cover the continuing reporting requirements, such as the annual reports, quarterly reports and certain other reports relating to the occurrence of specified events.

It is important to note that investment decisions involve risk and, as such, the ESEC should not be expected to pass judgment on the merits of securities offered for sale. That investment decision remains with the investor. The role of the ESEC should be to determine if there is satisfactory compliance with the applicable statutes and regulations and should be empowered to enforce penalties against those who present false or misleading information or those who commit other fraudulent acts. As previously described, this is how the U.S. Securities and Exchange operates, and much can be gained by learning from its experience.

2. Require Publicly Owned Companies to Disclose Financial and Other Information Through Initial Registration Statements and Annual Reports. Publicly owned companies should be required to provide a registration statement at initial offering of their shares to the public and should provide continuous disclosure of their activities through annual, quarterly, and special reports.

The principal objective of preparing a registration statement for a public offering should be to present all pertinent facts and figures that are needed by a prospective investor to make a judgement about a company's securities. Likewise, the continuous disclosures of financial and nonfinancial operating information is meant to provide shareholders, prospective investors, and government regulatory agencies with information they need to monitor the performance of these companies.

In the United States, a company that seeks to raise capital through an initial public offering of securities must file a registration statement. The registration statement should provide information about the nature of the business, capital structure, description of securities being registered; salaries and security holdings of key officers and directors; estimates of net proceeds and expected uses of the funds; detailed financial information on a proforma basis; and names of the directors and executive officers, their backgrounds, and principle responsibilities (Skousen 1987: Ch. 3).

3. Establish Accounting Standards by Adopting Existing International Accounting Standards. Although every sovereign country has the right to establish its own accounting and auditing standards consistent with its own legal, educational, social, economic, and commercial environment, it will be unwise to expend any effort and resource in trying to come up with a uniquely Eritrean approach to accounting and auditing standards. It does not make much sense to "reinvent the wheel" when those resources can best be used in other more pressing societal needs. The most logical thing to do is, therefore, to capitalize on the experience of other countries and adopt those standards that are relevant for Eritrea's needs. There is also a compelling reason to harmonize the accounting and auditing standards with the rest of the world. A country that is interested in international trade and investment should stand to gain by harmonizing the development of its financial reporting and auditing standards with the rest of the world. The principal advantage of harmonizing accounting and auditing standards is the increased comparability of Eritrean financial statements with those of other countries. Following an internationally practiced financial reporting approach would eliminate any suspicion as to the reliability of financial statements of Eritrean companies and would remove one of the most important impediments to the flow of international investment.

4. Establish Auditing Standards and Auditor Qualifications. The Eritrean Securities and Exchange Commission (ESEC) should be empowered to regulate the way auditors practice their profession and should set the qualifications for auditors. The Commission should also be responsible for establishing generally accepted auditing standards, covering all aspects of conducting an audit and how the auditor's report should be prepared. To ensure that audits are done properly, the Commission should set the framework for the auditors' legal liability.

VIII. CONCLUSION

The need for national reconstruction and accelerated economic development in Eritrea is obvious. This process can be facilitated through an introduction of an active and efficient securities market. To encourage the participation of Eritrean citizens residing within and abroad, in investment activities, it is important for the government to take the necessary steps in establishing an appropriate government agency that will regulate the stock market activities. It is also equally important that this agency moves fast to develop accounting and auditing standards that are compatible with the rest of the world. Eritrea does not have to reinvent the wheel when it comes to establishing accounting and auditing standards. The most cost-effective approach, for Eritrea at this point in time, is to adopt the existing International Accounting and Auditing Standards. These standards can be modified at a later stage to accommodate and to reflect any unique situations that might arise.

REFERENCES

Amer, Metwalli B. 1969. "Impact of Public Ownership on the U.A.R. Accounting Profession," *International Journal of Accounting Education and Research,* 4 (Spring):49–61.

American Accounting Association (AAA). 1978. *Accounting Education and the Third World.*

American Institute of Certified Public Accountants (AICPA). 1975. *Professional Accounting in 30 Countries.* AICPA.

Bait-El-Mal, Mohamed M., Charles H. Smith, and Martin E. Taylor. 1973. "The Development of Accounting in Libya." *International Journal of Accounting Education and Research* 8 (Spring):83–101.

Briston, Richard J. 1974. "The Accountancy Profession in a Developing Country: An Indonesian Case Study." *The Accountant's Magazine* 78 (August):314–15.

_____. 1978. "The Evolution of Accounting in Developing Countries." *International Journal of Accounting Education and Research* 14 (Fall):105–20.

Brombert, Alan R. 1973. *Securities Law: Fraud.* New York: McGraw-Hill.

Burton, John C. 1981. *The International World of Accounting.* Arthur Young Professors' Round Table, Council of Arthur Young Professors.

Carty, James. 1982. "Accounting Standards and the United Nations," World Accounting Report (September):9–15.

Central Auditing Agency. 1967. "The Uniform Accounting System." Cairo, Egypt: Central Auditing Agency. (In Arabic)

Choi, Frederick, and Gerhard Mueller. 1984. *International Accounting.* Englewood Cliffs, N.J.: Prentice-Hall.

Elliott, Edward L. 1972. "Accounting and Economic Development in Latin America." *International Journal of Accounting Education and Research* 8 (Fall):89–97.

Enthoven, Adolf J. H. 1975. *An Evaluation of Accountancy Systems, Developments and Requirements in Asia.* Ford Foundation.

_____. 1976. "Standardized Accountancy and Economic Development."
   Management Accounting 57 (February):19–23.
_____. 1980. "The Accountant in the Third World." *Journal of Accountancy*
   149 (March):76–78.
Holzer, H. Peter, and Doria Tremblay. 1973. "Accounting and Economic
   Development: The Cases of Thailand and Tunisia." *International Journal
   of Accounting Education and Research* 9 (Fall):67–80.
Jaggi, B. L. 1973. "Accounting Studies of Developing Countries." *International
   Journal of Accounting Education and Research* 9 (Fall):159–70.
Jennings, Richard W., and Harold Marsh, Jr. 1982. *Securities Regulations:
   Cases and Material,* 5th ed. Mineola: Foundation Press.
Lelievre, Thomas W., and Clara C. Lelievre. 1978. "Accounting in the Third
   World." *Journal of Accountancy*ᵢ 145 (January):72–75.
Mitchell, C. L. 1974. *Corporate Financial Reporting in Malaysia.* Kuala
   Lumpur Stock Exchange, Berhad.
Nobes, C. W., and R. H. Parker. 1981. *Comparative International Accounting.*
   Homewood, Ill.: Richard D. Irwin.
Qureshi, Mahmood A. 1974. "Private Enterprise Accounting and Economic
   Development in Pakistan." *International Journal of Accounting
   Education and Research* 9 (Spring):125–42.
Rueschhoff, Norlin. 1976. *International Accounting and Financial Reporting.*
   New York: Praeger.
Shuaib, Shuaib A. 1980. "Some Aspects of Accounting Regulations in Kuwait."
   Journal of Contemporary Business 9 (Third Quarter):85–99.
Skousen, K. Fred. 1987. *An Introduction to the SEC.* Cincinnati: South-
   Western Publishing.
United Nations Center on Transnational Corporations. 1982. *Towards
   International Standardization of Corporate Accounting and Reporting.*
   New York: United Nations.

CHAPTER 5

TRADE
AND INDUSTRY

TRADE POLICY PROPOSALS FOR THE TRANSITIONAL PERIOD

Prepared by
The Commerce Commission, EPLF[1]

I. INTRODUCTION

The importance of trade in developing countries in general, and the war- and drought-ravaged economy of Eritrea in particular, cannot be overemphasized. It plays a major role in the stimulation of industrial activity, the development of agricultural production and the provision of services. Taking into consideration the dilapidated condition of Eritrea's economy, we believe that the attention of the trade sector in the Provisional Government of Eritrea focus on the fulfillment of the following objectives:

1. Ensure fair distribution of domestically produced and imported commodities;
2. Increase foreign exchange earnings by improving the quantity and quality of exports; and
3. Ensure that imported goods do assist the processes of economic and social development of Eritrea.

To fulfill these objectives, one must become aware of the importance of intensive involvement of foreign and domestic private capital. This will definitely require an organizational structure that encourages such an involvement. This paper will thus mainly focus on the implementation of these objectives.

II. POLICY AND ADMINISTRATION OF TRADE UNDER ETHIOPIAN RULE

The advent of Ethiopian colonial administration frustrated the then thriving private sector of Eritrea's economy by dismantling communication facilities, forcing private investors to shift their attention toward Ethiopia and weaken the motivation of industry and trade, thus making the Eritrean economy a subsidiary. However, since private enterprises were given a relatively better scope of activity than what followed later, basic commodity and services were being rendered to the public.

When the Derg's regime took power in 1974, it nationalized almost all industries, commercial farms and trading activities under the guise of "socialization." Under this policy of socialization, the Derg established institutions like the Agricultural Marketing Corporation (AMC), the Ethiopian Domestic Distribution Corporation (EDDC), the Ethiopian Retail Trade Corporation

---

1. Presented by Tadesse Woldehannes

(ERTC), and the Ethiopian Household and Office Furniture (EHOF). A distribution network was also established where *Kebele* and Farmers Cooperatives' shops served as outlets. This method of distribution of basic commodities, through rural and urban cooperatives, made the trade sector open to corruption, and added to further deterioration of commercial activity, especially foreign trade.

III. ADMINISTRATION OF TRADE IN LIBERATED AREAS

In 1975, a separate section within the Economy Department of EPLF was set up mainly to issue trade licenses to traders, establish rural markets and community shops. However, the activities of that section ceased to operate during the strategic withdrawal in 1978–79. In 1984, the administration of trade was reorganized with the formation of the Trade Commission. The main aims of the administration of trade, as experienced up to now, could be summed up as follows: (1) encourage traders to satisfy market demand; (2) ensure fair distribution of basic commodities; (3) facilitate exchange by establishing new markets; and (4) gather information on prices and market trends.

To meet these aims, import, export and domestic trade licenses were issued. Because no price-control measures were exercised, the supply of goods to the market improved. In February 1990, a further improvement in the supply of basic commodities resulted after the announcement of a free trade policy.

However, the problems of now independent Eritrea are enormous and call for the adoption of appropriate trade policies and plans of action. The main problems currently facing the trade sector are:
1. The dominance of government ownership in trade, which has result ed in minimal private initiative;
2. Very low industrial output and near absence of agricultural produc tion to set trade in motion;
3. Lack of exportable commodities as earners of foreign exchange; and
4. Inadequate supply of basic consumer goods.

IV. TRADE POLICY SUGGESTIONS FOR THE TRANSITIONAL PERIOD

The solution for the above problems calls for an immediate and decisive action toward overhauling the administrative and operational sides of trade. However, since the Provisional Government is inheriting an economy with inappropriate organizational setup and an underemployed manpower, the course of action to be taken should be carefully chosen.

In accordance with the spirit of EPLF's National Democratic Program and the experiences of some third world economies, it is advisable to limit government participation to major economic activities such as banking, insurance, mining, energy and transportation and communication. Therefore, the following plans of action in the areas of domestic trade and foreign trade are suggested.

A. Domestic Trade

1. Distribution. (a) Immediately move toward privatizing the distribution of industrial products so that the whole function is taken over by the private sector at the end of the transitional period. (b) Introduce a marketing system whereby agricultural products are sold directly to private wholesalers and retailers and gradually transfer the function to the private sector. (c) Reorganize the Grain Marketing Corporation and limit its activities to purchasing grain for seeds and exports.

2. Price Control. Because of the drought and its after-effects, it is assumed that food and other basic commodities will remain in short supply. Thus, until the supply problem is solved, it is recommended that a separate unit be formed within the Domestic Trade Department with powers to set up price ceilings of basic consumer items.

3. Trade Licensing. To avoid the adverse effects of government monopoly in trade and to encourage the participation of private domestic and foreign capital in trade and commerce, it is recommended that the licensing unit formulate policies whereby Eritrean nationals are allowed to invest in the trade categories of their choice, and that foreign investors are allowed to participate in fields of trade that require special technical skills, managerial experience, market knowledge and acquaintance with foreign firms.

The licensing unit should also classify commodities into trade categories in order to carry out the licensing process in a systematic manner.

4. The National Commercial Register. Taking into account that all activities in manufacturing and service industry are of commercial nature and hence require proper registration in accordance with prescriptions of the commercial code, it is recommended that: (a) a national commercial register be set-up in the central premises of the Commerce Commission; (b) subsidiary registers be set up in the regional offices of the Commerce Commission with a requirement that a copy of the registration form be sent to the central registration office; and (c) the trade register contain all relevant information concerning names, addresses, trade names, trade marks and patent rights.

5. Trade Control. To ensure that traders abide by the law and refrain from unlawful and unfair trade practices, the following preliminary actions are recommended: (a) issue rules and regulations pertaining to trade control; and (b) set up a trade control unit to monitor traders for violation of trade regulations.

6. National Standards Unit. The production of goods for domestic consumption and export, and the importation of commodities for domestic use, require that they conform to certain standards in terms of quality, quantity and dimensions. Because the absence of such standards results in adverse effects on the national economy, it is proposed that the following measures be taken: (a) strengthen the present Standards Unit in staff and equipment; (b) introduce the metric system and ensure its applicability throughout Eritrea; (c) set up national standards of domestic products in collaboration with other government units; and (d) ensure that export commodities satisfy international standards of quality and are properly landed in ports.

B. Foreign Trade

The reconstruction and training of industry and the rehabilitation of commercial agriculture will be restrained by the existing acute shortages of foreign exchange and the present vacuum in the export of commodities. To ameliorate this condition we believe that our foreign trade policy must consider the following suggestions.

1. Import Trade. (a) ensure that priority is given to the importation of raw materials and machinery for industry and agriculture, that goods for general consumption do satisfy the immediate needs of the public; (b) encourage the process of import substitution in order to save our foreign exchange; and (c) control the import demand of traders through a system of import permit authorization.

2. Export Trade. Until recently, Eritrea exported T-shirts, raw hides and tanned leather, bone and animal remains, foul madames, salt oil cake, gum-arabic and other products in a very limited quantity. In order to strengthen the already established market of these products, it is desirable to ensure that their production meet market standards of quality and quantity.

A continuous effort is required to replace the export of raw materials with finished and semi-finished products and improve our export orientation through the dissemination of information and assisting traders to make the right choice.

3. Barter Trade. Traditionally, Eritrea has had a strong trade linkages with its neighboring countries, and barter trade has been the main feature of this relationship. At this stage of economy, we believe that encouraging this aspect of trade could be beneficial given the limited productive capacity of Eritrean industries and the general lack of foreign exchange earnings.

C. The Role of the Chamber of Commerce

Under the Derg's administration, the present Chamber of Commerce, although it had an independent status, did not play its assumed role of serving the trading community. It should, therefore, be encouraged to resume its proper functions and concentrate primarily on: (1) providing information and assistance to local traders and foreign investors through seminars and publications, and (2) cooperate with the commerce department in organizing local trade expositions, and encourage local producers to participate in international trade fairs.

APPENDIX

It is evident that the task of constructing the drought and war-torn economy cannot be accomplished by Eritrean nationals alone. Our trade policy should thus encourage the participation of foreign capital in certain areas of wholesale, retail, import and export trade. The following criteria may be considered in specifying trading activities open to foreigners: (1) the amount of capital required; (2) the professional qualification required and the special services involved in the trade; (3) the transfer of technology and know-how resulting from the trade activity; and (4) the market knowledge and the research activities required by the trade.

Based on these criteria, areas of trade reserved for Eritreans and those open to foreign nationals are proposed as follows (those that should be open to foreigners are indicated with an asterisk mark [*]):

A. Wholesale and Retail Trade — Domestic Distribution

1. Food, foodstuffs, washing active agents and other nondurable goods
2. Manufactures beverages — alcoholic and non-alcoholic
3. Butchery
4. Production and buying and selling of bread and pastry
5. Buying and selling of fish
6. Vegetables and fruit marketing
7. Honey and butter marketing
8. Red pepper, shiro and spices trade
9. Clothing, cloths, ready made or not, threads and bags
10. Footwear made of leather and other leather products
11. Kitchen utensils
12. Durable consumer goods
13. Office furniture and equipment
14. Drugs and pharmaceutical
15. Stationery and printed materials
16. Fuel and lubricants
17. Medical instruments
18. Sports appliances and apparatus
19. Gift articles and handicrafts
20. Cosmetics, adornments and apparels
21. Animal and livestock
22. Raw hides and skins
23. Animal feed
24. Wood and charcoal
25. Electric stove
26. Grain
27. Metal scraps
28. Milk and milk products
29. Electrical and electro-technical equipments and spare parts*
30. Musical instruments, sound recorders and reproducing equipment*
31. Photographic and cinematographic equipments and spare parts*
32. Clocks, watches and optical equipments and spare parts*
33. Heavy duty agricultural and construction equipments*

34.   Others*

B. Import Trade
1.   Food, foodstuffs, washing active agents and other nondurable domestic goods
2.   Domestic and household appliances
3.   Clothing, clothes, garments, threads and bags
4.   Footwear, leather and plastic shoes and other products
5.   Kitchen utensils
6.   Alcoholic beverages
7.   Fruits
8.   Spices
9.   Stationery and printed matters
10.   Sport appliances and apparatus
11.   Cosmetics, ornaments, jewelry and adornments
12.   Lubricants and lubricating oil, grease and grease paints
13.   Shoe industry materials
14.   Animal feeding stuff and fodder
15.   Office equipment*
16.   Medical goods and medicaments*
17.   Electrical equipments and appliances*
18.   Musical instruments, sound recorders and reproducers*
19.   Photographic, cinematographic and optical instruments*
20.   Clocks, watches and spectacles*
21.   Agricultural and construction heavy duty equipments*
22.   Vehicles and spare parts*
23.   Butane gas, fuels and petroleum*
24.   Others*

C. Export Trade
1.   Food, foodstuffs, washing active agents, and other nondurable domestic goods
2.   Beverages alcoholic and soft drinks
3.   Clothing, clothes, garments and undergarments, bags and threads
4.   Footwear and other leather or plastic goods
5.   Live animals
6.   Raw hides and skins
7.   Manufactures items
8.   Paper, plastic and textile sacks
9.   Salts
10.   Cereals, oilseeds and pulses
11.   Meat and fish
12.   Fruits and vegetables
13.   Others

D. Service Trades
1.   Restaurants, canteens, etc.
2.   Hotel
3.   Pension
4.   Bars, snacks, etc.
5.   Barber and hair dressing
6.   Laundry

7. Tailoring
8. Tailoring and sewing training
9. Typing school
10. Grain milling
11. Photography and photocopying
12. Car rental
13. Driving school
14. Tire repair and retreading
15. Garage servicing and car repair
16. Road transport
17. Carpentry
18. Fuel and petrol distribution
19. Tapestry for car seats, etc.
20. Motorcycle and bicycle repair
21. Soldering
22. Electro-technical repair*
23. Construction contracting and building*
24. Architectural works*
25. Clinical and medical services*
26. Others*

IMPORTANCE OF TRADE AND INDUSTRIAL POLICY FOR SOCIOECONOMIC DEVELOPMENT: REFLECTIONS ON THE ERITREAN ECONOMY

Woldai Futur

I. INTRODUCTION

This paper highlights the importance of efficient trade and industry for Eritrea's economic development. It attempts to identify the type of policies required to promote efficient expansion of these sectors in the context of the Eritrean economy's overall long-term potential. Based on lessons from the experiences of other countries, it draws broad conclusions and makes tentative recommendations for the Eritrean economy. The main objective is to identify issues and constraints to provoke discussion in favor of economic efficiency in policy-making in Eritrea. The paper's conclusions and recommendations are predicated on the notion that having a correct industrial and trade policy framework in place would ensure that the right industries are established in the right sequence, reflecting Eritrea's comparative advantage, its mastery of industrial technologies and the ability to penetrate foreign markets — both regional and global.

II. IMPORTANCE OF TRADE AND INDUSTRIAL EXPANSION

Given its limited potential, the agricultural sector of Eritrea is unlikely to become a significant source of economic growth. Continued soil degradation and unfavorable and uncertain climatic conditions have substantially reduced Eritrea's agricultural potential. The need for a rapid shift in Eritrea's economic base towards other sectors (industry, trade, finance, tourism and transport, etc.) is thus becoming increasingly apparent. Given its strategic location for accessing markets in Africa, Western Asia and Western Europe, as well as its dedicated and hardworking people, Eritrea probably has a better comparative advantage in industry and trade than in agriculture.

Hence, rapid expansion of industrial output and trade is going to be fundamental to Eritrea's economic growth and the structural changes of its society. An efficient expansion of these sectors is also a critical determinant of the acquisition and diffusion of advanced technologies required for its economic development. Rapid assimilation of advances in technological capability in the Eritrean society, to a large extent, would depend on the success in expanding industrial output and trade — enhancing the creation of entrepreneurs, managers, technicians and skilled labor required for sustained economic growth. Further, an efficient growth of these sectors would lead to the integration of Eritrean markets (factor, product and capital), encouraging specialization consistent with Eritrea's comparative advantage. It would also be important for attracting foreign collaborations (involving financial, technical and management contracts) that are needed to complement local development efforts.

If a sound economic policy approach is adopted from the outset, an efficient expansion of industrial output and trade of manufactured goods and services is feasible. Eritrea could be transformed from the present low-income agrarian to a middle-income industrializing society within the next twenty to thirty years. How quickly resources are shifted to industry and trade and the efficiency with which they are used will determine the rate of growth and structural changes of the Eritrean economy and the society. Thus, the Eritrean government's economic development strategy needs to give priority to accelerated industrialization and trade expansion commensurate with Eritrea's potential.

III. APPROPRIATE POLICY APPROACH

Economic policy measures are often closely interrelated, making the impact of a specific policy instrument on the economy difficult to isolate. If the formulation and execution of policy instruments are not carefully coordinated, unintended distortions in the incentive structure could adversely affect economic growth. In order to avoid undesired policy-induced results, the overall policy approach and the major policy instruments used would need to be coordinated and regularly evaluated against the national development objectives and the specific goals to be achieved.

A. The Need for Policy Intervention

No universal consensus exists on the type of trade and industrial policy framework a country should follow to achieve its economic growth and development objectives. Generally, most economists do not approve promotion of expansion of trade and industrial output based on high protective barriers, subsidies or restrictive regulatory measures. This reflects the weight that economists accord to allocative and operational efficiency considerations in the process of economic growth. Further, notwithstanding the lack of consensus on the nature of trade and industrial policy framework that nations should pursue, economists are keenly aware of the need for an efficiency-oriented policy framework with a closer coordination between its formulation and execution.

It should be recognized that the policy framework is important both when right and wrong. If applied correctly, it is a powerful means of efficiently allocating scarce resources to achieve economic objectives in accordance with society's potential and it could over time transform a backward economy to a modern and efficient one. Conversely, if applied wrongly, it causes major protracted economic stagnation and balance of payment crisis that require periodic costly adjustments. These have been the unfortunate features of many developing nations in sub-Saharan Africa, South Asia, Latin America and Eastern Europe. To appreciate the need for, and efficacy of, policy intervention — and to determine the optimal course of actions to be taken — the following two related questions should be answered prior to the execution of policy measures.

First, does the social benefit-cost calculation associated with economic activities to be regulated differ from the private benefit calculation of participants in the market place? If the private sector captures the full benefit and bears the full cost, then private profitability calculations will also work out just right from society's point of view. Under such a situation, the need for public policy to change the incentive structure cannot be economically justified. However, where market prices do not correspond to social values, private benefit-cost calculations are inadequate for generating economic activities in line with society's objectives. Under such circumstances, where market failure is obvious, government policy intervention to maintain the structural integrity of the different sectors of the economy and to promote rapid socioeconomic progress and well-being of society is justified. If governments could measure the discrepancies between the social and private costs and benefits of economic activities, they could then impose taxes, or provide subsidies, to close the gap — restoring parity between those of the private and the society as a whole.

Second, once the need for policy intervention is established, a question should be asked related to the policy actions: What action would most efficiently achieve the desired objective? Is the proposed policy the best way to solve the problem at hand? Are there other alternative measures that can address the problem more cost effectively? Policymakers would need to appreciate that establishing the need for policy intervention does not justify adopting any policy action. The proposed policy measures should be reviewed and evaluated in comparison with the prevailing situation and other options that could achieve similar objectives, to ascertain that both efficiency and consistency norms are satisfied.

B. The Levels of Policy Intervention

There is consensus among economists on the need to promote industrial production by: (1) providing general infrastructure, (2) improving efficiency of markets, (3) fostering overall macroeconomic stability, and (4) providing an efficient administrative and institutional framework. There is, however, controversy regarding the extent, mode and effectiveness of the policy interventions needed to promote trade and industrial output. The great differences in initial conditions between countries attempting to accelerate industrial output and trade, as well as the varying degrees of successes achieved by different nations pursuing different approaches starting from similar initial conditions, suggest that the trade and industrial policy framework need not be the same across countries. Furthermore, there are legitimate political and social considerations that should be taken into account in the formulation and execution of economic policy, suggesting that a country's policy need to reflect its specific situation, and to that extent could differ from what is usually available in a generic menu. The most common policy intervention levels often used to promote balanced economic growth, within which policy differences across countries could be appreciated, are outlined below.

1. Macroeconomic Framework. Actions and programs that affect economic activities throughout the economy are generally considered as part of the macroeconomic policy framework. Broadly, this includes policies which deal with the overall fiscal, monetary, financial and labor policy issues in the economy. Although affecting overall level of economic growth and efficiency, the macroeconomic policy framework is expected to remain neutral with respect to its effects on resources allocation between sectors. It is mainly concerned with general employment, price stabilization, income distribution and aggregate economic growth. At times, however, macroeconomic policy instruments (e.g., dual interest and exchange rates for different sectors) could be used to affect resource flows between sectors to address social and political issues, in which case there would be an overlap between macroeconomic and sectoral policy instruments.

2. **Infrastructure Policy.** Another type of macro policy is related to provision of basic infrastructure (physical and administrative). The importance of a strong infrastructural base to support efficient economic growth and social transformation is well-established. In recognition of its critical importance, public authorities consider provision of adequate support infrastructure as part of the overall macroeconomic and sectoral policy management framework. The state usually provides almost all general infrastructure and even some of the sector and firm-specific ones, depending on their importance. The general infrastructure that would need to be provided (or caused to be provided) by the state are usually related to the transport, power supply, communication, education and manpower training, and administrative/institutional support services. As these services are required in every region to allow smooth integration of national markets, they are usually part of the overall macroeconomic management strategy and usually fall in the domain of the public sector. However, varying degrees of private sector participation are also possible.

3. **Sectoral Policy.** In pursuing growth objectives in different sectors, governments use sector-specific policy measures. To promote expansion of industrial output, trade and industrial policy measures are usually combined. Generally, these are designed to protect local industrial output from import competition by creating barrier to imports (through tariffs and quotas) and from domestic competition by restricting capacity creation through licensing requirements. In addition, industrial output expansion is often promoted by directed, subsidized credit through commercial and development banks and direct public sector investments in industrial activities. These measures attract resources to industry beyond levels warranted by comparative advantage of the sector. Protection and subsidy artificially raise financial profitability of capital invested in the sector. Direct government participation in industry is usually based more on strategic considerations than economic and often tends to result in poor performance of the whole sector and limited private sector participation. In most instances, the justification for direct state participation is weak and usually not the best use of scarce national resources.

C. Trade and Industrial Policy

Within the overall national economic policy framework, trade policy refers to the direct and indirect government actions and programs that influence development and expansion of trade. Generally, it is comprised of exchange rate policy, commercial policy (tariffs, taxes, subsidies, etc.), and trade regulatory schemes (administrative restrictions, quotas and bans). As policy instruments, these are often designed to affect exports and imports of goods and services. In addition to trade policy, industrial policy includes regulatory measures that affect competition, ownership and the choices relating to technology, basic inputs and output-mix. The overall objective of the trade and industrial policy framework is to ensure the long-term integrity of the economy and to promote an efficient economic growth and structural change of the society. Toward this goal, the main thrust of the policy should be to engender an incentives structure that is neutral between exportables and importables. Further, to promote efficiency through competition, it should be neutral with respect to its effects on ownership (private versus public, or domestic versus foreign), size of operations (small, medium or large) and type of technologies used. To the extent that direct administrative controls are used, the system cannot be neutral and any expansion of trade and industry is unlikely to be as efficient as it could have been without such controls.

Considering its profound impact on economic growth and structural change in a society, the trade and industrial policy framework needs to be approached with the view of maximizing efficiency and sustainability of the benefits of rapid industrial and trade expansion. To minimize periodic economic disruptions, it should be designed to have built-in features that will engender flexibility in responding to changes in international market conditions. Thus, in formulating a trade and industrial policy framework, three points should be taken into account: (1) the policy measure in question is one of many affecting the long-term growth of industrial output and trade; (2) there is considerable uncertainty regarding future economic developments and that modifications would be needed to take into account actual and expected changes; and (3) future policy decisions are going to be constrained by the degree of flexibility afforded in past policy actions. Full appreciation of these points during policy formulation is critical so that the established policy framework is flexible and promotes efficient allocation of resources.

However, it is important to note that growth of industrial output is not simply the result of having a good trade and industrial policy. As mentioned earlier, there are many other factors that affect the rate and pattern of industrialization. These include the size of the host country's markets, its natural resource base, the level of its human capital, the stability and ability of its government to effect change, the nature and stability of its macroeconomic (fiscal, monetary and exchange rate) policy framework and the condition of its physical and administrative infrastructure. It is the net results of the interactions of all these factors combined that determine the pattern and rate of expansion of trade and industrial output in a given society. Hence, a good trade and industrial policy framework is one that is both flexible and efficient in coordinating these interactions throughout the economy to achieve the desired development objectives as rapidly as possible.

IV. LESSONS FROM EXPERIENCES OF OTHER NATIONS

From an operational standpoint, the importance of economic policy is in the direct and indirect incentives it provides to attract and regulate investments and business activities in the target sectors of a given economy. In most countries, trade and industry are highly regulated and relative prices are usually distorted. Due to these, private financial costs and benefits generated in certain activities within these sectors differ from the actual economic costs and benefits to society as a whole. Further, growth of economic activities based on distorted relative prices is not sustainable. It is well recognized that nations that follow distorted trade and industrial policies often suffer from periodic economic downswings and balance of payments crisis.

Countries that consistently pursue stable macroeconomic and undistorted trade and industrial policies, that are conducive for achieving a sustainable economic growth, are rare among developing nations. Based on economic growth performances to date, some of the good examples of such countries are found in East Asia (South Korea, Singapore, Taiwan, Hong Kong). Following largely the model developed by Japan, these countries have made remarkable progress in establishing an efficient industrial base, which has been critical for achieving the high and sustained successful economic growth rates of their economies. The major features of the Japanese and Korean economic growth strategies that could be adopted by other nations are:

- Assigning a leading role to exports in the overall process of economic growth by eliminating anti-export bias and providing incentives for high profits to export industries.
- Promoting the private sector to become the main engine of economic growth by limiting the role of the public sector to the provision of basic institutional and infrastructural services.
- Coordinating investments and maintaining neutrality of incentives between exportables and importables and between tradables and non-tradables.
- Supporting the national economic development strategy with an effective and efficient institutional arrangements through simple and flexible administrative mechanisms.
- Coordinating macroeconomic policy instruments (fiscal, trade, monetary and exchange rate policies) to provide appropriate and stable price signals to all actors of the national economy.
- Providing strong political backing to the publicly announced national economic development strategy.
- Creating strong partnership between the government and the private sector by providing a transparent and stable incentive structure for all concerned (investors, enterprise managers, laborers, consumers and civil servants) ensuring that each has a stake in the performance of the national economy.

The approach followed by Japan and Korea is known as *outward-oriented* (or export led) growth strategy, compared to the *inward-looking* (import-substitution) approach pursued by most developing nations, particularly those in Africa, Latin America and South Asia. However, the two models are not mutually exclusive. The difference between the two is only a matter of degree. A review of Japanese and Korean experiences shows that both countries have followed a highly protected import-substitution development approach in the early stages of their industrialization, allowing firms to sell at prices an oligopolist would enjoy in a protected market.[1] The protectionist stance taken by the Japanese government was evident in the high level of tariffs and restrictive quotas that characterized its imports in the 1960s.

However, both Japan and Korea, unlike other developing nations, did not deepen import-substitution by increasing anti-export bias in their growth strategies. From the outset, they realized that their internal markets were not adequate to sustain growth of industry without access to export markets. Having no natural resources to prime industrial development, they recognized that capital and raw materials required for establishing industry cannot be generated except through significant penetration of international markets with exports of manufactured products. Thus, both countries consciously decided to exploit their respective comparative advantage in labor-intensive manufactures as the core of their export-oriented development strategies. More recently, with the successful market penetration and mastery of advanced technologies, they have gradually been shifting toward more technology and capital-intensive manufactured exports.[2]

V. GROWTH CONSTRAINTS IN ERITREA

A. Background

Italian colonization brought both exploitation and modernization into Eritrea. The Italians generally organized the Eritrean economy around their own needs. In so doing, however, they had established a few light industries and a sizable trained manpower, which later on proved useful in Eritrea's industrial development. As a result, in the 1950s and early 1960s, Eritrea had a respectable industrial base by African standards. Its federal association with and subsequent annexation by a more backward Ethiopia, and the protracted war of liberation, which lasted for thirty years, have resulted in stagnation and substantial deterioration in Eritrea's economic, industrial and foreign trade position.

Since the mid–1970s, the Eritrean People's Liberation Front (EPLF) has been developing light industries in liberated areas to promote a self-reliant liberation struggle and to establish the basis for economic growth in post-independent Eritrea. Most of these activities were war-driven, and it remains to be seen whether they can withstand rigorous economic scrutiny in independent Eritrea, where inputs and outputs have to be valued at their economic opportunity cost. Nonetheless, the EPLF has succeeded in conserving, and in some cases even improving and expanding, Eritrea's industrial work ethic and overall technical capability. Notwithstanding the protracted and destructive war, which came to an end in May 1991, Eritrea has still relatively robust technical and organizational capability to embark on a reasonably ambitious industrialization program with a potential for success. If the government of Eritrea succeeds in motivating and mobilizing Eritreans for economic reconstruction and development, as the EPLF was able to do during the armed struggle, there should be no doubt that Eritrea can become an economically self-reliant nation within the next twenty to thirty years. It can even become an example of hope for the whole of Africa, a continent suffering from continuing economic malaise and political instability.

B. Constraints to Economic Growth

The rate and pattern of growth of trade and industry in Eritrea will depend on many factors. The most critical ones are: (1) the paucity of resources endowment; (2) the size of its markets; (3) the rate of improvement in technological capabilities; (4) the nature and evolution of the macroeconomic and microeconomic policies; and (5) the rate of transformation of its basic infrastructural and institutional support systems. Success would be a function of how quickly and to what extent these interrelated constraints are effectively addressed. The evolution of an appropriate overall macroeconomic policy framework — as well as sector specific policy measures, and the ability of the Eritrean government to motivate Eritreans and establish a transparent and efficient state apparatus will have much to do with finding a lasting resolution to these constraints. The most important constraints Eritrea will need to urgently overcome in order to achieve its economic growth objectives are briefly summarized below.

1. Market Size. In small economies, as Eritrea's is, industrial growth usually depends upon the ability to trade freely in order to take advantage of economies of scale and the benefits derived from specialization.[3] Even in larger economies, where size of domestic market and internal trade is adequate for realizing the benefits from economies of scale and specialization, import competition is required to force firms to cut costs, improve quality and develop new ways of producing and marketing products. Foreign contacts developed through trade are also essential in attracting foreign capital and the acquisition of new technologies required to complement national efforts to promote efficient industry. It would, therefore, be important for the government of Eritrea to explicitly recognize that expansion of trade will be a precondition for the development of a dynamic and efficient industry in Eritrea and to design an economic strategy that promotes efficient allocation of national resources. This means the private sector should be encouraged to develop its exporting capabilities, and the government must stand ready to provide the required logistic support for penetration of export markets.

2. Resource Constraints. At present, Eritrea does not have adequate resources to sustain rapid industrialization. The opportunity cost of resources that could be devoted to establish the basis for raising industrial output in Eritrea is going to be too high. Capital, needed for investment in industrial ventures and for rehabilitation of existing infrastructure, is going to be scarce. Energy and water resources, very critical factors for establishing industry, also are becoming increasingly scarce. Although mineral reserves are known to exist, economic deposits for their exploitation are yet to be proven, and economics of extraction under present international commodity market conditions has not been evaluated. Eritrea's entrepreneurs, industrial labor force and managerial manpower, though of good quality by African standards, have had limited experience and exposure to modern manufacturing processes to be able to produce goods that meet current world market standard. Scarcity of foreign exchange also will be a binding constraint on the process of industrialization and overall economic growth, at least in the earlier stages of post-independent Eritrea. To alleviate the scarcity of resources, the government will have to ensure that the limited resources are allocated and utilized from the very start to maximize value added for the Eritrean economy and to gradually expand its resource base. To do this, Eritrea's overall economic policy approach may have to be pro-growth; that is explicitly favoring growth over equity. Debates on growth versus distribution in the context of trade and industrial policy, when there is little to distribute, could only render adopted economic policy instruments totally ineffective — achieving neither growth nor equity.

3. Technological Gap. Growth of industrial output is determined by rate of expansion of productive inputs and by the efficiency with which inputs are combined and utilized, or total factor productivity changes. In most developing nations, early industrialization efforts tend to focus mainly on mobilization of investments for industry without paying attention to improvements in factor productivity and the technological capability required to generate such improvements. In the early stages of its post-independence existence, Eritrea's ability to adapt and develop appropriate technologies will be constrained by its underdeveloped labor, capital and financial markets and its rather low technological infrastructure. Eritrea will need to strive to rapidly improve its technological capability to achieve higher factor productivity throughout the economy. Improved technological capability will be critical for penetrating highly competitive export markets required to achieve economies of scale and rapid structural transformation of the Eritrean economy.

VI. TENTATIVE RECOMMENDATIONS

Generally, comparative experiences show that slower economic growth and periodic balance of payment and fiscal crisis are often mainly the results of: (1) unstable and uncoordinated macroeconomic policies; (2) highly protected and too restrictive trade and industrial policy framework; (3) excessive restriction on private sector activities and excessive state participation in production and distribution of goods; (4) mistrust and lack of strong partnership between the private sector and the state; and (5) a wavering political commitment to officially declared economic management strategy. The Eritrean government will be well advised to avoid pursuing such policies. Instead, the government should try to follow market-based policy measures and strive to maintain close coordination between its macroeconomic and sectoral policies through a continuing review process, stamping out creeping inconsistencies. This approach would, in the long run, prove to be successful. Within this general approach, Eritrean industrial promotion strategy should focus on achieving rapid expansion of economically viable import-substitution involving substantial exports based on a combination of the following policy measures.

1. Protection. A phased modest protection would be needed to encourage investors to take risk in pioneering and economically viable undertakings. However, uneconomic projects by rent-seeking enterprises profiting from high protection should not be allowed, as they are unlikely to be economically viable even in the long run. A combination of measures (such as avoiding exchange rate overvaluation, exemption of exporters from restrictions and tariffs on imported-inputs, cash export subsidies, etc.) may be used to offset anti-export bias from protection against imports.[4] On efficiency grounds, a relatively low and uniform effective protection structure should be preferred among the politically feasible options available for Eritrea. Customs duty on imported inputs and intermediates should be low and rebates for exports should be provided to enable exporters to compete in the international export markets.

2. Supporting Exports. Exporters of manufactured products must meet exacting and often changing product quality requirements and must deliver their products reliably on time to be able to penetrate highly competitive international export-markets. To do so, exporters need support in terms of efficient infrastructure and trade logistics (including transport and telecommunication services), appropriate export credits, quality control standards and technology development. Thus the Eritrean government needs to concentrate its scarce resources toward providing vital infrastructural and institutional services, leaving production and distribution of goods to the private sector.

3. Foreign Collaboration. Foreign collaboration can provide Eritrea with capital (loan and equity), production technology and marketing and management knowledge to establish a dynamic industrial base. Policies attractive to foreign investors include political and macroeconomic stability, protection of property rights, stable and transparent regulatory framework and liberal access to foreign exchange for profit remittances and imported inputs and service. The investment climate created by these types of policies is often superior to the provision of special incentives (such as protection and tax holidays) to foreign investors. Special incentives have the tendency of attracting rent-seeking and footloose industries that vanish when protection is withdrawn and the holiday is over.

4. Regional Cooperation. Eritrea's economic cooperation and integration with its neighbors could allow its manufacturing enterprises to realize gains from increased trade by taking advantage of economies of scale to produce for a larger regional market, providing useful initial exporting experience. A variety of mutually beneficial shades of economic cooperation (such as customs and currency unions), which could gradually lead to the development of a single regional market, could be considered with neighboring Ethiopia, Djibouti, Sudan and Somalia. Notwithstanding the discouraging experiences on interregional cooperation and economic integration (such as the East African Common Market) to date, economic benefits derived from a well functioning, step-wise economic integration of the nations in the Horn of Africa is probably attractive to all parties concerned and merits systematic consideration and support. To promote the desired pattern of economic integration of the region, a strong political commitment is necessary from each of the governments of the region's states. Eritrea should take the lead on this matter and initiate the process of cooperation.

5. Political Economy. The process of industrialization may be more politically acceptable and sustainable if it is carried out in partnership with the private sector. To achieve rapid economic growth, the private sector (both local and foreign) should have confidence on the durability and direction of the national economic policy framework and have adequate access to suitable financing sources. The Eritrean government should adopt a strategy that will make the private sector feel that it is the main partner in carrying out Eritrea's economic growth and development strategy. If this is not done systematically, private firms may waste scarce resources speculating on the durability and direction of public policy, taking a defensive instead of a proactive role in carrying out the national economic growth strategy. Eritrea cannot afford to waste resources in unproductive speculative activities.

VII. CONCLUSION

A preferred industrial and trade policy for Eritrea should be one that is less restrictive and closer to free market. Although departures from free market on account of externalities and dynamic effects may be justified under certain conditions (as implied by the recommendations above), quantitative restrictions and administrative controls as means of managing trade and industrial expansion should be avoided. Provision of long-term protection and subsidy to promote economic activities should be an exception. From the outset, it is important to ensure that protection does not become a permanent feature of the Eritrean industrial and trade policy framework. If temporary protection or subsidy is needed to promote a given economic activity, the conditions described below must be met.

First, the target industry after initial protection should have the potential to mature and generate sufficient dynamic effects within the economy to compensate for the initial costs of establishment.

Second, the dynamic effects and associated cost reduction would have to be non-accruable to the private firms operating in the target sector, otherwise there would be no need for distorting the economic incentives structure to promote economic activities in the sector.

Third, the protection or subsidy accorded must be removable without creating dislocations that result in large adjustment costs.

Finally, but most importantly, the exchange rate, which is one of the most powerful tools of economic management, should never be allowed to be overvalued. Market-based policy instruments should be used to ensure that the exchange rate remain always in line with the core objective of ensuring the competitiveness of Eritrean exports. The Eritrean government's economic policy interventions should aim at reducing market imperfections and promoting trade.

NOTES

1. About 60 percent of Japanese imports until 1960 were under quotas. And when pressure from its trade partners forced Japan to reduce (eliminate) restriction on imports in the 1960s, it increased tariff rates on 253 newly liberated imported items. The government was also quietly restricting imports by withholding foreign exchange allocation to certain imports to insulate domestic producers from foreign competition. Until the early 1960s, Japanese commercial policy (in the form of import barriers on goods and capital) was a major element of its industrial and economic growth strategy. Since then, however, protection of Japanese industry (through tariffs and stringent quantitative restrictions) has declined rapidly as it reached prominence in industrialization.
2. While encouraging private firms to expand in a protected market, the policy approach of Japan and Korea subjected firms to intense competition in export markets. This pressure, together with strong government commitment to follow through export drives, engendered optimization of scale economies derived from mass production technologies, prompting private firms to venture into production for exports. Increasing scale of operations and productivity, initially supported by protected domestic

market and subsidized export credits, eventually led to reduced unit costs of output and competitiveness. succeeds in motivating and mobilizing Eritreans for economic reconstruction and development, as the EPLF was able to do during the armed struggle, there should be no doubt that Eritrea can become an economically self-reliant nation within the next twenty to thirty years. It can even become an example of hope for the whole of Africa, a continent suffering from continuing economic malaise and political instability.

3. South Korea's phenomenal export-led economic growth performance would have been impossible without access to the large and sophisticated U.S. market. There is strong and clear evidence that the major breakthrough for both the Japanese and Korean economies has been their ability to penetrate the technologically sophisticated export markets (U.S and European) with products from economic size plants based on state of the art technologies.

4. A few East Asian countries (such as Japan, Hong Kong, Taiwan, Singapore and Korea) have been successful in developing sustainable growth of import-substitution and export-oriented industries side by side because of their ability to manage their exchange rate and fiscal policies correctly. As a whole, these countries have been able to maintain low fiscal deficits and inflation rates and stable and adequate real exchange rates. Hong Kong and Singapore essentially have had free trade regimes, with no (or very low) tariffs or trade restrictions. Countries like India, Mexico, Brazil, and Indonesia provide tariff waivers (and exemptions from other import restrictions) for imports of inputs for exports to compensate for lack of neutrality of incentives between importable and exportables arising from tariffs and other quantitative restrictions on imports.

REFERENCES

Finger, J. Michael, and Messerlin, A. Patrick. *The Effect of Industrial Countries' Policies on Developing Countries*. Policy and Research Series, Policy, Planning and Research. Washington, D.C.: World Bank.

Franco, de Silvio, Alberto Eguren, and David Baughman. 1988. *Korea's Experience with the Development of Trade and Industry*. EDI Policy Seminar Report No. 4. Washington, D.C.: World Bank.

Lal, Deepak. 1990. "International Capital Flows and Economic Development." In *Public Policy and Economic Development, Essays in Honor of Ian Little*, edited by Maurice Scott and Deepak Lal. Oxford University Press.

Leipziger, D. M., and S. Y. Song. 1991. "A Review of Korea's Trade Pattern." World Bank, Asia Regional Series, Discussion Paper (March).

Meier, G. M. 1990. "Trade Policy and Development." In *Public Policy and Economic Development, Essays in Honor of Ian Little*, edited by Maurice Scott and Deepak Lal. Oxford University Press.

Page, M. John, Jr. 1990. "The Pursuit Of Industrial Growth: Policy Initiatives and Economic Consequences." In *Public Policy and Economic*

Development, Essays in Honor of Ian Little, edited by Maurice Scott and Deepak Lal. Oxford University Press.

World Bank. 1987. *World Development Report 1987, Barriers to Adjustment and Growth in the World Economy, Industrialization and Foreign Trade.* Oxford University Press (June).

Yamamura, Kozo. 1988. "Caveat Emptor: The Industrial Policy of Japan." In *Strategic Trade Policy and the New International Economics,* edited by Paul R. Krugman. Cambridge: MIT Press.

FEATURES OF THE ERITREAN INDUSTRY: ITS PROSPECTS FOR DEVELOPMENT AND POLICY

Prepared by
The Manufacturing Commission, EPLF[1]

I. BACKGROUND OF INDUSTRY IN ERITREA

Modern industrial enterprises in Eritrea began with the advent of Italian colonialism. The objectives of Italian colonialism, however, were to retain Eritrea as a source of raw materials, a commercial outlet for Italian manufactured goods, a reserved territory for Italian settlers and a springboard for further colonial expansion in the Horn of Africa. Thus, Eritrea became a complete economic dependency of Italy.

Although Italy invested considerable amount of capital to build roads, railways, cities, seaports and airports, telegraph and telephone communication, military installations and other infrastructures, it did not pay as much attention to the industrial development of the country. The few factories established, mostly near the end of the Italian colonial era, operated primarily to satisfy the demands of the Italian community in Eritrea. After 1930, the building of infrastructure and the establishment and expansion of light industries were directly linked to Italy's design to invade Ethiopia.

Industrial activity began to stagnate during the eve of the Second World War. From 1941, when British occupation replaced Italian colonialism, until the end of the war, however, British and U.S. war programs and strategy created conditions that encouraged the revitalization of Eritrean factories and the establishment of new ones. Thus, 1941–45 saw a moderate revival of industrial activity. Several Eritrean industrial products were exported. As a brief expansion of industrial activity was stimulated by the special war conditions, however, several factories, unable to compete in the market, became bankrupt and were closed; others were forced to reduce their output and confine their products to the domestic market after 1945. Moreover, the British military administration dismantled and sold abroad installations that could have played an important role in the growth of the Eritrean industry. There was, thus, a severe economic crisis and unemployment during the last years of British rule in Eritrea.

Worse still, the Ethiopian colonial objective, as well as its economic and political policy in Eritrea, has been completely hostile to Eritrean economic growth and industrial development. The federation that the big powers imposed on the Eritrean people did not usher an era of development, prosperity and peace. The expectations and hopes for the elimination of unemployment, the securing of economic take-off and respect for human rights and liberties were thwarted. There prevailed almost no condition to encourage the

---

1. Presented by Tesfai Gebreselassie.

revitalization and renovation of the enfeebled and paralyzed factories during the federal period. After the abrogation of the federation, and especially during the Derg's fascist regime, a deliberate policy to destroy the economic life of Eritrea was implemented. To realize its dream of destroying the Eritrean revolution, crushing the resistance of the Ethiopian peoples and becoming a bully of our region, the Derg's regime, under the guise of socialism, nationalized all big factories in Eritrea in 1975 in order to procure the financial and material resources needed to build a huge army and to conduct offensives. In 1982, during the "Red Star Offensive," it issued a declaration nationalizing an additional twenty factories. All of the fifty-one nationalized factories were grouped into ten corporations under the management of the Ministry of Industry, except the Assab Oil Refinery, which was under the management of the Ministry of Mining Energy. Some of the small factories have been further regrouped on the basis of similarity of output, reducing the number of state-owned factories to forty-four.

Most of the existing big factories have long years of service and can be divided into four groups according to the year of their establishment.

Before 1928	3 factories
1929 – 1942	4 factories
1943 – 1951	11 factories
1952 – 1972	20 factories

In addition, there are privately-owned small-scale factories and handicraft workshops all over Eritrea. Of these, 644 have industrial license, 18 are cooperative associations and the remaining 78 operate with licenses from the Ministry of Internal Trade and Municipalities without being registered under the Ministry of Industry.

II. THE MAIN FEATURES OF ERITREAN INDUSTRY

As indicated earlier, the existing industrial base in Eritrea, dominated as it is by small-scale and light factories, has been laid down from the mid–1930s to the early 1970s. The productive capacity of the factories has been extremely weakened as most of them use obsolete machinery and technology and suffer from lack of spare parts and normal renovation. Because the generation and distribution of electric power in Eritrea is very expensive and the capital invested in industry is very small, the cost of industrial production has, despite low labor wages, remained so high that Eritrean goods have been unable to compete in the world market.

The overall capital invested in Eritrean industry is estimated at 281 million *birr*. This relatively very small investment is not evenly distributed among the various subsectors of industry. About 31 percent of the 220 million *birr* invested in the state-owned modern sector is in the chemical industry, the bulk of which is in the Assab Oil Refinery, 18 percent in the textile industry, and 14 percent in the food industry.

The total capital invested in the private sector of small-scale industry and handicraft workshops is 61 million *birr,* of which 95.5 percent is in private enterprises and 3.5 percent in cooperative associations. This does not include the capital of the seventy-eight private enterprises not registered under the Ministry of Industry whose amount is not known. Of the capital invested in the small-scale industries, 27.2 percent is in food, 18 percent in textiles and 15.5 percent in chemicals.

Eritrean manufacturing industry is underdeveloped. The Derg's nationalization in 1975 was a major cause for arresting as well as retarding industrial development. In the first place, this measure blocked the investment of domestic and foreign private capital in modern industry. Secondly, far from investing additional capital in the nationalized enterprises, the Derg appropriated the profits without even allowing for normal wear and tear maintenance. Thus, the Derg let all of the big factories decay while using their profits to wage war, build a huge army and develop and expand industrial plants in Ethiopia. It is to be recalled even before the advent of the Derg, Eritreans and foreigners were being forced to relocate their capital from Eritrea to Ethiopia.

Compared to agriculture, the Eritrean manufacturing industry offers an extremely low opportunity for employment. As of May 1991, there were 13,052 workers, excluding those working at the Assab salt work and electric power, employed in the state-owned sector and 4,648 workers in the privately-owned small-scale sector.

The regional distribution of Eritrean factories is uneven. Except for one or two in Massawa and Assab, all factories are located in Asmara.

The production capacity of Eritrean industry is also small. Although limited items such as hides, canned meat, garments and textiles, salt and shoes were being exported, the markets for most of them are Eritrea and Ethiopia. Although concrete information is lacking as to their quantities, the bulk of Eritrea's industrial output — alcoholic beverages, matches, glass, textile and garments, shoes, salt, mosaic, home and office furniture, and refined oil — have been exported to Ethiopia. Imports from Ethiopia include industrial raw materials and construction materials such as cotton, sugar, oilseeds, tobacco, wood, iron bars, corrugated iron, yarn and threads, cattle, skin, etc. Furthermore, all machinery and tools, most intermediate goods, crude oil and plastics, various metals, etc., essential for Eritrean factories, are imported from other countries. Thus, the accumulation of sufficient foreign exchange is an essential factor for ensuring the continuity of the Eritrean manufacturing activities.

Linkage within Eritrean industry is limited. There are virtually no factories that use the output of others as their inputs. There are domestic products, both in quantity and kind, which are represented as intermediate inputs. These are confined to cement, glass and hides. No domestically produced machinery and tools are available for Eritrean factories. Integration among productive enterprises has been weak and not set on the right track. There are virtually no enterprises that perform the various stages of a process necessary to manufacture a finished product. There was also no vertical integration except in the Baratollo Textile Factory, which used to grow cotton and process it into finished garments, and the Ela Bereid, Denadai's Agro-Industrial Complex.

The linkage between industry and agriculture is also weak. Industry has not made a sufficient push for the development of agriculture or other branches of the national economy. Nor could it lead to the expansion and improvement of the infrastructure due to the Derg's hostile objectives.

To summarize, Eritrean industry is: (1) light and oriented to the production of consumer goods, (2) composed of small-scale factories with a very few exceptions, (3) previously mostly owned by foreigners and later nationalized by the Derg, (4) concentrated in a single city, (5) dependent on obsolete technology and know-how, (6) constrained by high cost due to lack of reliable and sufficient electric power, (7) deficient in integration with other sectors, and (8) limited in providing employment opportunities.

Our endeavor to develop industry from the limited base built so far must thus pay attention to eliminating these weaknesses.

III. EPLF'S EXPERIENCE IN THE FIELD OF MANUFACTURING

The establishment of small-scale factories and handicraft workshops within EPLF was initially aimed at alleviating the problems facing the armed struggle and producing essential items which were not easily and continuously available in the market. As the establishment of our enterprises has generally evolved along lines of priority in terms of the front's military consolidation and expansion of economical tasks, the first ones to be set up and developed were those doing repair work.

Most of the small factories set up have been grouped under the EPLF's Manufacturing Commission. There are ten subcommissions comprising of metal, wood, electric, textile, leather, plastics, food, battery and sanitary towels.

As the primary national task of the past stage was the abolition of colonial rule, our economy was a war economy. Although the role played by our factories in alleviating the urgent problems faced at different stages cannot be underestimated, their productive capacity was limited because they were set up with very limited material and financial resources under difficult conditions of war and operating in unsuitable locations. They have not contributed much to easing the economic problems of the people. Nevertheless, it cannot be denied that they have, beyond the contribution of their concrete yields, served as a symbol of resolution and steadfastness as well as a source of self-confidence and pride for our people and fighters in the liberation struggle.

This, however, does not mean that our brief industrial experience has been all positive. We are fully aware that there were weaknesses in our management and methods of work which we should learn to avoid and fight complacency.

The main weaknesses calling for remedy are: (1) establishing productive enterprises without making sufficient study and preparations, (2) not mapping out our practical work schedules, (3) not sufficiently appraising our capacity to implement and manage, (4) working without proper cost accounting, and (5) not developing a regular procedure for preparing and deciding on projects.

IV. PROBLEMS AND PROSPECTS OF DEVELOPING INDUSTRY

A. Natural Resources

No extensive studies and surveys of Eritrea's potential resource, agricultural as well as mineral, have been taken. The limited surveys carried out, however, show that the country possesses substantial resources for industrial development. It is estimated that there are appreciable quantities of different minerals, metal and nonmetal. Oil and gas are available in quantities to warrant hopes that they could contribute to economic development. In addition, agricultural growth and development of the country's animal resources could spur food processing industries.

As has been noted previously, many of Eritrea's existing industrial plants, including those producing cement, glass, limestone, brick and ceramics, rely on local minerals and raw materials. It is also possible to provide local raw materials and agricultural produce for the food and beverage industries. Proper balance between agricultural and industrial growth could boost both sectors and propel national industry.

To give a more complete and balanced picture of the situation, however, it must be noted that on the basis of information available so far, Eritrea's mineral resources are few in kind and not very extensive. It should also be noted that scarcity of water and energy could hamper agricultural and industrial growth.

B. Human Resources

It is generally agreed that Eritreans are hardworking and resourceful. In the course of the long and bitter national struggle, they have also learned to work, strive and sacrifice for the attainment of common objectives. This human factor is bound to contribute positively to Eritrea's industrial growth as the population is ready to participate in national reconstruction with the same gusto it showed during the liberation struggle. Other positive factors are the existence of a small but skilled and experienced work force, which served as the backbone of industrial activity over the past sixty years, the exposure of the large Eritrean community in exile to modern industry and technology, and the existence of a substantial number of Eritrean skilled workers, experts and managers.

Conversely, there are some major human resource problems that could deter industrial growth: (1) a small population whose losses in the liberation struggle were very extensive, (2) a sizable community in exile, including a chunk of the country's elite, which cannot be expected to return in its entirety, (3) a low literacy rate, (4) the decline of educational standards and almost total disruption of educational activity in the past few years, and finally, the exclusion of Eritreans from all managerial and administrative posts that were reserved for Ethiopians by the Derg.

C. Capital

It is clear that the underdeveloped and war-devastated economy of Eritrea cannot generate all the capital necessary for the urgent task of national reconstruction and all-round development. The emergent Eritrean state will strive to channel effectively the capital that up to now was being wasted or sent outside the country, especially to Ethiopia. It will also create maximum opportunities for Eritreans to invest their capital in sectors that increase the country's productive capacity.

Domestic resource, however, is not sufficient to meet Eritrea's capital needs. Hence, there is a need for foreign capital in the form of grants, loans and private investments. But, where and how can this foreign capital be found and on what terms? This is a matter that requires urgent attention if we are to overcome the problem of capital scarcity, which is obviously the main hurdle to industrial growth, and the related problem of foreign exchange.

D. Infrastructure

What used to be Eritrea's relatively developed infrastructure including transport, communications and other facilities, power plants and financial institutions could have spurred growth in industry, agriculture and trade. Instead, the country faces major infrastructure problems because of the damage and destruction caused over the past thirty years. The railway system has been totally dismantled. Bridges have been destroyed, roads have fallen into disrepair. It is, therefore, essential to repair existing facilities and build and expand new ones so that lack of a supporting infrastructure does not become an obstacle to the progress of Eritrean industry.

E. Markets

The markets for Eritrean industrial products are essentially Eritrea itself and Ethiopia. Exports to other countries have been extremely limited. It is expected that the internal markets will expand and boost industrial production with the growth of agriculture and other economic sectors, a more equitable distribution of the national product and improvement in the variety and quality of industrial products aimed at satisfying the basic needs of the population, the demands of national reconstruction and the growth of the national economy. In addition, Eritrean industrial enterprises have to find foreign markets if they are to produce in sufficient quantities and at competitive prices, create jobs, introduce modern technology and earn foreign exchange for vital imports. Although further investigation is required, market possibilities exist in Asian and European countries and especially in our region. The Ethiopian market, whose continuity depends on future relations between the two countries, is also essential.

F. The Political Superstructure

It hardly needs to be stated that the political system or administration plays a decisive role in economic and industrial development. Economic objectives cannot be achieved if the administration lacks commitment to development, is unable to mobilize and efficiently utilize national resources, and fails to create a conducive atmosphere for all relevant elements to contribute their share effectively. The provisional Eritrean administration must therefore be competent, efficient and free from corruption and bureaucratic red tape. It has the responsibility of maintaining and passing on to an elected popular government the momentum of active popular participation so that the Eritrean people could follow up their political and military victory, which was nothing short of miraculous, with another miracle in economic and social development.

G. Industrial Strategy and Policy

The experiences of many countries show that industrialization is a difficult and complex process that requires continuous review and periodic readjustments. It is even more difficult in countries such as Eritrea, which have suffered from war-related destruction, natural calamities and massive dislocation of the population.

In discussing industrial strategy, the first issue that needs to be addressed is the relative roles of agriculture and industry. At this stage, industrialization cannot be contemplated apart from agricultural growth. For reasons already stated, the two sectors can only grow in tandem, with agriculture serving as the basis of the development strategy and industry as the "spearhead."

There are several other questions that have to be answered before meaningful industrial policy and strategy can be mapped out. Relevant questions that have to be asked to that end are: What branches of industry should be given priority in order to advance industrialization as a whole? Which strategy is better, import substitution or producing for export? Should we rely on advanced technology or "intermediate and appropriate ones"?

Although answers to these questions require in-depth studies, it is clear that in practice, as opposed to theory, one policy option does not necessarily exclude the other. Experience in other countries shows that the optimal policy is a flexible one that looks at the options not as mutually exclusive but as complementary ones and attempts to implement them at the same time albeit in different degrees. We must recognize, however, that the scope for flexibility is limited since industrial development requires massive infusions of investment capital, and there will not be sufficient capital to meet all identified needs.

For these and other reasons, Eritrea's policy for industrial development should have the following features:

1. It must encourage and provide wide opportunities for private investment, domestic as well as foreign.
2. It must selectively support newly set up national manufacturing plants to enable them to withstand the intense pressure of competitive goods for external markets. Since such support can harm other branches of industry and have other negative ramifications, it must be given in a way that prompts the support-receiving enterprises to stand on their feet quickly.
3. It must strive for an equitable distribution of industrial plants in different regions of the country. In this respect, attention must be paid to industries such as textiles, food and beverages, and construction materials that are more profitable if located near their markets and source of raw materials. The policy of gradual equitable regional distribution, however, has its constraints, since economic development favors concentration of industries in certain parts of the country.
4. At this stage, ours must be mixed economy which avails appropriate roles for the government and the market to develop and regulate the national economy. This means prices of industrial goods will generally be determined by the market. It also means that state enterprises, just like private ones, will have to compete in the market and bring in prof-

it.

5. Our industrial policy must encourage and support cottage industries as these create substantial job opportunities, meet a significant part of national needs in return for relatively small capital investment, and assist in domestic capital accumulation.

6. Those factories that had been expropriated by the Derg will largely become the property of the forthcoming Eritrean state and the bases of the public sector in industry. If, however, the national interest is better served by letting any number of these factories revert to private ownership, then the state should sell them.

V. INVESTMENT POLICY FOR INDUSTRY

Taking into account global political and economic trends and the small capacity and low development of national industry, technology and capital as well as the goal of rapid industrialization, we see as imperative the policy of unrestricted private investment in all branches of industry. It is therefore essential to proclaim clearly that our investment code for industry encourages investment, be it private, both domestic and foreign, government as well as mixed private-government cooperative. This policy is based on the convictions that the state can enhance its positive role in developing national industry and a more equitable distribution of the national wealth, without resorting to state monopolization of different branches of industry, and giving the state a dominant overall orientation, structure, distribution and scale of industrial growth by means of various policy instruments.

The ultimate objective of our investment policy in industry, just like in other sectors, is the success of our national development plan. More specifically, we want to encourage investment in industrial projects that serve our development goals and meet the following criteria in part or in full:

1. Substantially increase the national income and help in broadening the base of the national economy and making it more vibrant.
2. Contribute to the elimination of the bottlenecks of economic developments and growth.
3. Assist in making available essential services that strengthen economic and social growth.
4. Rely on locally available natural resources and raw materials or contribute to the setting up of other production plants that use local raw materials.
5. Raise the quantity and quality of manufactured products and introduce modern science, technology and modern methods of work.
6. Contribute to the success of the policy of self-reliance by producing export goods and earning foreign exchange.
7. Assist to an appreciable degree the balance of trade by earning or saving foreign exchange.
8. Create jobs for Eritrean nationals.
9. Help in realizing the goals of balanced regional and sectorial development in the socioeconomic field.
10. Have some other strategic importance for the country as a whole.

VI. PRIORITIES FOR THE TRANSITIONAL PERIOD

The following are suggested policy priorities for the Provisional Government of Eritrea to consider during the transitional period.

1. Make a detailed study of the present condition of the state-owned factories and endeavor to operate them at full capacity.
2. Determine which factories will remain state-owned and which ones will be returned to private ownership.
3. Alleviate the chronic shortage of water and electric power that has long obstructed the operations of existing industrial capacity all over Eritrea in general and in Asmara and Massawa in particular.
4. Revitalize and support the private industrial enterprises, small factories and handicraft workshops that have been idle.
5. Work to ensure a reliable source of raw materials and market for the products of Eritrean industries.
6. Give priority to domestic as well as foreign investment projects that help set up productive enterprises that process or use local natural resources and raw materials.
7. Start rapid programs of training and education to meet the requirements for skill in industrial management and administration as well as to produce professionals and technicians.

STRATEGIC PLANNING FOR INDUSTRIAL DEVELOPMENT OF EMERGENT ERITREA

Gebre Gebrekidan and Tsegay Moges

I. INTRODUCTION

The purpose of this paper is to discuss issues related to the planning and implementation of industrial development in Eritrea. We start with some questions. Does Eritrea need an industrial policy? What will be the content of such a policy? What will the industry's near- and long-term objectives be? How will the strategies be developed? What will be the role of the government, the private sector and international organizations in setting, or influencing the policy? What should Eritreans expect industry to deliver? What are the types of economic climate necessary for industrial development? Does Eritrea have the natural and human resources necessary to initiate a viable industrialization process?

Before these questions are answered, we note that in a number of industrialized nations there is a heated debate among economists, industrial strategic planners and industry observers on the subject of establishing national industrial policies. There are those who say it would be a grave mistake to let governments set industrial strategies and policies. They claim even the governments of highly developed nations do not have the expertise to distinguish between those industries that deserve support and those that do not. The result of such efforts, they say, would be to hamper market forces from freely allocating usually scarce resources to the most deserving ones. According to these experts, the market provides the most efficient process for allocating resources. Hence they dismiss all efforts to set an industrial policy by any government as simply meddling in the free market system.

The other group advocates the need for national competitive strategies. They point to the fact that countries like Japan and Korea were able to achieve their present industrial development stature through carefully planned industrial policies and market penetration strategies. This group explains that government led industrial policy helps focus attention to the major objectives of a nation. They claim industrial policies publicize campaigns for cooperative projects between industry, government and the academia for developing policies and setting directions for the introduction of emerging technologies and new manufacturing concepts.

Eritrea, as a country coming out of a brutal war, is starting with an obvious disadvantage. It does not have market tools that can be expected to efficiently allocate its financial and human resources. It has not as yet established private or public forums to debate and articulate the need and the process of development and implementation of its industrial policies. The only organized institution left that appears to be best positioned to attempt such a task in Eritrea is the Eritrean provisional government.

II. NATIONAL OBJECTIVES

Any industrial policy or strategy needs to be supportive of a country's short- and long-range national objectives. Thus, one needs to have a clear understanding of a nation's immediate and long-range needs before embarking on setting policies and strategies.

Eritrea's immediate national objectives are liberty, peace, stability, and the provision of basic necessities — food, clothing, shelter and health care — for its people. Eritreans have been subjected to one of the cruellest oppressions under Ethiopia's military regime for nearly two decades. That regime often used food as a weapon to weaken the determination of the Eritrean people in their quest for independence. Starvation, hunger and malnutrition have been rampant throughout Eritrea for quite a long time. Hence, Eritrea's immediate objective should be the elimination of hunger. Eritreans need to be provided with shelter from extreme heat in the lowlands and bitter cold in some of the highland areas. Health care, which is a basic necessity, has been totally neglected. These needs are absolutely essential for the continued physical, social and political survival of the people. That is why meeting them head-on, without delay, constitutes Eritrea's immediate national objective.

Eritrea's long-range objectives, we presume will include the establishment of stable democratic institutions and improvement of the standard of living for its people comparable to those in the developed nations. Through the expansion of literacy and provision of economic opportunity, Eritreans will begin to assert their place in the economic and political development of their country. Such an environment will provide a conducive atmosphere for accelerating industrial development plans.

III. INDUSTRIALIZATION IN THE SERVICE OF NATIONAL OBJECTIVES

A. Nature of the Problem

Given the main national objectives discussed above, how would industrialization support a nation's near- and long-term objectives? Many African countries developed elaborate industrial plans. They attempted to use industrialization as a means to move their nations away from being economies dependent on their former colonial powers. To this end, they opted to introduce industries which on the surface appeared to accelerate economic growth. Given the heavy dependence on imported goods from former colonies, a seemingly obvious objective became to substitute domestic manufactured goods for previously imported products. The obvious consequence of such a policy is to start a domino effect of borrowing to procure and install the needed machinery, to bring in skilled foreigners to operate the procured machines and to manage the enterprises, and in many cases to import the raw material or semi-finished products to complete the production process in these "African factories."

The problem is not with the policy of import substitution per se, but with the inability to identify real needs, the absence of objectivity in the prioritizing process compounded by lack of the essential requisites to establish an appropriate industrial base capable of meeting those needs. The challenge then is how to avoid the pitfalls. Given these problems, we ask: Are there lessons to be learned from the experience of other developing countries?

B. Industrial Policies: The Experience of Developing Countries

Many African countries considered that industrial planning was the best way to start organizing and giving impetus to the development of industries. Thus, industrial planning methods were developed and a chapter on industrial development was included in all national plans. The result, however, as African leaders themselves acknowledged in the preamble to the Lagos Plan of Action, was that "Africa was unable to point to any growth rate or satisfactory index of general well being from 1960 to April 1980" (UNIDO, Nov. 1990). The failure was due to deviations and errors that were accumulated by the planning process itself. All too often poorly conceived, for the most part purely theoretical, without any real or operational content, African industrial planning was rarely a genuine instrument for organizing and guiding industrial development. Industrial planning was mainly confined to defining groups of projects without any coherence. Most of the time the projects were poorly chosen. Compelling organizational needs of the budding industrial economies were ignored, real economic agents overlooked, economic constraints and demands largely underestimated. It was rarely the result of a coherent and rigorous work process, by properly staffed and adequately skilled teams. At the same time, it has been used to justify excessive intervention by governments in the economic life of their citizens. This type of industrial planning used as a technico-political structure can only serve as a political scapegoat, and result in the prevailing industrial crisis in contemporary Africa.

The crisis in the industrial sector of many African and other developing countries manifests itself as: overdependence on imported raw materials, machinery and equipment, underutilization of capacity and declining rate of productivity. It started during the debt-financed capacity expansion of the 1960s and 1970s which was to a large extent fueled by abundant international liquidity in the form of surplus petro-dollars or aid made available to the newly independent African countries. These external resources were available at very low interest rates throughout much of the 1970s. Since the early 1980s, however, certain external shocks and the ensuing debt crisis have overtaken this strategy of "growth with debt". The effects of unfavorable external shocks invariably caused a deterioration in the current balance account thereby reducing import capacity. This created a situation which made it difficult to maintain, upgrade, and boost export-oriented industries.

Restrictions on imports of industrial raw materials and machinery, which are vital to capital formation, also debilitates the capital good industries. The result is underutilization of capacity, production disruptions and the disappearance of domestic and foreign investments. Output and employment contractions in the manufacturing sector depresses the level of overall domestic economic activity from both the supply and demand side.

In the following sections we examine the paths taken by three developing countries to illustrate how different results of industrial policies can be depending on the policies themselves, and internal and external factors that influence their applications.

1. Yemen. The development of the national economy in Yemen following independence was largely funded from external sources. Burgeoning imports of consumer goods and materials for this development program were financed not from exports, which were negligible, but from the flow of migrants remittances from the oil-rich gulf states and foreign aid from supportive socialist and Arab countries. When these sources of external funding started to dry up in the 1980s, as a spillover effect of recession in neighboring Arab states, the economy lacked the means to sustain growth.

In response the government introduced stringent and arbitrary controls to curb the growth of imports; a measure based on national pride rather than national needs. Import restrictions covered not only consumer goods but the foreign exchange budgets of industrial enterprises. Inevitably in a country that imports the vast majority of its consumer goods, raw materials, and intermediate and capital goods, the austerity measures affected output. By 1985 the economy of Yemen entered a period of relative stagnation. For example, between 1970 and 1980 gross output fell by 16.7 percent.

One of the causes of the decline in gross national output and the relative stagnation of the economy in general was low capacity utilization rates, where the scale of production of the minimum viable industrial plant exceeds the needs of the limited local market. This is a situation where small-scale labor intensive industries would have been a realistic alternative. In some cases, however low capacity utilization rates resulted from the selection of inappropriate equipment, closures of production lines, poor maintenance due to the lack of skilled repair staff, and shortages of imported raw materials due to tightened foreign exchange budgets.

This is clearly the result of an industrial development strategy which placed the means of production in the hands of a rigidly centralized planning system of the state. It is clear the strategy did not take into account the resource base, strategy for import-substitution, export potential based on comparative advantage and did not attempt to integrate the industrial sector through internal linkages.

2. Djibouti. After years of sluggish growth, manufacturing value added (MVA) in Djibouti grew by 5.5 percent in 1979, as the sector benefited from the spurt in economic activity in the face of an enthusiastic rush on the part of the donors to help the new state during the years following independence. This momentum could not be maintained, and growth of MVA faltered to 2.9 percent in 1980 and plunged to a negative rate of .3 percent in 1981 (UNIDO, March 1989). The pace of industrial expansion suffered a marked contraction with stagnating and declining growth rates as a result of a pause in industrial investment.

Industrial performance recorded by UNIDO for thirteen selected enterprises revealed that eleven of them were working below capacity. The causes, as identified by UNIDO, were installed over-capacity, poor maintenance and interruptions in the supply of raw materials and spare parts which led to frequent and often prolonged breakdowns.

Undoubtedly the limited size of the country's internal market is a constraint on industrial development. But, the abrupt halt of industrial expansion, when the momentum of help from donors can not be sustained, also shows excessive external dependence for financial and material resource. For example, despite the availability of suitable mineral resources, Djibouti is almost entirely dependent on imported construction materials. The development of the country's food and beverage industry which employe 85 percent of the work force has been based on the processing of imported raw materials and the manufacture of products from imported semi-finished goods rather than domestic agricultural production.

Typically an industrial policy so heavily dependent on imported technology, material, expertise and finance can only serve to dazzle potential investors in donor conferences.

3. South Korea. In the initial phase of postwar economic development, Korea was like any other developing country, largely dependent on foreign aid to provide the key investible resources for its industrialization. Like Yemen and Djibouti and many other developing countries, the main emphasis was placed on a policy of import substitution until the early sixties when the policy shifted to export promotion on export expansion and diversification. It is this shift of policy that differentiates the Korean experience from the rest of the developing countries, and makes it a model of a successful industrialization process.

Manufactures constituted 96 percent of total exports in 1984, among the highest in the world. The high export dependence of the economy is beginning to become problematic in times of sluggish growth in international trade and as protectionist forces tend to increase. One of the aims of the government's export policy is to lessen the country's dependence on the U.S. market, which presently absorbs more than one-third of Korean manufactured exports.

In Korea an elaborate incentive system was used to attract foreign capital in the form of foreign direct investment loans and technology inducements were systematically used on selected industrial projects. These were utilized with specific forms of public/private sector participation and institutional interlinking. Market signals were used to guide strategic decisions without, however, leaving industrial development entirely to the unrestricted working of market forces. Scientific manufacturing techniques were developed to improve productivity and quality, which made Korean manufactured goods competitive in the world market.

It is interesting to see Korea's outstanding economical achievement in contrast to other developing countries. The industrial planning system in Korea was indicative of "administrative guidance." It was based on strong cooperation between government agencies and the private sector. The centerpiece of Korea's plan was a sophisticated ensemble of incentives together with a financial system which has been so purposefully designed and systematically utilized as an instrument for targeted industrial development. In other developing countries the industrial planning system though imperative was not effective. In many African countries it was not even genuine. Investable resources, depended on foreign aid and grants, was not specifically targeted to selected industrial projects capable of consistently producing good quality competitively priced products.

Given the Republic of Korea's poor natural resource endowment (including the high import dependence to meet its energy requirements), the successful economic performance over the past two decades could only result from the efficient use of investment capital, scientific manufacturing techniques, and the industriousness and work commitment of the country's labor force.

IV. ERITREA'S RESOURCES FOR INDUSTRY

Most published reports on Eritrea's resources are of colonial origin. They were gathered and analyzed to serve colonial interests and must be used with care. Although Araia Tseggai (1983) made an excellent case in his attempt to put to rest opposition to Eritrea's independence on claims that the country lacked adequate natural resources, the real picture of Eritrea's national resources is yet to be unveiled. This task of compiling data on natural resources should be of high priority. It is a prerequisite to the development of sound economic and industrial plans. Any industrialization effort that does not start from an appropriate assessment of natural resources is bound to run into serious difficulties.

A. The Need for Census Data

Eritrea's most valuable resources are its people. For a long time Eritrea's population has been estimated at around 3.5 million. A first order of business should be establishing a statistically correct count of all Eritreans. Additional challenges involve determining the various types of population parameters: the rate of population growth, migration, population distribution by urban, and rural regions, by sedentary and nomadic life, by employment type (such as in agriculture, industry, and services); by sex, age, educational background, etc.

All planning efforts including human resource development, establishment of schools, adult education programs, hospitals, residential and industrial zones, and communication infrastructures are dependent on census data. Reliable and detailed demographic data are an essential input to the decision-making process of the government, developers, national and international investment banks, and entrepreneurs.

B. Agriculture Should Be a Sector of Priority

Agriculture is the principal source of employment and income in Eritrea. As such any industrial development will have to be structured to complement the country's agricultural potential. Work needs to be initiated on identifying fertilizers, water resources, improved agricultural tools and new farming techniques to change the now subsistence into sustainable agricultural production.

Livestock data, vaccination requirements, sizes, location, future potential for expansion of pastures and large-scale irrigation projects to increase acreage of cultivable land areas that need to be addressed. The country's water resources: rainfall, irrigation systems, and wells need to be studied and development requirements identified. The long-term impact of drought which ravaged the country for a number of years should be studied.

C. Potential Marine Wealth

Eritrea is blessed with a long and beautiful coastal line along the Red Sea. The coastal land and the Dahlak Archipelago are rich in marine resources. Research should be conducted to determine the types of species, the level of stock, migration and breeding patterns, and habitats. To encourage widespread consumption, educational programs should be provided to the general public on nutritional values, refrigeration, cooking and serving of seafood.

D. Mineral and Energy Resources

Eritrea is very rich in a number of minerals with large amount of deposits (Araia Tseggai 1983, pp. 42–45). These include gold, copper, iron ore, salt, potash and potentially petroleum. It is important to consider world market conditions and environmental impact when planning to exploit the country's mineral resources. Minerals should not be excavated solely for export purposes. Mining should provide an impetus for local related industrial development.

For its energy resources Eritrea will have to depend on a combination of alternative energy sources such as solar, hydroelectric, and potentially energy from wood and charcoal. Wood and charcoal may not contribute significantly for some years to come due the drought and neglect that has adversely affected Eritrea's forests. The refinery at Assab will probably contribute to the national economy through reduction of foreign exchange expenditures. Just like other requisite areas for industrial development requirements and development of alternative energy sources needs to be studied.

E. Communication Infrastructure

Communication infrastructure, particularly railways and roads, assist not only in the economic development of a country but also contribute to an even distribution of economic benefits. Eritrea's railways have not been functional for some time. The system was built to link Massawa on the Red Sea with Asmara, the capital and cities in the western lowlands. The roads built during Italian occupation comprise an excellent transportation network. Even during the war of liberation, Eritreans have been busy building roads. The next step is to improve and expand them to regions targeted for economic development.

V. INDUSTRIAL POLICY CONSIDERATIONS IN ERITREA

The quest for survival in the short run, leading into a better standard of living and eventually narrowing the development gap between Eritrea and other developed countries, should be the centerpiece of all Eritrean national development plans. This will require passing through phases during the course of development in general and industrial development in particular.

A. Phase One

At this stage the objective is survival — attention to the basic necessities of life for the entire Eritrean population. In this regard, the manufacturing sector has an important role to play in providing consumer goods and inputs to agriculture, in processing its outputs and creating job opportunities. Eritrea's underground cluster of small-scale industries, which have earned international acclaim for their miraculous performance in serving the war front, and the old industrial base mostly crippled during the war, will have to be restructured and revitalized to serve as the core for the budding

Eritrean manufacturing sector. The restructuring and/or revitalizing of these industries should take the following public policy issues into consideration:

1. The manufacturing sector as defined above could be converted into pub-lic, private and mixed sector enterprises with the state playing the role of the "guardian" of public interest. The government of Eritrea should particularly be aware of the benefits to be reaped by strengthening the private and mixed sectors' contribution to industrial development. In the context of an acute shortage of development funds and the govern-ment's wide range of commitments to social and other development pro-jects, the private sector can serve as an important source of investment. Legislation to promote private sector investment could be introduced with a range of tax exemptions and customs duty exonerations on approved investments, with the duration of these privileges defined according to the size of the proposed investment. Enterprises approved and designated as having priority may fall within the following sec-tors:
   a. Agro-industrial companies engaging in both agriculture and the transformation processing of agricultural products in Eritrea, as well as those companies developing and/or transforming Eritrean crops and livestock.
   b. Companies transforming, manufacturing, assembling or distrib-uting articles for general domestic consumption from domestic and imported raw materials or semi-finished products.
   c. Building and construction companies providing low cost housing or engaged in rebuilding or expanding national infrastructure.
2. Highest consideration must be given to the framework in which the restructuring of the manufacturing sector takes place, that is, efficient management practice, human resources development, establishment and implementation of an incentive system that aims at improving the public and private sector, mobilization of domestic investable resources and promotion of private initiatives.
3. In this phase, heavy dependence on imported manufactured goods could be inevitable. Given the magnitude of devastation due to war and drought, domestic sources for most manufactured goods will under-standably be insignificant. This trend, however, cannot be allowed to continue indefinitely. Efforts should be made to limit imported goods to the immediate needs of the population, and to develop an indigenous capability to produce most consumer goods thereby reducing depen-dence on imported manufactures. To achieve these capabilities, it will be necessary to import carefully selected sets of production equipment, including capital goods.

B. Phase Two

In this phase the objective is to minimize dependence on imported con-sumer goods by developing the manufacturing sector to a technological level capable of producing manufactured goods for the domestic and possibly the foreign market. This requires the establishment of an indigenous capability to produce tools, machinery and other essential means of production for selected sectors without excessive dependence on foreign aid. The effort to establish this indigenous capability can be supported by policy measures such as: (1) restriction of capital goods imports in selected sectors, (2) promotion of imports of appropriate technologies for the domestic capital goods industries, and (3) development of local technological base.

C. Phase Three

Passing through a successful implementation of the first two phases of industrial development, the country will have solved excessive dependence on imported consumer goods by developing a capital goods sector with technological capability to produce consumer goods for both domestic and foreign markets. This leads to rising income, availability of more resources for leisure and the shifting of capital into expanding industrial sectors.

At this stage the most significant constraint to further expansion can be the limited market size, heavy dependence on imports of advanced technologies for the production of capital goods and the limitation of key investable resources. For this reason, the overall economic strategy and the industrialization process should take the following measures into consideration:

1. Formulate a strategy to expand and promote the export of consumer and capital goods. Initially, this strategy should emphasize and capitalize on Eritrea's proximity to the Sudan, Ethiopia, Djibouti, Somalia and Arab countries across the Red Sea.
2. Develop a sustainable capital goods industries on the basis of indigenously developed designs. This will require a restriction of some foreign technologies, promotion of indigenous technological capabilities, and establishment and expansion of research and development institutes.
3. Inducement of foreign capital through a careful design. Import of foreign capital, if not carefully planned and targeted selectively, can lead to the exploitation of material and human resources of the country by foreign investors. To prevent this, the selection of industrial sectors falling under a foreign capital inducement act should be based on well thought-out criteria. Such criteria could include: contribution to the advancement of technology, promotion of employment opportunities, efficient maximization of local resources and contribution to the balanced development of the overall national economy. It can be followed by a foreign capital inducement act regulating priorities in the industrial sector as to where the foreign capital is to be applied.

With Eritrea's commitment to industrialization and an outward-looking, industry-based policy, and with the help of foreign capital investment rather than foreign aid, it will be possible to generate an export expansion whose impact will be embodied in the achievements of the national economy. Such achievement will have to be measured by increased per capita GNP and the growth in the share of the manufacturing sector as a percentage of GNP.

Once the nation's economy grows, as measured by the above indicators, subsequent national plans should emphasize: (1) an economic structure for self-sustaining growth, (2) promotion of social development, and (3) technological innovation and improvements in productivity and efficiency.

VI. INSTITUTIONAL FRAMEWORK FOR INDUSTRY

To develop a meaningful industrial policy and to enhance its chances for a successful implementation, the formulation of an appropriate institutional framework is an essential precondition. The government must provide leadership by establishing a Department of Industries whose mission will be to develop a short- and long-term industrial policy for Eritrea and to guide its implementation. The department needs to be chartered to actively seek and encourage the involvement of all sectors — public, private and international institutions — in the industrialization process of Eritrea. The government should also enact the legislation and provide the necessary resources to the department.

In attempting to accomplish its mission the Department of Industries will face three major challenges: (1) coordinating Eritrea's industrial policy with the overall national economic policies, (2) identifying the right functional elements within the department itself to support the entire policy formulation and execution activities, and (3) involving the public at large.

The problem with coordination and creation of linkages to the national economic objectives could be effectively dealt with by creating an Industrial Development Coordination Committee (IDCC) comprising of government and private agencies involved in the country's economic and industrial development. The IDCC function could include prioritizing of new business ventures, development of industrial incentives, identifying critical technologies and opportunities for technology transfer, providing guidelines on importation of consumer, intermediate and capital goods based on the national objectives.

In order to develop a sound industrial policy and to make necessary periodic revisions, changes or updates to the policy, the department should insist that policy decisions are made based on sound research and facts. To promote and cultivate such a practice and to assist local and foreign industrial investors, the department may include the following institutes:

Policy Analysis: to conduct economic research and policy analysis; to measure and report on progress; and to evaluate the effectiveness of the industrial policy.

Standards Bureau: to set standards; to monitor and ensure that Eritrean industrial products meet or exceed national and international accepted standards; to promote the concept of quality and provide total quality tools such as statistical process control.

Data Bank: to gather, store and retrieve industry-relevant data and to provide access to those who need them.

Investments: to advise, guide and support Eritrean and foreign investors on procedural matters and investment proposals. To finance industrial projects, especially small-scale industries.

Research Institute: to promote public and private R&D in developing local raw materials for industrial input; focus on development and adaptation of industrial transferred technologies to the Eritrean environment.

Science and Technology: to promote the development of a "critical mass" of Eritreans capable of conducting basic research in science and technology as it pertains to industrial development.

VII. SUMMARY AND CONCLUSION

Eritrea's proven record of implementing a pragmatic policy of self-reliance during the struggle for independence in the past thirty years should continue to be the foundation of all national development plans. Such plans, by properly taking into consideration the prevailing international economic conditions, will provide the direction necessary to a continuously improving environment in Eritrea.

Eritrea has the human and material resources to successfully implement a well-planned and flexible industrial policy as outlined in this study. We thus recommend an immediate action to initiate an objective assessment of Eritrea's short- and long-term needs and the establishment of an organization to lead a national industrial policy-making process. The policy must be guided by Eritrea's national objectives. There should be a clear mapping from Eritrea's national objectives to the industrial policy documents.

Industrial policy should consist of approaches for phased stages of implementation. Initially it should be directed at meeting survival objectives, to be followed by a stage that emphasizes the development of locally manufactured goods and industrial support of agricultural objectives. The last stages should foster the creation and expansion of external markets through provision of quality and cost competitive products.

REFERENCES

Beije, P. R. (ed.). *A Competitive Future for Europe, Toward a Stronger Europe.*

Day, Charles R., Jr. 1991. "We Need a Better Policy," *Industry Week,* March 18, 1991.

Donovan, J. J. 1990. *Crisis in Technology.* Cambridge, Mass.: Cambridge Technology Group.

Cliffe, Lionel, and Basil Davidson (eds.). 1988. *The Long Struggle of Eritrea for Independence and Constructive Peace.* Trenton, N.J.: Red Sea Press.

Congress of the United States, Office of Technology Assessment. 1979. *Technology and East-West Trade.* Washington D.C.

Fisher, A.G.B. 1939. "Production: Primary, Secondary and Tertiary," *Economic Record* (June).

Henderson, Bruce D. 1989. "The Origin of Strategy," *Harvard Business Review* 6 (November/December):139–43.

Industry Africa. *Unido,* Vol. 4, November 20, 1990.

Industrial Development Review Series. *Unido,* June 1989.

_____. *Unido,* March 1989.

Meier, Gerald M., and William F. Steel. 1989. *Industrial Adjustment in Sub-Saharan Africa,* EDI Series in Economic Development. Oxford University Press.

Porter, Michael E. 1990. *The Competitive Advantage of Nations.* New York: Free Press.

Schultze, Charles. 1984. "Industrial Policy: A Dissent." In *National Industrial Policy,* edited by Thomas E. Petri. Boulder: Westview Press.

Tseggai, Araia. 1983. "Independent Eritrea: Economically Viable," *Horn of Africa,* 6(2):39–49.

Wriston, W. B. 1988/89. "Technology and Sovereignty." *Foreign Affairs* (Winter 1988/89):63–75.

MICRO AND SMALL-SCALE ENTERPRISES IN ECONOMIC DEVELOPMENT STRATEGY

Yacob Fisseha

I. INTRODUCTION

In the 1950s and 1960s, the accepted sustainable developmental model was investment in large, capital-intensive industries and vast integrated agricultural projects. Such a growth model was expected to benefit from economies of scale in modern production and management as well as overcome problems of lump-sum (indivisible) investment requirements. It was expected to accomplish this, at the same time generating adequate employment to absorb the growing labor force and pulling the rest of the economy along the path of economic growth.

In many developing countries, both private and public efforts and funds were marshalled toward this end. As one writer describes the situation, "Governments and the institutions they have set up, have tended to concentrate scarce financial and skilled human resources on projects which, like a good story, have a beginning, a middle and an end: on large industrial and agricultural schemes" (Glaser 1989).[1] The expected benefits never materialized; instead, many states incurred large external financial debts from which they have not been able to extricate themselves. Local investment resources were mobilized by siphoning a large share of the agricultural "surplus" production with no compensating benefits going back to the rural areas whose purchasing power was sapped by this very action.[2] Despite the passage of concessional and often discriminatory policies favoring large-scale enterprises (LSEs),[3] the result was for the most part a disappointment. Many such investments never became fully operational; if they did, they were enclaves of economic and social isolation in the midst of general impoverishment and technological backwardness. The employment they generated as a group was not sufficient enough to even put a dent on the unemployment rate of a growing labor force.[4] The major impact in fact was unintended factor (input) price distortions between the large- and the small-scale enterprises; thus, making certain factors of production artificially expensive or cheap.

Over the past twenty years or so, a new interest has been growing to promote what are commonly called micro and small-scale rural and urban enterprises (MSEs). MSEs could be defined as non-farm enterprises whose total labor force is at most 25 to 50 people; the very small among these, employing one or two people are called micro enterprises.[5] Such enterprises are involved in market-oriented production, commerce and service activities.[6] In many developing countries, enterprises with employment of ten or less account for up to 95 percent of their entire (non-farm) establishments.

The major characteristics of MSEs are as broad as their size spectrum is wide. Some common basic attributes include the dominance of rural MSEs, small size, high participation rate by women, and employment of a fifth to a third of the total national labor force.[7] Some MSEs are truly micro and others are modern small-scale establishments. It is important to remember the wide diversity of sizes, types, locations and production techniques when one speaks of MSEs as a group. Efforts at policy formulations should also keep in mind this diversity of characteristics. The basis for increased attention for these types of small enterprises was the fact that quite a large number of them were already in existence employing thousands of the unskilled and those with little formal education (i.e., a group of labor force with diminished employment opportunity in the formal or LSEs sector).

In many developing countries, MSEs are usually not only ignored or forgotten by policymakers, particularly those MSEs at the lower end of the size spectrum, but also swim against a policy tide of official bias, indifference and outright hostility toward them. In fact, until the likelihood of failure of the large-scale, capital-intensive principal approach to economic development became increasingly apparent, MSEs were not only neglected but often actively discouraged. Even the less informal units are victims of such bias. One observer notes, "Indeed, to some extent, governments are hostile to these almost-informal operators, seeing in their marginal status an affront to a tidily-organized economy" (Glaser 1989). It must be noted that what is faulted is the sole reliance on large-scale investments for economic development; otherwise, both MSEs and LSEs could and should play an integral and complementary role depending on the nature and market relationship of their products in a competitive pricing system.

The organization of the remaining part of this paper is as follows: First the role of the MSEs in developing countries is discussed. This is followed by a brief discussion on characteristic constraints of MSEs. The third part deals with forms of assistance and modes of delivery; and the final part is summary and conclusion.

II. MICRO AND SMALL-SCALE ENTERPRISES IN ECONOMIC DEVELOPMENT

Both Marxist and capitalist economic thoughts rationalize the existence of MSEs as a sign of a "pre-capitalist" economy that has not yet made a complete transition to an industrial state. However, such an explanation could not be convincingly sustained, given that small-scale enterprises account today for a major share of the production and employment in the industrialized countries, including the United States, Japan and Germany. For example, MSEs with employment size of 1 to 4 people accounted for 19% in Japan as of 1975; the corresponding figures were 60% for India (as of 1973), 36% for South Korea (1975), and 49% for Kenya (1969). In the United States, where small MSEs are defined as those that employ 1 to 99 people, they accounted for 22% of the labor force in 1967 (Cortes et al. 1987). There is no indication that their shares have fallen in these countries. In Italy too, the "informal" sector accounts for 26% of the non-agricultural labor force and 15% of the total national gross domestic product (GDP) (Sardoni 1990). In fact, the major surges in export and employment generated during the late 1980s and early 1990s in these countries were primarily due to the small-scale enterprises sector.[8]

Current pressing problems in Eritrea are of different nature and leave very little room to maneuver. As a result, the available alternative choices during this difficult time of national reconstruction and rehabilitation are bound to be highly constrained. In the short run, both small-scale and large-scale establishments will need some sort of assistance to help them stand on their feet. And long-term development decisions will have to be made in an environment of invariably limited resources. Nevertheless, it is proper to ask whether MSEs can play a critical role in Eritrean economic scene and what benefits can be gained by deliberately incorporating them in a strategy of broad-based economic development. Historically, Eritrean commercial and industrial strength has fluctuated widely due to an economic environment heavily influenced by external factors. Formal employment grew substantially after the mid–1930s due to increased demand in transport, housing and manufacturing to enhance Fascist Italy's colonial expansionist intentions. For example, there were only 56 industrial firms before 1930; but by 1939, the number jumped to 2,198, plus 2,690 commercial firms (Yohannes 1991). Industrial products included "leather goods, cement, boots and shoes, boot polish, hand tools, buttons, matches, lamp shades, canned foods, fish meal, fish oil, pickles, flour, seed oil, tomato sauce, pottery, paints, alcoholic beverages, sodas and refractory bricks" (ibid.).[9]

After a period of a steady and continued growth during the Second World War, Eritrean industrial output started to decline.[10] Beginning with the early 1950s, the decline became an outright deterioration and disintegration as a result of deliberate Ethiopian policy both to consolidate its political hold on Eritrea and to secure a stranglehold on the latter's economy.[11] During the federation period alone, Eritrean industrial and commercial employment (excluding farming and animal husbandry) declined by 17 percent between 1950 and 1961 while the labor force increased by 28 percent; the number of commercial license holders declined by 90 percent during the same period (Ellingson 1985).[12] After Eritrea's annexation by Ethiopia, the situation became worse. Sherman notes, "What was once a moderately productive light industrial economy has, in the 1970s, been almost totally dismantled by the Ethiopian government . . . Since 1974, the Ethiopians have systematically transported industrial equipment out of Asmara, transferring it to various destinations in Ethiopia itself." Examples include the canning and slaughtering facilities and the nail factory.

The surge of interest in promoting MSEs throughout the world is a belated acceptance of the important role they play in the national economies. One source notes, "Experience gained from economies which have exhibited success in developing shows that micro-enterprises are a major engine in industrial and commercial development" (Morgan 1989). Before discussing the various benefits to be gained from active promotion of MSEs in the Eritrean scene, one needs to pay attention to the following caveat: MSEs do not in themselves solve the employment or income problems of a country. However, if a substantial part of the national economy and the people that depend on it are not to be left out, MSEs must be fully and consciously integrated into the national policy environment. Similarly, "Small firms must not be regarded as an isolated sector for which suitable solutions must be found, but as the general norm around which everything is organized — currency stability, free trade (including foreign trade), tax incentives, soft loans, etc." (see Glaser 1989).

Eritreans have gained a unique and invaluable experience of social and economic survival through a strategy of self-reliance during the arduous armed struggle for independence. The importance of small or "petty" producers, traders and craftsmen to make local and regional economies function properly was gradually and firmly accepted and encouraged during this time. There are hundreds of skilled workers who were trained in the basics of production, maintenance and improvisation during the war years, who can easily start their own ventures or work in small and large firms. Thus, it seems logical to place the MSEs at the center of a national economic recovery program.

There are at least four compelling reasons why such a move should be at the forefront of an economic policy: they are economic, technological, social and environmental benefits.[13] Each is briefly discussed below.

A. Economic Benefits

Relative to the large-scale establishments, there are a few key economic issues which justify the promotion of MSEs in an overall sustainable economic development strategy. Such comparative analysis could be divided primarily into supply and demand side empirical issues.

1. Supply Side Question. On the supply side, the major issues are related to the quality and relative quantity of factors of production (e.g., labor and capital). Policy measures affect the accessibility of these (and other) resources and services) to MSEs, which in turn determine their relative levels or intensity of use in production. MSEs are particularly well suited in their accessibility to unskilled labor, in creating new jobs at lower cost, efficiency in the use of scarce capital, modest demand for foreign exchange, backward and forward linkages with other sectors of the economy, and creating and marshalling scarce family savings into productive activities.

It is well known that the cost (total investment per worker) of job creation is much cheaper in MSEs compared to their large-scale counterparts. The cost in large scale enterprises is five to ten times more expensive.[14] In addition to creating jobs, MSEs also produce every year a cadre of trained workers and entrepreneurs experienced in entry-level technical and management skills (thus, raising a country's pool of trained human power). This is made possible through employment modes that include on-the-job vocational and entrepreneurial skills training and apprenticeship arrangements.

A basic issue currently debated in development expert circles is whether MSEs are more efficient in the use of capital (that is, more output from a given size of capital investment) than their large-scale counterparts. There is increasing evidence that they are at least as efficient. Both their lower cost of job creation and capital efficiency make MSEs labor-intensive outfits ideally suited to utilize a country's most abundant resource, labor, while economizing on the most limiting resources, investment capital and large scale management.

By going with labor-intensive activities, MSEs also place less demand on foreign exchange needed for the purchase of imported techniques of production (both embodied and disembodied technology).[15] The saving in foreign exchange is even greater as some MSEs also produce goods that substitute for imports or that can be exported directly.

Another major advantage of MSEs is that because bank loans are usually inaccessible to them, their entrepreneurs tend to mobilize their own or family savings, a financial mobilization that may not otherwise occur.

Finally, MSEs could have both backward and forward linkages that help boost other sectors. For example, blacksmiths have forward linkages with agriculture through the production of vital tools and implements. The major backward linkages consist of primary products used as inputs for MSEs in the processing area. Further, among the most important linkages both for rural and urban settings are consumption linkages where low-income consumers buy a large share of the output produced by MSEs. This consumption demand is believed to induce rural households to exert more effort to raise their income through increased agricultural production.[16]

2. Demand Side Issues. One of the most crucial determinants of success among MSEs is the availability of product demand. In practice there could be three main sources of demand for MSEs products: final consumers (private or public), various forward linkages with other sectors (including limited subcontracting), and the export market. Whatever the source of their product demand, relevant questions include (a) the staying power or continuity of MSEs product demand in the face of growing consumer income levels, and (b) the marketing skills of entrepreneurs to at least maintain their relative product market shares during such growth.

A greater part of the demand for MSEs products comes from lower and medium income consumers both in urban and rural localities — demand that is not normally met by LSEs due to their high-priced products. However, because the majority of the MSEs are located in rural settings, rural consumers are the main buyers of their products. This can have positive impact on promoting growth of the MSEs sector to raise general rural incomes (or arguably improve income distribution). Government purchases are not usually substantial; however, direct or indirect (tourist-related) export demands are sometimes considerable, particularly for "culturally-oriented" craft items.

An important question on the demand side is whether products of the labor-intensive MSEs are "inferior" goods whose consumption will decline as general income levels of consumers rise. The reasoning behind this is that consumers would shift to "better" quality goods and services imported or produced by capital-intensive, large-scale domestic enterprises sector as their income level rises. Empirical evidence shows that MSEs are growing both in size and in number and that their products are not necessarily "inferior goods" whose consumption declines as consumers' income rises (Liedholm and Mead 1987).[17] In any case, because the rise in income has to be quite substantial in many developing countries before consumers will abandon MSEs products in favor of modern, capital-intensive products (either locally produced or imported), the demand for MSEs products will remain high for quite sometime. The existence of an MSEs sector that substantially contributes to income and employment in the developed countries supports this assertion.

The overwhelming majority of MSEs being located in rural or near rural settings, measures takes to increase the per capita level of income in the agricultural sector translate into growth in the MSEs sector; agricultural incomes produce surplus value, which in turn creates markets for MSEs products.

B. Technological Benefits

Benefits, in the form of appropriate technology, include MSEs employing local expertise to fix, run or make machinery adaptable to local conditions utilizing local resources. Although MSEs will utilize new techniques of production and management consistent with their needs, their demands for such resources are largely met from local resources. Historically, Eritreans have been good at adopting and maintaining new techniques to suit their specific needs. Experiences of self-reliance under difficult situations gained during the struggle for independence were both an expression of such adaptability as well as a solid foundation for future technical adeptness. Thus, given the right policy and market environment, Eritrean ingenuity and enterprising disposition bode well for a thriving MSEs in the country.

Another major contribution by MSEs, which often goes unrecognized, is the informal or on-the-job training (e.g., through apprenticeship system) of hundreds of unskilled individuals in all facets of business activities such as production, marketing and management.[18] Many of the workers end up establishing their own MSEs or are hired by LSEs as skilled workers.

C. Social and Economic Benefits

There are a number of social benefits obtained from promoting MSEs in the economy. The occupational environment in MSEs is thought to involve more interpersonal and human interactions than in bigger establishments. MSEs are usually well distributed among small towns, villages and other rural areas; consequently, benefits such as employment and income generated by MSEs are distributed geographically.[19] Further, empirical data from other countries show that MSEs usually employ women, the unskilled and the poor. All these benefits tend to alleviate rural poverty and contribute towards a more equitable distribution of economic benefits.

In the political sphere, MSEs' employment in many developing countries has effectively averted potential urban social unrest and dissatisfaction. Furthermore, by diluting the control by few powerful economic entities, MSEs contribute toward more autonomy of the state, to make independent (unbiased) economic policies for the good of the whole country.[20]

D. MSEs and Ecology

The micro or small MSEs tend to use renewable resources (such as forest-based raw materials), recycle old ones (such as metal scraps) and emit far less toxic discharges, which are harmful to health and the environment, compared with their large-scale counterparts. They also consume less energy, require less communication and transportation networks, which means less investment in and maintenance of infrastructure.

This is not to say that everything about MSEs is positive. There are a few aspects of MSEs activities which could degrade the ecology or human health. In fact, if proper steps are not taken, certain activities, such as basket-making and firewood/charcoal production, could have a deleterious impact on the environment. Unregulated, such activities contribute to deforestation and subsequent soil erosion.

Roadside or open market vending is another activity that requires careful regulation in terms of sanitation and product handling. This is particularly true with food items. Food items spread out at ground level in the market, by the roadside or other places for sale collect dust and other impu-

rities and spoil easily. What is required of such activities is education of proprietors and the securing of places that are suitable and accessible to both
consumers and vendors. With proper policy measures, such MSEs have benefits that far outweigh any negative impacts incidental to their activities.

III. CHARACTERISTIC CONSTRAINTS OF MSEs

The incidence and severity of problems associated with MSEs vary by
age, size, type, and location of the MSEs as well as the quality of entrepre-
neurship. Major and typical problems faced by MSEs include shortages of raw
materials, intense product competition (demand shortage), shortage of investment and working capital from formal sources (e.g., banks), and lack of commercial and technical informational assistance. Problems related to
management weaknesses also exist but are less tractable to document.

Problems related to lack of raw materials are often a direct result of a
country's inability to generate sufficient foreign exchange, inefficiencies in the
delivery system of inputs, or dependence on depleting resources. The problem could be exacerbated by policies that distort the relative prices of factors
or inputs. Furthermore, even though the imported raw material used by
MSEs is usually very small, it could be an integral part of the production
process. Such a small but vital ingredient could still be the limiting factor in
the production process.

Keen competition, and thus shortage of demand for individual MSEs
products, is not surprising. The sector is characterized by a high turnover
rate. Each year thousands of MSEs enter a market that is already experi-
encing cutthroat product competition and result in thousands of failures.
The enterprises that survive and persevere seem to pay more attention to
product quality, marketing skills and to avoiding any diversion of badly needed business funds into other ventures.

The question of corroborating financial sources is a typically problematic constraint. Because lack of finance is such a common complaint by MSEs'
proprietors, there is a tendency to dismiss the obvious need as unimportant
or as an excuse for some other underlying enterprise shortcomings. It is true
that MSEs proprietors may be more readily disposed to cite financial problems than others, particularly if the researcher is perceived as coming from
a government agency intending to "help" them. Nevertheless, study after
study in many countries have shown that lack of finance, especially short-
term or working capital, is a serious handicap to the survival and growth of
MSEs. Lack of access to formal credit is one of the most common complaints
expressed by MSEs entrepreneurs. Empirical evidence has shown again that
this problem exists. Typically, micro enterprises lack formal bookkeeping
and budgetary procedures as well as adequate loan collateral even for their
small loan applications. As a result, formal credit sources, such as commercial banks, find it time consuming and costly to evaluate, extend and monitor small credits to small enterprises. However, some of the reluctance by
such institutions to extend credit to MSEs is due to lack of understanding of
how the MSE sector functions. Training of bank credit officers on MSEs activities could be extremely helpful.

Technical needs of MSEs is a multifaced issue that requires careful examination. MSEs may have carved out a market niche for their products that their large-scale counterparts do not cater to, but they may also be in direct competition with large-scale establishments in some markets. For this reason, technical training must be provided to MSEs' proprietors in accordance with the size of their enterprises and type of product they present to the market. For example, there is little justification to urge the very small MSEs to adopt standard bookkeeping procedures; all they require may be simple recording of key transactions consistent with their needs and with the demand on their time and ability. Training of production techniques particularly in wood, metal, leather and garment works is typically very crucial. Such training becomes even more vital as MSEs producers compete with large-scale enterprise products (local or imported) and as they move to higher quality products for higher income consumers. The finishing stage of a production process is usually the weakest area as far as MSEs ability to compete in the formal market is concerned.

Finally, a proprietor's capacity to deal with a problem depends on his or her experience, the size and location of the enterprise and the availability of supportive services or organizations to help solve a given problem.

IV. FORMS OF ASSISTANCE AND MODES OF DELIVERY

Whether their problems are related to finance, product marketing, production technique or raw materials, there are a number of key issues involved in considering assistance to MSEs. These issues include the following: (1) types of intended beneficiaries, (2) objective of the assistance program, (3) the complementarity of some assistance schemes, and (4) the mode of delivering assistance to MSEs. Following is a brief discussion of each issue.

A. Intended Beneficiaries

At any given time, there may be literally tens of thousands of small, diverse MSEs scattered in a given country. Even though the MSEs subsector may be defined with an upper "employment" size limit of ten (or twenty-five or fifty, as the case may be), the average employment is only about two people per enterprise. Indeed, two-thirds of them are usually one operator running his or her own enterprise; about a fourth are those that employ up to three people. In fact, less than a tenth of the MSEs would have a total employment of six people or more. It was indicated earlier that many of them will face problems whose effects vary by individual enterprise. It is impossible to give each proprietor facing constraints individual attention even if there existed a strong "industrial" extension service.[21] Fortunately, given the right policy environments, micro enterprises are resilient and highly resourceful, and direct individualized government assistance may not always be critical. This is particularly true with the micro or very small outfits. Therefore, one needs to make a careful assessment of the objectives of any assistance scheme and weigh its potential impact in order to avoid spreading available project resources too thin. There should be a careful balancing between issues of equity and efficiency in providing assistance.

Although certain assistance schemes will not reach all deserving units, there are certain policy measures that can generally and positively affect a large number of enterprises. Such desirable policy measures that can open ways for MSEs to help themselves include: (1) quick and easy licensing and taxing procedures with minimum transaction costs; (2) preventing factor price distortions, which adversely affect the MSEs relative to the LSEs sector (or vice versa); (3) relaxing restrictive commercial or industrial area zoning that impede growth of MSEs (better to build market stalls and sheds in strategic locations); and (4) weighing carefully steps, such as pricing regulations, intended to help the MSEs sector; for example, interest rate ceilings could be counterproductive if private commercial credit institutions are forced by such a move to divert credit to more lucrative sectors, such as LSEs, or to raise MSEs collateral requirement. The impact of concessionary credit in the context of national development objectives needs to be carefully and objectively examined for efficiency and equity in resource allocation.

B. The Objectives of Assistance Scheme

To have clear overall objectives of an assistance program is very important for efficient use of limited resources. Examples of relevant questions that should be addressed include the following: Is the assistance to foster the creation of new MSEs or to improve existing ones? Is the scheme intended for individual producers of a given socioeconomic status (e.g., the very poor) or is it for group or community producers (e.g., all women engaged in basket production individually or as a co-op)? Is the assistance scheme intended as a welfare (humanitarian), developmental or is it to be operated on the basis of commercial sustainability? All three objectives could be justified; what is important is that the goals are clearly stated and the basis of evaluation clearly understood. Whether the goals have humanitarian, developmental or commercial ends, it is important to continually monitor the scheme and steer it toward the intended goals. Well-intentioned assistance schemes could end up being counterproductive if they are not scrutinized for their technical, economic or welfare integrity.

C. The Complementarity of Assistance Schemes

Certain types of assistance need other schemes in order to succeed. For example, any credit program may have to be accompanied by some technical assistance to improve product/service quality and productivity. Again, what is needed may be first to remove unintended barriers to accessibility of services (e.g., credit) and then concentrate on direct assistance to certain groups or industries that show promising features for job creation or product export. Sometimes the provision of relevant commercial and technical information on a timely basis might be all that is needed.

D. The Mode of Delivery of Services

Although the state has to assume the delivery of certain services, others could well be provided by nongovernmental organizations (NGOs). Some NGOs have specialized resources and flexibility which a government may not have. Nevertheless, it is important to understand the goals, capacity and complementarity of NGOs services before their involvement. In certain situations, for example, the state could provide market information more effectively through its media coverage on newspapers and the radio, and NGOs could concentrate on individualized technical assistance in production, marketing or management.

To see how the above-discussed four major issues come together, let's consider credit. One way to indirectly help all MSEs could be not to impose an interest ceiling on commercial loans to MSEs and to educate the banking institution on the workings of the MSEs sector and on the potential benefits of making financial services widely available throughout the country. Also, selective credit could be provided to certain categories of industries that promise to generate more jobs, export products or alleviate poverty. NGOs could be allowed to help the selected MSEs prepare credit worthy bookkeeping, including budgeting, and production and marketing plans; the state could help provide specialized services such as technical assistance and management-related training. Assured of an acceptable risk (perhaps through a credit guarantee scheme), banks would be willing to extend credit to such MSEs.

A number of novel ways have been tried to help MSEs. These include the extending of credit under the responsibility of a group and not an individual proprietor although the credit might be used by the individual. Thus, a group of five to ten proprietors borrow funds for individual use; however, the monitoring of use and repayment of loans is done by the group as a whole. Such successful credit schemes have been tried with urban and rural micro and small-scale enterprises as well as landless and poor farmers. Small credits, say $500, could be extended to small proprietors who apply as a group. Peer pressure and desire to maintain good reputation keep repayment rates very high, usually above 90 percent. Another attempt to help MSEs proprietors is to use what is called a "One-Stop Office" where proprietors can deal with all or most government formalities and requirements at a single place or office. Such offices must also provide the entrepreneur with information relevant for decision making.

V. SUMMARY AND CONCLUSION

After a faltering beginning relying solely on a highly capital-intensive development model, many countries are belatedly paying attention to the labor-intensive mode of production by micro and small-scale enterprises (MSEs). The advantage from MSEs are several: They generate more employment per unit of capital; they are at least as efficient as their large-scale counterparts in capital productivity; they present less damage to the environment; and they are geographically well distributed throughout a country, thus distributing widely income and employment benefits. Also, MSEs cater to specific market segments that may not be met either through local large-scale producers or imports.

MSEs have a number of constraints. The major ones are intense product competition from fellow MSEs producers, unavailability of investment and working capital, shortage of raw materials, and lack of technical assistance. In this situation, the state has a vital role to play either directly or indirectly.

Eritrea had a long history of experience in small- and medium-sized industrial and commercial enterprises. Unfortunately, many of such enterprises were weakened, dismantled or transferred to Ethiopia during the past forty years, beginning in the early 1950s when the federal arrangement with Ethiopia was instituted. On the other hand, under the principle of self-reliance, during the armed struggle years, small-scale productive units were effectively utilized by the Eritrean nationalists, and private entrepreneurs were increasingly encouraged to be involved. This bodes well for the promotion of and progress in micro and small-scale enterprises in Eritrea.

However, to make progress in such productive activities, a clear policy direction that incorporates such activities in overall economic development strategy must be stipulated. Above all, rules and regulations must be carefully examined for inadvertent discrimination against MSEs either in favor of LSEs or otherwise.

Finally, one cannot make intelligent and prudent decisions about the Eritrean MSEs subsector without adequate empirical knowledge about the subsector. For understandable reasons, there does not currently exist a comprehensive nation-wide data base that one can draw from for policy formulation. The collection of such information (on both rural and urban localities) should be seriously considered in order to have at least the order of magnitude on the current size, geographical distribution and economic effectiveness of the subsector. Such information would serve: (1) to put the MSEs subsector employment and income in a national context for purposes of setting priorities, and (2) to provide a benchmark of information against which future evaluations of the subsector could be compared.

NOTES

1.   case, small- and medium-sized enterprises (SMEs) are defined as those that employ fifty people or less.
2.   One researcher found that 76 percent of Kenya's gross capital formation was supplied by agriculture (Sharpley 1981).
3.   It will be helpful to the reader to note the following acronyms used in this paper:

LSEs	Large-scale enterprises (including manufacturing, trade and service activities);
LSIs	Large scale manufacturing (industrial) Enterprises;
MSEs	Micro and small-scale enterprises (micro refers to the very small units);
SSEs	Small-scale enterprises (including manufacturing, trade and service activities);
SSIs	Small-scale industrial (manufacturing) enterprises;
SMEs	Small and medium enterprises (including activities in manufacturing, trade and services).

Less commonly used acronyms include:

SSC	SSEs in commercial or trade (SST) activities only;
SSS	SSEs in service activities only;
LSC	LSEs in commercial or trade (LST) activities only;
LSS	LSEs in service activities.

4.   There are rare cases when investment on large scale is absolutely necessary either to take advantage of economies of scale or necessitated by lump sum (indivisible) capital investment.
5.   Two things should be noted here: One, total employment includes proprietors, family members, hired workers and apprentices working in the enterprise. Two, in many cases MSEs have also been defined as enter-

prises with employment less than twenty-five and in some cases less than fifty. How MSEs are defined is usually a function of the stage of economic development of a country; a small size establishment for developed countries may be one with as high as 250 to 500 employees. For many African countries, an employment of fifty is a large number and accounts almost for 95–98 percent of their entire commercial and manufacturing establishments; a 50 employment upper size limit was first used in Kenya by the ILO and has been used since in several countries. MSEs activities are also sometimes known as micro, cottage, or "informal."

6.   Examples include furniture making, trade, blacksmith, tailoring, metal works, tannery, handicraft, flour mills, vending, etc.

7..   The following tabular presentation demonstrates the basic features of MSEs in four African countries of varying resource endowments and socioeconomic characteristics:

	Lesotho	Niger	Zambia	Botswana
Population (Million)	1.7	7.25	8.25	1.33
Estimated # of MSEs	103,000	728,480	340,000	48,000
Estimated # Employment[a]	160,000	1,122,000	575,000	88,000
Total of Labor Force in MSEs Employment (%)	20	33	17	20
Percent of MSEs Employment in MSEs Employing < 6 [b]	97.7	97.9	98.6	95
MSEs in Rural Areas (%)	80	93	85	69
MSEs in Rural Towns (%)	8	3	8	7
MSEs owned by Women (%)	71	62	60	75
Women in MSEs Employ(%)[c]	59	56	54	72
Households with 50% or more of their Income from MSEs (%)	50	53	45	56

Source: Author's research in the four countries.

a This total number includes proprietors, family members, hired workers, and apprentices working in MSEs.

b That is MSEs whose total employment is five people or less.

c This is the proportion of all the labor force (including female proprietors) accounted for by females.

8.   But, this begs the question of what determines relative survival and adaptiveness in time of economic stagnation or decline; suffice it to say that faced with the same weak economic environment, the smaller enterprises often seem to be more adaptive and flexible than their large-scale counterparts.

9.   For details of Eritrean industrial growth during the Italian colonial period, see Okbazghi Yohannes (1991), pp. 13–15.

10.   Some of the products manufactured during this period included beer, bottles, glassware, brandy, chemicals, cigarettes, dairy products, glue, lime, marble, margarine, matches, mineral water, nails, oxygen, paper, plywood, soap, soft drinks, textile products, tiles, tires, wine and wires.

11.   For details of Ethiopian economic policy in Eritrea, see Araia Tseggai (1983), Richard Sherman (1980:118); and Okbazghi Yohannes (1991:13–15).

12. For details see Ellingson (1985:218).
13. The rate of return to private investment in MSEs is very high, sometimes close to 30 percent. On first impression, such level of return may imply that resources should flow to this attractive subsector. There are three fundamental reasons why this may not happen: (1) the scale of operation is so small that those with investible resources are not attracted to such activities; (2) for the very small would-be entrepreneurs, lack of initial investment and operating capital is a major deterrent; and (3) the degree of commitment of MSEs proprietors to their businesses is such that separation of business from family affairs is usually blurred.
14. The average capital investment per worker was small in forest-based (i.e., using raw materials such as wood, reed, twigs, bamboo, etc.) manufacturing MSEs: $1,515 in Jamaica, $391 in Honduras, $254 in Sierra Leone and $94 in Bangladesh (Fisseha 1985). The figure is even much smaller for other kinds of MSEs.
15. "Embodied" and "disembodied" refer to whether advanced knowledge is incorporated into the physical design of the machinery.
16. Among the most important linkages of agriculture with forest-based MSEs are the following: (1) farm households serve as source of demand and (seasonal) labor for the F-B enterprises, and (2) savings or supplementary income from agriculture may be used to start or expand the F-B enterprise. In turn the MSEs provide agriculture with (1) inputs such as ox carts, wooden agricultural tools, crates/boxes, grain baskets and other containers, (2) rural construction materials and services, and (3) channel some income generated in the MSEs sector to investment in agriculture. Because of the nature of their activities, the backward linkages of F-B MSEs to agriculture are weak. A good example of such linkage is the use of cotton fibers and leather in upholstery work.
17. A demand study in Sierra Leone showed that MSEs products are not inferior and thus a general rise in income levels leads to higher consumption of such products. The elasticities of income for forest-based MSEs products was 1.61 indicating that a 10 percent rise in general income level of households would result in a 16.1 percent increase in the consumption of these items. The Sierra Leone study also indicates that development strategies that result in more equitable income distribution (such as enhancing rural household income through alternative income generating activities) would result in more consumption of MSEs' products (and hence more employment in micro and small-scale enterprise).
18. From a study the author conducted in Jamaica, about 4,000 individuals are trained on the job by the thousands of MSEs in manufacturing activities found throughout the country. About three-fourths of the proprietors obtained their training from on-the-job training in manufacturing MSEs. Such informal training was particularly prevalent in woodwork, metal works, shoemaking, garment and craft works and repairs (Fisseha 1982).
19. Given the facts that MSEs account for a fourth to a third of a country's labor force and that more than two-thirds of them are found in rural areas, any measure that increases the income of MSEs or helps create viable ones would also help to raise the general level of income in rural areas.

20. In comparing South Korea and Taiwan with Argentina, Brazil and Mexico, Rhys Jenkins states, "The key to the superior industrial performance of the East Asian Newly Industrialized Countries (NICs) does not lie in the general superiority of export-oriented industrialization strategies over import substitution, or of market-oriented policies over state intervention, as some writers have suggested. It is rather the ability of the state to direct the accumulation process in the direction which is required by capitalist development at particular points in time which is crucial. . . . Such observations serve to reinforce the argument that the relative autonomy of the state is a crucial factor in explaining rapid industrial development in the Newly Industrialized Countries" (1991). According to Jenkins, all five countries practice major state intervention; what makes the East Asian NICs' intervention *effective* is its "flexibility, selectivity, coherence and promotion rather than regulation" (ibid).

21. One fact about industrial extension service is that it can be very expensive, and it usually deals with the supply side of issues leaving the demand side unattended. Thus, products may be produced but there may not be buyers.

SELECTED REFERENCES

Cortes, Mariluz, Albert Berry, and Ashfaq Ishag. 1987. *Success in Small and Medium-Scale Enterprises: The Evidence from Colombia.* Oxford University Press, published for the World Bank.

Ellingson, Lloyd S. 1985. "Eritrea: Separation and Irredentism, 1941–1985." Unpublished Ph.D. dissertation. East Lansing: Department of History, Michigan State University.

Fisseha, Yacob. 1982. "Management Characteristics, Practices, and Performance in the Small Scale Manufacturing Enterprises: Jamaican Milieu." Unpublished Ph.D. dissertation. East Lansing: Department of Agricultural Economics, Michigan State University.

_____. 1985. *The Contribution of Small-Scale Forest-Based Processing Enterprises to Rural Non-Farm Employment and Income in Selected Developing Countries.* Rome: FAO publication MISC/85/4.

Glaser, Tom. 1989. "Small and Medium-Sized Enterprises," *The Courier,* No. 115 (May/June); a publication of the Africa Caribbean-Pacific-European Community.

Jenkins, Rhys. 1991. "The Political Economy of Industrialization: A Comparison of Latin American and East Asian Newly Industrialized Countries," in *Development and Change* 22, 2 (April).

Liedholm, Carl, and Donald Mead. 1987. *Small Scale Industries in Developing Countries: Empirical Evidence and Policy Implication.* MSU International Development Paper No. 9. East Lansing (48824): Department of Agricultural Economics: Michigan State University.

Sardoni, Claudio. 1990. "The `Informal Sector': An Estimate of its Impact on the Italian Economy," in *Development 1990:3/4,* a journal of the Society of International Development (SID).

Sharpley, Jennifer. 1981. "Resource Transfers Between the Agricultural and Non-Agricultural Sectors: 1964–1977," in Tony Killick (ed.), *Papers on the*

Kenyan Economy: Performance, Problems and Policies. Nairobi: Heinemann.

Sherman, Richard. 1980. *Eritrea: The Unfinished Revolution.* New York: Praeger.

Tseggai, Araia. 1983. "Independent Eritrea: Economically Viable?" *Horn of Africa* 6(2).

Yohannes, Okbazghi. 1991. *Eritrea: A Pawn in World Politics.* Gainesville: University of Florida Press.

CHAPTER 6

NATURAL RESOURCE DEVELOPMENT AND CONSTRUCTION

WATER RESOURCE DEVELOPMENT
AND MANAGEMENT IN ERITREA:
PROBLEMS AND POLICY IMPLICATIONS

Prepared by
The Water Resource Subcommission, EPLF[1]

I. INTRODUCTION

The importance of proper utilization of a nation's water resources to the overall national economic development should be obvious. The presence of ample water resources is a vital boost to the development of an economy; its absence would be extremely detrimental to development efforts. Thus, it is justifiable to consider water resources as one of the main sectors of a national economy.

Eritrea's economy is basically dependent on agriculture. Over 80 percent of the population is rural. The main rural activities are rain-fed agriculture and/or animal husbandry. The rural population, at present, is completely dependent on rainfall, which has been not only inconsistent and irregular, but at times nonexistent during the past twenty years or more. Consequently, the Eritrean population has been adversely affected. A sizable proportion of the population has been displaced due to the drying up of water points and a complete lack of harvest. Tens of thousands of herds have been completely wiped out for lack of drinking water and fodder. This has resulted in the near total breakdown of the socioeconomic fabric in wide areas of the country. As a result, the majority of the Eritrean people have become completely dependent on food donations from humanitarian organizations.

To alleviate the existing dependency on food aid and to set the Eritrean economy in motion again, major water conservation projects have to be undertaken. These projects could be aimed at both the rehabilitation of existing structures and the construction of new structures. The Water Resources unit, the main responsible authority in the field, has to play its role effectively.

The precarious nature of the rainfall is affecting not only the agricultural sector but also the drinking water supply system. Needless to say, water is one of the basic human needs; without water no life can exist. Thus, drinking water is a question of life and death. For a community, to ensure its existence, a dependable source of drinking water has to be guaranteed. As previously mentioned, the recurrent drought has resulted in the drying up of many water points. The rehabilitation of these water points and the construction of new ones are also one of the main responsibilities of the Water Resources unit.

A healthy population is a prerequisite for the development of a country's economy. According to the World Health Organization (WHO), devel-

1. Presented by Haile Weldetensae.

oping countries are victims of water-related diseases. These diseases cause a general weakening of the affected population, which in turn is believed to have detrimental effects on the national economy. Eritrea, being a developing country, has a population affected by such diseases. The Water Resources unit, with the cooperation of other departments of the Provisional Government, has to effectively deal with this problem by carrying out sanitary education, protecting surface water bodies, and ensuring that hygienically safe water is supplied to the population.

In the development of the national economy, the role that the water resource sector has to play is tremendous, and thus, due consideration has to be given to the sector.

II. CURRENT SITUATION

The responsibilities of the Water Resources unit include: surface water, groundwater, and sea water surveys and development as well as meteorological and hydrological studies and services. Sewage disposal and treatment is also a component of the unit's activities. The current situation pertaining to water resources can be described as follows:

1.   Groundwater is the most reliable and quickest resource to be tapped; it is hygienically fit, in that it can be consumed without any treatment.
2.   Digging or drilling wells is the only solution to the present acute drinking water supply problem.
3.   Surface water is almost nonexistent in most of Eritrea at present. Dams that were constructed by nongovernmental organizations (NGOs) have very little water or are practically dry. At the same time, some of them have been completely filled with silt in a very short period of time.
4.   Sea water resource could not be used for drinking and agriculture presently due to lack of necessary tools, equipment, etc.
5.   Sea water resources that could help the national economy at the present time include fisheries, transportation, tourism and salt production.
6.   The overwhelming majority of the rural people and a fairly large number of the urban people have no access to portable water.
7.   With the exception of the Setit, all Eritrean rivers are dry during the long dry season.
8.   The majority of surveys carried out so far are of a reconnaissance nature. Some foreign consulting firms have done feasibility studies in some areas.
9.   The only meteorological station at present is at the International Airport in Asmara. Some small stations operated by the EPLF exist in the Barca and Sahel regions. (During the Italian occupation sixty-five different kinds of meteorological stations existed in Eritrea.)
10.   There are no hydrological stations at present.
12.   Preliminary feasibility surveys indicate that there are no areas where groundwater could be used for irrigation purposes.

III. THE MAIN PROBLEMS

The major problem affecting the proper utilization of the nation's available water resources include the following:
1. Lack of trained manpower with the necessary skills and specialization;
2. Unavailability of necessary machines and equipment;
3. Limited organizational capabilities;
4. Inadequate transportation facilitie;
5. Lack of aerial photographs and decent maps of the country;
6. Complete lack of hydrometeorological historical data;
7. Low level of consciousness about sanitation and health among the population; and
8. Unpredictable nature of the rainfall.

IV. OBJECTIVES

The Water Resources unit has outlined the following objectives:
1. To supply clean and reliable water to the population in both rural and urban areas;
2. To maintain existing water pipelines and extend new lines in the urban areas;
3. To rehabilitate old water points in the rural areas;
4. To rehabilitate water structures all over the country;
5. To ensure proper maintenance of existing water-related machineries;
6. To administer proper utilization of the nation's water resources;
7. To conduct surveys and studies that will help in water conservation projects;
8. To oversee the works of consulting and construction firms working in water-related projects;
9. To protect the nation's water resources from contamination, pollution, etc.;
10. To study the hydrometeorological conditions of the country;
11. To extend sewage collection services in the urban areas; and
12. To build water structures where the private sector is unable to.

V. PLANS OF ACTION

To maximize the contribution of water resources to the national development efforts, the following plans of action have been formulated.
1. Train manpower in relevant technical and administrative fields.
2. Employ appropriate technology that can easily be applied and maintained by the rural population.
3. Procure the necessary heavy machinery and transport facilities.
4. Strengthen operation and maintenance capabilities for rural and urban water supply schemes.
5. Investigate and study sources of water for rural areas and the urban water supply systems.
6. Conduct studies to help locate large aquifers for the use in irrigation schemes.

7. Educate the rural population about clean water and health.
8. Install hand pumps in rural water supply wells.
9. Encourage community participation in the areas of drinking water supply as well as sanitation and proper waste disposal.
10. Establish hydrometeorological networks and collect information for analysis and documentation.
11. Encourage private companies and individuals to be actively involved in drinking water supply and sanitation works.
12. Encourage NGOs to participate in alleviating the current shortage of drinking water.
13. Prepare an all-encompassing national laws on water resources.
14. Oversee the construction of all water structure in the country.
15. Ensure adequate sources are available for the sector's investment needs.
16. Prepare a master plan for national water development.
17. Prepare projects to be funded by foreign governments and NGOs.

VI. INVESTMENT AND PARTICIPATION

As mentioned in the general introduction, the economy in Eritrea is of a mixed type wherein the public and private sectors complement each other. Thus, one has to see the sectors as two sides of the same coin. In some areas of the water resources development the public sector may dominate while in other fields the private sector may have the dominant role. During the Ethiopian occupation, the private sector did not play any role in water resource development activities. All of the water resource activities were dominated by three governmental authorities: (1) the Water Resource Development Authority (WRDA), (2) the Ethiopian Water Works Construction Authority (EWWCA), and (3) the Water Supply and Sewage Authority (WSSA).

Furthermore, the Ethiopian colonial administration was not interested in developing the water resource potential of Eritrea. Thus, even though EWWCA and WSSA were represented in Eritrea by branch offices, they were understaffed and lacked any financial resources. On top of that, these institutions were primarily involved in helping the military personnel of the colonial administration.

For quick and efficient development of the national water resource, active participation of the private sector is essential. A conducive atmosphere has to be created to attract the private sector for involvement in water resource activities. Historically, the water supply systems of many small Eritrean towns, as well as drilling or digging of wells, were run by private firms in Eritrea. These private firms used to run their business more efficiently when compared to the running of the same systems by the public sector in the recent past. It is, therefore, envisaged that:

1. drinking water supply systems be run by private firms in towns where there are well-organized municipalities;
2. the private companies work on a contract basis; and
3. the national Water Resources unit monitor to ensure that the companies are serving the population properly.

National and international private firms can play an active role in conducting surveys and studies and in actual construction activities. This is because the present national water resources unit is understaffed and under-equipped to effectively deal with the effect of recurrent drought. Rules and regulations dealing with participation of both national and international private firms in water works need to be established. Priority should be given to private firms owned by Eritrean nationals provided they meet certain necessary minimum requirements.

Active participation of NGOs in water works also should be encouraged. There are some NGOs that worked in Eritrea prior to independence. These NGOs have substantially helped the Eritrean population in solving drinking water supply problems and are recognized as such by the people. Besides, the Provisional Government of Eritrea will not be able to financially meet all water work needed. Therefore, those NGOs that have already established good reputation in the country, and others who are willing to finance water works, should be encouraged.

As already stated, the financial resources available in the country at present are very minimal. Yet, the construction of large water structures requires substantial financial resources. To resolve the problem of financing, long-term loans or bilateral and multilateral aid should be encouraged by the Eritrean government. Without such an input, the role of this sector in the development of the national economy will be very inadequate.

Even though it is envisaged that the private sector would be engaged in water resource development activities, it is unlikely to happen in the immediate future. Currently, there are no private water firms in Eritrea. Therefore, the public sector, understaffed and under-equipped as it is, will definitely remain dominant in the country's water resources development activities for some time.

STRATEGIES FOR WATER RESOURCE DEVELOPMENT MANAGEMENT IN ERITREA: PROBLEMS AND POLICY IMPLICATIONS

Berhane Meskel Abraha

I. INTRODUCTION

Now that Eritrea is independent, the national priority is that of long-term economic and social development, including the restoration and reconstruction of the infrastructures that have been destroyed by the long war. A major part of the development efforts will necessarily be the restoration and development of Eritrea's natural resources including water resources and soil conservation.

Analysts recognize that the threat to the long-term stability and development of Black Africa is the breakdown of the ecosystems that sustain development. They appropriately argue that the long-term development strategy that does not include as its major activity the "conserving of soils [and] restoring forests and woodlands" is unlikely to succeed. This, of course, includes the need for management of the critical, scarce and unrenewable water resources for its conservation and optimal development use (Brown and Wolf 1985; Postel and Hiese 1988; Postel 1989).

Eritrea has suffered an excruciating experience from drought, war, famine and underdevelopment. As part of the Horn of Africa region, Eritrea has experienced its share of environmental degradation as waters have dried up, forests disappeared and fertile soils eroded precipitously during the past fifty years. In addition, rains failed or faltered in Eritrea for seven of the past ten years. Drinking water shortages are frequent. Many people have died from water-borne diseases as well as from malnutrition and the war.

For Eritrea to develop, strategies and policies that will encourage the husbanding and the harnessing of its natural resources, including its water resources potential, are essential.

This paper deals with planning and management strategies for water resource development in Eritrea. Its main purpose is to raise issues and questions that must be addressed in the formulation of a national plan and policies for water resource development programs. It is hoped that the paper will stimulate discussion and exchange of ideas among participants. It attempts to review the role and importance of water resources in national development and explore options and strategies open for Eritrea. It is based on a review of the literature on the water resources systems development and the writer's experience gained by working with the United Nations and government agencies on water resources management in developing countries such as Mexico, Saudi Arabia, Taiwan, Pakistan and Ethiopia. Lessons to learn from their success and failures are reflected in this paper. This paper makes policy recommendations, which are hopefully useful for the action by Eritrea's decision-makers.

II. WATER RESOURCE DEVELOPMENT EFFORTS

A. During the Liberation Struggle

Effective strategies to protect Eritrea's natural resources have been carried out during the Eritrean liberation struggle. The EPLF was one of the few political institutions that combined both military and development strategies. The Front adopted a comprehensive development strategy combining activities in agriculture, including afforestation, soil conservation, and water supply. The comprehensive approach in agriculture is best exemplified by Rora-Habab agricultural project implemented by EPLF (Araia 1990; Firebrace and Holland 1985). The project combined various strategies, including soil conservation efforts. A Forestry, Soil and Water Section was established to protect the environment against erosion and reduction in soil fertility. Work begun on terracing, afforestation and the management of surface water by building small dams in the gullies. Such work is vital for the long-term agricultural security of Eritrea. It is especially essential in the highland areas where erosion and soil exhaustion is already severe (Firebrace and Holland 1985:87). More land can also be brought into use if the underground water supply potential is tapped with modern drilling techniques and fuller use made of river water by constructing dams and irrigation schemes (Pateman 1990:203). Rehabilitation programs have been implemented in close collaboration with people's assemblies, in the areas of agriculture, water supply, health, and education. Alongside the rehabilitation and development programs, the Eritrean Relief Association (ERA) had carried out a large-scale emergency relief program (ERA 1990; EIAC 1991).

The Eritrean Inter Agency Consortium (EIAC) was involved in supporting water programs since 1984. Friends of Eritrea in Europe formed this consortium to assist in rural water supply development. This support started with a small-scale well digging program and continued in 1987, with a more comprehensive and country-wide Water Supply Development Programme. The Eritrean Relief Association (ERA) drilled 200 boreholes between 1987 and 1991. Very recently, the ERA has benefited from a training and research mission on (1) the application of remotely sensed data in water exploration, geological, soil classification and environmental monitoring, and (2) checking on the ground what has been observed on the satellite imagery. As this program covered only the Sahel region of Eritrea, and because it proved extremely useful, the ERA decided to extend its funding of the research to the southeast and western parts of Eritrea (EIAC 1991).

The Water Supply Development Programme implemented by ERA helped to curb the massive migration of people due to drought. The experience gained by the ERA can be effectively used throughout Eritrea during this transitional period and in the future.

B. Strategies for Future Water Resource Development

Institutional and legal structures and mechanisms must be established to carry out water resources planning and management at the national level. One viable recommendation is the setting up of National Water Resources and

Environment Commission to delineate and implement the policies related to water resource development in the country. Implementation and executing agencies can be instituted both centrally and regionally to carry out programs and multipurpose projects related to this sector (for example, for urban and rural water supplies and environmental protection, irrigated agriculture, hydro-electric power generation, tourism and recreation, etc.).

Water resource programs tend to be very expensive, more so in developing nations where capital, trained personnel and trained managers are scarce. Thus, it is of utmost importance for Eritrea to clearly define its objectives, identify its priorities and develop a realistic and well integrated policy and infrastructure for water resource development.

III. THE IMPORTANCE OF WATER RESOURCE DEVELOPMENT PLANNING AND MANAGEMENT

The need for effective water management and the use of multidisciplinary approach to planning water resource development are stressed in this section. Laws regulating water development within developing countries also are discussed briefly to provide a conceptual background.

A. The Need for Effective Water Management

Management of water resource is very important for general national economic activity. The quality and availability of water determine levels of public health, food production, the productivity of industry, the production of energy, and other important aspects of the quality of life. Water is the life blood of national development.

By "management of water" is meant people's control of water as it passes through its natural cycle, with balanced attention to maximizing economic, social, and environmental benefits. Because planning is one of the most important tasks of management, it follows that planning for water management is a critical activity. The basic difficulty faced is conflict between various demands and interests. This has always been true, as even primitive societies fought over scarce water. The conflicts still exist but they are more sophisticated.

Water planning is needed at different levels and for different purposes of water management; for example, to site a new irrigation project to increase agricultural production or for a water supply and sanitation project for a rural community. Planning is also needed to develop integrated, multipurpose development plans for a river basin. Further, planning is needed to develop policies for the regulation of contaminants that are discharged into water ways. Such purposes are interrelated and form the general water planning picture. The planning for water resources must take into account the integration of different purposes and interests, if it is to be effective (Grigg 1985).

Internationally, the subject of water management has been recognized as critical. The desertification of parts of Africa in the 1970s, great losses from floods and droughts in Asia every year, lack of access to sources of safe drinking water, and the ever-present problems of world hunger, all underscore the need for good water management.

Due to the recognition of the international aspect of water management, the 1980s had been declared the International Water Supply and Sanitation Decade, with appropriate goals for supplying safe drinking water and appropriate sanitation to the world's population. Much of the work of water planners in the future will be in developing countries. With rapid rising world population, many of the most pressing and basic water problems are located in those countries.

Lately, there has been media attention to the "water crises" in different parts of the world. There are indications that future global water crises will be more severe and more important than the "energy crises" that are retarding development in many third world countries. There will be hydrodiplomacy for peace in the future between countries and regions prompted by the global water crises.

B. Water Resources Management is Multidimensional

As mentioned earlier, water resources management is multidimensional. It embraces planning, design, construction, operation and maintenance. Its ingredients include technological capability, social attitudes, economic realities, political viewpoints, and environmental goals. Being able to effectively manage water resources often depends more on our ability to maneuver within institutional constraints than to design technological fixes. Our engineering capability is more advanced than its application; yesterday's methods are being applied to tomorrow's problems, and regional problems are begging for solutions because we try to solve them on a local scale. The need for institutional reform is clear, but the key to accomplishing it is elusive (Viessman 1990).

Development and management of water resources involves modification of the hydrologic and hydrogeologic cycle to regulate the natural water supply to better meet human needs. Therefore, planning for water resource development and management is based on recognition of the close interrelationships of the hydrologic cycle with other systems such as land use, soil conservation and watershed management, groundwater supply and use, drainage and aquatic weed control, demographics (population characteristics and distribution), economics, social well-being, flora and fauna, and public health and control of disease vectors.

Early in the planning process interrelationships of such systems must be defined as primary or secondary so that the scope on planning can be limited to manageable dimensions while assuring that all relevant factors are considered (Petersen 1984:1–3).

The need for long-range planning of water resources has become more evident in recent years with population growth and increased development and utilization of the world's resources. There is no substitute for water, and the objectives of planning center on wise use of water resources to avoid future shortages that might otherwise limit a nation's economy or the social well-being of its people.

C. The Need for Impact Assessment

Water resources management activities and future developments are affected by the decisions of planners. According to Barrow (1978:66–67), when water resource management identifies the objective(s) that are to be met by water resource development, there should be adequate pre-project/pre-program appraisal sufficiently in advance of proposed developments. The appraisal must sufficiently be thorough to ensure that problems which might arise are identified and dealt with. Such an *impact assessment* should consider environmental, socioeconomic and sociocultural costs and benefits of the strategy(s) available to achieve the objective(s). Effort should also be made to research and evaluate relevant hindsight experience and there should, wherever possible, be consultation with the people who are likely to be affected by the development.

Once a particular strategy is selected it has to be implemented and then maintained. To do this satisfactorily, it requires an ongoing monitoring of environmental and human impacts. Without adequate monitoring it is difficult to identify whether it is necessary (and practical) to alter the plan or program should unforeseen problems arise. Without monitoring, it would be difficult to assess the degree of success of the project or program.

D. Laws Controlling Water Use Within Developing Countries

Any effort made towards an integrated and planned use of water could fail if it is not made within the framework of a comprehensive water legislation. Lack of comprehensive water legislation, in many developing countries, has been one of the main stumbling blocks for the integrated and planned use of water resources.

Water is frequently a *common resource,* not owned or controlled by any one individual or organization, and used by many. Under conditions of relative abundance, use of a common resource is unlikely to cause difficulties. However, under conditions of relative scarcity, such as in Eritrea and many other developing countries, the use of a common resource must be regulated. If there is no regulation, users are likely to damage or destroy the water supply. Thus, there is a need for water legislation.

Land and water are often treated as separate "entities"; ideally there should be integrated planning and management of land and water resource development. To achieve this, legislation controlling water resource development must be coordinated with laws relating to land tenure, land use and inheritance. Unfortunately, water resources managers often have little control over anything other than their water sources and supply system (Falkenmark 1984).

E. Managing Shared Water Resources

Another area of importance in water resource development involves the managing of shared water resources as demand upon them increases. Increasingly, water resource development involves the use of river systems or groundwater shared by more than one user, region, state or country. It is worth noting that roughly one-third of developing countries are federations, and that federal and state authorities often do not see eye to eye. Even within one region different, often conflicting, interests may wish to develop water; for example, hydroelectric generation may compete with fisheries or irrigation needs. To develop such resources fully and to minimize harm to the interest of any of the parties involved to maintain, and where necessary, to improve flow and quality, may require interregional, interstate or international cooperation (Barrow 1987:67).

Management approach will be necessary during the development of river basin shared between Eritrea and Ethiopia and between Eritrea and

Sudan. For example, Mereb flows between Ethiopia and Eritrea. Mereb surges to Gash which flows to the Sudan. Similarly, River Setit, which also borders with Ethiopia, flows to the Sudan. River Barka joins Ansaba at Selea on the border and then flows to the Sudan. Transboundary agreements are necessary between these countries in order to develop the water resources on a good footing using river basin planning approach.

IV. THE ROLE OF WATER FOR SOCIOECONOMIC DEVELOPMENT IN ERITREA

The natural resources endowment of Eritrea is conducive to water resource development in the country. There are, however, major constraints and problems that have to be tackled. Water resource development planning has to be integrated with the country's national economic planning.

A. Natural Resources Potential of Eritrea

Eritrea, located in the Horn of Africa, displays a variety of natural resources which are conducive for water resource development in order to increase its agricultural production, tourism and industrialization. It has diverse climatic regions, soils, geological formations and long coastline along with relatively extensive infrastructures of roads and railways connecting the major cities and towns.

Eritrea is moderately endowed with several types of land resources such as minerals, forest wealth and wildlife, yet there are many problems related to water resource. Not only is drinking water in the semi-desert lowlands scarce, but the erosion-producing flow of rivers and streams from the highlands is not yet adequately controlled to irrigate the numerous valleys and flatlands for agricultural production. Some of the rivers have been dammed and used to support irrigated agriculture, especially in the eastern lowlands of Semenawi Bahri, and the Tessenei–Ali Ghider areas of western lowlands. The rainfall pattern in the lowlands is an extension of the same pattern in the highlands, and with a range of 250mm to 875mm per year, can be made sufficient, using storage. There is a potential for greater agricultural output through extensive development of irrigation.

Eritrea's main rivers are Setit, Gash, Barka, Anseba and Mereb, which can be dammed for irrigation, for water supply to urban and rural communities, for hydroelectric power, recreation and other uses. The most important and dependable water supply source in Eritrea is the groundwater.

The groundwater resource is the biggest and, as yet, virtually untapped resource that Eritrea has. Subsurface or groundwater potential of Eritrea is probably the most extensive but the least known of the water resources that are available. For instance, no studies have been conducted that define the regional and hydrogeologic extent of aquifers in Eritrea.

The potential areas for groundwater are the highlands, the Tessenei-Ali Ghider areas of western lowlands, the eastern lowland of Semenawi Bahri, the escarpments, the northeast coastal plains and Danakil Alps, and southeast lowlands. The Bahri is a narrow strip of land in eastern Eritrea. The colonial government of Italy had encouraged cash crops irrigation farming in the Bahri lowlands. Long-term investments, such as deep water wells and high-wall soil conservation terraces, characterize these farms (Abraham 1990:112). There is a long tradition of using groundwater wells and well digging in Eritrea.

At this stage, however, the extent of Eritrea's groundwater resources is not sufficiently known to be of any use for comprehensive planning purposes. Studies must be made to determine the real extent of potential groundwater areas and their hydrogeologic characteristics to facilitate proper water resource development planning and management and groundwater conjunctive use with surface water supplies.

The lack of large-scale irrigation projects has so far prevented the realization of higher agricultural production levels, which have the potential to feed the country's growing population. Its potential, in fact, lies in its agricultural productive capacity to provide not only for its own requirements but to serve as a potential exporter to neighboring Arab and African markets. All in all, the cultivable area of Eritrea is nearly 6.5 million acres. With proper water resource development policies and needed construction of irrigation facilities, Eritrea could easily be agriculturally self-sufficient.

B. The Role of Water Resource Development

The development of the water resources in Eritrea is an essential prerequisite for the development of its agricultural and industrial potential, besides being critical to the survival of human and animal life. The surface waters have yet to be used on a significant scale for increasing agricultural production. Production in the areas currently under cultivation can be increased by means of improved technology, such as the introduction of irrigation facilities, fertilizers, improved seed varieties, and so on. In fact, it will be possible to draw maximum benefit from the other inputs only when water supplies are assured at the right time in the right quantity.

The development of hydroelectric power provides relatively cheap energy for industrial and mineral development. Hydropower can assume a key role as energy source, particularly in the present global petroleum situation. Due to the character of the topography and the amount of streamflows that can be stored in reservoirs, Eritrea possesses a fairly reasonable potential for the development of hydroelectric energy. For example, River Barka has the potential of about 299 GWH (gega watt-hours) gross theoretical capability and 77 GWH of annual generation of hydroelectric energy. Similarly, Mereb-Gash have a potential of about 1,745.6 GWH gross theoretical capability and 569.2 GWH of annual generation. Tekezze-Setit have an enormous potential for hydroelectric power (14,846 GWH and 5,048 GWH respectively) (United Nations Water Conference 1976; ECA 1976).

In addition to its use as an energy source, water is directly necessary for almost every sphere of industrial activity and development. Almost all industries — food products, beverage, chemicals, petroleum and synthetic fuels, mining, quarrying, automobile plants, thermal electric stations, and so on — require sizable quantities of water.

Over vast areas of Eritrea, there is an acute problem of water supply in urban as well as rural communities. The lack of water over extensive areas, as in the drought-prone lowlands, and war zones caused enormous suffering of the people as well as livestock.

The dangers of man's total dependence on rain, and disastrous consequences of failure of rain or inadequate rainfall, not only over Eritrea but also in several parts of Sahelian Africa, have caused so much suffering and hardship that combatting drought has now been assigned the same high priority as liberation by the policymakers of Africa. The effort to combat drought needs to be redoubled in the areas of meteorology and hydrology. There is also the need for ensuring a greater participation of the people in the control and use of rivers.

The shortage of rain, not only does affect agriculture and livestock, but also the recharge of groundwater aquifers. Recharge under arid and semi-arid conditions are low because of evapotranspiration, and the lack of soil and vegetation causes torrential and damaging runoffs. Because the ecosystem in Eritrea is fragile, land use has to be monitored in order to stop soil erosion caused by deforestation and overgrazing. Major increase in agricultural production could be achieved through proper land and water use management which will involve terraced field for soil and water conservation. Wise management of the water development projects could play a vital part in the rural development program, while at the same time ensuring protection of the environment (ERA 1990).

The development of fisheries is of great importance in view of the vast potentialities of the Red Sea and the rivers in Eritrea. Not only would such a development help to improve the nutritional standards of the people but also provide exportable surpluses to earn foreign exchange. The rivers and the Red Sea of Eritrea have also an enormous potential for the development of recreational facilities and tourism.

V. POLICY RECOMMENDATIONS

In this section some pertinent policy strategies for action by decision-makers of Eritrea are recommended on the basis of the discussions on the concepts of water resource planning and management in the preceding sections.

A. Water Resources Plan and Policy

Eritrea's basic national objectives of policies on water resources should be: (1) the development and proper utilization of water resources; (2) the proper regulation of the resource development for its conservation and use; and (3) the integration and coordination of water resource development activities in the country.

Successful implementation of the national objectives will require the formulation of national structure(s) for: (1) formulating policies and plans related to water resource development, conservation and use; (2) identifying and prioritizing appropriate water resource development programs and projects; (3) setting up guidelines for development of the sector; (4) coordinating all water resource activities that might be taking place in different sectors of the government as well as in industries established for economic development; (5) regulating water resource development for proper conservation and use of this scarce resource; and (6) budgeting for identified water resource development activities and/or programs that are linked to the national development objectives.

The government can and should facilitate the main instruments of the water resources policy by making it possible, through appropriate state budget allocations, by instituting appropriate and democratic laws and policies for participation in the process of water resource development.

The need for coordinated water resource development activities cannot be overemphasized. In order to effectively develop the water resources of a nation, a clearly stated policy of coordinated development must evolve.

The policy should be aimed at ensuring complete coverage of the problems of water resource development and providing adequate means of implementation. A prerequisite to coordinated development is that there must be cooperative effort among central, provincial and local governments, water related agencies and industries and the agricultural economy. Independent efforts of these agencies will not produce the results that can be obtained by a combined enterprise.

B. National Structure for Water Resource Development

As national activities in water resource development becomes more significant to Eritrea's economic and social development, it is essential to have a central authority or commission for administering, coordinating and monitoring these activities. Therefore, the main policy recommendation is to urgently establish a central commission with all-embracing executory, regulatory, supervisory, directory, coordinatory and advisory powers. It is suggested that this central agency be named the Eritrea Water Resources and Environment Commission (EWREC).

The suggested EWREC will have the following specific functions: (1) manage and develop the utilization of water and water resources; (2) authorize or license water uses on the basis of the relevant general and project plans and in accordance with corresponding regulations; (3) regulate, authorize or license the utilization, purpose of use and supply of water and water resources; (4) regulate, authorize or license the exploitation of water and water resources; and (5) determine and regulate legal acts and relationships among individuals and/or corporations in respect to water and water resources uses.

This central commission can be an interministerial agency composed of, but not limited to, ministries of public works, agriculture, health, economic planning and finance. Or it can be a special semi-autonomous body that reports directly to the supreme authority of the state.

In summary, the purposes for which the commission will be established is to ensure the optimum development and use of the nation's inland water resources; to ensure the coordination of all activities which may influence the quality, quantity, distribution or use of water; and to ensure the application of appropriate standards and techniques for the investigation, use, control, protection, management and administration of water.

C. Provide the Appropriate Legal Arrangement for Water Resource Development

In accordance with its statutory functions and powers, the government should formulate specific water resources management policies, in particular, with respect to: (1) the determination of the conditions and procedures for project planning and for water and water resources utilization, exploitation, policy and licensing; (2) the permanent regulation and implementation of water resource development; (3) the prevention of pollution harmful to water uses and to the environment; (4) the control of, and protection against harmful effects of water; (5) the survey and inventory of water resources (both surface and groundwater); and (6) the need to specify clearly that all water resources are the collective property of the Eritrean people and that the state shall take all necessary and proper measure for the conservation, preservation and augmentation of water resources.

VI. SUMMARY AND CONCLUSION

In addition to drought, war, famine and underdevelopment, Eritrea has experienced its share of environmental degradation as waters have dried up, forests disappeared and millions of fertile soils eroded precipitously over the past fifty years. Drinking water shortages are frequent. Many people have died during the war, and from drought, malnutrition, and water-borne diseases.

As Eritrea embarks on a new road of peace, its national priority is socioeconomic development, including the restoration and the reconstruction of the infrastructures destroyed by wars. A major part of this development effort will focus on the restoration and development of its natural resources including water resource development and conservation.

Effective development management of the country's water resources will ameliorate the severe situations and improve the quality of life of its people. As part of this strategy, what is urgently needed is the formulation and implementation of an integrated water management and water development program that emphasizes the efficient development, use and conservation of the scarce and unrenewable water resources.

From the discussions in this paper of concepts on multidisciplinary planning and management of water resource development, and relevant experiences of selected countries, one important theme stands out as the main thesis of this essay: The institutional and legal arrangements and mechanisms to direct and regulate the development and use of water resources in Eritrea is indispensable. Two pertinent policy recommendations have been brought to the attention of Eritrea's decision-makers in this area: the establishment of (1) an interministerial commission, Eritrean Water Resources and Environment Commission (EWREC) with an all-embracing executory, regulatory, supervisory, directory, coordinatory and advisory powers; and (2) a comprehensive legislative framework in the field of water resource administration and management. Such a legal provision will empower the recommended national commission to regulate and engage in activities related to water resource development.

REFERENCES

Anderson, T. L. 1983. *Water Rights: Scarce Resource Allocation, Bureaucracy, and the Environment.* Cambridge, Mass.: Ballinger Publishing.

Barrow, Chris. 1987. *Water Resources and Agricultural Development in the Tropics.* New York: John Wiley & Sons.

Bokhari, S.M.H. 1977. "Institutional Arrangements for Planning and Management of Water Resources in Pakistan, A Case Study," *National Resources Forum* 1, 2 (January). New York: United Nations.

Brown, Lester R., and Edward C. Wolf. 1985. *Reversing Africa's Decline,* World

Watch Paper 65, World Watch Institute, Washington, D.C. (June).

Commission Del Plan Nacional Hidraulico. 1975. *Plan Nacional Hidraulico. 1975 – Resumen,* Tepic #40, Mexico 7.

Economic Commission for Africa (ECA). 1976. "Problems of Water Resources Development in Africa," Regional Report - ECA, United Nations Water Conference, Africa Regional Meeting. (September 20–24, 1976), Addis Ababa, Ethiopia, Report #E (CN.14/NRD/WR/1/Rev 2, October 21, 1976).

Eritrean Inter Agency Consortium (EIAC). 1991. "Eritrea Emergency Water Drilling Programme," *Groot Hertoginne Laan,* 34 2517 EH Den Haag, Holland (February).

Eritrean Relief Association (ERA). 1990. "Emergency Water Development Programme in Eritrea" (November/December).

Falkenmark, M. 1984. "New Ecological Approach to the Water Cycle: Ticket to the Future," *Ambio* 13(3):152–60.

Firebrace, J., and Stuart Holland. 1985. *Never Kneel Down: Drought, Development and Liberation in Eritrea.* Trenton, N.J.: Red Sea Press, p. 70.

Gelawdios, Arai. 1990. "The Politics of Famine and Strategies for Development in Ethiopia." Doctoral dissertation, Columbia University, pp. 169–70.

Grigg, Neil S. 1985. *Water Resources Planning.* New York: McGraw-Hill.

Gunnerson, C. G., and J. M. Kalbermatten (eds.). 1978. "Environmental Impacts of International Civil Engineering Projects and Practices." Proceedings of a session sponsored by the Research Council on Environmental Impact Analysis of the ASCE Technical Council on Research of the ASCE Convention, San Francisco, October 17–21, 1977. New York: American Society of Civil Engineers.

Petersen, Margaret S. 1984. *Water Resources Planning and Development.* Englewood Cliffs, N.J.: Prentice-Hall.

Postel, Sandra. 1989. "Water for Agriculture: Facing the Limits." World Watch Paper 93, World Watch Institute, Washington, D.C., April 1988, pp. 35–40.

Tseggai, Araia. 1981. *The Economic Viability of an Independent Eritrea.* Doctoral dissertation, University of Nebraska, July 1981 (Economics/Political History).

United Nations Water Conference. 1976. "African Preparatory Meeting — Country Report of Ethiopia" (January).

Viessman, Warren. 1990. "Water Management: Challenge and Opportunity," *Journal of Water Resources, Planning and Management,* ASCE, 116, 3 (May/June).

Wiener, Aaron. 1977. "Rural Water Supply Management in Developing Countries," *Natural Resources Forum* 2.

ORGANIZING THE MARINE AND PORTS AFFAIRS OF ERITREA

Prepared by
Marine and Ports Affairs, EPLF[1]

I. INTRODUCTION

In this brief paper, proposals are presented for discussion on how to organize the Marine and Ports Affairs. First, however, some background information will be helpful to gain a better understanding of the problems.

What does Marine and Ports Affairs (MPA) deal with? As is well-known, the resources and problems of the Red Sea are continuously being identified by various researchers and interested bodies. Among the economic resources, mining, transport, fishing and tourism can be mentioned. The problems are, of course, largely reflections of the geopolitical and economic tensions and conflict that manifest throughout the region.

It would require a longer paper to deal with the many resources and problems, therefore, this discussion will focus on the sea transport as the most likely aspect to be vigorously explored first by the Provisional Government of Eritrea. The Marine and Ports Affairs now being considered concerns the activities of ports, shipping and transit agencies, ship-owning and operating, both passengers and cargo, marine engineering and maritime affairs.

These activities were all nationalized by the former military government of Ethiopia and, as a result, the current Eritrean government is inheriting a state-owned and operated system that requires reorganization. In this attempt, one can and should begin from what has already been established by the Ethiopian government without having to start from scratch or initiating a detailed study. The Derg had conducted an interesting study, through the Public Administration Services (PAS), in 1981 for the reorganization of the MPA, whose findings and recommendations we can still adopt by modifying them to suit our objectives and conditions. Another study was also conducted in 1982 by Roy Jorgensen Associates of the United States.

Notably, the duties and responsibilities of the Marine and Ports Affairs institutions are universally similar. If they differ it is probably in the way they are organized and managed to serve the needs of each country. For example, the MPA in the Sudan falls under the Ministry of Defence; in Djibouti and Somalia it stands as a ministry by itself. In Kenya, Mozambique, Comoro and Ethiopia the unit is attached to the Ministry of Transport and Communications (MTC). In Ethiopia in particular, due to nationalizations and repeated structural changes, all power and authority were concentrated within the MTC in the past ten years.

When the port of Massawa was reopened for shipping under the EPLF

---

1. Presented by Berhane Abrehe

administration by the end of 1990, a new Marine and Ports Office was set up to run the port. It housed the Massawa Port Administration and a Shipping and Transit unit within the port compound. Later when the whole country was liberated in May 1991, the Marine and Ports Affairs added to its responsibilities the management of the port of Assab, and MTC branch offices in Eritrea, mainly in Asmara. All links between the MTC head office in Addis Ababa and its ex-branches in Eritrea were therefore terminated and replaced by this new national Eritrean establishment. The former Ethiopian Marine Engineering Development (EMED) unit of Massawa and the Haleb Port project of Assab are now administered by the Eritrean Navy.

II. WHAT IS TO BE DONE NEXT

As answers to this question, a number of proposals could be forwarded. However, for the purpose here, we will focus on those aspects dealing with policy and structural organization. The objective is to aid the appropriate policymakers of the Provisional Government and those specialists in administrative organization who should be working on these issues.

At this juncture of history it is very crucial that a clear national policy on marine and port affairs be formulated which address the short- and long-term strategic interests of Eritrea. The policy should (1) delineate the roles and participation of private and state investments in the various sectors of the industry, and (2) establish the way marine and port activities will be handled and organized nationally. As a matter of policy, the meaning of "free port" as it relates to Assab Port should be spelled out clearly.

Three organizational structures are subsequently proposed in this paper. At this point though, the question of privatization should be discussed as the answer to that question will influence the type of organizational formula to be adopted. The experiences of the Derg in this respect will be informative.

As already stated, the Derg's government owned all maritime and ports activities and organized them under the umbrella of one ministry. The advantage of it, as claimed by some people, was that the government effectively controlled the foreign currency dealings of the industry and sealed off the possibility for flight abroad of this vital national asset by private enterprises. The disadvantages were said to be inefficiency, corruption and too much bureaucratic wrangling.

If we go by the general global experiences, it is not uncommon to find a port being privately owned and operated. This system, at least at this time, is not recommended for Eritrea. Exchange of ideas among colleagues so far favor that Eritrean ports be state-owned and operated. However, privatization could possibly be encouraged in cargo handling, transit agency services, marine engineering, ship owning and operating. The opening of stevedoring and shipping agency to privatization is very controversial among Eritrean experts. Some of them advise to keep the two under state control, gradually freeing them for privatization. The need for a smooth continuity, justifies the continuation of the major port and marine activities under state ownership despite the disadvantages associated with it.

The concern in permitting private capital operation in the maritime industry is that the large volume of hard currency revenue it generates could be lost to foreign interests unless some sort of control mechanism is devised to discourage it. According to some options, this can be accomplished either by excluding privatization or limiting the right to participation to Eritrean nationals only. The state, of course, can compete anytime and anywhere it wishes.

III. PROPOSAL FOR ORGANIZATIONAL STRUCTURE

We propose three organizational structures for the Marine and Ports Affairs in Eritrea. These structures are represented by the three charts presented at the end of this paper.

At the national level the body responsible for Marine and Ports Affairs must be (1) simple and require a small number of officials and office workers, and (2) organized to have a section that will answer queries from private owners and operators when applicable. As an interim arrangement, it is proposed that this institution in our country be organized roughly as shown in Chart 1, and its establishment immediately announced through proclamation.

In the administration of ports, experts usually recommend that when there are more than one port in a country their structure and management procedures be made similar and standardized. In the case of the Eritrean ports it is partly applicable and partly not. Assab and Massawa were developed differently for different objectives.

The Derg as well as the Haile Selassie regime deliberately strangled the development of Massawa and accelerated that of Assab in a typical exploitative colonial fashion. Assab largely handles Ethiopia's sea-borne trade and requires a different organizational setup to reflect its difference from Massawa, especially now that it has been declared a "free port" as it relates to Ethiopia. Thus, the general outline of an organization applicable to both ports is as shown in Chart 2 at the end of this paper.

The Eritrean body that is to guide the National Shipping and Transit Services — which, by recommendation, is stated-owned and operated — is proposed to have an interim organizational structure both at the head office level and at the Assab branch office roughly as shown in Chart 3 at the end of this paper.

There are other matters that require policy proposals. We know that the physical structure, general manpower and managerial facilities of the whole marine and ports system, and especially that of Massawa have been heavily damaged by war. The Provisional Government of Eritrea should, therefore commit itself to invest to rehabilitate and\or reconstruct these facilities. A good organizational setup will be useless unless a complementary action is taken to improve on the said facilities. Training programs for personnel must be immediately initiated.

Another proposal is to immediately set up insurance, banking and communication systems which are essential for smooth operation of the marine industry. Finally, the Provisional Government of Eritrea should consider to replace soon the letterheadings, emblems and formats of the existing forms and documents with an appropriate Eritrean version.

Chart 1. The National Office

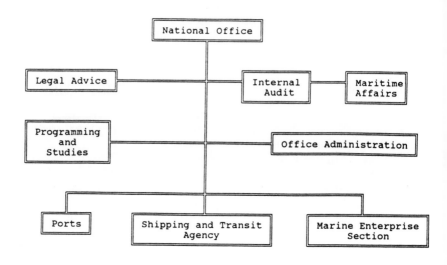

Chart 2. Port Administration

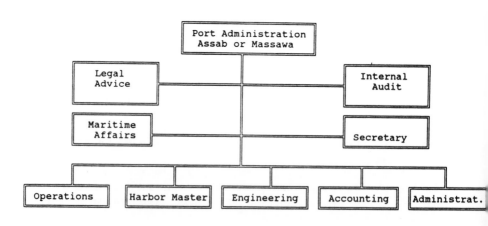

Chart 3. Shipping and Transit Agency

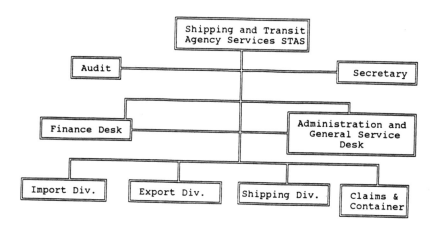

PROSPECTS OF PETROLEUM EXPLORATION AND PRODUCTION IN ERITREA

Ytbarek Cuddus

I. INTRODUCTION

After almost a century of colonial rule and thirty years of bitter war, Eritrea is an independent country. At this time, the country finds itself devastated with virtually no standing structure of economic value except its untapped natural resources.

The purpose of this brief paper is to provide an account of Eritrea's petroleum exploration history and to suggest, in a broad sense, some ideas and recommendations that may be helpful in formulating policies, laws and regulations on the exploration and development of natural resources in Eritrea.

The exploration for natural resources began in Eritrea in the late 1930s during the Italian colonial rule. The exploration has gone through different phases during the successive colonial rules, but it has never achieved any appreciable production.

Because water is a matter of life and death in most parts of Eritrea, the task of finding groundwater, using seismic and electrical methods, is presently undertaken by the "Water for Life" project.[1] The focus of this paper, however, is the development of energy resources. This development will require contracts and agreements for investments by newly formed national corporations and foreign investors, as well as technical and financial assistance from foreign governments and international financial institutions.

In the remaining parts of this paper, a brief history of Eritrea's petroleum exploration activities is presented first, followed by a description of past and current experiences, including the associated politics and economics of hydrocarbon recovery. The paper concludes by providing recommendations for the formation of a Department of Petroleum to be entrusted with, among other responsibilities, the task of writing the laws and regulations that will guide future hydrocarbon and petroleum exploration and production activities in independent Eritrea.

II. HISTORY OF PETROLEUM EXPLORATION IN ERITREA

Petroleum exploration activities in Eritrea began in the late 1930s during the Italian colonial rule. After the Second World War, especially from the early 1960s through the end of the 1980s, several oil and seismic survey companies conducted exploration activities in Eritrea both onshore and offshore. The majority of the surveys, however, were conducted offshore (see map appended at the end).

1. A project launched by the Eritrean Relief Committee just before independence and is currently raising funds for bigger drilling rigs to alleviate the shortage of water.

The exploratory wells that were drilled during the period between 1938 and 1977 are listed in Table 1, with an indication of their status.

Table 1: Wells Drilled Between 1938 and 1977 in Eritrea

Well	Operator	Depth (ft)	Year	Status
Adal 1	AGIP	2,638	1938	Abandoned
Adal 2		8,118	1938	Abandoned
Suri 1-7	AGIP	1,043–8,210	1940	Abandoned
Dhunishib 1	Gulf	12,698	1965	Abandoned
Amber 1	Mobil	11,671	1966	Abandoned
Secca Fawn 1	Gulf	9,000	1968	Abandoned
B-1	Mobil	9,730	1969	Abandoned
C-1	Mobil	9,874	1970	Gas shows
Massawa J-1	GAO	10,291	1973	Abandoned
MN-1	GAO	9,404	1973	Abandoned
Thio-1	Shell	10,233	1977	Abandoned

As shown in Table 1, all drilled wells except one were abandoned. The most recent and most promising well, C-1, was drilled by Mobil and Exxon. This well was recorded as a discovery well because a gas blowout occurred at 9,874 feet. As the term "gas blowout" implies, natural gas blew the drilling rig and fire was raging for several weeks. Although remarks on the well history record indicate that the gas blowout died before a relief well, C-1A, reached the necessary depth, two wells were drilled three years later. Massawa J-1 spudded July 5, 1973, and completed on August 27, 1973. This well is located 8 kilometers northwest of C-1. The same drilling rig, Shilloh, was moved to spud MN-1 at a location 19 kilometers south of C-1 on September 1, 1973. This well was abandoned because of political unrest in the region.[2]

II. POLITICAL AND ECONOMIC CONSIDERATIONS

Given the current political and economic changes sweeping the Soviet Union and Eastern Europe, it is believed that there is a global tilt toward a market economy. Countries of what used to be the Eastern Bloc are asking for financial assistance for development; and many Western governments and private firms are likely to divert economic assistance and investment funds to these countries. However, because these countries lack the legal framework needed to govern agreements for such investments, their natural resource exploration activities are likely to be slowed down, delaying the realizing of the potential of their natural resources.

Some developing countries that gained independence beginning in the 1950s have enjoyed exploration activities for the past twenty to thirty years. Such countries typically experienced relatively peaceful periods, which

2. The writer was on the drilling rig at the time the decision was made to pull out.

enabled them to explore and produce hydrocarbons, which contributed to their prosperity. In contrast, countries such as Eritrea, Ethiopia, Sudan, Somalia and Mozambique, to name a few in Africa, suffered long periods of political instability and civil war, which severely curtailed their exploration activities.

As Eritrea emerges from a long and destructive war, it has the opportunity to develop a legal framework that will provide the specific laws and regulations for the exploration and production of natural resources. To begin, Eritrea must create environmental laws that would regulate industrial practices and ensure cleaner air, soil and water.

Although exploration for natural resources has never attained a level of development, Eritrea has potential in the following:

1. Petroleum. Continued interest in the offshore region of Eritrea in the Red Sea by various oil companies indicates the potential for oil find. If farming and industries are to be modernized, if educational and medical needs are to advance, if the standard of living is to be higher and if the people are to prosper and enjoy happiness, then Eritrea needs to explore and exploit its oil as soon as possible.

2. Natural Gas. As indicated by the gas blowout at C-1, drilled by Mobil and Exxon in 1970, the Red Sea basin is believed to contain natural gas. Because refining is bypassed, this could be a fast way to achieve energy independence.

3. Geothermal. Beneath the eastern part of Eritrea is a geothermal region that could produce enormous energy if dry steam methods were used to produce electricity.

Eritrea, like many other developing countries, needs alternative sources of energy. Excessive dependence on firewood and charcoal for cooking is fast depleting Eritrea's remaining trees and shrubs. Electricity, kerosene and/or gas appliances are viable alternatives. To realize such alternatives, the search for hydrocarbon must become a priority.

IV. RECOMMENDATIONS

The following recommendations are based on a review of the practices of other countries in the area of petroleum exploration and production and, in particular, their various contracts, articles of petroleum laws and corporate taxes.

- Establish a Department of Energy within the Ministry of Mines to deal with the country's energy concerns.
- Establish the economic territorial boundary in Eritrea's offshore region and use existing or modified or newly drawn blocks for lease purposes.
- Form a National Oil Company under the Department of Energy to direct all oil activities, including the signing of contracts and the commissioning of required studies.
- Establish a task force with mandate to gather and analize all existing seismic, gravity, magnetic survey data, and core sample analytical results from various exploration contractors and oil companies that have conducted surveys in Eritrea under previous contracts.
- Enact laws and regulations governing all phases of exploration, production, transportation, and refining of the final product. Such laws,

among other provisions, should include provisions for: (1) performance of minimum work and minimum expenditure; (2) preference for local employment and supplies; (3) insurance and indemnity payable by contractor for industry-related injury or damage; (4) mandatory training of Eritrean nationals in the petroleum industry; (5) need for incorporation and/or registration in the country.

• Develop a model petroleum production sharing agreement with clause specifying the duration of the exploration period, contractor's obligations during the period, cost of oil and oil profit sharing, government participation in such decisions, import and export of products, foreign exchange requirements, etc.

• Enact a Petroleum Operations Income Tax Act that establishes taxable income after production, allowable deductions, and rates of taxes, and levy taxes of petroleum service subcontractors.

V. CONCLUSION

The writer strongly believes that sound laws and regulations and viable agreement articles constitute a good start for petroleum exploration and production activities in Eritrea. The surest resource Eritrea has is, undoubtedly, its industrious and hardworking population. However, efforts should also be made to exploit the country's natural resources, including petroleum. According to this writer's estimation, there are more than fifty Eritreans in the diaspora who have expertise in geophysics, geology, petroleum engineering, drilling, hydrology, water engineering, earth science, and geophysical positioning both in the field and in the processing/analysis of data for hydrocarbon and hydrology. This is a good resource and if utilized can greatly contribute to the country's natural resource and general economic development efforts.

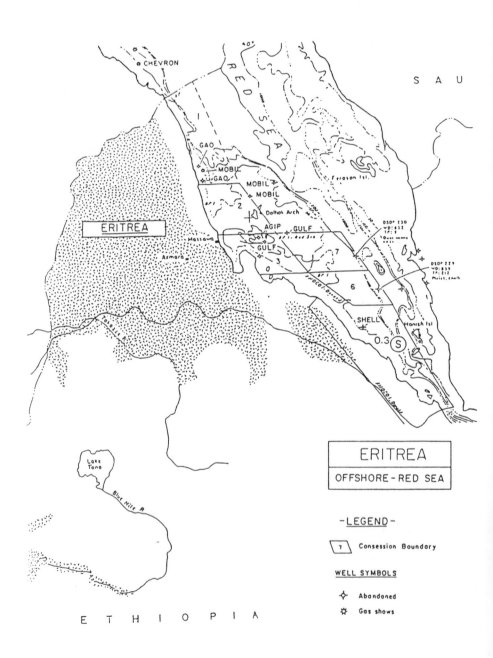

ERITREA

OFFSHORE - RED SEA

-LEGEND-

Consession Boundary

WELL SYMBOLS

◇ Abandoned

✿ Gas shows

CONSTRUCTION:
PLAN OF ACTION AND POLICIES

Prepared by
The Construction Commission, EPLF[1]

I. INTRODUCTION

The importance of a development plan to improve a country's economy and raise the standard of living of its population is beyond doubt. To be effective, the development plan should be based on the country's needs and capabilities. Furthermore, planning is indispensable for the rational utilization of human, financial and material resources of a nation. This kind of planning will accelerate economic development ensuring the well-being of the nation.

The economy of Eritrea is of a mixed type wherein public and private sectors have to play their respective roles. Any economic plan has to guide and coordinate public and private efforts and ensure that the two sectors complement each other. Various development projects concerning either economic activity or social services are to be undertaken by the public as well as the private sectors having in mind the highest efficiency and national interest. Being equally important to the national economy, both sectors are closely interrelated and each will have to contribute to the national development in its own way.

Construction gives service to different economic sectors through the provision and maintenance of buildings, highways, water works and other physical structures. Thus, good planning and proper implementation of construction works, are prerequisites for a national development, and the construction sector can have a large portion of the share in the formation of the National Gross Fixed Capital.

Eritrea, being a newly "born again" country, is not yet on its footing, and an enormous task is awaiting for its development; construction will have to play a key role in this endeavor.

Major construction activities were undertaken during the Italian colonial period. Extensive transport facilities such as roads, railways, ports, airports and a cableway were built. Moreover, towns, agricultural centers, administrative and market centers, and several buildings serving different purposes were constructed during the almost sixty years of Italian rule.

During the British colonial rule, the federation period, and Haile Selassie's reign, construction work had been progressing minimally. Building construction for the enhancement of manufacturing industries, public health, education and other purposes was effected to some extent. With regard to transport facilities, few roads were constructed although some rehabilitation and maintenance was undertaken. Little construction of new or reha-

---

1. Presented by Habteleul Gebremedhin.

bilitation of old airports and ports was done. One of the world's longest cableways was dismantled during the British rule in the late 1940s.

During the Ethiopian Derg's rule, the situation went from bad to worse. Construction activities were almost at a halt. The systematic and deliberate policies of the Derg to destabilize, depopulate and ruin Eritrea's economy, the thirty-year duration of the armed struggle and the intermittent droughts contributed to the stagnation of construction activities. Let alone undertaking new constructions, the regime never endeavored to rehabilitate and maintain existing building and transportation facilities unless they served its militaristic purposes. The primary objective of the Derg was to subjugate the Eritrean people and make the country very dependent on Ethiopia in every respect. Overall, developmental programs and construction projects were confined to Ethiopia proper. For example, the amount spent on transport facilities, building construction, and urban and housing developments in Ethiopia in five years was about a hundred billion *birr,* compared to only about thirty million in Eritrea over the same period for the same purposes.

Because the seat of all governmental institutions was at Addis Ababa, the regional office at Asmara was devoid of centralized institutional setup. Under the guise of "security" reasons, almost all construction activities in Eritrea were stopped; manpower and equipment were transferred to Ethiopia. For example, the number of skilled and semi-skilled employees in Building Construction branch office in Asmara dwindled from 414 in 1987–88 to merely 35 in 1990–91.

II. CONSTRUCTION UNDER THE EPLF

Under the EPLF, construction activities have been undertaken since 1975–76. Over 4,000 kilometers of roads were constructed, rehabilitated and maintained in the past fifteen years. Housing and building construction for different purposes — public health, education, administration, stores, small manufacturing industries, settlements for displaced people — were undertaken. Housing and building administration and maintenance in liberated towns were being affected. However, given the general war situation, the main aim of the Construction Sector was to promote the armed struggle and, to a limited extent, help alleviate the living conditions of the Eritrean people. Thus, construction programs implemented were specific and short-lived, with limited contribution to the bases of infrastructure. However, the role construction played in the Eritrean struggle for independence and its triumph was indispensable.

III. CURRENT SITUATION IN CONSTRUCTION

The background of the Construction Sector has been described in the introduction. The following is a description of the current situation of this sector.

A. Transport Facilities

Transport facilities include roads, railway, cable/ropeway, ports and harbors, and airports.

1. Roads. Prior to the advent of the Derg, Eritrea had a more or less developed system of road networks and organizational setup. The Public

Work Department and the then Imperial Highway Authority (IHA) administered and maintained the road networks. The maintenance of all-weather roads that radiate from Asmara to Massawa, Decamere-Senafe-Zala Ambessa, Adi Ugri-Adi Quala-Mereb, and Keren-Agordat-Barentu-Tessenei, were managed by IHA, and the secondary and/or feeder roads were managed by the Public Works Department. However, with the coming of the Derg's regime almost all of the established management and maintenance work was disrupted. Consequently, most all-weather roads (asphalt and gravel-surfaced) have reached a stage of no repair mainly due to extreme neglect.

The existing road system was designed almost 60–100 years ago and could only foresee the transport system and truck capabilities that existed then. At this stage, the existing road system cannot accommodate the anticipated rapid economic development in the country. Therefore, there is a need to construct new truck roads connecting the main port of Massawa to Asmara, the towns of Decamere and Keren, as well as the western lowlands where economic potential in agriculture and mining is bright. In addition, the rehabilitation of existing roads will meet immediate needs of a transport system and serve as secondary or branch roads to the truck roads that will be constructed, thereby increasing the efficiency of the transportation system.

2. Railroads. During the Italian colonial era, the railway system was intended to connect Massawa to Asmara, and Asmara to the towns of Keren, Agordat, and Tessenei, a town at the Eritrean-Sudanese border. However, construction was disrupted at Bisha, west of Agordat, probably due to World War II and the defeat of the Italians. The bulk of the transportation system from Massawa to Asmara to Agordat and vice versa was made of the rail system. But, this was also discontinued with the escalation of the armed struggle. During the Derg's rule, the rails were dismantled and used for fortification in the front lines, thereby destroying the system completely.

The rehabilitation of the rail system is debatable. An extensive study on the development of transport facilities and formulation of options and priorities need to be undertaken prior to setting programs of rehabilitation.

3. Cableway. A cable/rope linked Asmara to the port of Massawa during the Italian colonial period. This transportation system is said to have had a capacity of transporting about 200 tons one way. The whole system was dismantled during the British rule in the 1940s.

4. Seaports and Harbors. There are two main seaports, Massawa and Assab, and several harbors on the Red Sea coast. The port of Massawa was constructed about 400 years ago and was developed by the Italians in the early 1900s. However, since the Derg's policy was to paralyze Massawa and develop Assab as the main gate to and from the Ethiopian hinterlands, no rehabilitation and development measures were take for the port of Massawa. Thus, currently Massawa needs urgent rehabilitation and development as it has the best geographical and natural harbor positions to serve the Eritrean economy and some parts of neighboring countries.

The port of Assab is relatively well-developed despite the malicious intentions of the Derg. As such, it can serve Eritrea's as well as the Ethiopia's economic needs.

Rehabilitation and development of harbors on the Red Sea coast will depend on the agricultural, fishery and mining developments on the coast line and its hinterlands.

5. Airports. There is an international airport in Asmara, a well-developed one at Assab, and several small ones in the country. However, most of them were damaged during the war, and thus require immediate rehabilitation and development in order to increase the efficiency of the transportation system.

B. Building Construction, Town Planning and Housing

The greatest challenge confronting the Construction Sector is perhaps in the areas of building construction, town planning and housing. Due to the Derg's policy, there is a serious shortage of buildings for all purposes. During the war, most of the towns and villages were bombarded by air and as a result, heavily damaged. People were forced to abandon their towns and villages and flee to neighboring and other countries. Some had to flee to settlement camps in EPLF's liberated areas. Therefore, it is anticipated that there will be a large influx of Eritreans returning to their country, and for obvious reasons the towns, will be the magnetic centers.

Given these facts, the rehabilitation of the war-damaged towns is critical. Massive building and housing construction is needed to accommodate the returning nationals, to house industrial, agricultural, commercial and mining enterprises, to house rehabilitation and social services such as public health and education, and to furnish government and private firms with administrative offices. Further, there is the need to develop plans for the towns. All of these are urgent challenges confronting the Provisional Government in general and the Construction Sector in particular. To solve these problems, active participation of nationals, public and private firms, international agencies, foreign governments and NGS's in investment aids, long-term loans, and in consulting is vital and would be highly appreciated.

C. Institutions and Firms

As was mentioned in the introduction, there is a centralized body in Eritrea that guides, controls, monitors, designs and supervises construction activities. But there is an absence of consulting firms and well-equipped construction firms in the country. Except for very few ill-equipped firms, the bulk of building construction was dominated by the public sector, the Ethiopian Building Construction Authority (EBCA). Even this very authority was poorly equipped and eventually paralyzed.

As far as transport construction is concerned, there are neither public nor private specialized contractors. If at all any construction project was undertaken, the public sectors, EBCA and the Ethiopian Transport Construction Authority (ECTA) with the help of small private contractors, undertook them. At any rate, the ETCA had the capacity to only maintain the existing road system and not undertake new constructions.

Thus, considering the small construction unit of the EPLF, it is important that a well-organized and well-equipped centralized organization is established immediately to provide guidance in design and construction, and monitor the establishment of private consulting and construction firms, both domestic and international.

D. Shortage of Manpower

Currently, there is a chronic shortage of manpower in construction, especially skilled and semi-skilled. Presumably, there is a good number of

Eritreans abroad who are skilled in building, transport construction and other construction-related activities. Hopefully, the return of these Eritreans in the future will alleviate the now acute shortage of manpower.

E. Construction Material, Machinery and Equipment

It is unfortunate that one of the constraints in this sector is shortage of construction materials. Enterprises which used to produce construction materials are paralyzed except for the cement factory in Massawa, which has just started to produce. Imported materials are not available either. The revitalization of existing construction material producing firms, and the establishment of new ones as well as the immediate importation of materials require priority attention.

Comparatively speaking, construction equipment and machinery, although not diversified, are available. However, proper investigation is required to identify and check the appropriateness of the quantity and quality of construction equipment and machinery needed during procurement.

F. Finance

The Provisional Government, as a new and transitional government, faces financial shortages in seeking solutions to the various problems at hand. The government is taking off from scratch. The Construction Sector is no exception in this regard. To revitalize and develop construction activities, the acquisition of foreign aids, long-term loans and the contribution of the private sector are of paramount importance.

G. Summary of Current Problems

The current problems facing the Construction Sector can be summarized as follows: (1) shortage of financial resources, (2) shortage of skilled manpower, (3) absence of consulting firms, (4) absence of established and well-equipped contractors, (5) lack of a central organization with the expertise to guide and coordinate construction activities, (6) shortage of materials, equipment, and tools, and (7) absence of firms producing building and construction materials.

IV. BROAD OBJECTIVES OF THE CONSTRUCTION SECTOR

Given the current conditions of the country in general and the Construction Sector in particular, rehabilitation of war-damaged and deteriorated buildings and transportation facilities will have top priority. To achieve overall development of the construction industry, the following objectives have been formulated.

1. Establish and develop an institution that guides, monitors, sets standards, procedures and methods of construction and design, coordinates professionals, consulting and construction firms.
2. Develop production capacities in building and transport facilities to facilitate prompt plan implementation in the different economic sectors.
3. Develop and strengthen local production and of construction materials by type, quantity and quality.
4. Develop plans and coordinate the growth of urban centers and their housing needs.
5. Establish building and transport maintenance capabilities.
6. Increase manpower requirements in all sectors of construction.

7. Develop management capabilities of the Construction Sector.

V. PLAN OF ACTION

Considering the objectives listed above and the immediate rehabilitation works at stake, the following plan of action has been formulated.

1. Identify immediate needs and prepare work programs of specific projects. These include rehabilitation works of existing roads, ports, airports, war-damaged towns and the construction of new and immediate building and transport facilities.
2. Establish the organization that prepares building and transport construction procedures, codes of practice and contractual agreements.
3. Establish a laboratory for testing and setting standards to determine quality and appropriateness of construction materials.
4. Establish and develop training centers to train the required manpower and improve technical and administrative skill of employees and managers of Sector.
5. Introduce appropriate technology and use the proper mix of machinery and manpower to generate job opportunities and ensure speedy implementation of programs.
6. Develop town plans of existing towns and promote the construction of housing to accommodate the anticipated influx of nationals from abroad.
7. Register professionals, consulting and construction firms, and help develop their management skill.
8. Locally produce construction materials and save foreign exchange spent on imported materials.
9. Assist and encourage the participation of rural people and cooperatives in the construction, maintenance and management of basic social services and self-help projects.

VI. INVESTMENT AND PARTICIPATION

As stated in the introduction, the Eritrean economy is a mixed economy. In the Construction Sector in general, and the Building Construction in particular, investment from and full participation of the private sector is important. Establishment and growth of local firms in construction materials will definitely enhance the development of the construction sector. Community participation and investment in the construction, maintenance and management of self-help projects and basic social services should be encouraged.

It is obvious that, at the very outset, the public sector will dominate the construction and design of building and transport construction until the private sector develops. This is because, at present, the existing quasi institutions are the Construction Commission of EPLF, the feeble public sector inherited from the Derg's regime and some small private construction firms. However, it should be understood that the public sector currently is understaffed and ill-equipped, and cannot run all-round construction activities by itself. Therefore, the participation of international construction and consulting firms will be vital for the institutional building of the construction department, the preparation of economically viable large and specialized projects and their implementation. Moreover, it is quite clear that international aids and long-term loans are needed immediately for a healthy takeoff of the Construction Sector.

Thus, the ultimate goal of the construction department is to encourage and develop the full participation of private firms in construction, consulting and production of local construction materials. The participation and investment of the national communities in the construction, maintenance and management of basic social services and housing will also be enhanced. However, the construction department will remain as the main body to guide, coordinate, monitor, set standards and procedures, in addition to filling the gaps in actual construction activities as needs arise.

CHAPTER 7

TECHNOLOGY
AND
INFORMATION SYSTEMS

NATIONAL TECHNOLOGICAL CAPABILITY SYSTEMS FOR SUSTAINABLE ECONOMIC AND SOCIAL PROGRESS: IMPLICATIONS FOR ERITREAN ECONOMY

Woldai Futur

I. INTRODUCTION

Over the past three decades, many developing nations have managed to achieve impressive records of economic and social development. A few are, in fact, rapidly closing the gap between them and the more advanced nations in the West. Rich natural resources endowment (such as oil and minerals) accounted for the economic and social transformation of some. For most nations, however, economic and social progress depended on the overall national capacity to absorb advanced technologies and adapt them to their specific local conditions to promote efficiency. Such improvements gradually engender stronger national technological capability (NTC) systems that sustain rapid socioeconomic transformation and structural change.[1]

Comparative studies show that the overall national policy framework (economic, educational and sociopolitical) has considerable impact on the pattern and rate of growth of NTC systems. Variations in technological achievements between nations, to a large extent, are attributed to differences in policies. Some countries consciously adopt an overall national policy framework that is conducive for continuing technological changes, and provide basic support infrastructure for establishing stronger NTC systems that promote rapid economic and social progress. Others provide no such support infrastructure and tend to pursue policies that unintentionally discourage technological advances, and thus retard the development of their NTC systems and socioeconomic growth.

This short paper attempts to identify policies that are conducive for building up stronger NTC systems. Policy differences between nations and their effects on the growth of NTC systems and the resulting economic and social progress are briefly qualitatively analyzed. The paper then makes recommendations for the Eritrean economy. In view of Eritrea's present status and uncertainties regarding resources availability, these recommendations are necessarily broad and tentative.

II. NATIONAL TECHNOLOGICAL CAPABILITY: THE CONCEPT AND ITS DETERMINANTS

A. The Concept

For purposes of this paper, national technological capacity is the use of human, technical, financial and institutional resources to find ways of achieving economic and social objectives in a sustainable and more cost-effective manner. NTC is often embodied in people, institutions and the machinery and equipment with which they work. It comes in the form of both hardware and software, and by its nature it is a systemic, forward-looking and complex process. Weak NTC systems manifest themselves in a systemic ineffectiveness in dealing with economic, political and social issues. Conversely, stronger NTC systems are characterized by high degree of efficiency and profound agility and flexibility engendered in the effective management and resolution of socioeconomic issues throughout society.[2]

B. The Main Determinants

Acquisition of strong NTC systems is a systemic process. It involves all sectors of the economy and segments of society. It often requires changes in traditions, institutions and strong and sustained links between domestic and international markets. Among the essential prerequisites and determinants for rapid development of stronger NTC systems are:

- Well-developed and efficient factor and product markets based on a transparent economic incentives structure that rewards innovative and risk-taking behavior;
- Free access to international factor and product markets based on an efficient mode of transportation and communications;
- Legal framework for defining and enforcing property rights and standardization processes;
- Well-developed and efficiently managed physical, institutional and administrative infrastructure;
- Accessible and integrated modern educational system, and labor market laws that are conducive to labor mobility;
- Stable political system and sociocultural values and attitudes that are conducive to technical changes; and
- A well-designed state-sponsored technology program that addresses market failure and encourages private investments on general development and new technologies.

As could be inferred from these prerequisites, growth of stronger NTC systems is not merely the result of advances in the physical and natural sciences. It is also closely related to, and significantly affected by, the advances in the behavioral sciences and humanities. Technological advances are usually the cumulative result of small productivity gains achieved in the factor and product markets and the institutional environment within which their activities are conducted. Sustained improvements in process changes, quality of inputs, design and quality of products and organizational efficiency are among the major indicators of the development of stronger NTC systems in a given society.

It is also important to keep in mind that, contrary to general perceptions, acquisition of stronger NTC systems rarely involves a radical break with the past. It is usually gradual, with changes taking place over time based on small but sustained productivity gains spread throughout society. It is the cumulative impact of these small changes in productivity that forms the basis for stronger NTC systems. Policy measures aimed at achieving stronger NTC systems, therefore, need not be concentrated on getting large technological changes in limited segments of the society, as is often the case in many developing nations, leading to dual economies. Instead, efforts could better be focused on inducing small productivity changes and on effectively spreading them throughout the society.

III. POLICY LESSONS FROM EXPERIENCES OF OTHER NATIONS

As indicated earlier, the critical importance of stronger NTC systems for achieving rapid economic growth and structural change is well-recognized.[3] However, the net impact of the national policy framework (economic, educational and sociopolitical) on the acquisition of stronger NTC systems is not yet fully understood. Many nations appear to be pursuing policies that are inconsistent with their own stated objective of establishing stronger NTC systems. In most cases, the spatial and intergenerational implications of policies on the acquisition of stronger NTC systems are neglected while formulating and executing development strategies. In view of this, a regular and critical review of the process of policy formulation and execution is a sound practice.

A. Economic Policy Variations Across Nations

The nature of the overall national policy framework varies considerably across countries and over time. Notwithstanding this variation, the fact that sustained improvements in productivity requires a consistently conducive and stable structure of economic incentives is well recognized and widely shared. Where the structure of economic incentives is inconsistent with the desired technological objectives, technological advances are usually slow. On the basis of the types of economic incentives structure they pursue, countries could be broadly divided into the following three groups:

1. Countries that follow *a stable, outward-oriented,* liberal trade, investment, industrial, financial and commercial policies, which stimulate acquisition and development of stronger NTC systems and socioeconomic progress. The economic incentives structure rewards risk-taking behavior and encourages the competitive spirit of firms; the liberal policy approach induce efficient allocation of resources, leading to a more dynamic economy, flexible institutional settings and stronger NTC systems.

2. Those that pursue *a stable inward-looking,* restrictive trade, investment, financial, industrial, and commercial policies, which, by according high protection and reducing competitive pressure on firms, eliminate the need to be innovative and negatively impact the development of NTC systems. An inward-looking and restrictive policy approach allows the continuing use of uneconomic and obsolete technologies and suboptimal-scale plants, leading to substandard products at high unit cost. Thus, inward-looking policy unintentionally retards socioeconomic progress and structural transformation of society.

3. Countries that pursue *frequently shifting* trade, investment, industrial, commercial and fiscal policies. Quite often, the shifts involve rapid swings between extreme positions, creating uncertainties in the overall economic incentives structure, thus retarding the acquisition of stronger NTC systems and socioeconomic progress. Depending on the frequency and magnitude, the shifts produce substantial instability in the overall business environment, adversely affecting the growth of the

NTC systems and limiting socioeconomic achievements.

B. National Technology Program

No matter how well-designed and coordinated, the economic incentives structure alone is not sufficient for achieving stronger NTC systems. An efficiently run educational system and mission-oriented technology program, among many others, are also critical. As was indicated earlier, access to relevant education is a prerequisite for the acquisition of stronger NTC systems. In addition, a well-designed, state-sponsored technology program, focused on addressing pressing socioeconomic issues of strategic consequences, is essential. This would be especially critical where the issues involved are country specific and technological advances are needed to achieve the most cost effective solutions.[4] Comparative studies show that nations that combined market-based economic incentives with well-focused educational systems and state-sponsored technology programs have achieved better results in reaching their goals compared to those that relied on market based research and development efforts by private sector alone.

A certain level of NTC systems development and socioeconomic progress is, of course, possible even without direct state intervention. Private sector firms and individuals could invest in technology development and a gradual modest growth of the NTC systems could be achieved. But, due to factor and product market conditions that are usually highly imperfect, such investments are usually suboptimal. Hence, to achieve an optimum investment profile to rapidly establish stronger NTC systems, state intervention that complements, but not supplants, private efforts is essential.[5]

The most important issue is not whether or not governments should intervene to promote the growth of their NTC systems and socioeconomic progress, but when, where and how to intervene to achieve the intended results. Comparative research on the role of direct technology policy intervention show that nations:

- that developed a stronger capacity to search out and evaluate foreign technology have usually been able to acquire technologies on satisfactory terms and assimilate them effectively;
- that extended their factor and product markets have been able to improve overall NTC systems and achieve higher total factor productivity;
- that maintained a close and coordinated links between industry and science and technology education have been able to rapidly develop stronger mastery of modern production technologies and thus stronger NTC systems;
- that provided incentives and allowed experimentation with alternative technologies, have been able to develop stronger technological capabilities; and
- that allowed foreign collaborations have been able to raise the level of their NTC systems much faster and acquire higher levels of national agility and flexibility, compared to those that viewed foreign collaborations with suspicion and restricted their involvements.

C. Development of Entrepreneurs

A sound economic incentives structure is a necessary, but not sufficient, condition for the rapid acquisition of stronger NTC systems. A critical mass of high quality entrepreneurs, managers and technicians, as well as an efficient government bureaucracy, staffed with committed and incorruptible officials, are also important factors. Because these groups are the main actors in the process of technological and economic development in any nation, they should be produced quickly and placed in a position where they can understand, adapt and modify technologies to local conditions.

The ability and propensity of citizens to understand and acquire advanced technologies is often a function of their educational background and motivation. As was previously mentioned, in addition to establishing sound incentives structure the government should play a leading role in providing universal access to education and the training and development of entrepreneurs/managers necessary for achieving rapid technical changes. Acquisition of effective and flexible NTC systems usually depends on establishing a close partnership and cooperation between the public and private sector in the provision of these services.

IV. STRATEGIES FOR DEVELOPING AND APPLYING TECHNOLOGY

Developing nations attempt to advance their NTC systems in many different ways. However, depending on the nature of the overall economic policy framework they adopt, the most common routes they take are:

1. A freer absorption and diffusion of imported technologies with little attention given to indigenous technology development;

2. Initially pursue a freer absorption of imported technologies with the intent of creating modified versions suited to local conditions as soon as possible; and

3. Make intensified efforts to create indigenous technology with little attention given to advantages of importing technology.

Each route has its own economic, social and political merits and demerits, and thus would have to be evaluated in the context of the stage of development of a country, size of its economy and the political climate. It should also be noted that the propensity to follow any one or any combination of these routes, is also influenced by several other factors, such as prior exposure of the entrepreneurs, managers and technicians to advanced technologies; the ease of access to and cost of imported technology. For a small country like Eritrea, a combination of the first two routes is usually considered appropriate, considering the very high up-front cost associated with complete indigenous technology program implied in the third route.

V. NEED FOR STRONGER NTC SYSTEMS IN ERITREA

A. Determinants of Economic Growth

Eritrea is now suffering from the after effects of protracted drought and a thirty-year war that just ended. Presently, it does not have significantly known and commercially proven natural resources and financial means to prime and stimulate critically needed economic activities. The transition toward a sustained economic growth and transformation of the society is thus likely to be protracted and difficult. When viewed against this reality,

Eritrea's economic development options are going to be limited; the process will require careful optimization of efficiency across sectors and time, balancing allocation of investments between the main sectors and subsectors of the economy.

Fortunately for Eritrea, the basis for economic growth is shifting from natural resources intensive towards advanced technology and skill intensive growth. As shown by the experiences of the resource-poor countries, such as Singapore, Taiwan, South Korea, Japan, and Hong Kong, lack of natural resources is not a binding constraint on economic growth anymore. Many natural resources superpowers are loosing their relative position in competitiveness and market share in international export markets, or are yet to penetrate it — particularly in manufactured products. On the other hand, the above mentioned countries are expanding their trade and accumulating considerable surpluses.[6]

Consistent with these shifts in the major determinants of economic growth, Eritrea's future is likely to depend on its human resources and technological capability systems. These could compensate for Eritrea's relative scarcity of resources endowment. The quality and number of its educated and skilled people and the rate and pattern of growth of its NTC system will determine the rate of its economic development and transformation of its society. Thus, Eritrea's economic motto must be articulated toward this objective and its strategy carefully delineated right from the very beginning. This means, Eritrea will have to devote substantial resources to the production of sophisticated and aggressive entrepreneurs and skilled managers and technicians capable of searching, evaluating and adapting modern production technologies to quickly strengthen its NTC systems.

B. Acquiring Foreign Technology

Economic progress in Eritrea, especially establishing an internationally competitive industry from the very beginning, will depend on the type of access Eritrean firms will have to foreign technology. However, foreign technology imports should not be seen as substitutes for local technology efforts. Instead, these should be viewed as complementary and transitional means of getting access to advanced technologies. In time, local capabilities should be developed to substantially modify imported technologies to suit the evolving Eritrean conditions. In some circumstances, imported technologies could eventually be substituted by domestically produced ones. Four major policy areas for technology and technological support infrastructure need to be in place in order to establish a competitive economy in Eritrea:

1. Acquire foreign technology in such a way as to reduce the gap between best domestic and international practice in the shortest possible time;
2. Diffuse acquired technology effectively, especially to reduce dispersion in economic efficiency among firms and sectors of the Eritrean economy;
3. Improve acquired and locally developed technology to keep up with the latest developments keeping in mind existing and potential markets for Eritrea's exports; and
4. Develop adequate technical manpower and conducive organizational structure and incentive scheme.

C. Areas of Special Emphasis

While concentrating on long-term efforts of acquiring stronger NTC systems, the Eritrean government will need to pay special attention to the resolutions of some critical priority issues in its overall economic development management strategy. The strategic development constraints that require special and immediate attention in order to accelerate the long-term process of Eritrea's economic development and to ensure its sustainability are summarized below.[7]

1. Security of Food Supply. As Eritrea starts its existence as an independent state and plans for its long-term economic and social development, *no task is going to be more urgent than feeding its people.* To provide adequate food for its people, Eritrea will have to accelerate its agricultural development potential. Given the limited arable land, solution to Eritrea's food problem is likely to be in improved factor (land, capital, labor, etc.) productivity through use of modern inputs (improved seed varieties, irrigation, fertilizer, etc.) and improved farming and management techniques. A state-sponsored and mission-oriented agricultural technology policy, accompanied by market based input-output pricing system, would perhaps be the best approach to ensure reasonable levels of self-sufficiency in food production. Although substantial proportions of Eritrea's demand for food could be met economically through imports, Eritrea will need to develop its agriculture to insure itself against large fluctuations in world food prices and the politics associated with large procurement of food in the international market. Aiming at 50–60 percent food self-sufficiency may probably be a prudent long-term objective in managing the Eritrean economy. While ensuring security of food supply, it is important that the long-term goal should be achievement of self-reliance and not self-sufficiency.

2. Energy Supply. At present, Eritrea's energy balance is very precarious. Its natural and conventional energy resources (wood and agricultural residues) are dwindling rapidly. Due to the accelerated deforestation over the past several decades, many parts of Eritrea are showing the characteristic features of desertification. Nonconventional energy resources (hydrocarbon fuels), currently imported, are too expensive to serve as feasible substitutes for natural and conventional energy inputs. The technology for use of solar energy, which is abundantly available in Eritrea, is not yet commercially viable. Hydroelectric potential from rivers is limited, and harnessing the Red Sea for power is likely to be too expensive, at least in the short run, as opportunity cost of available capital is expected to be too high. Given this situation, it may be strategically advantageous for Eritrea to undertake an aggressive state-sponsored technology program (including coordinated search, adaptation, modification and development of new technologies), with a view of developing economically viable substitutes for the existing but dwindling conventional energy resources. The scheme could include harnessing solar and wind power (at least for rural electrification, groundwater pumping and windmills) and an accelerated exploration and development of hydrocarbon fuels (such as petroleum, natural gas, coal and lignite, etc.).

3. Water Resource. That water shortage is already a critical factor and a binding constraint in Eritrea's economic management is quite obvious. The importance of water in determining the rate and the pattern of agricultural and industrial development in Eritrea, and the need for making every possible effort to conserve existing water and optimize its use, is also well recognized by Eritreans. How Eritrea could optimize the use of and conserve its scarce water resources (underground, rivers, lakes and sea) is, however, a subject that could benefit from the adaptation of advanced and economically optimal water management techniques, including new methods of waste water treatment methods and applications. To accord the management of Eritrea's water resources the critical attention it deserves, it would be necessary to constitute a National Water Resources Authority (NWRA) with a strong mandate to formulate Eritrea's overall long-term water resources development and management strategies, adequate staffing and budgetary support to carry out its duties.

4. Export Strategy. Given the small size of the Eritrean economy, Eritrean firms will need to seriously consider the export market in planning domestic production capacities. Plants set up without such consideration are likely to be suboptimal in scale and would need excessive tariff and nontariff protection to be financially viable, entailing substantial costs in economic efficiency and domestic resource cost. To succeed in its export efforts, Eritrea will need to produce higher quality products than those produced in its target export markets (such as the Sudan and Ethiopia). To do that, Eritrean firms will need to optimize the scale and technology base of their production facilities, and make continued efforts to stay ahead of their competitors in terms of product design and quality, cost, delivery time and after sale services. At the same time, the Eritrean government will need to develop an open trade and forward-looking export strategy and strong infrastructural support system. During the early stages, the state may have to provide adequate export financing facilities and share the initial costs of market penetration, including expenses on research and development efforts required for technology acquisition and new product development. Without such government support, it is unlikely that Eritrean firms would be able to face the competition from already established producers in other countries.

VI. CONCLUSIONS

Eritrea's short-term development outlook appears difficult. The productive base of its war-ravaged economy (both basic infrastructure and the limited productive asset base) need to be urgently rehabilitated. The challenges to Eritrea's economic growth management are thus massive and intense. Within the overall broad agenda of economic management issues, looking ahead for next ten years, three critical ones loom large: (1) securing adequate food supply to feed the people; (2) marshalling adequate resources (financial, technology, technical and management skills, etc.) for reconstruction of existing productive base and building new ones; and (3) establishing effective institutional and policy framework to engender a self-reliant and dynamic economy. These are interrelated and systemic problems of far-reaching significance for Eritrea's economic growth prospects.

Eritrea's long-term economic growth outlook however is not as dismal as the short-term. Critical for Eritrea's economic growth would be the Eritrean people themselves. Having fought and won against a formidable

Ethiopian colonial army which was alternately supported by the United States and the USSR, they are now at work executing reconstruction and development strategy of their nation with great dedication and determination. Considering their tenacity in struggle, the prospects for achieving reasonable economic growth in the medium to long run are good. A vital factor in ensuring success during the liberation struggle against Ethiopian occupation was the EPLF's capability to motivate Eritreans to make the utmost sacrifices for a national cause. Success in tackling the present binding economic constraints will also depend on the government's capacity to motivate Eritreans to continue working harder for a common national cause of a different sort, economic development.

Acquiring a stronger NTC systems in Eritrea is likely to be a protracted and difficult process. However, in view of its importance as the main determinant of socioeconomic progress, it would have to be at the core of the Eritrean development strategy. To a large extent it will be a function of an overall national policy framework and the guidance and nurturing accorded to it through a committed and vigilant government schemes. To avoid inconsistencies within the policy framework that could unintentionally impede the growth of stronger NTC systems, the major elements of the policy will need to be subjected to periodic critical reviews That is, all policy measures related to: (1) the overall economic incentives; (2) the regulatory schemes regarding public and private sector operations; (3) the accessibility and quality of the educational system; and (4) access to foreign collaborations (financial, technology and management) would have to be regularly evaluated and corrective actions taken if needed.

To effectively tackle the pressing issues related to securing adequate supplies of food, water and energy inputs and to rapidly develop export markets for Eritrean products and services, Eritrea will need to seriously consider executing a phased and result-oriented technology development program. Although the private sector should be allowed and aggressively encouraged to participate in finding solutions to these urgent problems and constraints of Eritrea's development, its overall capability is limited to meet the challenges alone. Thus, the state needs to take the leading role in developing a technological solution to these pressing economic constraints by establishing the necessary sectoral technology institutes, providing required funding and political support and creating conducive incentives scheme.

NOTES

1. The importance of rapid structural change may be sometimes questioned on grounds that it brings with it an erosion of traditional social values - creating conflicts between the old and emerging ones. The benefits (economic, social, political, etc.) of advances in NTC systems, however, are far greater than the associated costs. In addition to enhancing the potential for higher and sustained economic and social growth, stronger NTC systems engender agility and flexibility in the overall national effectiveness of managing and resolving social conflicts. As one of the most critical determinants for achieving sustainable economic and social progress, acquisition of a stronger and widespread NTC systems is a strongly

shared and an overarching objective of most nations.

2.   The marked differences in effectiveness in addressing economic, social and political issues between developed and developing countries, or even among developing nations themselves — such as those in East Asia and those in Africa — are mainly attributed to differences in NTC systems growth and distribution within these respective societies.

3.   The main reason for the success of Japanese and West German firms in penetrating the world market with manufactured products, based on imported raw materials and energy, is attributed to continuing improvements in their NTC systems. The success achieved by some East Asian nations (Taiwan, Korea, Singapore, Hong Kong, etc.) is also based on the rapid and sustained improvements in their NTC systems.

4.   Free market advocates may argue that state intervention is unnecessary on the grounds that market-based private initiatives are adequate. The need for direct state-sponsored technology program is, however, quite obvious, particularly in the early stages of development, considering the externalities associated with rapid technological advances. Stronger NTC systems generate benefits that cannot be captured by the private sector in the marketplace alone.

5.   The Japanese, Korean, and German governmental efforts toward achieving improved NTC systems in industry have been extensive. The technological superiority and cost competitiveness their products enjoy in the international market today are attributed to state support for technology development in partnership with the private sector.

6.   Natural resource–rich nations, such as Indonesia, Argentina, Brazil, India and many more in Africa and the Middle East, are trailing these resource-poor but technologically advanced countries of East Asia and the Pacific. Similarly, Switzerland, with neither natural resources nor a large domestic market, continues to have trade surpluses. Its remarkable success is attributed to its industrious, highly educated and skilled people and its private sector approach to economic growth.

7.   Satisfactory long-run resolutions to these issues are likely to be a function of the overall evolution of Eritrea's long-run NTC systems. However, considering their importance, a well-coordinated and concentrated research effort to find technological solutions would be warranted.

REFERENCES

Ergas, Henry. 1987. "Does Technology Policy Matter." In *Technology and Global Industry: Companies and Nations in the World Economy*. Series on technology and social priorities, edited by Bruce R. Guile and Harvey Brooks. Washington: National Academy Press.

Kobayashi, Iwao. 1990. *20 Keys to Workplace Improvements*. Cambridge, Mass., and Norwalk, Conn.: Productivity Press.

Ohmae, Kenichi. 1987. *Beyond National Borders: Reflections on Japan and the World*. Dow Jones–Irwin.

Womack, J. P., D. T. Jones, and D. Roos. 1990. *The Machine That Changed The World*. New York: Rawson Associates.

INFORMATION TECHNOLOGY: A STRATEGIC FACTOR IN PROMOTING PRODUCTIVITY-TRANSFORMING ORGANIZATIONS IN ERITREA

Tewelde B. Zerom

I. INTRODUCTION

In a country's long-run pursuit of well-being, the single most important objective, the one that should guide all economic policies, is said to be higher productivity growth. The one ingredient in this respect is "human capital," meaning a skilled work force and skilled management. Historical data pertaining to currently advanced economies suggest that, because of compounding, a sustained small increase in the rate of productivity per worker can make an enormous difference in the long-run growth of living standards (Krugman 1990).

Currently developed countries required a century to industrialize. This transformation, which Simon Kuznets (1966) calls "modern economic growth" and which Eritrea will perforce undergo, involves large systematic shifts in the structure of production, demand, employment, investment and trade (Dervis et al. 1984). Comparatively today, some fast developing countries are achieving a similar transformation in a quarter century. The so-called Four Dragons in the Pacific Rim are a case in point. As The Economist (1991) observed, "During the past few decades four East Asian economies — South Korea, Taiwan, Singapore and Hong Kong — have achieved the fastest rates of economic growth the world has ever seen. . . . In 1962 South Korea was poorer than Sudan; by 1986 it was richer than Argentina. Today the four `dragons' account for 10% of manufactured exports worldwide, not far short of America's 12%."

It is this writer's conviction that an emerging Eritrea, although devastated and dislocated by a long and bloody war, need not reinvent the wheel. It is in an opportune position to achieve economic transformation — provided that appropriate policy mixes and sustainable long-term goals are formulated and implemented.

The primary purpose of this paper is to advance the alternative idea that, despite the prevailing technology base and knowledge base in Eritrea, information technology (IT) could play a strategic role in promoting the nation's productivity and transforming its organizations. This paper is premised on the following generalized propositions (Nolan 1990): (1) an underlying technology drives the transition of economies and organizations; (2) productivity gains require both new technology and changing the organizational structure for doing work; (3) new technology enables new ways to do work; and (4) transformation of organizations is the outcome of economic transition.

II. DEFINITIONAL/CONCEPTUAL ASPECTS OF INFORMA-
TION TECHNOLOGY

A brief overview of the definitional and/or conceptual aspects of IT is, we believe, in order before dwelling on the Eritrean context, which is the focus of this paper.

Information technology is a generic name that reflects the convergence of several streams of technical developments over the past two decades, including software engineering, microelectronics, telecommunications, computer science and systems analysis. It is a technology that has transformed organizations and dramatically increased the ability to record, store, analyze and transmit information in ways that permit flexibility, accuracy, immediacy, geographic independence, volume and complexity. IT is said to have a unique capability to restructure operations that depend upon information for the purposes of transaction, record keeping, analysis, control, or communication (Zuboff 1989).

There are several characteristics that distinguish IT from earlier generations of machine technology. Foremost among the distinguishing features is its ability to accomplish tasks and translate them into information. Computer-based, numerically controlled machine tools or microprocessor-based sensing devices not only apply programmed instructions to equipment but also convert the current state of the equipment, product, or process into data. Similarly, scanner devices in supermarkets automate checkout process and simultaneously generate data that can be used for inventory control, warehousing, scheduling of deliveries, and market analysis (Gilder 1989; Strassman 1985; Zuboff 1989; *Fortune* 1991). In addressing perhaps the most fundamental element of the IT revolution, an author stated:

> In the microchip, combing millions of components operating in billionths of seconds in a space the size of the wing of a fly, human beings built a machine that overcame all the conventional limits of mechanical time and space. Made essentially of the silicon in sand, microchips find their value not in their substance but in their intellectual content, their design or software. (Gilder 1989).

Among the latest manifestations of IT are electronic data interchange (EDI), the workstation, and enterprise-wide network. EDI is the direct computer-to-computer exchange of standardized data to streamline the interactions any organization has with its customers, distributors, suppliers, carriers, and service providers. Similar in some respects to electronic mail, EDI is different in that it deals with specific documents used for transaction of all kinds of business, such as requests for quotes and purchase orders. EDI can convert paper-intensive activities into an all-electronic event, once initial data are entered. The benefits of EDI are many, including reducing human errors in recording data and lessening filing requirements. However, the major payoff of EDI is reducing the time it takes to exchange information required to initiate action: (1) forms that can be generated in minutes rather than hours and received in seconds rather than days compress the entire order-payment-delivery cycle, (2) transport companies can accurately track shipments, and (3) finance departments can send and receive invoices and undertake electronic funds transfer to facilitate immediate payment (World Communication Works 1990).

Proliferating personal computers and more powerful workstations continue to expand the number of individuals who can use a wide range of digital-based communications. The latest advances in IT suggest that single purpose users, like word processing, spreadsheets, and data base management are expanding into communications-intensive applications like electronic mail, fax networking, enterprise data base access, and work group computing (*Fortune* 1989).

A workstation, any networkable device a person uses to transform computer-aided tasks (defined broadly), is becoming the centerpiece of the workstation-network-software complex. Building networks of workstations (both the local area network and the wide area network varieties) improves communications and more effectively distributes information throughout the organization or a nation at large.

Moreover, advances in communications standards and technology are changing the mission of the network. Computers were originally networked in order to share access to peripheral resources, such as printers and data storage devices. It was a centralized, hierarchical network based on the traditional mainframe computing model. The decentralized model that has emerged in the past ten years or so is termed "distributed processing." In such a system, which depends on a mix of computers, data are collected and processed closest to where they are obtained. Results of such computing are subsequently transmitted via the network to where the summary data are needed (*Fortune* 1989).

III. THE ERITREAN CONTEXT: RATIONALE FOR INFORMATION TECHNOLOGY

It is public knowledge that three decades of the War of Liberation and the enemy's incessant total war campaigns have resulted in the devastation and dislocation of the Eritrean economy; with a serious drain on the precious human resources of the nation. Nevertheless, it should be possible to adopt a working framework of the present structure of the Eritrean economy, namely: (1) agrarian, (2) service, and (3) manufacturing.

Although the paucity of credible data makes any attempt at describing the structural division of the Eritrean economy using quantitative measures of magnitude virtually impossible, it would be safe to assume that the agrarian sector is the dominant sector of the economy. Most of the Eritrean labor force is engaged in agriculture and the sector accounts for the lion's share of the gross domestic product (GDP). The technology base of this sector is low and labor intensive. Moreover, decades of neglect and deliberate depopulation and displacement policies of the enemy, overuse and misuse of land resources, and creeping desertification processes and drought have rendered the nation a net importer of food and/or dependent on food aid and other agricultural products.

It is possible the service sector is the second dominant area of the economy (as is typical of many developing economies). This sector includes the food service activities, transport, retail, construction, entertainment, banking and finance, and the services/professions of education, health, `defense,' clerical, administration/management, and related activities.

Although manufacturing was vibrant and significant in its heyday, it may be accounting for a small share of the GDP. Ethiopia's wanton destruction of the industrial base and the infrastructure, the dismantling of factories and physical plants, and the concomitant loss of the resilient and skilled Eritrean labor force and management have to date probably reduced this sector to be the Achilles' heel of the Eritrean economy.

One could advance the plausible argument that, given the prevailing resource constraints and low technology base, it is rather inopportune, unrealistic, and ironic that information technology is being prescribed as a strategic asset in the nation's development agenda. Although such a contention is valid and well taken, this writer submits that IT could indeed play a strategic and essential role in the following policy areas: (1) enhancing the generalized productive capacity of the economy; (2) the establishment of a management information systems (MIS); (3) the design and operationalization of a macro and micro data generation, processing, storing, retrieving, dissemination and management system(s); (4) improvement in the communication and policy- and decision-making capabilities of the nation; and (5) saving scarce factor/labor resources.

Equally, IT has in the long run the promising potential of playing a major role in improving the competitive edge and planning activities of business, in the design and management of Eritrean education, public health, agriculture, trade, banking and finance, and transport, be they in the private or public domains.

IV. SUGGESTED POLICY ACTIONS

In the dynamic environment of economic development, decision making under conditions of uncertainty is the rule of life. The element of uncertainty is compounded in situations where credible historical and/or cross-sectional data are absent; or the capability to generate, process, disseminate, retrieve, and manage data/information is lacking. These shortcomings may be characteristic of present-day Eritrea and it is suggested that this paucity of dependable data and the general lack of capability be given prominence in the nation's development agenda. Suggested below are some possible alternative courses of action that Eritrea's policymakers and decision-makers could consider and implement to lay the foundation for a full-fledged information technology system as a basis for transforming the economy and the country's various decision-making entities (both in the private and public sectors):

A. Formulate and Implement a Long-Term Strategic Plan for Information Technology

As indicated at the outset of this exposé, this paper is premised on the following generalized propositions: (1) an underlying technology drives the transition of economies and organizations; (2) productivity gains require both new technology and changing the organizational structure for doing work; (3) new technology enables new ways to do work; and (4) transformation of organizations is the outcome of economic transition. Hence, any long-term strategic plan for information technology needs to be contemplated and formulated within the context of the nation's development agenda. Moreover, it needs to be emphasized that a strategic plan is vision and mission driven. It is suggested that the underlying mission of the IT being proposed needs to be the creation of a Wide-Access Integrated Eritrean Data/Information Base (WIEDB) with the singular purpose of helping the nation's policymakers formulate and implement informed decisions. The need to link the strategic vision of the IT system with the development agenda cannot be over-emphasized. The WIEDB could become a reality only if micro/individual department (decision-making entities big or small) functions and data are viewed as part of a comprehensive picture.

B. Create Core Personnel and Structure to Operationalize and Manage IT System

Information technology is having profound impacts on communication patterns and organizational structures. The hierarchical organization, with a single line of authority headed by a chief executive officer and based on a traditional line and staff structure, is a paradigm/model that may not be suited for an IT system. Organizational paradigms of the information age are more and more characterized by flatter organizational structure with information processing professionals (faculty, analysts, programmers, technicians, etc.) in critical roles and managers who are planners, coordinators, problem mediators, and team organizers. The literature on IT demonstrates that when good strategic planning converges with the appropriate technology and is implemented by motivated, creative professionals, the process of organization and/or national transformation begins.

C. Establish a Wide-Access Integrated Eritrean Data Base

The articulation of the nation's development agenda will call for the construction and integration of both historical and cross-sectional data to develop, implement, and evaluate plans and policies and to continuously improve the processes. The integrated system being advocated will become a reality only if the nation's individual department/unit functions and data are viewed as part of a comprehensive picture.

Powerful, relatively inexpensive, easy-to-use computers and user-friendly software have enabled professionals (in many countries) at virtually every operational level to participate in the collection and analysis, reporting, and managing of data. The acquisition of such hardware and software and the training of information processing professionals and managers may be the critical initial steps that Eritrea needs to adopt.

V. CONCLUSION

It is appropriate to conclude this paper by alluding to Japanese management philosophy and to the organizational dynamism of the Eritrean Peoples Liberation Front (EPLF), which successfully and heroically led and concluded Eritrea's war of liberation.

The Japanese have two management terms/practices that other economic systems are attempting to adopt as their own: *Kaizen* and *Ishinsuru*. *Kaizen*, which means a process of continuous improvement, is an evolutionary philosophy where constant incremental improvements build from generation to generation to achieve quality, competitiveness, and success.

Ishinsuru means to "revolutionize." "Taken together, the concepts of constant improvement and a predisposition to revolutionize when appropriate provide significant insight into the management philosophy of Japanese business. This philosophy has helped to propel Japan to the forefront of competitiveness . . ." (*Cause/Effect* 1991).

Although Eritreans may not need to import ideas and concepts wholesale, they don't have to reinvent the wheel either. Eritreans can always learn from other successful applications — foreign or domestic. In keeping with this modus operandi, it does not take a genius to realize that it was the time-tested and history honored organizational dynamism and structural set up of the EPLF and its ability to generate, process, manage and disseminate data/information that were decisive in out-foxing, out-hustling, out-smarting, and out-maneuvering the enemy. The rest, as the adage goes, is history. This writer, a confirmed optimist, would submit that a macro version of the EPLF organization supplemented by information technology and a wide-access integrated nationwide data base would definitely transform the country's economy and its decision-making entities.

REFERENCES

Cause/Effect. 1991. "Concepts for Reengineering Higher Education." Vol. 14 (Summer):10–17.

Dervis, Kemal, et al. 1984. *General Equilibrium Models for Development Policy.* Cambridge, Mass.: Cambridge University Press.

Fortune. 1989. "Workstations and Networks: Enhancing Personal and Group Productivity" (November 6).

Gilder, George. 1989. *Microcosm: The Quantum Revolution in Economics and Technology.* New York: Simon & Schuster.

Krugman, Paul R. 1990. *The Age of Diminished Expectations.* Cambridge, Mass.: MIT Press.

Kuznets, Simon. 1966. *Modern Economic Growth: Rate Structure and Growth.* New Haven, Conn.: Yale University Press.

Nolan, Richard L. 1990. "Too Many Executives Just Don't Get It." In *Cause/Effect* (Winter):5-15.

Strassman, Paul A. 1985. *Information Payoff: The Transformation of Work in the Electronic Age.* New York: Free Press.

The Economist. 1991. (June 1).

World Communication Works, Inc. 1990. *Productivity Through Messaging: New Tools for Business Communications.*

Zuboff, Shoshana. 1989. *In The Age of Smart Machine: The Future of Work and Power.* New York: Basic Books.

ALLOCATING RESOURCES TO SATISFY CONFLICTING GOALS

Amdetsion Kidane

I. INTRODUCTION

During the Second World War, military scientists and scholars of the Allied Forces were prompted by the size and preparedness of the German army to devise techniques that would enable them to counter the enemy effectively. One of the mathematical models they conceptualized and developed was the linear programming (LP) technique. Since then, the technique has been expanded, diversified and refined both in complexity and use. Currently, the model and its extensions are popularly used by decision-makers both in the public and private sectors.

It is an indubitable fact that developing nations face resource constraints. Eritrea is no exception in this regard although human resource, which is one of the major components necessary for economic development, is believed to be Eritrea's strength. Properly guided and utilized, the human resource that gained Eritrea world recognition in military prowess will likely lead her to economic success. However, Eritrea, as a nation emerging from a thirty-year armed struggle for independence, has challenging tasks of reconstruction ahead. Needless to say, there are several social programs competing for the same limited resource. In view of the fact that the programs are all important, they are, in essence, conflicting. The purpose of this paper is then to demonstrate how one of the extensions of LP, goal programming (GP), can be used to resolve such conflicting economic goals. The underlying concepts of GP will be addressed in the process of developing and solving a hypothetical situation relevant to economic development.

II. THE PROBLEM SCENARIO

Assume that Eritrea is drawing a five-year development plan for education, public health and agriculture with $2.5 billion earmarked for the period. Further, assume that the plan envisions the following goals:

- Priority level 1. Forty percent of the budget will be devoted to three of the eight provinces with the highest total "need index" for education, public health and agriculture.
- Priority level 2. Equitably, 50 percent of the budget earmarked for education, public health and agriculture will be devoted to Provinces 2, 4 and 5 where 50 percent of the population lives.
- Priority level 3. Functional education to 50,000 people, public health care to 100,000 patients and agricultural services to 100,000 farmers will be provided.

Let us further assume, as a matter of policy, the government requires

1. Presented by Berhane Abrehe

that each of the eight provinces receives at least 10 percent of the budget. Note that this is not a goal, but a requirement which has to be strictly observed.

The objective is to allocate the budget to the eight provinces for the implementation of the programs in education, public health and agriculture in such a way that deviation from targets is minimized. In order to achieve this objective, the goals are expressed sequentially in terms of priority of their implementation. However, mere listing of goals in sequence does not indicate the priorities of goals. What defines the real priority of goals is the magnitude of penalty assigned to deviation from targets. The greater the penalty assigned to a goal the higher is the priority level of the goal to which that penalty is assigned.

III. FORMULATING THE MODEL

In formulating the model, we should first define the notations to be used.

X_j = Total amount of fund allocated to Province j.
X_{ij} = Amount of fund allocated for program i in Province j.
b_i = Budget allocated for program i in deserving provinces.
n_i = Number of people receiving services in program i.
d_{io} = Overachievement of goal i.
d_{iu} = Underachievement of goal i.
p_{io} = Penalty for overachieving goal i.
p_{iu} = Penalty for underachieving goal i.

In view of the fact that the total budget is $2.5 billion, $1 billion (i.e., 40 percent) will be earmarked to the three provinces with the highest total need indices. Referring to Table 1, the three provinces falling into this category are 3, 5 and 7. Thus, the goal with the highest priority is expressed mathematically as follows:

$$X_3 + X_5 + X_7 = 1.0$$

Table 1. Need Index of the Eight Provinces for Education, Public Health and Agriculture

Program	1	2	3	4	5	6	7	8
Education	2.0	1.0	3.0	1.0	2.0	1.0	1.0	1.5
Health	1.5	2.0	1.2	2.5	3.0	1.0	2.0	2.0
Agriculture	0.5	0.5	0.5	0.1	0.3	1.0	2.0	1.0
Total	4.0	3.5	4.7	3.6	5.3	3.0	5.0	4.5

Writing the equations given above so as to reflect deviations from the goal, we have:

$$X_3 + X_5 + X_7 - 1.0 = d_{1o} - d_{1u}$$

where, $d_{1o} - d_{1u}$ is the difference between overachievement and underachievement of allocation of fund to the three provinces with the highest total need indices for education, public health and agriculture. Modifying the expression on the right hand side so that the penalties of overachieving and underachieving are incorporated, we have the expression, $p_{1o}d_{1o} - p_{1u}d_{1u}$ where p represents penalty.

Consistent with the notations already established, the subscripts p_{1o}, and p_{1u} refer to the penalties for overachieving and underachieving goal 1. The general expression of the penalty associated with the deviation from goal i is $p_{io}d_{io} - p_{iu}d_{iu}$.

According to Goal 2, \$1.25 billion (i.e., 50 percent of the total) will be allocated to Provinces 2, 4 and 5. Note that Province 5 which was identified as one of the provinces with the highest total need indices is also one of the densely-populated provinces. Be it as it may, deviations from Goal 2 in Priority level 2 can be expressed as:

$$X_2 + X_4 + X_5 - 1.25 = d_{2o} - d_{2u}$$

To express Goal 3 mathematically, the data given in Table 2 is used.

Table 2. Number of People in 1,000 Served per \$1 Million of Allocated Fund

Program	1	2	3	4	5	6	7	8
Education	2.0	3.0	4.0	3.0	2.0	4.0	2.5	3.5
Health	5.0	3.0	5.0	5.0	7.0	6.0	9.0	1.0
Agriculture	3.0	5.0	8.0	3.0	5.0	2.0	5.0	4.0

Assuming that X_j million dollars is allocated to Province j, we can formulate the tertiary goals of providing functional education to 50,000 people, public health service to 100,000 patients and agricultural service to 100,000 farmers and their deviations as follows:

$$2X_{11}+3X_{12}+4X_{13}+3X_{14}+2X_{15}+4X_{16}+2.5X_{17}+3.5X_{18} - 50 = d_{3o} - d_{3u}$$
$$5X_{21}+3X_{22}+5X_{23}+5X_{24}+7X_{25}+6X_{26}+9X_{27}+1X_{28} - 100 = d_{4o} - d_{4u}$$
$$3X_{31}+5X_{32}+8X_{33}+3X_{34}+5X_{35}+2X_{36}+5X_{37}+4X_{38} - 100 = d_{5o} - d_{5u}$$

The highlighted expressions in the constraints above represent the number of people in thousand who can be served theoretically in each of the social programs given the respective parameters of Table 2. A difference between a theoretical value and a projected goal represents deviation from a goal.

In addition to the constraints given above, it is also required that (1) the total fund allocated for the eight provinces equal \$2.5 billion and that (2) each province receives at least 10 percent (i.e., \$0.25 billion) of the budget. Writing these requirements symbolically, we have the following additional constraints:

$$X_1 + X_2 + X_3 + X_4 + X_5 + X_6 + X_7 + X_8 = 2.5$$
$$X_j => 0.25 \text{ for } j = 1 \text{ to } 8$$

The overall objective of minimizing deviations from goal targets and constraints could be compiled in a more concise but complex form. However, this option is dropped in favor of a non-mathematical choice as is stated below:

Minimize the overall deviations from goal targets the objectives of
- allocating, on the basis of need index, $1 billion to Provinces 3, 5 and 7,
- earmarking, on the basis of population, $1.25 billion, to Provinces 2, 4 and 5, and
- providing functional education to 50,000 people, public health service to 100,000 patients and agricultural services to 100,000 farmers while at the same time observing the following requirements:
- the utilization of $2.5 billion; and
- allocation of at least $0.25 billion to each province.

The model is expected to give a satisfactory allocation of budgets to the eight provinces depending on how much deviation is tolerated for each priority level. In assigning penalties, the various goals are usually grouped into priority levels, with level 1 having the highest priority and, therefore the highest unit penalties. Under a preemptive assignment of penalties, the non-zero unit penalties decrease significantly from priority level to priority level — by a factor 10 or 2.

IV. ANALYSIS OF RESULT

Calculations in such complex models, to obtain results of optimal allocations of funds, are usually performed with the aid of computers and appropriate computer software. Such a software is the Linear INteractive and Discrete Optimizer software, which, in short, is known as LINDO. Subjecting the model discussed above to LINDO and simulating it for different penalty levels, the optimal allocation of fund is found to be $500 million each for Provinces 2 and 5 and $250 million each for the remaining provinces. As a result of the optimal allocation of fund 57,200 people will receive functional education, 114,900 patients will receive public health care and 111,150 will get agricultural services. Note that Goal 3 is overachieved in a sense that 7,200 more people than planned are getting functional education, 14,900 more patients are getting health care service and 11,500 more farmers are getting agricultural services. Needless to say, the total deviation from goal targets is minimized when the aspiration levels are assigned penalties of 1,000, 100 and 10.

A. Sensitivity Analysis

Analysis can also be made to check sensitivity of the model to changes to any of the parameters in the model.

1. Referring to Table 3, note that there is no slack or surplus money associated with the constraints relating to need, equity, education, public health, agriculture and budget implying that the budgets allocated have been used. This is expected since these factors involve equality constraints. On the other hand, since the budget constraint for the provinces is given in terms of minimum requirement, surplus budget is expected. Consistent with this expectation, Provinces 2 and 5 are using surpluses of $250 million each meaning that $500 million is allocated to each of these provinces.

Table 3. Partial Output of Sensitivity Analysis Observed

Constraints	Type of Constraint	Slack/ Surplus	Dual Price
Need	=	0	-3.00
Equity	=	0	-1.00
Education	=	0	1.00
Health Care	=	0	1.00
Agriculture	=	0	1.00
Budget	=	0	-10.00
Province 1	=>	0	0.00
Province 2	=>	250	0.00
Province 3	=>	0	-4.00
Province 4	=>	0	0.00
Province 5	=>	250	0.00
Province 6	=>	0	-2.00
Province 7	=>	0	-3.50
Province 8	=>	0	-7.50

2. The dual prices represent the improvement in the optimal value of the objective function per unit increase in the right-hand side value of the constraint. The dual prices for need, equity and budget constraints are negative indicating that deviation from respective target values decrease as more fund is allocated to the provinces. On the other hand, the dual prices for educational, health care and agricultural services are positive suggesting over-achievement of goals in the social services as more fund is allocated to the provinces. The dual prices of 0 associated with Provinces 1, 2, 4 and 5 mean that an increase in funds allocated to these provinces will not improve any further the target values already arrived at. Thus, looking at the dual prices we can determine what action to take in relation to the goals that we like to achieve beyond what was recommended initially. For example, it does not benefit to allocate more funds to Provinces 1, 2, 4 and 5 because their dual prices are all zero.

B. Significance of Change

In some cases, a change in allocation of fund may not make much of a difference unless the change is significant.

1. Recall in the hypothetical example that the provinces with the highest total need index were to be assigned $1 billion for provision of services in education, health care and agriculture. Table 4 shows that the allocation of fund to these provinces can be reduced or increased by $250 million and still have the optimal solution unchanged. On the other hand, any amount of funding ranging from the targeted allocation of $1.25 to $1.00 to Provinces 2, 4 and 5, on the basis of equity, will not change the current optimal solution. The allocated fund, on the basis of need and equity, within the specified range may result in as many as 7,200, 14,900 and 11,500 more people than planned receiving educational, health care, or agricultural service respectively.

Table 4. The Ranges Within Which the Ranges Remain Unchanged

Row or Variable	Objective Coefficients Allowable		Right-Hand Side Allowable	
	Increase	Decrease	Increase	Decrease
d_{1o}	∞	1030		
d_{1u}	∞	970		
d_{2o}	∞	110		
d_{2u}	∞	90		
d_{3o}	90	10		
d_{3u}	∞	20		
d_{4o}	10	0		
d_{4u}	∞	20		
d_{5o}	0	8		
d_{5u}	∞	20		
Need			250	250
Equity		0	250	
Education			7200	∞
Health Care			14900	∞
Agriculture			11500	∞

2. The penalties assigned may vary within a range without causing the optimal solution to change. For instance, the penalty for overachieving the primary goal, d_{1o}, may be increased to ∞ or decreased by 1,030 from 1000 to -30 and still have the optimal solutions unchanged provided that the penalties associated with the other priority levels are changed in accordance with the preemptive assignment of penalties.

V. CONCLUSION

At this point a word of caution is in order. Although, the underlying concept of goal programming is mathematically sound, the plausibility of the solution depends on the validity of the parameters used. Thus, assuming that the parameters are sound, goal programming can identify a satisfactory and equitable allocation of funds for the implementation of the three social programs in the eight provinces as in the hypothetical situation discussed above. But even then, goal programming cannot guarantee realization of the goals relating to social programs because effective implementation of the solution recommended by the model depends on the decision-makers' ability to execute. Thus, it is mandatory that the analyst consults the decision-makers throughout the model-building process to see to it that all important factors are taken into account. In the event that these factors cannot be incorporated into the model, the recommendations suggested by the mathematical model should be supplemented with subjective judgement of the analysts and the decision-makers. In the absence of such a collaboration between the theoretician and the practitioner, the recommended solution is no more than a mere outcome of mathematical manipulation.

In summary, it should be reemphasized that an empirical study should be conducted, or data should be captured as they occur, in order to determine the parameters used in the model. The sets of information shown in Tables 1 and 2 in the hypothetical example have to be replaced with actual data to make the situation realistic.

REFERENCES

Anderson, David R, Dennis J. Sweeney, and Thomas S. Williams. 1982. *An Introduction to Management Science: Quantitative Approach to Decision Making*, 3rd ed., St. Paul: West Publishing Company.

————. 1989. *Quantitative Methods for Business*, 4th ed., St. Paul: West Publishing Company.

Baumol, W. J. 1977. *Economic Theory and Operations Analysis*, 4th ed., Englewood Cliffs, N.J.: Prentice-Hall.

Charnes, A., and W. W. Cooper. 1975. "Goal Programming and Constrained Regression — A Comment," *Omega* 3(4):403–9.

Childress, Robert L. *Mathematics for Managerial Decisions*. Englewood Cliffs, N.J.: Prentice-Hall.

Dantzing, G. B. 1963. *Linear Programming and Extensions*. Princeton: Princeton University Press.

Ignizio, J. P. 1976. *Goal Programming and Extensions*. Lexington, Mass.: Lexington Press.

————. 1982. *Linear Programming in Single and Multiple Objective Systems*. Englewood Cliffs, N.J.: Prentice-Hall.

Lee, S. M. 1973. *Goal Programming for Decision Analysis*. New York: Van Nostrand Reinhold.

Lee, S. M., and M. M. Bird. 1970. "A Goal Programming Model for Sales Effort Allocation," *Business Perspectives* 6(4):17–21.

Lee, S. M., and L. J. Moore. 1973. "Optimizing Transportation Problems with Multiple Objectives," *AIIE Transactions* 5(4):333–38.

Lee, A. M., and R. Nicely. 1974. "Goal Programming for Marketing Decisions: A Case Study," *Journal of Marketing* 38(1):24–32.

Moskowitz, Herbert, and Gordon P. Wright. 1979. *Operations Research Techniques for Management*. Englewood Cliffs, N.J.: Prentice-Hall.

Plane, Donald R., and Claude McMillan, Jr. 1971. *Discrete Optimization: Integer Programming and Network Analysis for Decision Making*. Englewood Cliffs, N.J.: Prentice-Hall.

Shogan, Andrew W. 1988. *Management Science*. Englewood Cliffs, N.J.: Prentice-Hall.

Turban, Efraim, and Jack R. Meredith. 1985. *Fundamentals of Management Science*. Business Publications.

THE ROLE OF MASS MEDIA IN ERITREA'S SOCIAL AND ECONOMIC DEVELOPMENT

Yemane Girmatzion

I. INTRODUCTION

Eritreans are celebrating their military victory and enthusiastically waiting for the day their country joins the world community of independent nations. But this celebration will be short-lived if the ravaged Eritrean social and economic structures, devastated for three decades by the Ethiopian war machine, are not reconstructed. The task of reconstruction will require a tremendous amount of human resources and capital, as well as an effective mass communication network. According to the UNESCO publication *Culture,* mass media are indispensable tools in human endeavor: "Firstly, they are instrumental in creating awareness of the developing countries' problems, goals and capacities, among its own population and within the world context; and secondly, they are indispensable for all forms of coopera-tion — industry, trade, banking, agriculture, education, etc." (quoted in *Media Development* 1986:6).

Throughout the war of liberation, the Eritrean People's Liberation Front (EPLF) owned and operated printed media and a radio station known as the Voice of the Broad Masses of Eritrea (VBME). The EPLF used such media to promote Eritrean nationalism and raised the consciousness of its people. In addition, it provided news for local and international audiences. Now in postwar independent Eritrea, the media can play a significant role in mobilizing Eritreans to reconstruct the war-torn country and in helping its people to adjust to the transition from a situation of constant conflict to that of peace. Thus, for new Eritrea, there is a need for a theory-based media model to guide the development of mass media operations.

The purpose of this paper is to suggest a mass media model for devel-opment in Eritrea. First, five theories of the press and the concept of devel-opment are discussed. Then development communication and development support models, their use in various countries and their applicability in Eritrean economic development are examined. This is followed by a section which presents a set of recommendations regarding a model, and appropri-ate technology for Eritrea.

II. THE NEED FOR A MASS-MEDIA MODEL

The function and role of the media in a nation depends on the democ-ratic principles the nation follows. For example, Ethiopian media during the rule of its authoritarian leaders — the late Emperor Haile Selassie and his successor, the recently deposed Colonel Mengistu Haile Marian — were echo-ing the viewpoints of those rulers and were the tools for the government's distortion of facts on economic, political and other issues affecting Ethiopians. Similarly, before the collapse of communism, the state-owned mass media in Eastern Europe were serving the Communist Party which represented a few elite and ignored social issues that affect the majority of the people in those countries.

Despite the circumstances under which the EPLF clandestine media operated (war and jamming), the front provided a considerable service to Eritreans as well as to those who sought reliable information on the Ethio-Eritrean conflict. It was reported in 1989 that the VBME had nine hours of broadcasts a day, in the following five languages spoken in Eritrea: Afar, Arabic, Kunama, Tigrinay, and Tigre. The radio station also had broadcasts in the Ethiopian language, Amharic. Its programs could be heard in Ethiopia, parts of Somalia, Djibouti, Kenya (up to Nairobi), part of Sudan and Saudi Arabia (Sagem 1989:18). The Eritrean media depicted the true history of Eritrea which until then was deliberately distorted by Ethiopia. Further, the VBME was an "alternative" and reliable source of information for internal and external consumption. Lawrence and Nichols wrote: "During heavy fighting between the EPLF and Ethiopian troops during 1981–82, the clandestine station kept the world informed about the conflict" (1987:129). The capture of the port city of Massawa by EPLF was confirmed by VBME and monitored by major international media such as the BBC, *The New York Times,* and the *Arab News,* while the state-owned Ethiopian media continually denied that Massawa was captured by EPLF. The reliability of VBME was also confirmed by *The New York Times* as follows: "The estimate on casualties in the Eritrean fighting came from the rebels, but diplomats in Addis Ababa say they are generally reliable" (*The New York Times,* April 17, 1990). In addition to news, the EPLF media provided various programs on education, health care, and agriculture. In order to continue and expand their work and to fulfill their goals of reconstruction, Eritrean media need a theory-based model to ensure their success. Haule, writing on the media in Africa, expresses the need for a framework or model for Africa's development:

> Much more lacking is a coherent body of knowledge based on a theoretical formulation which is predictive and which could guide the implementation of African development programs including communication development at the national, regional and continental level (Haule 1984:7).

Realizing the significance of a model for the media, five theories of the press are discussed below, after which the writer suggests an applicable and workable model for the media of postwar Eritrea, which could promote socioeconomic and sociocultural growth and foster national integration. Needless to say, a model is useful only when it is properly applied.

A. The Authoritarian Theory

This theory was developed in Europe and North America in the sixteenth and seventeenth centuries and it has been practiced since then in many parts of the world. Hachten describes the authoritarian theory's main purpose and the operations of the mass media under a country led by an authoritarian leadership as follows:

The press is always subject to the direct or implied control of the state or sovereign. A printing press or broadcasting facility cannot be used to challenge, criticize, or in any way undermine the rule. The press functions from the top down; the kind or ruler decides what shall be published because truth is essentially a monopoly of those in authority (Hachten 1981:16).

The Ethiopian media, during the late Emperor Haile Selassie's rule fell under the authoritarian theory. The media were serving the emperor and a small elite of that country.

B. The Libertarian Theory

The Libertarian theory emerged in the seventeenth and eighteenth centuries, first in Europe and later in North America, to provide a guideline for the media in democratic governments. The scholars who developed this theory were influenced by "the social, political, and economic events of their times" (Siebert et al. 1979:40). The main purpose of the media according to this theory is: "to inform, entertain, sell — but chiefly to help discover truth, and to check on government" (ibid., p. 6). It emphasizes the need for free expression of ideas and dissemination of information. The theory sees the media as a business venture, thriving on the desire for profit.

C. The Social Responsibility Theory (SRT)

This theory was developed in the nineteenth century in England and the United States. The social responsibility concept appeared as a "goal model" in the United States and the model "soon swept the world," as it was widely accepted by media practitioners in the aftermath of World War II (Altschull 1984:179). The major purpose of the social responsibility theory was to balance between freedom and responsibility of the press. As Siebert stated:

> Freedom carries concomitant obligations; and the press, which enjoys a privileged position under our government, is obliged to be responsible to society for carrying out certain essential functions of mass communication in contemporary society. To the extent that the press recognizes its responsibilities and makes them the basis of operational policies (Siebert et al., p. 74).

Merrill, in his writing on the success of the SRT model indicates that the most stable liberal democratic press systems are found in Japan, Australia, New Zealand, India, and some Pacific Island countries. According to Merrill, these countries have a philosophy that tends to follow the social responsibility theory (Merrill 1983:178). The countries that follow this model have privately owned mass media. The media's obligation in such nations, as noted above, is to provide information to the public taking responsibility for the society. The idea is "that the people are the ultimate decision makers and that the role of the press is to provide them with news and commentary important to them" (ibid.).

D. The Soviet Communist Theory

This theory emerged at, and was practiced in, the Soviet Union, although it was exercised in Germany and Italy during the rule of the dictators — Hitler and Mussolini respectively (Siebert 1979:7). Its primary purpose was "to contribute to the success and continuance of the Soviet socialist system, and especially to the dictatorship of the party" (ibid.). The theory was also practiced in almost all Soviet-allied countries around the world, including Ethiopia during the now deposed Mengistu's regime. The failure of media in countries that follow this model was discussed by Adzotsa as follows:

> The far-reaching changes in Eastern Europe have just shown us that a people who are badly informed can lead their country into stagnation and other evils like the cult of personality. Journalists in these countries used to write that "everything is perfect," that "our country has everything it needs." (Adzotsa 1990:24)

For decades the Ethiopian media, as was true in Eastern Europe, were telling stories that reflected the viewpoints of the rulers. The media in these countries were prohibited from reporting objectively on social, economic, and political issues that affect the people. The media were reporting that "everything is perfect." For instance, the Ethiopian media presented no objective reporting of the Ethio-Eritrean war throughout its duration of three decades, nor did they report on the devastating famines which occurred in the early 1970s and mid–1980s in the country and shook the conscience of the world when it was brought to the world's attention through the Western media.

E. Development Theory

This theory is practiced in third world countries, and according to Hachten it advocates: "All the instruments of mass communication — newspapers, radio, television, motion pictures, national news services must be mobilized by the central government to aid in the great tasks of nation building: fighting illiteracy and poverty, building a political conscious, assisting in economic development." Hachten added, "The media therefore should support authority, not challenge it. Dissent and criticism have no place, in part because the alternative to the ruling government would be chaos, it is argued" (1981:31). The development concept as noted above has similarities with the authoritarian and communist theories. As explained by Hachten the theory is: ". . . to some extent a critique of and reaction against the West and its transnational media. It also reflects the frustrations and anger of poor and media-deficient nations of the Third World" (ibid., p. 30).

F. Which Model for Eritrea

These theories have been adopted in different countries, and each suggests a framework within which mass media can operate. Certainly, over time modifications of the theories have occurred. For instance, the "Soviet Communist Theory" was developed from the oldest, the Authoritarian Theory, whereas the "Social Responsibility Theory" is a modification of the "Libertarian Theory" (Altschull 1984:183), and the "Development Concept" emerged from the authoritarian and the Communist theories (ibid., p. 30). From the five discussed models the Social Responsibility Theory is suggested to be adopted as a model for the Eritrean media and the reason of adopting it will be discussed in section IV.

Regardless of which model is accepted, it is imperative that an independent Eritrea design a communication policy that would take into account the country's historical and sociopolitical circumstances. The MacBride Commission on media policy, published by the UNESCO subscribes to the view that "every country should develop its communication patterns in accordance with its own conditions, needs and traditions, thus strengthening its integrity, independence and self-reliance" (quoted in Domatob and Hall 1983). However, the commission believed that ". . . if expertise were available, and a commitment made by the national governments, then the media could become a powerful tool for development (ibid.).

III. DEVELOPMENT COMMUNICATION

A. The Concept

The concept of "development communication" was conceived by development scholars who believed that mass communication can play a significant role in third world countries to boost the ailing economy and address social issues in areas such as education, nutrition, health care, and agriculture, where there is a great need for development (Menon 1986:5). This media strategy has had a remarkable impact on third world countries, and the media acts as an agent for the promotion of economic growth and social change. Menon describes the factors that led to the success of this strategy when he states: "Development communication by its very nature requires that the professional must be both theoretician and practitioner" (ibid.). In the Philippines, for example, development communication has led to a significant improvement in food production. Menon stated that how the Philippines moved, ". . . from a rice-importing to a rice-exporting nation in less than five years, is an outstanding example and perhaps, one of the oldest" successes of development communication" (ibid.). The Philippines' experiment later came to be replicated in India and, more recently, in Indonesia. The success of this program was partially due to the interaction between the mass media and the project designers, on the one hand, and the beneficiaries of the agricultural program, on the other, working to increase agricultural productivity.

Development Support Communication (DSC) also advocates information sharing and participation of the people who benefit from the program in planning, decision making, and implementing the plan with the designers. The Food and Agriculture Organization (FAO) policy document resulting from a 1987 conference, defined the DSC policies, as quoted by Agunga: "Training local communication workers in the principles and practices of their profession; training extension workers in the techniques and strategies in the use of audio-visual tools; and developing and providing improved teaching/learning methods that will facilitate the acquisition of knowledge and skills by both field-level development workers and rural people" (Agunga 1990:152–53).

According to Menon, the mass media strategies used in the Asian countries were "localized radio programs, community newspapers and posters made by local youths, community organizations and multi-agencies co-ordination" (1986:5). As in those Asian countries, the media in Africa too played a significant role by disseminating development information in ways the intended beneficiaries understand through such media as dramas and short stories in vernaculars. In addition, efforts were made in the areas of agriculture, health care, nutrition, and education. To disseminate the programs, local radio dramas were used.

B. The Need for Media Regulations

The importance of continued "flow of information" in a country cannot be overemphasized. However, the government must pass laws and regulations that ensure freedom of expression and flow of information. Guidance and assistance are given to the media in many countries: Most governments in the world consider the flow of information a vital part of national life and have developed and implemented a variety of policies to encourage the circulation of newspapers and magazines. According to Wilcox: "In some countries, such as the United States, the encouragement is indirect through reduced postal rates for printed matter. In many Third World countries, however, the encouragement may be more direct, in the form of governmental budgetary allocations" (Wilcox 1975:48). How the media's freedom could be affected by the assistance they receive is also explained: "The kind of government encouragement often determines the level of control over a particular publication. A newspaper primarily dependent upon government subsidy and allocations, for example, often feels pressure to support and endorse governmental policies. By the same token, a newspaper receiving most of its revenue from subscriptions and commercial advertising feels less pressure to strictly follow the government's wishes" (ibid.).

Of course, there must be some government regulation of privately owned media, but in African countries mistakes have been committed in an ostensible attempt to foster national unity by controlling the press. Concerning the line of reasoning that advocates that control of the press is necessary for national unity, Ali Muzri stated: "There are fundamental fallacies in this whole line of reasoning. One is the assumption that avoiding conflict is the same thing as achieving integration. And so African governments often go to great lengths to avert the appearance of dissension in the country and try to eliminate every risk of serious conflict, either between groups or between the state itself and some groups. What is overlooked is that there is such a thing as artificial 'absence of conflict.' National integration does not consist merely of our being forced to smile sweetly at each other" (quoted in Wilcox 1975:28). Muzri added: "This then is the first fallacy of those who argue that open clashes of opinion are harmful to nation-building. They are wrong in assuming that to avert conflict between groups is the same thing as to integrate these groups. They forget that the groups could never be integrated unless risks of conflict are taken" (ibid.).

However, freedom of the press must be tempered with a great deal of responsibility, particularly in the case of Eritrea, freedom for this country came after three decades of war and the sacrifice of over 50,000 Eritrean lives. Therefore, the media should recognize their responsibility to preserve national unity, the hard-won independence, and the welfare of the society.

IV. RECOMMENDATIONS

Eritrea's economy and social structure have been destroyed by three decades of war. Thus, economic reconstruction should be the immediate task in postwar independent Eritrea. The mass media could function as an agent for mobilizing the Eritrean masses in that endeavor. Areas which require immediate media attention are: agriculture, family planning, health care, illiteracy, nutrition, land conservation, food production, including fishing, and fostering unity in the Eritrean society. In dealing with the areas, the role of the media should be not only to revitalize the economy, but also to tackle social problems by providing adequate and accurate information. Well-informed citizens can make wise decisions. In sum, journalists and other members of the media should do responsible reporting on national issues that fosters development.

To accomplish goals in these areas, a well-developed plan for communication infrastructure is necessary. The following steps are recommended to rebuild Eritrean mass media: (1) adopt an appropriate model of mass media, (2) utilize appropriate media technology, (3) establish a national news agency, and (4) establish a school of journalism. Each step is briefly discussed below.

A. The Social Responsibility Model is Most Appropriate for Eritrea

Of the five media models discussed in section II, the social responsibility model appears to be the most appropriate for independent Eritrea. This model allows people to express their opinions freely but at the same time requires the media to assume social responsibility for its reporting. The following points have been considered in recommending this choice:

1. The Eritreans deserve responsible mass media that serve as a bridge between the decision-makers and the public by reporting objectively with a sense of fairness.
2. In the EPLF's National Democracy Program, "establishing a People's Democratic State" and "protecting the democratic rights of freedom of speech, the press" are stated objectives. (Cliffe and Davidson 1988:205).
3. Those countries which have espoused freedom of the press have proven to have stable governments and have a higher standard of living: Australia, New Zealand, and Japan are some good examples.
4. The other models are doomed to failure as in East European countries and in Ethiopia.

Currently, the Provisional Government of Eritrea (EPG) and the economy of the country are in transition. Considering the importance of a free flow of information for a country, the EPLF-owned and operated media, which so far have been successful, should continue to bring information to the people. However, privately owned media also should be encouraged in order to foster business and communication in Eritrea. Further, competition between government and privately owned media would probably lead to more thorough and quality news coverage. Given the economic situation in Eritrea, privately owned media may not be able to support themselves financially through advertising and subscriptions. Therefore, the government should support the private mass media by advertising development programs on topics such as nutrition, primary health care, education, and agriculture and by providing other types of assistance.

B. Appropriate Technology Should Be Adopted

Overall, the electronic devices the media use for disseminating information should provide efficient and long-term service but also be affordable. In addressing appropriate communication technology, Jipguep, Deputy Secretary-General of the International Telecommunications Union (ITU) rec-

ommends the following:
- the technology must be technically appropriate to meet the present and expected future demand;
- the implementation of the technology must be economically viable;
- it must call for a minimum of power and space requirements;
- it must be able to withstand the prevailing climatic environment (Jipguep 1988:67).

Radio, newspapers, and television should be adopted as major information disseminators for Eritrea.

1. Radio. There are several advantages to radio as a means of communication. (a) radio transmission is not expensive: more channels can be made available; (b) illiterate as well as literate people can listen to the message; (c) receivers also are relatively inexpensive, radio is easy to operate, maintain, and repair; (d) programs can be listened to at work or while traveling; and (e) although the majority of the people are unable to afford a radio, a large audience can be reached through loudspeakers at the market and other public places (Girmatzion 1990:10). Radio's effectiveness was explained as follows: "The radio, in most of rural Africa, has the force of the Bible. It is not uncommon for someone to substantiate whatever statement or claim he or she has made by adding `the radio said so'" (Domatob and Hall 1983:16–17).

2. Newspapers. (a) can be read in spare-time and can be read repeatedly; (b) can be used as a learning tool for illiterate people; (c) can be reasonably prices; and (d) one newspaper can be shared among many people.

3. Television. It is the most advanced method of communication, as it combines visual as well as audio messages. Though TV appears to be the best method of conveying information, it can only be operated at great cost, requiring highly skilled manpower. In the beginning stages of reconstruction, TV could be used to a limited extent with videotapes on educational programs to be circulated by the government throughout the country's cities and towns to show on televisons placed in market areas and other public places. In this way large audiences could be reached.

Almost all communication equipment is currently imported; effort should be made to assemble and manufacture devices such as radio sets and dry-cell batteries within Eritrea so they can be distributed to the people at minimum cost.

C. Establish an Eritrean National News Service

A national news agency, Eritrean National News Service (ENNS), per se can aid in the work of reconstruction of the Eritrean economy and help solve other sensitive social issues by providing needed domestic information from all corners of the country to the ENNS main office in Asmara, to the nation's radio, television stations, and newspapers. In addition, ENNS can foster acceptance of the true and positive image of Eritrea to the world through responsible reporting by its correspondents.

For example, ENNS information on commodities, stock exchange, banking, and other commerce-related news could be reported in all parts of the country and thus help buyers and sellers to be up to date on internal commercial activities. Information about social and economic reforms and achievements of various development schemes could be readily available to all citizens.

D. Establish a School of Journalism

To meet the challenges facing the media, independent Eritrea needs a school of journalism to train dedicated Eritreans with the requisite code of ethics and skills of the profession. A school of journalism could help in training many young Eritreans so they could translate important and useful information into the various Eritrean languages.

The significance of responsible journalism has been echoed by many African journalist, one of whom was Alhji Babtunde Jose, former chairman of the *Daily Times,* who said: "[I]n the new nations and traditional societies of Africa . . . a journalist has additional responsibilities to help in building a nation out of the multilingual, multicultural societies in countries where economic resources are inadequate to meet the expectations of the people." Jose added: "In the final analysis, the journalists are part of the Nigerian society. If a society decays, the journalist cannot claim to be healthier than the body and if law and order breaks down and there is chaos, there would be no newspapers, no journalists and no readers" (Wilcox 1975:25).

V. CONCLUSION

The primary concern in developing countries is meeting basic needs such as food, drinking water, shelter, electricity, primary health care, and basic education. The function of the mass media in such countries should be tied to these concerns. Eritrea today is lacking in almost all basic needs. Thus the type of mass media to be established in the country should be primarily concerned with such basic needs.

The suggested media model for new Eritrea is the Social Responsibility (SR) model. As the name implies, the media have a responsibility in their reporting; they must be objective, fair and informative about issues which affect the public and their country; program on citizens' responsibility to their country also should be part of the reporting. Well-informed citizens can make wise decisions that affect them and their country. Today, about 80 percent of Eritreans live in rural areas and the overwhelming majority are illiterate. Therefore, development programs should focus on areas such as literacy, agriculture, health care, and similar social services that affect these people.

For these programs to be successful, the beneficiaries must be trained and made to participate in programming and decision making. On the part of the government, laws and regulations must be passed which will ensure freedom of expression and the operation of the mass media. According to Adzotsa, "Freedom of the press is an integral part of democracy and actively contributes to development by allowing the public to diffuse ideas and exercise some form of control over government" (1990:12). If founded on the SR model, the media in Eritrea can serve as a bridge between the public and the leaders, bringing the viewpoints of the people to the decision-makers. Further, the media can be helpful in disseminating information about development programs on agriculture, health care, education, etc.

Eritrea achieved its political independence through its people's resilience under the able military and political leadership of EPLF. Now the struggle is for economic independence; the energy and resources should be channelled into efforts to reconstruct the country and turn it into a prosperous and stable nation. An effective mass media infrastructure could be an important tool toward achieving this goal.

REFERENCES

Adzotsa, Edouard. 1990. "The Demystification of Information." *The Democratic Journalist* 37(12).

Agunga, Robert. 1990. "Development Support Communication and Popular Participation in Development Projects, *Gazette* 45(3).

Altschull, Herbert J. 1984. *Agents of Power.* New York: Longman.

Cliffe, Lionel, and Basil Davidson. 1988. *The Long Struggle of Eritrea.* Trenton, N.J.: Red Sea Press.

Domatob, Jerry Komia, and Stephen William Hall. 1983. "Development Journalism in Black Africa," *Gazette* 31(1). See also: Sean MacBride. 1980. *Many Voices One World.* New York: UNESCO.

Girmatzion, Yemane. 1990. *Clandestine Radio Stations in the Horn of Africa.* Unpublished paper.

_____. 1990. *Appropriate Technology for Communication Systems for Africa.* Unpublished paper.

Greenberg, Bradley, and Tuen-Yu Lau. 1990. "The Revolution in Journalism and Communication Education." In the *People's Republic of China* 45(1).

Hachten, William A. 1981. *The World News Prism.* Ames: Iowa State University Press.

Jipguep, J. 1988. "Appropriate Technology for Development Countries." *Telecommunication Journal* 55(1).

Menon, Vijay. 1986. "What Hope for the Future of Development Communication?" *Media Development* 33 (2/1986).

Merrill, John C. 1983. *Global Journalism.* New York: Longman.

Sagem. 1989. "Let's Introduce You to the VBME," 2(18).

Soley, Lawrence C., and John S. Nichols. 1987. *Clandestine Radio Broadcasting.* New York: Praeger.

Wilcox, Dennis L. 1975. *Mass Media in Black Africa.* New York: Praeger.

CONTRIBUTORS

Berhane Meskel Abraha, Ph.D., P.Eng. (Colorado State University), is Program Coordinator in Water Resources and Environmental Management at Colorado State University, Fort Collins, Colorado.

Ytbarek Cuddus is Manager of Navigation Services, Western Geophysical Company of America, Houston, Texas.

Araya Debessay, Ph.D. (Syracuse University), CPA, CMA, CIA, is Professor of Accounting at the University of Delaware, Newark, Delaware.

Eritrean People's Liberation Front
    Agricultural Commission
    Commerce Commission
    Construction Commission
    Finance Commission
    Manufacturing Commission
    Marine and Ports Affairs
    Water Resource Subcommission

Yacob Fisseha, Ph.D. (Michigan State University), is Associate Director of African Studies at Michigan State University, East Lansing, Michigan.

Tekie Fessehatzion, Ph.D. (University of Pittsburgh), is Professor of Economics at Morgan State University, Baltimore, Maryland.

Woldai Futur, Ph.D. (Southern Illinois University at Carbondale), is Senior Economist with the World Bank, Washington, D.C.

Gebre Gebrekidan is an Engineer in Los Angeles, California.

Tesfa G. Gebremedhin, Ph.D. (Oklahoma State University), is a professor of Agricultural Economics at West Virginia University, Morgantown, West Virginia.

Yemane Girmatzion, M.A., M.S. (Ohio University in Athens, Ohio), is a professor of African Affairs and Journalism at Ohio University–Lancaster, Lancaster, Ohio.

Berhe Habte-Giorgis, DBA, (Louisian Tech University) is a professor of Marketing at Glassboro State University, New Jersey.

Yegin Habtes, Ph.D. (University of Illinois–Champaign-Urbana), is a professor of Education at the University of Virgin Islands, St. Thomas, Virgin Islands.

Yohannes Habtu, Ph.D., is a Development Consultant in London.

Amdetsion Kidane, DBA (University of Colorado), is a professor of Quantitative Methods and Statistics at Howard University, Washington, D.C.

Kidane Mengisteab, Ph.D. (University of Colorado), is a professor of Political Science at Old Dominion University, Norfolk, Virginia.

Tsegay Moges, Ph.D. (Syracuse University), is Senior Engineer with MacDonald Douglas, Los Angeles, California.

Veronica Rentmeesters is Director of Research and Information with the Provisional Government of Eritrea Mission to the United States and Canada, Washington, D.C.

Ghermay Habte Selassie, M.A. in Economics (Sweden).

Gebre Hiwet Tesfagiorgis, Ph.D., J.D. (University of Wisconsin–Madison), is Director of Institutional Research and Planning at the University of Nebraska system, Central Administration, Lincoln, Nebraska.

Brhane Tesfay, Ph.D. (University of California, Los Angeles), is Professor of Management and Department Chair at California State University–Dominguez Hills, California.

Arefaine G. Yohannes, Ph.D. (Northwestern University), is Professor of Economics at the University of Michigan–Dearborne, Dearborne, Michigan.

Tewelde B. Zerom, Ph.D. (University of Pittsburgh), is Executive Director of Institutional Research and Planning at Grambling State University, Grambling, Louisiana.

INDEX

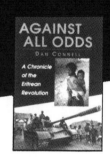

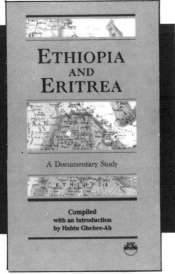